Flying against Fate

Flying against Fate

Superstition and
Allied Aircrews
in World War II

S. P. MACKENZIE

University Press of Kansas

Published by the University Press of Kansas (Lawrence, Kansas 66045), which was organized by the Kansas Board of Regents and is operated and funded by Emporia State University, Fort Hays State University, Kansas State University, Pittsburg State University, the University of Kansas, and Wichita State University.

Library of Congress Cataloging-in-Publication Data
Names: MacKenzie, S. P., author.
Title: Flying against fate : superstition and Allied aircrews in World War II / S. P. MacKenzie.
Description: Lawrence, Kansas : University Press of Kansas, 2017. | Includes bibliographical references and index.
Identifiers: LCCN 2017020138 | ISBN 9780700624690 (cloth : alk. paper) | ISBN 9780700624706 (ebook)
Subjects: LCSH: World War, 1939–1945—Psychological aspects. | Superstition—History—20th century. | World War, 1939–1945—Aerial operations.
Classification: LCC D744.55 .M33 2017 | DDC 940.54/4973—dc23
LC record available at https://lccn.loc.gov/2017020138

British Library Cataloguing-in-Publication Data is available.

Printed in the United States of America

10 9 8 7 6 5 4 3 2 1

The paper used in this publication is recycled and contains 30 percent postconsumer waste. It is acid free and meets the minimum requirements of the American National Standard for Permanence of Paper for Printed Library Materials Z39.48-1992.

CONTENTS

ACKNOWLEDGMENTS

This book would not have been completed without access to the holdings of many important libraries and archives. In particular I sincerely thank the staff members at the Air Force Historical Research Agency, Maxwell AFB; the Australian War Memorial, Canberra; the Research Room, Imperial War Museum; the National Archives, Kew; the Roger A. Freeman Research Center at the National Museum of the Mighty Eighth Air Force, especially Dr. Vivian Rogers-Price; Special Collections, Joyner Library, East Carolina University; Special Collections, University Library, University of Leeds; the Archive and Library, Royal Air Force Museum, Hendon; the Rutgers Oral History Archives, Rutgers University; Special Collections, Willis Library, University of North Texas; Thomas Cooper Library (notably Elizabeth Sudduth in her role as custodian of the Gilbert S. Guinn Military Aviation Collection, as well as the members of the interlibrary loan office), University of South Carolina; and the Center for the Study of War and Society at the University of Tennessee, Knoxville.

I am also grateful for the comments provided by the two external readers who received a draft manuscript from the University Press of Kansas. Thanks also go to the UPK editorial staff. All interpretations and opinions expressed in the following pages are my responsibility alone and do not necessarily reflect the views of those who have assisted this project.

—*S. P. MacKenzie*
Columbia, South Carolina
February 2017

INTRODUCTION

That fliers can be superstitious has long been acknowledged within the aviation community.[1] Especially in reference to the Allies in World War II, furthermore, the subject has been touched on repeatedly by popular writers; but, with very few exceptions, academic historians have tended to ignore this aspect of the military aircrew experience.[2] The trend thus far among the latter has been to concentrate on aspects of strategic bombing and various other air campaigns along with the thoughts and actions of leading air commanders.[3] This gap is unfortunate, given how powerful belief could be among pilots and other combat crewmen in the efficacy of various supernatural means of avoiding destruction and ensuring survival, as a number of physicians perceived at the time.[4] Recent work in the behavioral sciences, moreover, offers important insights into the psychological mechanisms that could make otherwise rational and discerning men become, as cultural historian Martin Francis has written, "intensely superstitious."[5] Given the extent to which supernatural belief has been recognized by scholars as an important psychological coping mechanism among Allied soldiers fighting on the ground in both world wars, furthermore, a full-scale study of the phenomenon among those men flying for the American, British, and associated dominion air forces as well as naval air arms in the war against the Axis appears worthwhile.[6]

Why, though, concentrate on these particular fliers? Superstitious thought and action, after all, also occurred in enemy air forces and among Russian fliers.[7] What is more, magical thinking was by no means confined to World War II: belief in the supernatural also influenced combat pilots in, for example, World War I, Korea, Vietnam, the Falklands, the Gulf War, and most recently Afghanistan.[8]

The Allied air endeavor, however, was much larger than that of the Axis opposition, and collectively it exceeded the not insubstantial Soviet air effort on the Eastern Front. The aerial campaigns of World War II, furthermore, were much greater in scale and scope than either those that came before or those that have occurred since.

In World War I, the US Army air service produced around 17,500 pilots, only a limited number of whom went to France in 1918; while in World War II, even after heavy losses and not counting the navigators, bombardiers, flight engineers, and air gunners needed to man the heavy bomber fleets, the United States Army Air Forces (USAAF) were fielding over 140,500 pilots by the time hostilities ceased.[9] On top of this were the almost 50,000 United States Navy (USN) pilots and over 10,000 United States Marine Corps (USMC) pilots on duty.[10] In 1968, about 47,500 air force personnel, the vast majority ground crewmen rather than combat fliers, were committed to air operations over North Vietnam: this was in contrast to August 1945, when the USAAF around the globe had fielded over 2 million personnel.[11]

Meanwhile, the Royal Air Force (RAF), at the end of World War II, was over three and a half times bigger than it had been at the end of World War I and would shrink to under a tenth of its wartime size in the second half of the twentieth century.[12] The same basic pattern of expansion and contraction also held true for the Fleet Air Arm (FAA) of the Royal Navy.[13]

The comparative scale of the Allied air effort directed against the Axis powers means a proportionately larger number of the kind of first-person written and oral accounts exist that are crucial to developing an understanding of superstition among combat airmen. At the same time, the inclusion of fliers from not only the United States but also the United Kingdom as well as the British Commonwealth and Empire serving either in the RAF, the FAA, or in national air forces modeled on the former—principally the Royal Australian Air Force (RAAF), Royal Canadian Air Force (RCAF), and Royal New Zealand Air Force (RNZAF)—allows for a wider transnational picture to be drawn.

In order to understand the appeal of the supernatural to these pilots and other crewmen, it is first necessary to discuss context. The prevalence of superstition among those of similar age and intelligence needs to be outlined, along with the extent of such belief in wider populations in the timeframe under consideration. Even more important, the stresses and uncertainties induced by aerial combat need to be laid out in order to explain why large numbers of comparatively intelligent and educated volunteers "in a modern scientific war," as military historian Mark Connelly has put it, "still clung to animal-like rituals to appease the gods of battle."[14]

The consequent reliance on the supernatural, though, took many forms, so subsequent individual chapters are devoted to: appeals for specific and direct intervention by a monotheistic deity; reliance on personal or group talismans and charms; a tendency toward ritualistic words and action often not directly associated with religion; the appearance of apparently hexed persons, objects, or events; numerology and magical symbolism; and, finally, supposed supernatural premonitions of doom.

Gremlins are not discussed. Although these mythical creatures appealed to the whimsical nature of certain fliers, notably of course Roald Dahl, and the term became a useful rhetorical means of attributing blame for undiagnosed electro-mechanical problems or odd atmospheric phenomena like St. Elmo's fire, there is no indication that any flier thought gremlins, as such, actually existed.[15]

Chapter 2, it should be stressed, does not consider religious faith per se to be a form of superstition—"an unreasonable or groundless notion"—insofar as the existence of God is inherently untestable in scientific terms.[16] As for the utility of calling on the Almighty for help, though scientific trials indicate that mass intercessory appeals have no discernable effect on recovery from medical procedures or disease, if each miracle is unique and hence nonreplicable, then the effect of prayer too is simply not subject to the scientific method.[17] A case can certainly be made, however, that the prospect of imminent and untimely death drove even those without much or any religious conviction toward pleas for salvation on earth as opposed to entry to heaven.[18]

As we shall see, some forms of superstitious thought among Allied combat fliers were not entirely lacking in rational content. Just as important, as a number of recent studies have shown, even the most completely irrational beliefs, while having no direct physical impact on the future of the people concerned, can still have an effect on self-confidence and thereby performance.[19]

It was easy enough for more rational contemporary observers to be rather dismissive about aircrew superstitions, writing them off as backward and childish examples of magical thinking.[20] More than seventy-five years on, historians can approach the subject more dispassionately, not only chronicling the extent of such thinking but also explaining why it became so prevalent, as well as the role it played in buttressing or undermining morale and operational effectiveness. A fair amount of scholarly attention has been devoted to the policies adopted toward those who eventually refused to fly any more combat missions. It is time to shed more light on one of the mechanisms through which the vast majority were able to keep going.[21]

CHAPTER ONE
MEN AGAINST ODDS

That some of those who volunteered for aircrew duties on either side of the Atlantic in World War II brought supernatural beliefs with them into the air should come as no surprise. Mass-Observation surveys in Britain indicated that about half of adult males accepted at least one common superstition, while around 20 percent offered up prayers outside church, these often being of an intercessory nature.[1] Meanwhile in the United States, Gallup polls revealed that nearly half of those surveyed admitted to having at least one superstition, over 40 percent of families prayed aloud in thanks before meals, and over 80 percent of people believed in the efficacy of intercessory prayer even half a century later.[2]

Normally, though, superstitious thought and behavior is negatively correlated with cognitive ability and educational attainment; and those young men trained as fliers in World War II were among the best and brightest of their generation.[3] Surveys, indeed, suggest a much higher than average level of skepticism regarding common superstitions among a group of civilians of similar intelligence and education to those who volunteered to be USAAF and USN pilots in 1941; less than one in ten, for example, believed Fridays in general and Friday the 13th in particular to be unlucky at a time when this was perhaps the most popular superstition in the country.[4] Thus the hazardous conditions under which wartime fliers operated, and more specifically the odds against survival they encountered, need to be examined in order to understand what a leading RAF physician described as "the mushroom growth of superstition among aircrew."[5]

Flying in World War II was a dangerous business right from the start. The pressures to produce the maximum number of aircrews as quickly as possible to build up forces meant that training crashes were common and often fatal. The RAF lost more than 5,000 men due to training accidents, with another 3,000-odd suffering nonfatal injuries.[6] In the continental United States, the USAAF lost over 3,500 budding aviators to primary, basic, and advanced flight training mishaps.[7] The situation was similar in the USN and FAA. In the middle of the war, one station in Florida was reputed to be suffering one fatality for every six flights, while another in Texas was rumored to be losing on average one cadet each day.[8] Carrier training added extra hazards, the two ersatz flattops used for the purpose on Lake Michigan losing over a hundred planes in the course of the war.[9] Thus a great many of those who successfully completed the various stages of air training remembered men who had been killed along the way.[10] As newly minted Fleet Air Arm pilot Eric Rickman put it, "We all knew of, and had seen, fatal accidents in training."[11]

Acquaintances and friends would continue to be lost in aerial mishaps before and after airmen began operating from frontline airfields or carrier decks. Flying by day, the US Eighth Air Force lost over a thousand men killed in this manner between 1942 and 1945.[12] Operating mostly at night, RAF Bomber Command suffered just over 2,000 such fatalities in 1943–1944 alone.[13] The USN, USMC, and FAA, meanwhile, lost more aviators in crashes than they did in aerial combat.[14]

It was enemy action, however, that demonstrated most vividly to those concerned that war operations were a matter of life and death. In all, the USAAF suffered over 121,000 casualties in the various theaters of operation, the vast majority as a result of aerial combat, while the RAF lost approximately 55,500 men in Europe alone.[15] Over 3,200 USN and USMC fliers were also killed in this way, along with over 400 FAA aircrew.[16]

Depending on period and place, Allied aircrew loss rates could be dauntingly high. The length of aircrew tours, designated as either a certain number of hours flown (usual for fighters) or a specified number of operations or missions (common among bombers) varied over time and from one war zone to another.[17] Yet air staffs, while recognizing the need to hold out the prospect to fliers of a temporary or permanent rest from operations, sought to maximize in combat the investment made in training. In practice this meant tours in which, statistically speaking, the chances of being killed, wounded, or taken prisoner usually exceeded those of emerging unscathed. The overall casualty rates for both RAF Bomber Command and the US Eighth Air Force, for example, exceeded 50 percent, producing approximately 26,000 American and 55,000 British and Commonwealth fatalities.[18] At times when enemy defenses were particularly successful, things could get worse. In the first six months of 1944, the battle casualty rate for the USAAF in the European Theater approached 60 percent.[19] Arthur Harris, who directed RAF Bomber Command between 1942 and 1945, admitted in his memoirs that at times the aircraft loss rate was so great "that scarcely one man in three could expect to survive his tour of thirty operations."[20] An internal Eighth Air Force statistical study completed in February 1944 revealed that only 25 percent of heavy-bomber crewmen were emerging unscathed from their twenty-five-mission combat tours.[21] When they began operations against Japan from Saipan toward the end of the same year, the four B-29 groups that constituted the 73rd Bomb Wing of the Twentieth Air Force suffered casualty rates about twice what had been anticipated.[22]

The level of attrition aboard aircraft carriers tended to be lower but still significant. "On each tour," F6F pilot James D. Billo recalled of his two nine-month operational periods at sea between 1942 and 1944, "we lost about 1/3 of our squadron pilots to enemy fighters, anti-aircraft fire or operational accidents."[23] Moreover, there were episodes in the wartime aerial history of both the Royal Navy and the United States Navy when entire units were practically wiped out in a single operation through enemy action.[24]

Not surprisingly, care was taken not to advertise such gloomy statistics. As *Stars and Stripes* reporter Andy Rooney explained, the "Air Force brass" did not "want to discourage the crews with details of the carnage."[25] What held true for Eighth Air Force headquarters was also the case in RAF Bomber Command. "Stringent precautions were taken," junior operational research scientist Freeman Dyson remembered, "to ensure that any of our Command headquarters documents that discussed survival rates should not reach the squadrons."[26]

Allied fliers, though, had their own ways of calculating the odds. Media reports, along with intelligence briefings and scuttlebutt, though not always entirely accurate, did give a sense of cumulative attrition.[27] There was also direct awareness, as time went on, of the number of aircraft within a particular USAAF group or RAF squadron that failed to return, exploded on or over the airfield, or came back damaged with dead and wounded aboard. "Anyone's arithmetic can figure out how many missions you are likely to last if ten go out and only five come back," P-40 pilot James Morehead observed of the critical situation in the 17th Pursuit

Squadron facing the Japanese in 1942.[28] "We all knew, very accurately, what chance we had of surviving a tour," confirmed Australian navigator Robert Nielsen in reference to the losses incurred over Europe within 460 Squadron in 1942–1943.[29] "One did not have to be a brain surgeon to figure out one's odds of finishing a combat tour," as Samuel Fleming, a B-17 navigator with the 360th Bomb Group in 1944, later explained.[30]

The results might not be encouraging. Though he had successfully completed ten of the then required twenty-five missions over Europe by the start of March 1944, B-17 radioman George Webster of the 92nd Bomb Group noted that "my friends are being killed, one after another, and I know that my probability of dying is increasing with each mission."[31]

Similar trains of thought could arise in the RAF: "Something that very definitely affected my thinking," admitted Bill Grierson, a Halifax navigator flying with 35 Squadron in 1942, "was contemplating the odds of being shot down." Though he did not fully digest the implications of average losses of 5 percent per operation for a thirty-operation tour, he was aware that the future looked distinctly grim.[32]

This sort of observation was by no means confined to RAF and USAAF bomber crews. "I remember thinking on the way home that it truly would be a miracle if one could survive very long with missions like this," P-47 pilot Bill Wright of the 368th Fighter Group reflected after his first exposure to the perils of ground-attack strikes in the autumn of 1944.[33] "The high percentage of losses made us all aware," wrote another P-47 pilot, Marvin Bledsoe, of his tour with the 353rd Fighter Group that spring and summer, that "it was only a matter of time before percentages could catch up with each one of us."[34]

Navy fliers could also reach depressing conclusions. "I don't think I was the only one to do some calculations that summer," the commanding officer (CO) of 835 Squadron, operating from HMS *Nairana* on Atlantic convoy protection duties that same year, later wrote. "In the last four months we had lost seven pilots, observers and telegraphist air gunners, and come within a hair's breadth of losing a great many more. We were a small squadron and if we kept up this sort of mortality rate you didn't need to be Einstein to work out that by the end of the year there wouldn't be many of us left."[35] Dennis Scranton, a US Navy radio operator flying in PB4Y-2s with VPB-108 in the Pacific in 1945, recalled that "I had come to realize that death was more than likely inevitable."[36]

Casualty statistics, in short, could make the odds of being killed all too obvious. Depending on the group or squadron and the period, educated guesses as to chances of survival ranged from as high as about 60 percent to as low as under 10 percent.[37]

At the headquarters of RAF Bomber Command and the USAAF Eighth Air Force in England, it soon became evident that crews were aware that their chances were poor. "Every commander in the Eighth was reporting the same thing" in early 1943, recalled the commander of the 305th Bomb Group, Curtis LeMay, of the mood among fliers: "In the end everyone was going to get shot down."[38] The chief of RAF Bomber Command, Arthur Harris, recognized around the same time that his crews had often worked out the unfavorable statistics. "They were in fact—and they knew it—faced with the virtual certainty of death," he wrote, adding "probably in one of its least pleasant forms."[39]

Indeed, the fragility of the human body could become glaringly evident when observing the fate of those who fell victim to the enemy. Allied fighter jockeys engaged in air-to-air combat might on occasion glimpse the death of a friendly fighter pilot as well as that of adversaries. Briefly distracted from his own difficulties during a Battle of Britain sortie, Spitfire pilot Geoffrey Wellum of 92 Squadron was "transfixed" by the sight of a Hurricane going down, "a long trail of black smoke behind it, and at its base, a bright angry flame." The RAF pilot, perhaps trapped, did not bail out: "Poor sod."[40] Easier to spot than in a frenetic dogfight, an American or British plane badly hit by flak during a dive-bombing or strafing run tended to crash and explode with what one Canadian pilot aptly described as "heart-stopping finality."[41] It was Allied bomber crews, however, whether Americans flying in tight formation by day or Britons semi-independently by night, who were most often the unwilling witnesses to the various nasty ways in which they themselves might die or be maimed in the near future.

The aircraft of USAAF bombardment groups operated in close proximity to one another in order to maximize defensive firepower and, over Europe, flew virtually always in daylight. This meant that most crew members had a grandstand view of what could happen to other aircraft when struck by antiaircraft shells—flak—from the ground or cannon and machine-gun fire from attacking fighters.

Contact between a bomber and a heavy-caliber shell usually meant either near-complete disintegration or a mass of flaming wreckage with observable "body parts, aircraft metal, and other debris," as Mike Morgan, a B-17 copilot in the 384th Bomb Group, recorded.[42] In circumstances like these, the men inside the plane did not stand much of a chance. "Saw a ship in the lower left formation take a direct hit," B-24 pilot Kenneth Jones of the 389th Bomb Group related after a mission in December 1944: "He disintegrated. Flaming gasoline spraying outwards and down and the chunks of debris trailing smoke as it arched downward in slow motion. No chutes seen." Seeing this, he added, had been a "bad nightmare."[43] Two aircraft inadvertently colliding with one another tended to have the same catastrophic effect, as did hits from bombs dropped accidentally onto aircraft below from higher up in formations.[44] Machine-gun and cannon strikes from attacking fighters or a flak burst nearby could cause enough internal damage for a bomber to begin dropping out of formation with a prop or two feathered, engine perhaps already smoking or visibly on fire. Men in nearby ships would look for parachutes; but it was very rare to see everyone get out before the stricken bomber, if not lost to sight, went into a fatal spiral dive or simply blew up. "It was sickening," pilot Vince Fagan of the 450th Bomb Group remembered of watching the final moments of a nearby B-24 in which at least four men perished.[45]

Seeing crew members falling away from their doomed aircraft was not necessarily reassuring. If the plane fell apart, fliers might not have time to attach their parachutes and could "tumble out like tattered rag dolls," B-17 pilot Jim O'Leary of the 303rd Bomb Group confided to his diary.[46] Jumpers might hit other aircraft with likely fatal results; and if they bailed out from a burning plane, such men might find their parachutes smoldering and be seen to become "twisting, blazing torches falling towards the ground," in the words of a radio operator from the 92nd Bomb Group. "What a hell of a way to get it," as 379th Bomb Group pilot Ray Carré commented.[47]

Damaged bombers might make it home, but with dead or wounded men aboard in a gory state. In the wake of a fighter attack on a mission in late June 1943, for example, though the copilot and the rest of the crew managed to get the ship home, the pilot of a B-17 from the 92nd Bomb Group had much of the back of his skull blown away while the flight engineer had most of his left arm severed in combat.[48] Others might hear about this sort of thing from those who had survived comparatively unscathed among the crews concerned, like the escaping gunner of a crashed and burning Liberator from the 98th Bomb Group who had nonetheless heard his trapped pilot's agonized screams.[49] Especially if not flying themselves that day, crewmen could also sometimes find themselves helping extricate the dead and wounded after crippled ships had landed.[50] Ray Matheny, a flight engineer with the 379th Bomb Group, lent a hand when a B-17 damaged on a mission skidded to a halt off the runway at his base:

> Medics removed a wounded waist gunner who had been shot through the chest and he looked dead to me. The tail gunner was dead at his post, and two men removed his bloodied body. The ball turret operator was still strapped in his turret; I unlatched the small egress door, pulling him out by his parachute harness with the help of the others. He had been shot through the stomach . . . but he was still alive. . . . The poor radio operator's head had been blown off by a cannon shell leaving a terrible mess in his compartment.[51]

"We looked at this terrible sight," a member of a crew from the 489th Bomb Group recalled of the corpse of a headless B-24 top-turret gunner, "and prayed that none of us would end up that way."[52]

The handling of dismembered cadavers could be distressing. Aerial gunner Jack Novey, who knew four deceased members of the crew of a B-17 from the 96th Bomb Group that had crash-landed in a nearby field, decided to pay his respects at the hospital morgue. "I looked in the door," he remembered, "and the medics were going through a pile of body parts. . . . It looked like a mess of garbage. It was a horror."[53] 99th Bomb Group radioman Alvin Kotler, after returning from a mission, walked to an isolated B-17 around which there appeared to be some unusual activity only to witness the bloody remains of the ball-turret gunner being washed out into buckets: "These things you don't imagine until you've seen them."[54]

USAAF very heavy bomber operations against Japan, to be sure, like most RAF Bomber Command sorties against Germany in the latter half of the war, might be flown at night. Darkness, however, only magnified the visual effect when an aircraft in the same general area, perhaps as a result of an accidental collision or, more commonly, after being stalked by a fighter or trapped in searchlight beams and hit by flak, caught fire, plunged down, and exploded. Tail gunner Kevin Herbert recalled the "terrible sight" during one of the May 1945 night raids on Tokyo of another

B-29 blowing up "in one vast globe of flame" and then falling away burning in a shallow arc.[55] Parachutes might be spotted occasionally in the glare, but also men falling miles to their deaths, sometimes as human torches. "It was indeed the stuff of nightmares," a Lancaster pilot confirmed.[56]

For those RAF aircrew who survived an encounter with flak or fighters but collectively did not emerge unscathed, the graphic nature of what shrapnel or bullets could do to crewmates was hard to ignore. The pilot of a Boston light bomber of 266 Squadron that had been riddled by anti-aircraft fire, for instance, found on landing that his gunner had received a direct hit to the head from a 40mm shell so that, as the navigator related, "bits of skin, bone, blood and hair had been plastered by the slipstream all over the rear of the aircraft."[57]

The authorities took care to try to shield other crews from gory visual evidence of enemy action or crashes. Badly damaged aircraft, especially with not easily extricable dead onboard, might be towed to hangers and secluded spots where the medical or engineering staff could collect the body parts.[58] The location of station mortuaries, meanwhile, was kept rather quiet.[59] There were times, however, when RAF aircrew on the ground, seeking to rescue trapped colleagues from aircraft that had crashed, saw the remains of men who had been literally torn apart, or, worse yet, witnessed survivors who were still conscious but burning to death before their eyes. "It was a horrible experience," a 308 Squadron wireless operator recalled.[60]

Visiting an RAF hospital could also expose men, as an Australian air gunner noted, to "limb cases, the belly wounded, the eye cases, the head wounds, in fact every damned wound, injury and laceration you could conceive."[61] Encountering burn victims could be particularly shocking. "At Australia House in London I saw a pilot who had been badly burned on the face and hands," remembered 102 Squadron wireless operator Ross Pearson. "I only just recognized him as a fellow who used to travel on the same train to the city as me before the war. . . . His face was covered in scar tissue."[62]

There were instances where the cumulative strain of bad survival odds and shocking visual and other experiences induced psychological collapse in the air.[63] A few men simply refused outright to continue operational flying once back on terra firma.[64] Others might try to avoid the stigma

and potential penalties involved in such overt declarations through generating simulated medical or mechanical problems.[65] There were even
suspicions that some aircrew were deliberately choosing to land and be
interned in neutral Sweden or Switzerland rather than head for home in
aircraft that could still make it. The latter was not in fact the case, though;
and the number of those who failed to carry on flying against the foe was,
in fact, quite tiny. [66]

Most wartime fliers either possessed, or were able to develop, successful psychological coping mechanisms. These, though, varied a good deal.
Some men were able to distance themselves emotionally from what they
saw or heard about in the way of grisly ends, while a few others simply
avoided calculating their odds.[67] There were those adventurous types who
knew full well that their chances of survival were statistically question-
able, yet some found the risk of death in combat actually quite "exciting,"
even "addictive," in the words of P-51 pilot Bud Anderson of the 357th
Fighter Group.[68] Some fliers erroneously argued that their odds were in
fact quite good because the losses for each individual trip against the enemy were proportionately low.[69] Some thought that the experience gained
as time passed outweighed the greater odds of being hit. James Kyle and
other veteran Typhoon pilots in 197 Squadron during 1943 "believed in
the philosophy that the danger was receding in proportion to the number
of missions completed" and asked for more.[70]

Others felt they were somehow being looked after by a higher power.
Having cheated death in a prewar crash, FAA pilot John Wellham felt
that "I either had a guardian angel or, more likely, it was a case of the
Devil looking after his own." In any event, during the war "I could not
escape the feeling that I was not designed to be killed or badly injured
in an aircraft," he later wrote.[71] "God and I have our own arrangement,"
was how Wade Rodgers, an Australian pilot flying Lancasters with 630
Squadron in 1944–1945, put it.[72]

Among American fliers in particular there were some who felt that
they were being shepherded personally by the Almighty. P-40 pilot Robert Scott of the 23rd Fighter Group in 1942 famously titled his wartime
memoir *God Is My Co-Pilot* out of the belief that He was "watching out"
for him.[73] After a number of narrow escapes, P-47 pilot Herky Green
experienced a revelation in February 1944 to the effect that "God finally
made me understand that I was going to live through it."[74] There even

might be literal belief in a guardian angel.[75] "I knew that whatever happened, the man upstairs would take care of me," remembered Dean Bloyd, a B-17 copilot with the 487th Bomb Group in 1945.[76]

Other aircrew, through self-confidence, lack of imagination, or a combination thereof, evidently thought that even without divine protection they were essentially indestructible.[77] Beirne Lay, who in 1943 flew B-17s with the ill-fated 100th Group and cowrote one of the most prominent American war novels of the postwar years, *Twelve O'Clock High*, remembered that "I had been sure I would come home safe and sound."[78] David Evans, who commanded the Boston light bombers of 88 Squadron in 1944–1945, felt the same way: "I always thought I would survive the war," he confirmed in an interview.[79] "We knew that we would not be shot down," Wellington navigator George Bury remembered of his 115 Squadron crew in 1940.[80] A good number of fighter pilots also assumed they were bulletproof: "Death is something that happens to someone else," as an FM-2 pilot flying off the USS *Petrof Bay* in 1945 put it.[81] "It never occurred to me that I would not survive," John Truluck, a P-47 pilot with the 56th Fighter Group in 1943–1944, wrote in his memoirs. "I did not even consider such an outcome."[82]

More generally, youthful optimism could insulate the minds of fliers from the possibility of death or dismemberment. "There's a certain kind of immortality that everyone feels when they're twenty," reflected P-51 pilot Roscoe Brown of the 332nd Fighter Group, a view shared by others.[83] "Each of us younger flyers had the advantage of thinking that we were immune to harm," B-24 navigator John Stewart of the 467th Bomb Group recalled of operations in 1944–1945. Dick Stouffer, a B-17 copilot with the 34th Bomb Group in roughly the same period, agreed. "Being young," he explained in an interview, "this sense of immortality is serious. It never even occurs to you that you won't come back."[84] Youths in the British and Dominion air forces often felt the same way. "I was like most Bomber Command aircrew," Frank Dennis, who joined Lancaster Squadron 419 in the summer of 1944, "young and full of enthusiasm and in spite of knowing the heavy losses still being suffered, it was difficult to imagine, at that age, your own life coming to an end."[85]

That there were casualties and gore was irrefutable; but these could be argued away as irrelevant to personal survival. "I always thought it was going be the other guys that got hit—never me," admitted Charlie Weddell, an A-36 pilot with the 27th Fighter Group in 1944.[86] "Of course, we did not think of dying," RAF fighter pilot Meron Naydler, who began operational flying in North Africa in 1943, affirmed: "The other chap might, probably would, sometimes did, but it never happened to oneself, always to the other poor bastard."[87] Bomber crews might think along similar lines. "I didn't have a feeling that I was going to get killed—my friends were, but not me," remembered B-17 pilot Bob Nelson of the 398th Bomb Group: "I'm going to miss these guys around me, but I'm going to be OK."[88] Laurence Deane, flying Hampdens in 1941–1942 with 144 Squadron, admitted how faith that "it would always be the other chap that got the 'chop' kept us going."[89]

A consciously upbeat attitude also might be helpful. "My answer [to the nasty sights and bad survival statistics] was to think positively," Robert Morgan, skipper of the famous B-17 *Memphis Belle* of the 91st Bomb Group, later explained, the result being that "I always believed, at rock bottom, that my airplane, my crew, and I were going to make it."[90] A similar frame of mind could be found among some RAF Bomber Command fliers. "I never really believed that I wasn't going to come home," asserted Kiwi navigator Des Andrews. "I wouldn't let myself think that."[91]

There was also faith that superior skill lengthened the odds against aerial disaster. "If I learned all I could and did my job right," as B-17 flight engineer Ray Matheny put it early in his 1943–1944 tour with the 379th Bomb Group, "maybe I and my crew mates would be safe."[92] In part because of "a very competent crew and outstanding pilot," B-17 tail gunner Kenneth Tucker of the 97th Bomb Group believed in 1944–1945 that "I stood a good chance of making it back."[93] Confidence in his pilot and the rest of the crew meant that Lancaster bomb aimer Les Bartlett of 50 Squadron "never thought that anything would happen to us . . . never had a thought that we would be shot down."[94] Andrew Maitland, a Halifax bomb aimer with 76 Squadron in 1943, was more conscious of the statistics, but "I consoled myself with the fact that our crew was knitting together like a good team and so together I hoped we could beat the odds."[95] There was also a related belief that experience counted in your favor; that if a pilot or crew survived the first five to ten clashes with the enemy, then they were less likely to be shot down.[96]

Official statistical analyses tended to confirm this last idea.[97] Unfortunately, though, skill and experience could not prevent men from losing their lives later in their tours. "The attrition rate on experienced crews has been quite heavy [by February 24, 1944]," noted B-24 lead navigator Hal

Turell of the 445th Bomb Group; he decided that this had brought down his chances of survival to one in three.[98] Less than two months later, C. C. Cole, a six-mission and no-longer-neophyte B-24 radio operator with the 458th Bomb Group, noticed one morning that he knew almost nobody among the 150 aircrew seated for breakfast at Horsham St. Faith:

> Wanting to call this to the attention of fellow crew member and buddy Jim Wedding [the crew's flight engineer], but not too harshly, I said, "Hey, Jim. Do you notice anything different about the mess hall?" Jim was munching away on his rather tasteless powdered eggs and brownish-grey English bread. He casually glanced around the room and said, "Nope. Looks like the same old mess hall to me." "Jim, take another look. Who do you see that you know?" He began to scan the room . . . after a very long look. . . . "Well, there's Reynold's crew . . . there's Manker's crew. . . ." Then realization struck! Astounded, he turned. . . . "We're strangers in our own mess hall!" "Yeah, Jim, does that tell you anything?" "It sure does. Time is running out on us. We're probably not long for this place!"

"Losses had indeed been heavy," as Cole noted.[99] Fliers were very much aware that, as B-17 copilot James O'Conner noted in his diary in October 1944 as he contemplated the final five missions of his tour with the 388th Bomb Group, crews "had been known to be shot down on their very last trip."[100]

The same underlying unpredictability concerning the correlation between skill and repeat exposure, on the one hand, and end-of-tour survival, on the other, was evident in RAF Bomber Command. "We used to think that experience counted for a lot because most of the guys would be lost on number two or three," Canadian rear gunner Jimmy Moffat noted of his time with 427 Squadron during 1943–1944; "and then a bunch of guys would be lost between twenty-five and thirty. And you wouldn't know what the hell to think."[101] Geoff Copeman, a Lancaster flight engineer who joined 57 Squadron about the time Moffat was shot down, concluded after a popular veteran flier was killed at the end of July 1944 that while experience "must be a help," the fact remained that "no-one was invulnerable; it seemed you were just as likely to get what we called 'the chop' on the last as on the first—or the next?"[102] The mix of "training, experience and ability," admitted RAF fighter pilot K. B. McGlashan, who flew operationally from 1940 through 1944, might not be enough in the "environment of loss" characteristic of wartime flying.[103] The bottom line, as Lancaster skipper Jack Thompson noted of his 1944 operational tour with 12 Squadron after witnessing the death of a highly experienced pilot, was that "you never knew what the next trip over the continent held in store for you, veterans or not!"[104]

As time went on, it might not be possible to avoid the inevitable conclusion that, in combat flying, whether one lived or died was in the end highly arbitrary. "The fickle finger of fate had spared many and killed many for reasons that are impossible to explain," reflected P-38 pilot Stubb Hatch of his tour with the 1st Fighter Group in 1944, adding: "The sheer inconsistency of life in a war is inexplicable."[105] Fate could appear so random. "Some got killed on their first mission while others survived a tour of 35 trips or so and some even completed two tours," reflected Canadian pilot Donald Smith, who flew Halifaxes with 425 Squadron in 1944. "Some never encountered enemy fighters or flak, while others encountered them every time they went out. Sometimes one or more crew mates were wounded or killed while the rest of the crew returned [unharmed]."[106]

The apparent randomness of death and injury in combat flying, coupled with general knowledge of the overall odds, made it more difficult for some to go on believing in long-term survival. "It's hopeless!" a B-17 copilot angrily shouted one summer morning in 1944 at Polebrook as crews of the 351st Bomb Group were awoken for yet another mission. "If they don't get you one day, they'll get you the next! There's just no way you can make it without being shot down sooner or later!"[107] Though few expressed such sentiments aloud, they were quite common. "So far as I could see, we should go on flying until we were killed," Miles Tripp, a Lancaster bomb aimer, concluded after some months on operations with 218 Squadron in 1944–1945.[108] Even that most self-confident of types— the American fighter pilot—might become pessimistic. By early September 1944, after a month of aerial combat, P-51 pilot Richard Curtis of the 52nd Fighter Group was starting to develop "strong doubts that I would ever get back [to the United States] alive."[109]

Faced with all this, some fliers became fatalists. "When it's your time, it's your time," B-17 pilot Tex Holmes of the 303rd Bomb Group told his navigator in late 1944. "There's nothing you can do to change that."[110] F4F pilot Joe Foss, who flew with VMF-121 against the Japanese from Guadalcanal in 1942, remembered another USMC pilot arguing that if "your number's up, you're going to get it" no matter what.[111] As F6F pilot Charles Moutenot reflected while flying off the deck of the USS *Essex* in 1944, "If it's going to happen, it's going to happen."[112] RAF aircrew might also develop the attitude that "whatever happens, happens," as Roger Coverley, a Halifax pilot with 78 Squadron in early 1944, put it.[113] According to Doug Johnston, flying Whitleys as a wireless operator/air gunner with 76 Squadron in 1941, "You reconciled yourself to the inevitable."[114]

Embracing the strong likelihood of death might be liberating, allowing for a carpe diem approach. As Richard Byers, a B-24 waist gunner, confided to his diary on August 16, 1943, after six months of combat flying: "If you're going to get killed—so what?"[115] But it could also be dangerous, causing aircrew to fight less hard to survive. Fatalism could result in fliers "doing less and less to help themselves since they were convinced that they could not change the inevitable result," RCAF Mustang pilot Robert Brown argued; it led to "auto-suggestion which whittled away at the instinct of self-preservation and led to carelessness and attendant disaster," according to bomb aimer Ron Mayhill, flying with 75 Squadron in the summer of 1944.[116] "They let themselves be killed," B-17 copilot Jesse Pitts of the 379th Bomb Group in 1943–1944 stated bluntly.[117]

Yet recognizing the potential dangers of fatalism did not solve the problem of poor survival odds and the limits to which a positive attitude and emphasis on honing skills could counteract them in the context of operations (the British term) or missions (the American term) in which fortune seemed to play a leading role in determining who did and did not return in one piece. After observing how even the veterans in 460 Squadron could suddenly get the chop in August 1944, Halifax pilot Ted McGindle concluded that "no matter how experienced an operational crew is, survival is still largely a matter of luck."[118] Even those who made it through might agree. "How much of our successfully completing our missions," B-17 flight engineer Bill Williams and his crew debated after completing their fifty-mission tour with the 463rd Bomb Group in the summer of 1944, "was due to skill and how much to chance?"[119] There were naval fliers who concurred. "You needed a lot of luck," F6F pilot Ted Crosby reflected, "no matter how well you could handle your aircraft."[120] Some fliers thought that skill still counted more than luck; but many seem to have thought the opposite was true, ratio estimates ranging from 75 percent luck versus 25 percent skill to as high as 90 percent luck versus only 10 percent skill.[121] "Everyone knew that without luck you weren't going to make it," recalled Melvin McGuire, a B-17 waist gunner with the 2nd Bomb Group in 1944–1945.[122]

Even fighter pilots confident in their abilities had occasionally to admit that skill alone was not enough. The factor "that cannot be underrated by the fighter pilot is luck," opined a veteran RAF flier.[123] "The best of us needed luck to survive," argued James Vernon of VBF-87, flying F6Fs from the deck of the USS *Ticonderoga* in 1945.[124]

Awareness of the extent to which survival depended on sheer chance often drove fliers to contemplate how lucky they had been thus far and to worry about their apparent good fortune ending before they completed their tour in one piece.[125] Logic and reason suggested that there was nothing that could be done to influence more-or-less random events, that beyond a certain point whether one lived or died was "like a roll of the dice," as B-24 pilot Robert Capps of the 456th Bomb Group stated.[126] Yet a variety of behavioral studies have demonstrated clearly that when the future seems particularly uncertain people are much more inclined to engage in magical thinking and superstitious action as a means of trying to assert agency and impose control than otherwise would be the case.[127] Thus, while it might be incontrovertible that some airmen had experienced "a bad roll of the dice," it was still possible to influence the outcome for oneself: "if I shook mine carefully, and spit on them" as B-17 navigator Robert Grilley of the 401st Bomb Group put it, "they'd land right."[128]

How, though, to make fickle Lady Luck, as young men often conceptualized this mythical arbiter of their fate, smile rather than frown?[129] As the following chapters illustrate, there were a variety of means through which frightened fliers experiencing an "intense need for help and protection," as a pair of USAAF doctors explained, would try to bring about good fortune while staving off the bad.[130]

CHAPTER TWO
ASKING FOR MIRACLES

In the context of considerable danger, it was natural that aircrew should turn to God as a means of saving body as well as soul. This might involve talismanic or ritualistic elements, to be discussed in the chapters ahead. The most widespread form of entreaty, though, came in the form of requests for help directed at what American fliers might euphemistically dub "the Command Pilot" or more commonly "the Man Upstairs."[1]

Chaplains were employed by both the RAF and RN and by the USAAF and USN, but their role as intercessory figures differed somewhat, with American clergy often being expected to take a more active role in publicly mediating prayers for personal safety. In both navies, chaplains might be asked to say a prayer or two over the public address system on aircraft carriers and other large warships before action commenced; but as far as can be ascertained, unlike their USN counterparts, RN chaplains were not in the habit of visiting the aircrew ready room to offer fliers their services prior to a strike being launched.[2] As in the USAAF, there were regular church services in the RAF; but except for Catholics, fliers were generally not given the opportunity, as they were on the more permanent American bases, to attend a denominational service of their choice either before or after being briefed for action.[3] It was virtually unheard of for a chaplain to lead an assembly of British airmen in asking for divine intervention—"Almighty and everlasting Father, we humbly beseech thee to protect those of us who will be flying today," for instance—at the beginning or end of the briefing itself, but this could and did happen in the USAAF.[4]

This likely reflected the diverging trajectories of religious practice and belief in Great Britain and the United States. In the former, though a strong majority still seem to have identified with a particular denomination, formal affiliation had been gently declining through the first half of the twentieth century, such that in 1940 only about a fifth of the population was a church member.[5] "To many," the authors of a Mass-Observation study compiled later in the decade concluded, "religion has come to mean little more than being kind and neighbourly, doing good when opportunity arises."[6] Within the RAF, the final report on a succession of chaplains' conferences held through 1944 lamented, three-quarters of the men and women wearing air force blue lacked even basic religious knowledge.[7]

By way of contrast, the number of those with a strong religious affiliation in the United States grew significantly in the first four decades of the twentieth century, reaching around 50 percent of the population during the war years, with belief in God nearly universal.[8] Popular aviation culture in America was already saturated with religious metaphors and imagery; and in stark contrast to the RAF chaplains' lament mentioned above, the religious teachings embraced by the majority of American airmen were both deep-rooted and extensive, according to the official historian of the wartime USAAF chaplaincy.[9]

Catholics tended to engage in religious practice with greater regularity and enthusiasm than many other denominations, and about 30 percent of the chaplains working with the USAAF in England were Catholic.[10] The great majority of chaplains within the RAF, though, were from the Church of England and other Protestant denominations, and much of their effort seems to have been directed toward general welfare rather than interceding with the Almighty on behalf of those who flew operationally.[11]

American chaplains—Catholic, Protestant, or Jewish—who conducted short services for those who voluntarily gathered around before or, more often, after briefings on mission days were catering to a demand. Sometimes the response might be limited. "As I recall," wrote B-24 navigator John L. Stewart of the 467th Bomb Group in his memoirs, "only a small fraction of airmen participated in this."[12] Yet much of the time "a lot of the fellas," as B-17 tail gunner Arnold Willis of the 303rd Bomb Group put it, who "depended a lot on their religion, they would see the chaplain before [missions]."[13] Richard R. Johnson, a B-17 pilot with the 303rd Bomb Group in 1944, estimated that "about half the combat crews would go to the chapel for prayers" before setting out toward their aircraft.[14] Especially once it was clear that the mission was going to be against a distant and well-defended target, young men like B-17 pilot Les Rentmeester of the 91st Bomb Group, who figured "that I needed all the help I could get," took advantage of the opportunity to have their prayers for survival mediated by a professional.[15] "A few words are offered by the Chaplain, for those who are interested," noted P-51 pilot Frank Speer of the 4th Fighter Group, "and there are few who are not."[16]

The fact that such "spiritual insurance" (as it was sometimes dubbed) was not simply a matter of religious habit is illustrated not only by a noticeable spike in Sunday service attendance once combat commenced but also by the way in which men of varying religious backgrounds took advantage of the presence of a chaplain of a different denomination. A B-17 pilot with the 398th Bomb Group, for example, though a Methodist, was quite happy one day in August 1944 to take up the offer of Father Sullivan, the padre ministering to the Catholics among his crew, to "say a few words to try and insure your safety on this mission."[17] The more missions flown, the greater the reliance on clerical help often became. "Time spent with the chaplain became more important with each successive mission," B-17 ball-turret gunner Randall Rasmussen of the 91st Bomb Group noted in his war memoirs.[18]

In the RAF, the situation was different. "I have never been an overly religious person," wrote navigator John Harding of 103 Squadron, adding that on Sundays "like many aircrew I would have preferred to skip church parade."[19] It was usually only the Catholics, fewer in number than in the USAAF, who routinely sought and received clerical help before flying in supplications for divine protection.[20] Basil Spiller, a Halifax navigator with 102 Squadron at Pocklington in 1944, recalled the ministrations of Father Searby, an Australian, who would routinely visit the dispersal point before takeoff and give his blessing to the three Roman Catholics among the seven-man crew.[21] An Irish padre working on a station from which another Halifax squadron was operating in 1942–1943 noticed that the number of Catholic fliers attending the RC chapel—always high to begin with—tended to increase when the target was a "sticky" one like Berlin.[22] Protestant chaplains in the RAF might also pay visits to the dispersal points but tended to confine themselves to cheery optimism, offering sweets or "wakey-wakey" pills and wishing the men concerned the best of luck.[23] Aboard the aircraft carriers of the Royal Navy, meanwhile, the role of the Church of England chaplain tended to be as much secular as pastoral.[24]

Sometimes knowledge that a family member was praying on one's behalf offered hope.[25] On occasion those manning bombers in either air force might also pray as a team before boarding their aircraft. "My crew always held a short prayer service on the flightline before takeoff," B-17 waist gunner Melvin McGuire of the 2nd Bomb Group remembered.[26] A senior pilot and the other six fliers in a Halifax crew in 158 Squadron did the same thing. "It was common knowledge on the squadron that before each trip he and his crew held a little prayer session together, after boarding their aircraft," related the navigator of a different crew in his memoirs.[27]

More commonly, either before or as they lifted off into the unknown or upon their return, crew members might make individual requests for divine help in surviving their tour. Beaufort navigator William Hunter recalled how, just before the aircraft began to taxi during his time with 217 Squadron in the spring of 1941, he silently offered up the following: "Please God take us safely into the air and back to land at the end of our operation."[28] Canadian pilot Sydney Smith, about to take off in a Hampden of 115 Squadron on his first operation to bomb Dusseldorf in the autumn of 1942, sat in the cockpit and silently mouthed: "Oh God, now that this night has come, I pray to thee to protect with thy loving care myself, my crew, and our dear ones who are far away from us."[29] Each night of operations in 1943–1944, as his Lancaster began the climb to cruising altitude, Les Bartlett, a bomb aimer with 50 Squadron, offered up a silent prayer for a safe flight.[30] Ronnie Waite, a Halifax pilot with 78 Squadron based at Middleton St. George, had in 1942 habitually prayed before heading out. "It usually took the form of a brief request that I should return safely," he remembered. "If the mission was expected to be particularly hazardous, I sometimes made my supplication on bended knee at the iron bedstead in my room."[31] Starting his tour two years later, Lancaster pilot Richard Kelly began as he meant to end. "Every trip we made," he recalled, "about five or ten minutes before we reached the target, I used to say a few prayers, hoping that the good lord would look after me and see me safely out of the target area."[32]

To judge by memoir and interview references, USAAF airmen were even more inclined to believe in the power of prayer. William H. Dowden, a B-24 radio operator with the 389th Bomb Group, thought that, like him, "everybody" prayed to improve their chances.[33] Phrasing might vary, but the general thrust was often similar. "Nothing fancy," remembered Leonard Herman, a Jewish B-17 bombardier flying with the 95th Bomb Group in 1943, "just 'God, please get us home alive. Please let us live through this mission.'"[34] About to start his tour as a B-17 pilot with the 401st Bomb Group toward the end of that year, William Maher asked the Lord "for the best of providential protection in the days ahead."[35] Another devout Christian, B-24 flight engineer John Shiver of the 98th Bomb Group, "asked him to take care of me each day" during his tour in 1943–1944.[36] Requests might be quite specific. "I prayed shamelessly to be spared a death from fire, drowning or explosion," remembered Granholm Jackson of his occasional visits between missions to Norwich Cathedral while serving as a B-24 navigator with the 458th Bomb Group in 1944–1945.[37] "Please, dear God, help get us through this last one safely," radioman Thomas Wilcox remembered asking aboard his B-26 just before it taxied out for what would turn out to be the sortie on which he was shot down and captured by the Germans.[38]

An entreaty might take the form of an offer. "God, give me my life," pleaded B-24 navigator Donald Currier of the 449th Bomb Group in the wake of particularly rough trip, "and I will never ask for anything else again."[39] During one hair-raising mission, remembered B-17 pilot Keith Lamb of the 100th Bomb Group, "I prayed—the only time I ever did on a mission. I said, 'God, if you get me through this one, I'll never doubt you again.'" Landing safely, he lived up to his side of bargain.[40] Terms, though, might be subject to eventual renegotiation even by the devout, as B-24 radioman Michael Donahue of the 93rd Bomb Group later related. Facing the prospect of death on his penultimate trip over enemy territory, he called on God, the angels, and the saints for protection, vowing to become a priest if it was given. "I survived the mission and completed my tour, but 'the Lord works in mysterious ways.' The Big Guy up there told me to forget the vow; instead, get married, have four children, and become a dentist."[41]

This sort of thing was by no means confined to bomber crews. "I struck a deal," P-51 pilot Richard Curtis recalled: "If God would return me safe and sound from this crazy war, I'd train for the ministry."[42] Indeed, it appears to have been fairly common within the single-seat fighter fraternity for pilots to pray before takeoff. "There was ample opportunity during taxiing, and it certainly was an appropriate time, for prayers for a safe return from the combat mission about to be flown," observed P-47 pilot Al Zlaten of the 373rd Fighter Group, adding: "I am certain I am not the only pilot who started a mission with a prayer on his lips."[43] He was quite correct: "I always said a little prayer on the runway before I pushed the throttle forward," wrote Hal Shook of his time flying the same fighter type with the 404th Fighter Group.[44] Some who looked to heaven were devout, others less so. "Sitting there in the cockpit [waiting to taxi out on his first mission]," remembered Marvin Bledsoe of the 353rd Fighter Group, another P-47 jockey operating at the same time, "I prayed. I had never been a religious person and had very little faith in a higher being, but I didn't want to miss out on any possible help. I heard my voice say out loud, 'Lord, I don't know what I'm up against, so I want you to help me over the hurdles. Just get me back to my family.'"[45]

Perhaps most prevalent of all were supplications made amid aerial emergencies. "Many a prayer was said during the heat of battle or other crises," remarked B-17 copilot Craig Harris of the 457th Bomb Group— "even by those who were not particularly religious."[46] There is plenty of evidence from Allied airmen to support this view. "I can remember what I call 'relearning the Lord's Prayer,'" recalled B-24 bombardier David Lundy of the 93rd Bomb Group in relation to a particularly dangerous takeoff in foggy conditions: "I started and forgot it; then I remembered it. That was one case where I was scared, afraid," he added.[47] "In panicky desperation," confessed Tony Tabor, a B-17 radioman forced to operate one of the waist guns during a fighter attack, "I pleaded with the Blessed Virgin, reciting every prayer I remembered since childhood."[48] Realizing in the course of a mission that he had inadvertently forgotten to take aboard his parachute, B-24 nose gunner Bill Fili of the 450th Bomb Group looked for divine help. "Christ, I need you now," he remembered pleading, "please let this be another milk run."[49] Paul Katz, a navigator with the 91st Bomb Group, found one day in February 1945 during the return leg of a mission to Dresden that his damaged B-17 had inadvertently drifted over the formidable flak defenses of the Ruhr: "I don't know what the rest of the crew was doing," he noted in his diary, "but I was praying like I never prayed before."[50]

Sometimes the prayer came naturally. Clay Akin, a radioman with the 498th Bomb Group and a devout Catholic, turned to prayer when his B-29 was caught by searchlights over Japan after more conventional counter-measures had been exhausted.[51] But even confirmed atheists might discover the benefits of supplication. A flight engineer in the 100th Bomb

Group who refused to attend any religious services admitted to one of the waist gunners on his crew that when the flak bursts were close "I pull my head down behind the [top-turret] gun-sight and pray."[52]

Crises in the air could make British and Commonwealth bomber crews turn their thoughts heavenward as well. After a Halifax of 420 Squadron was so badly damaged by flak that it looked as if the crew might have to ditch in the English Channel on the night of July 25, 1944, the flight engineer noticed the wireless operator, a staunch Irish Catholic, on his knees in the fuselage praying for God's help.[53] As B-17 copilot Craig Harris noted, however, one did not need to be devout to call on the Lord in a tight spot. Wireless operator Eddie Wheeler of 97 Squadron recalled how his Lancaster was caught in a cone of searchlight beams over Mannheim in early 1944 for no less than six minutes: "If ever I prayed, it was never more earnestly than on that night."[54]

Those flying fighters for the USAAF might also call on the Lord for emergency assistance. P-51 pilot Bob Schimanski, who rarely if ever felt the need to call on the Almighty, found himself doing so one day in early 1945 while leading the 357th Fighter Squadron on instruments in combat formation through low cloud. Though sure he himself would survive, "I prayed that I wouldn't make a mistake. I felt that lives were entrusted to me and I was going to do the best I could, and I didn't want to make a mistake. That was my only prayer."[55] Busy trying to stay aloft and alive while flying alone, single-seat fighter pilots might only have the chance to make the briefest of entreaties. "God, please. Don't fail me," John Godfrey, a veteran P-47 pilot with the 4th Fighter Group, remembered thinking while in a tight spot over Europe.[56] "Okay, God, this is it," Harold Rosser of the 33rd Fighter Group explained when lost in bad weather over Burma flying a P-38: "I'd sure like to be out of this mess."[57] Both men emerged unscathed. "Dear God, please give me enough pressure to help drop my flaps," A-36 pilot Mark Savage prayed as his Allison engine quit while he tried to land in Italy. He too remained uninjured.[58]

American bomber crews, meanwhile, were particularly prone to entreating the Almighty at length for protection during the bomb run—the stressful few minutes when enemy flak was heaviest and formations had to fly straight and level. "I strongly suspect that most men offered a prayer or two during this time," B-26 navigator Carl Moore of the 344th Bomb Group commented, adding: "I know I did."[59] Another navigator, John Stewart, who flew aboard B-24s with the 467th Bomb Group, did not normally pray but found himself doing so amid very accurate flak over Hildesheim on February 22, 1945. "Although out of character," he wrote subsequently in his diary, "I really prayed today for our crew."[60] According to B-29 pilot Gordon Robertson of the 29th Bomb Group, the bomb run over a flak-defended Japanese target in 1945 "was the moment of greatest anxiety for many crew members and resulted in a lot of believers and nonbelievers alike trying to make a deal with God."[61] Fighter attacks and damaged engines could also generate calls for help. "Need I say we were all praying?" B-17 pilot Bruce Muirhead wrote in his diary of a heavily contested trip to Brux on May 12, 1944.[62]

With or without the assistance of a chaplain, and with or without much prior religious instruction or conviction, Allied fliers used prayer as a potential means to improve their chances of survival. "They want to live," a pair of newspapermen reporting on the bomber crews of the Eighth Air Force observed, "and prayer, like an extra oxygen mask and long underwear, is an added precaution."[63] Even among the religious, however, looking for supernatural assistance would by no means be confined to asking for God's protection. A variety of other methods—often more occult in nature—would also be employed by the atheistic, agnostic, and devout alike as a means of beating the odds.

CHAPTER THREE
TALISMANS AND MASCOTS

The veneration of objects with sacred associations has long been a feature of organized religion, notably within the Catholic Church. In the context of the perilous air war, various personal items would take on added importance as individual protective devices both among those who looked to the Pope for spiritual guidance and among those who did not. A wide variety of other material things, meanwhile, inanimate and occasionally animate, were invested with supernatural significance.

Medals portraying the patron saint of travelers were fairly common among Allied fliers. Ian Gleed, for example, flying Hurricanes with 87 Squadron in 1940, always wore one on a chain around his neck.[1] They were the most popular talisman among crews of the 303rd Bomb Group in 1944, according to B-17 radioman Ben Smith.[2] By no means did all of these men happen to be Roman Catholic themselves. "Around my neck I always wore a medal of St. Christopher that a Catholic friend had given me," recalled Canadian bomber pilot Sydney Smith of 115 Squadron.[3] "As a 'just in case' my Roman Catholic cousin in Philadelphia had impressed upon me a St. Christopher medal that had a special place in my wallet," wrote B-24 pilot Keith Schuyler of the 44th Bomb Group.[4]

Other objects of religious significance might be carried aloft, including crucifixes, sacred heart medals, and even vials of holy water.[5] Rosary beads, of course, were popular among the devout and might also serve the needs of non-Catholics. Recalling his tour as a B-17 navigator with the 490th Bomb Group late in the war, E. J. Johnson noted that, when things got really rough in the air for his plane and crew, his pilot, Ray Hann, would call up radio operator Michael Quagliano over the intercom: "Mike, we're in trouble—better get your beads and get us some help from above!"[6]

Short written tracts or homilies of one sort or another could also take on talismanic significance. Sidney Munns, a Whitley navigator with 77 Squadron in the early war years, was sent a Prayer to the Holy Cross by a friend of his mother with a cover note explaining that it "will protect you from many dangers."[7] Toward the end of the war pilot Jack Pitts of the 371st Fighter Group was sent a page containing a favorite hymn by his mother and pastor, and he always took it when climbing into the cockpit of his P-47 in 1944–1945.[8]

Religious mementos dating from the previous war might be kept about the person. At least two Australians in 44 Squadron had inherited pocket Bibles used by their father or grandfather in the trenches during World War I, while Bill Jackson, a Canadian rear gunner flying aboard Stirlings with 218 Squadron in the middle war years, stowed in one of his tunic pockets a small prayer book that his father had carried during the Great War: "I was determined to carry it through this war also."[9] A B-17 gunner was overheard explaining around the same time that "I carry this bible with me every time, damn right I do," adding: "My Dad, he carried it all the way through the Argonne in the last war and he came out okay."[10]

It was in the USAAF, in fact, that testaments most often seem to have taken on quasimagical protective properties. "I wouldn't be without it," B-29 pilot Van Parker of the 19th Bomb Group wrote to his family in early April 1945 of the metal-plated New Testament they had given him, which he had carried in his pocket through his first thirteen missions.[11] There were plenty of them about: in addition to the innumerable personal Bibles carried overseas, the Americans printed and distributed 11 million Protestant, Catholic, and Jewish versions to the armed forces.[12] Often encased in stainless steel and engraved with the legend "MAY THIS KEEP YOU SAFE FROM HARM," these items seemed to offer a combination of spiritual and physical protection. Stories circulated of fliers' lives being saved through carrying them, such as that of B-17 navigator Albert Simon of the 303rd Bomb Group, hit in the lower abdomen by a flak fragment that penetrated his armored vest and flying clothing but miraculously left only a bruise rather than severing a main artery.[13] To help generate "good luck," B-17 ball-turret gunner Kenneth Drinnon of the 487th Bomb Group carried his Good Book over the heart in an upper-left jacket pocket on every mission he flew.[14] He was by no means alone. "In one pocket over my heart I carry my prayer book with the metal armored cover,"

John Briol, a devout Catholic serving as a B-17 ball-turret gunner with the 457th Bomb Group, confided to his diary, adding: "It would stop a light piece of flak."[15] This train of thought was by no means confined to churchgoers. "Many of the crewmen carried the testaments," explained a B-17 radioman of the 303rd Bomb Group, including him (despite being far from devout), since word had gotten around "of an instance where one of them had deflected a piece of shrapnel."[16]

Meanwhile the popularity of crucifixes and religious medals was matched if not dwarfed by that of a host of personal and collective lucky charms in the Allied air forces. These usually came in three basic forms: small trinkets, items of clothing, and toy figures.

Items traditionally thought to bring good fortune—a rabbit's foot, horseshoe, or four-leaf clover, for instance—were often acquired as is or in miniature facsimile. "I had my father send me a rabbit's foot," related Lancaster flight engineer Ted Peck of 622 Squadron, "which accompanied me on all my ops."[17] Lancaster wireless operator John Marsden of 115 Squadron, to cite another case, carried a rabbit's paw on the right side of his battledress blouse for "good luck" when flying, as did many other aircrew in the RAF.[18] This particular trinket was also very popular among Americans. Ground crew chief Herbert L. McKibbin, for example, dangled a rabbit's foot from a small chain on the instrument panel of the P-51 flown by Bud Fortier of the 355th Fighter Group. "It wasn't lucky for the rabbit," McKibbin explained, "but it'll bring you lots of luck!"[19] Horseshoe trinkets might also be carried. Though claiming "I am not superstitious," Spitfire pilot E. A. W. Smith of 127 Squadron did concede in his diary that "I *do* carry the silver horseshoe with me every day."[20] Fresh four-leaf clovers were perhaps harder to acquire, but after searching successfully amid the airfield grass, wireless operator Bill Copley of 460 Squadron had a specimen mounted in Perspex and carried it on every operational trip.[21] Not surprisingly, a pair of loaded dice might also be considered talismanic.[22] Ted Fahrenwald, flying with the 352nd Fighter Group, glued a Joker—a playing card of potentially great benefit in games of chance like poker and euchre—to his lifejacket.[23] Presumably in an attempt to combine the supernatural idea that reflective surfaces can be used to repel evil and the material strength of high-tensile metal, air gunner Mike Henry of 110 Squadron "always carried a steel shaving mirror in the left breast pocket of my uniform" while manning the turret of his Blenheim in 1940.[24]

More region-focused superstitions might also influence what were considered good-luck charms. While in transit to England, B-24 flight engineer Ken Covington of the 34th Bomb Group picked up a "Giddy-Giddy" talisman in Dakar of a kind that the local Senegalese wore as protective charms.[25] B-17 navigator Harry Crosby was given a sprig of white heather by a woman of Celtic ancestry while in training: "Keep this and you will always be lucky."[26] And B-17 flight engineer Vern Kling of the 398th Bomb Group always carried a buckeye—or horse chestnut— because it was considered particularly lucky in the state of Ohio.[27] Bob Gates, flying Lancasters with 467 Squadron, habitually wore the desiccated remains of part of a foot from a kangaroo from his native Australia around his neck, while Hurricane pilot John Ellis of 85 Squadron, a Cockney, always wore as a pendant a small boomerang lucky charm sent from Down Under by a favorite aunt.[28]

A wide variety of more personal trinkets, meanwhile, might be brought aloft as good-luck pieces. Special items of currency were popular, such as lucky pennies or—in the case of American fliers—silver dollars.[29] Veteran RAF bomber pilot Tom Sawyer recalled in his memoirs "a bent ha'penny which I always carried. By the end of the war it had become brightly polished and much thinner through being permanently in my pocket."[30] Given a gold farthing by his FAA engine fitter—"Something to bring you luck, sir"—Swordfish pilot John Godley displayed outward nonchalance but was inwardly delighted.[31] In addition to his four-leaf clover and horseshoe, Ralph Schneck carried an oversized 1937 Indian Head nickel.[32] Their size and durability made special coins and medallions a natural talismanic choice, but sometimes special bank notes might also be prized. "My lucky charms, which justified themselves by their excellent results," wrote RAAF Lancaster pilot Rollo Kingsford-Smith, "were an American Dollar Bill and an Australian ten shilling note signed by all my friends in a bar at Bairnsdale in Victoria in 1942."[33]

Other small items might also be adopted. Fighter pilot Desmond Scott "always carried a small [1.5-inch] pink [glass] elephant [with a broken trunk] in my pocket" that had been given to him by a well-wisher before he left New Zealand for the United Kingdom, while Jock Wilson of 214 Squadron carried a small yellow rubber duck with "BERLIN OR BUST" written on it.[34] On arrival at his Heavy Conversion Unit, Halifax navigator Colin Dudley adopted a paper-and-wire Armistice Day poppy, which he carried throughout the rest of the war.[35] From the start of his first tour,

Lancaster flight engineer Norman Ashton of 103 Squadron wore a pin with a red bead head in his lapel; Halifax flight engineer T. W. Fox of 77 Squadron attached a tiny pair of wooden clogs to his; Lancaster bomb aimer Geoff King of 57 Squadron "carried a little tiny ornament of a black cat minus tail"; Miles Tripp, another Lancaster bomb aimer, adopted a "tiny bone elephant"; and Halifax mid-upper gunner Harry McLean of 427 Squadron linked "a tiny brass Lincoln imp" to his identity tags.[36] It was the same in the USAAF. "I have carried a fishhook for a long time," admitted B-17 pilot Robert Tays to others in the 392nd Bomb Group, adding that on missions "I won't go without it."[37] Melvin McGuire, a B-17 waist gunner with the 2nd Bomb Group, adopted an old metal gunner-qualification badge as "my good luck charm."[38]

Rings, often obtained during training, were favored by American fliers. "I wore my 'lucky' air cadet ring through all my twenty missions," B-17 radio operator James Hutchinson of the 490th Bomb Group recalled.[39] Fighter ace "Kid" Hofer of the 4th Fighter Group swore by a big snake ring he wore on the third finger of his throttle hand.[40] Paul Thayer, a F4F pilot with VF-26, considered his fraternity ring his "good luck charm."[41]

Lucky finger bands, though, were not unknown in the RAF and dominion air forces. "My mother had given me a gold signet ring on my joining the [Royal New Zealand] Air Force," 16 Squadron Corsair pilot Bryan Cox wrote, "inscribed with the ancient family crest of an upraised arm with the hand holding a dagger, and the words 'Nil Desperandum.'" He wore it on operations and thought that on one occasion it had "saved my life."[42] Another New Zealander, Typhoon pilot Desmond Scott of 486 Squadron RAF, recalled: "An old Danish couple had given me a gold ring that had travelled round the world several times in old windjammer sailing ships. 'Keep it on your finger, dear boy, and God will return you to your native shores.'" Scott added in his memoirs that "to disregard such a message one would have needed a heart of stone."[43]

Objects that had narrowly missed bringing a tour to a fatal conclusion could become prized tokens. "On one occasion an aircraft returned with telephone wires wrapped around its loop aerial," related Stirling bomb aimer Hugh Russell of 149 Squadron, noting that "thereafter the crew all wore a piece of the wire attached to their battledress as a lucky charm."[44] An American air gunner flying B-26s kept in his pocket a spent slug that had narrowly missed him as a good-luck souvenir, as did B-17 copilot Hamilton Mero of the 398th Bomb Group with a piece of antiaircraft shell shrapnel. "A piece of flak came through the pilot's side, bounced off his knee, hit somewhere on my side, then hit me right in the throat," he recalled. "It never cut the skin, but it was a piece about this big [size of small finger]. I kept that in my pocket for quite a while. If that was for luck, I don't know. I still have it."[45]

Almost any object would do as a charm, though, if it appeared to bring good fortune.[46] The officers of a B-17 crew with the 100th Bomber Group in 1943 refused to remove a piece of decomposing baloney attached to one of the bunks in their quarters because the man who had put it there originally had survived his tour and returned to the United States. Even as it turned green, remembered navigator Robert Culp, "nobody wanted to take it down because it was a good luck symbol." To take a less malodorous case, Johnny Corbin, after downing an enemy floatplane over the English Channel while flying Spitfires in September 1940, recalled that after landing:

I removed my helmet and as I strolled towards the dispersal hut I became aware of a hard lump in my trouser pocket pressing against my leg. I reached down and pulled out the champagne cork [picked up at a party] I had been idly playing with before we'd been scrambled. I must have slipped it into my pocket without realizing it. I'm not a superstitious man, but I decided then I would hold on to that champagne cork.

Like more than a few other fliers—including Culp and his bunkmates—Corbin was succumbing to the logical fallacy *post hoc ergo propter hoc* ("after this, therefore because of this"); but that did not stop the champagne cork assuming "its rightful status as my lucky mascot and it accompanied me on all operational flights."[47] When air gunner Dave McCausland of 21 Squadron SAAF discovered that the parachute stored underneath his Marauder turret seat had stopped a piece of flak, the remains became talismanic. "I have a piece of that parachute still," he related decades later, "and in fact, my wife wore a piece of it on her wedding dress."[48]

Particular items of clothing might also be worn to generate good fortune. Various lucky caps and scarves were worn.[49] A radio operator with the 392nd Bomb Group adopted a single sock, while a B-29 copilot in the 499th Bomb Group wore his "lucky shoes."[50] As a B-24 pilot with the 445th Bomb Group, former and future actor Jimmy Stewart put on the same tie each time he flew.[51] Ace pilot "Kid" Hofer of the 4th Fighter Group always donned a blue football sweater with the number 78 stenciled in bright orange on the front before climbing into his cockpit.[52] Ed Megin-nies, a B-17 copilot with the 388th Bomb Group, always wore a special pair of lucky polka-dot shorts on missions, while Stanley Peterson, a navigator with the 96th Bomb Group, later explained that "I called my underwear lucky" and wore the same pair throughout his tour.[53] "We nearly all wore lucky charms or garments," related Lancaster pilot Robert Wannop of 90 Squadron, "which in my case consisted of a rather tatty school scarf tied very loosely around my open necked shirt."[54] Lucky neckwear and service caps were apparently quite common in the RAF and dominion air forces.[55] John Goulevetich, an Australian bomber pilot, had a top hat he had picked up at a pub and carried with him on each operational sortie.[56] He was not the only Aussie skipper to adopt exotic headgear, as bomb aimer Frank Tolley of 625 Squadron related: "Bruce Windrim had a bowler hat which someone had given him in a pub. He had it painted in the airfield ob-struction colours of black and yellow squares and wore it on every raid on top of his flying helmet. It was a talisman for him."[57] Doug Harvey, flying Halifaxes and Lancasters with 408 Squadron in 1943–1944, always wore a sweater he had worn playing ice hockey in Toronto. "I wouldn't fly without it," he explained.[58] Just about any article of clothing could do duty as a lucky charm: "I used to wear an old leather belt," remembered Lancaster bomb aimer Geoff King.[59]

Such items often became lucky simply as a result of being worn or carried on one or several operational flights that ended without incident, thereby generating the impression that it was because of the item that disaster had been averted. Thinking about the billed cap that he wore aloft, B-17 pilot Harry Task of the 305th Bomb Group reflected that "it had somehow assumed a special power, because it (and you) have survived all the raids so far." He admitted to "an irrational feeling that should you take off on a mission without it, you will have diminished your chances to complete the mission!"[60] Even regulation flying kit (e.g., battledress, headgear, parachute, and survival kit) could easily take on magical prop-erties through *post hoc ergo propter hoc* thinking. "Well," as B-17 radioman James Stivender of the 34th Bomb Group put it, "if I wore that [set of clothes] and got back okay, I'll wear it again."[61] This line of thought was supplemented by fears that to replace old items with new ones was to tempt fate unnecessarily. "To me the implication [of obtaining new kit] was that you were taking for granted an indefinite stay on the planet," ex-plained Australian bomb aimer Syd Johnson, "the sort of attitude which was asking for correction by the Grim Reaper."[62] Hence, some or all of the same footwear, headgear, undershirts, shorts, shirts, trousers, flying suits, flying jackets, and so forth were worn on every trip. "Many pilots," Murray Peden of 214 Squadron wrote, "and I was one of them, refused to buy a new hat while they were on operations."[63] Though his flying boots began to fall apart in the second half of his tour with 158 Squadron, Halifax navigator Harry Lomas would not contemplate discarding them: "I would be a fool to risk ending the good luck I had so far experienced."[64] Wellington air gunner Bill Belton always wore the same pale-blue RAF shirt and black service tie when on ops with 156 Squadron, just as John Walter, a B-17 pilot with the 95th Bomb Group, would later wear the same "lucky" khaki-drill shirt for all his thirty-five missions.[65]

Such clothing was usually never laundered during a tour in case the process drained away the luck.[66] The results were not pleasing in either ocular or olfactory terms. By the time his tour finished, the shirt that Walter wore had crusty salt rings under the armpits of monumental size and an inside collar with "a nice layer of grease."[67] As B-17 waist gunner Jack Novey of the 96th Bomb Group admitted, the wool gabardine trousers he habitually wore eventually became "so stiff with filth that they could almost stand up next to my bunk."[68] As B-17 copilot Bert Stiles of the 91st Bomb Group admitted with reference to his lucky undershirt: "If you got close to it, you were sure there was a goat in the room."[69] Eddie Camp, a B-17 flight engineer with the 2nd Bomb Group who wore the same lucky set of clothing each mission, eventually began to smell so bad that his crewmates made him sit on the tailgate when they were picked up by truck from the hardstand.[70] And Eddie Klein, a bombardier with the 381st Bomb Group, wore the same unwashed set of flying clothes throughout his tour. By his final mission, Klein's coveralls were in tatters and the whole ensemble so disreputable that it was burned from the underwear on out afterward.[71] Putting up with worn-out, dirty, and malodorous garments, though, seemed a small price to pay for survival.

Figurines, dolls, and soft toy animals were the third common category of lucky charm. B-17 ball-turret gunner George Moffat of the 95th Bomb Group always hung a four-inch wooden soldier named "Willie" from his guns and refused to fly without him.[72] The same was true for B-17 copilot Bill Marvin of the 91st Bomb Group and his wooden Indian encased in Plexiglas.[73] For the captain of a B-17 from the 385th Bomb Group it was a stuffed pink elephant, as it was for Johnnie Houlton, a fighter pilot from

New Zealand.[74] A B-24 pilot in the Fifteenth Air Force, Bill Carrigan, always took aboard "my lucky rag doll" as "insurance for getting back."[75]

Soft toys were favored because they were harder to accidently misplace than trinkets yet often could be compressed so as to fit inside flying clothing. Lancaster flight engineer Geoff Copeman of 57 Squadron, for example, always "tucked a little stuffed rabbit into my battledress."[76] These were popular personal mascots in the RAF, along with golliwogs, because they represented something considered lucky.[77] There were, though, also plenty of teddy bears along with stuffed koalas, pandas, penguins, and other knitted dolls taken aloft both in the RAF and in the FAA.[78] Lancaster rear gunner Bob Pierson related how he acquired one of the latter after he and the rest of his crew befriended a family living next to the pub they frequented:

> The family's name was Lancaster, which made them special to us, and she [the daughter] was called Sally. She was fifteen and had been in a wheelchair from birth but she was a cheerful soul, always smiling. Every time she went to the pub, she would be sitting in the window in her wheelchair and knitting little patriotic red, white and blue dolls. One night she said to me: "This will take care of you," and gave me one of those dolls. I wasn't even superstitious but there was something about her, and I was very touched by her gift. I carried it pinned inside my battledress all the way through the war. I promised her I would always go flying with it and I always did.

Pierson added that "it must have worked because I'm still here."[79]

This category of charm could often do double duty in bombers, becoming a mascot not only for the owner but for the entire crew. Though bought by one of the waist gunners, "Smitty," a stuffed toy horse, served as the "faithful little good-luck mascot" of a complete B-24 crew with the 460th Bomb Group.[80] Provided by Lancaster flight engineer Norman Ashton of 103 Squadron, a knitted doll named "Joe" was charged by his owner "with the task of ensuring the safe return of crew and aircraft."[81] Sometimes provided with their own miniature flying kit, such inanimate mascots could become indispensable additions to aircraft crews.[82]

Attempts might even be made to endow the aircraft in which men flew with talismanic power. Bob Vickers, for instance, when presented with a brand-new B-24 in the 392nd Bomb Group, had a four-leaf clover painted below the cockpit in honor of his father's faux-Irish sobriquet.[83] Scantily clad Vargas-type pinup girls were the favored images for the nose art of American bombers; but the names given to the ships might be designed to signal the crew's wish to go on living. "The plane normally flown by my crew was *The Fighting Mudcat*," remembered B-24 pilot Richard Feldman of the 459th Bomb Group, "so named because the catfish is a survivor."[84] The crew of a B-29 on Saipan "finally settled on a name for the plane," wrote the copilot Chester Marshall: "We called her 'Lil' Lassie,' borrowing the name from the smart dog in the movies who always comes home."[85] Five other B-29 crews had the same idea.[86] No less than twenty-six B-29s, fifty-four B-24s, and over sixty B-17s had the adjective "lucky" in the ship names painted on their noses at the instigation of crews.[87] On the principle that such objects always came back or turned up again, eighteen B-17s, fourteen B-24s, and a pair of B-29s were dubbed *Boomerang*, while two B-29s, fourteen B-17s, and sixteen B-24s were named *Bad Penny*.[88] The aim of the eleven B-17 and nineteen B-24 crews who chose *Heaven Can Wait* is obvious.[89] More unique but no less significant was the French name given to a B-17 of the 483rd Bomb Group—*Je Reviens*, "I Shall Return."[90]

USAAF fighter pilots might also name their ships along similar lines. P-51 jockey Dick Kenyon of the 354th Fighter Group, for example, flew a *Bad Penny*, while Robert Johnson of the 56th Fighter Group had the word *Lucky* painted under his P-47 cockpit.[91] This sort of thing could happen in the US Navy as well. Paul Thompson, a pilot of Air Group 35, flying off the USS *Chenango*, decided to call his replacement TBF Avenger *Lady Luck* after his first plane, which he had dubbed *Southern Comfort Express*, was written off in a landing accident.[92]

Records of nose art in the RAF and Commonwealth air forces are much patchier than for the USAAF, but similar superstitious attempts to ensure good fortune through painted names or symbols were made.[93] There are photos of a Mosquito in 418 Squadron dubbed *Lady Luck* and a Lancaster from 420 Squadron called *Lucky Lady* and of two other RCAF Lancs each featuring a painted pair of dice showing three and four—lucky seven.[94] A little green tiki figure was painted under the pilot's window of a Wellington of 75 Squadron in 1942 that was meant, according to New Zealand navigator Alf Drew and air gunner Bill Gibbs, to "bring you [the rest of the crew] luck."[95] Canadian pilot Pete Peters of 419 Squadron had an Indian Hiawatha head painted on the side of his Wellington that year with the same end in mind, while an American bomber pilot in the RCAF, Joe McCarthy, had a facsimile of his crew's lucky charm—a stuffed panda bear—stuck to the side of each aircraft he flew.[96] Fighter pilots might also seek to make their aircraft lucky. Tim Vigors, hailing from neutral Ireland yet flying Spitfires with 22 Squadron during the Battle of Britain, drew up a personal emblem he thought "brought me luck" and had it painted just in front of his cockpit: "It consisted of a green shamrock with crossed swords over it and the Irish Tricolour beneath it."[97] Fellow fighter pilot Alan Deere, a New Zealander and like Vigors a Battle of Britain veteran, had a Kiwi emblem painted on the fuselage of his Spitfire with the same end in mind.[98]

More animate creatures might also become valued mascots. Fliers adopted pets of all descriptions during the war—everything from a crow to a donkey—and sometimes invested them with supernatural significance. It was considered an excellent omen if the station mascot at Mildenhall, a bulldog named Butch, wandered in front of the camera while an RAF bomber crew was being photographed.[99] A P-47 pilot with the 4th Fighter Group in England owned a poodle he named Lucky: according to John Godfrey, "Lucky was my talisman of good luck."[100] At Wyton, a Stirling crew had a bulldog mascot, Prune, whom they occasionally took on operations.[101] The crew of B-17 *Hell's Belle* of the 379th Bomb Group took their canine mascot on a few practice missions, while Penny, the cocker spaniel mascot of a B-24 crew with the 453rd Bomb Group, was taken along on an actual raid.[102] Homer, the canine mascot of a B-17 crew with the 303rd Bomb Group, became so much "our talisman" that he was taken on no less than five missions, fully equipped with modified oxygen mask and parachute.[103] Antis, the boon German Shepherd companion of a Czech air gunner, was considered so powerful a talisman that he was taken on over a dozen bombing operations by a Wellington crew with 311 Squadron.[104] Blackie, the cocker spaniel mascot of 407 Squadron, accompanied crews on so many antisubmarine patrols that it was later estimated he must have flown the equivalent of at least a half-dozen operational tours.[105] It was not just dogs, though, who might find themselves aloft in an aircraft fuselage: a B-24 crew with the 11th Bomb Group in the Pacific had an eleventh crew member, a young mongoose, a creature that they regarded as their good-luck talisman.[106]

On occasion, individual homo sapiens might be felt by others to possess talismanic power. Jim Brierley, a Lancaster mid-upper gunner in 622 Squadron, was thought by the rest of his crew to imbue them all with good luck on account of his red hair.[107] Having flown his first mission without having had time to shave, a flier in the 381st Bomb Group decided he should always fly this way, and his increasingly unmanageable moustache—cut off only after the tour was complete—came to be seen as a vital safety accoutrement by the rest of his B-17 crew.[108]

Elmer Haynes of the 308th Bomb Group, based in China, was a sought-after pilot for those assigned to the B-24s he flew "because I lead a charmed life."[109] A neophyte B-24 crew with the 446th Bomb Group thought that Albert Pishioneri, a gunner assigned to them for their first trip, must embody good fortune after having survived twenty-four missions unscathed and hoped some would—quite literally—rub off: "They touched my flying suit for good luck."[110] In the case of B-17 flight engineer Edward Tye, the fact that he was forced to fire his top-turret guns only once in thirty-five missions made him a human lucky charm whose presence protected the entire crew from fighter attacks.[111]

Regardless of the form of the object or creature concerned, fliers particularly valued items given by a loved one with the intention of bringing good luck or warding off bad fortune for the recipient. Such charms were reminders that someone cared about one's safety and of a world beyond that of armed conflict.

Sometimes the donors were family members. "I always used to carry with me a piece of black rock with a hole in the middle, shaped like a cone," remembered Beaufort air gunner Bill Carroll of 217 Squadron. "I'd found it between Deal and Hastings on the southern English coast when I was four. I'd been walking with my father[,] a Cockney who'd been gassed in the First World War. He brought me a ring to put that little stone on, and he said to me: 'Bill, this is a good luck charm—never take it out of your pocket.' I flew with it everywhere."[112] Harley Tuck of the 447th Bomb Group hung the Swiss watch and special knife his father had given him in the radio compartment of his B-17, explaining that "I liked to have those things where I could see them."[113] Ted Hitchcock, a wireless operator on Bostons with 226 Squadron later in the war, was given a drilled thrupenny-bit by his father that he attached to his flying helmet as a good-luck talisman; while Frank Moody, a Lancaster flight engineer in 625 Squadron, always carried one of his uncle's Great War medals.[114]

Married men were particularly grateful for charms that reminded them of hearth and home and were meant to impart luck. Tom Rebello, dropping bombs from his position in the nose of a B-24 in the 446th

Bomb Group late in the war, always wore the lucky sweater his spouse had sent him.[115] George McGovern of the 456th Group had a photo of his bride, Eleanor, taped to his instrument console in front of the pilot's seat.[116] Recently married, B-24 pilot John Schuyler of the 44th Bomb Group was given a mascot named Pete by his bride, Eloise, before he departed for Europe: "Pete was actually a little stuffed doll, shaped somewhat like a gingerbread man, with cotton stuffing in a pink exterior. About ten inches long, Pete was properly equipped with a seat-pack parachute with ribbon straps. His chute was packed with Friendship Garden sachet, a frequent gift to Eloise from me on special occasions. Button eyes completed the absurd likeness to an airmen." It became a habit for Schuyler "to tuck Pete inside my shirt as regular preparation for the mission before leaving my hut." As he fully understood, Pete was meant both to remind him of Eloise—a "whiff of Friendship Garden could quickly take me back to some of the wonderful experiences my bride and I had shared"—and serve as a good-luck mascot.[117]

For couples with toddlers or expecting newborns, baby shoes or knitted booties might be the preferred talisman given by wives to husbands. A navigator from New Zealand flying Stirlings with 218 Squadron always carried a bootie knitted for his infant daughter, as did a Canadian bomb aimer in 37 Squadron under his flying helmet.[118] Emil Kantor, a B-24 pilot with the 460th Bomb Group, also treasured the blue baby booties that his wife knitted and sent him. "Those booties took on nearly mystical significance for me," he later wrote, adding, "I carried them everywhere in my shirt pocket, and on missions I hung them on the instrument panel in front of me for luck."[119] Other items from wives or fiancées, such as scarves, jumpers, photographs, or locks of hair, might also do duty as talismans.[120] More intimate apparel could also be forwarded—stockings in particular—which, according to RAF rear gunner John Wainwright, were worn on operations by the men concerned to serve "the dual purpose of bringing them luck and keeping their legs a bit warmer."[121]

The majority of the youthful men who flew in World War II were neither married nor engaged, but they might often have girlfriends and sweethearts eager to offer them tokens. These too might consist of lingerie, but also scarves, snapshots, and sundry other items ranging from coins and trinkets to locks of hair, dolls, and stuffed toys.[122] P-51 pilot Robert Frisch of the 339th Fighter Group recalled:

I needed all the luck I could get to make it through the war in one piece [during 1944]. My lucky charm was a "worry bird" my girlfriend sent me from back home. My worry bird was a small figure that you could mount on top of a glass and let it tilt forward, as if it was sipping your drink. I carried it with me on my missions. When my crew chief saw it on my instrument panel, he was afraid I'd lose the bird during a high-G turn, so he manufactured a bracket for it and screwed it into my panel.[123]

For pilot Ken Lee of 501 Squadron, flying Hurricanes in 1940, the equivalent gift was a toy Jiminy Cricket, while for Canadian navigator Robert Kensett, flying Halifaxes in 158 Squadron in 1945, it was a toy leprechaun: "When I arrived in England, Madalyn sent me a gift. It was a little leprechaun made out of pipe cleaners. They had been twisted to make arms and legs on a two-inch body. The whole was covered with a dark green felt including a little cap." This figurine became "my good luck charm, and I carried him everywhere with me tucked into the breast pocket of my battledress."[124]

Items passed along as gifts also made it easier on those who did not want to admit they were susceptible to magical thinking. "I had a little good-luck charm that I carried with me," admitted Bennie Hatfield, a B-17 pilot with the 447th Bomb Group, "but [I was not] superstitious, just [acknowledging] the fact that someone had given it to me."[125]

Whatever the attitude taken, a single talisman might not seem enough. It is worth reemphasizing that one token could be supplemented by a second or even more. Harry Yates, a Lancaster pilot with 75 Squadron, possessed a two-in-one charm: "It was the wishbone of my favourite hen, Blackie, whose demise enriched the family table on Christmas Day 1942. This hallowed relic was garlanded by my mother with a sprig of dried lavender which she fixed by means of some black wool."[126] So too did Ralph Schneck, a B-24 pilot with the 445th Bomb Group, who was given a 1936 US penny pressed into a miniature aluminum horseshoe.[127]

More commonly, fliers might wear several individual charms. Warren Ellis, a Canadian gunner who flew Wellingtons and later Stirlings, recalled how "the 4 leaf clover my mother sent me was with me on every flight, along with a rabbit's foot the mother of our neighbor sent to each member of our crew."[128] Another RAF air gunner, Thomas Quinlan, flew in the rear turret of a Lancaster with several lucky charms—"a pair of pandas," a "little wooden doll," and a "scarf that always went around my neck."[129] Lancaster bomb aimer Miles Tripp noted that among his quite superstitious crew "I flew with more tokens than anyone—a silk stocking, a Land Army broach, a pink chiffon scarf and a tiny bone elephant."[130] He was not, however, by any means a record-holder. Bomb aimer Les Bartlett had a chain of charms that he draped around the bombsight of his Lancaster that included "a rabbit's foot, a Cornish pixie, a silver threepenny bit, a Lincoln imp, and a suspender."[131] One USN dive-bomber gunner aboard the USS *Lexington*—where fliers often possessed lucky pieces—carried no less than six whenever he flew: a pipe, an ivory die, a screwdriver, two nuts and bolts, and a pinecone worry-bird.[132] Ralph Schneck had a grand total of eight good-luck charms.[133]

Even so, more might be thought necessary to bring about good luck and ward off ill fortune. With or without an associated talismanic object present, specific words spoken or actions carried out in a particular order could be considered equally vital to survival.

CHAPTER FOUR
INCANTATIONS AND RITUALS

In the struggle to improve the odds over enemy skies, saying and doing the right thing might extend well beyond the proficient exercise of military aviation skills, or, indeed, either silent prayer or faith in magical objects. Certain repeated words and deeds could take on an incantational and ritualistic quality that made them an indispensable part of efforts to survive an operational tour.

A religious upbringing could be helpful in conjuring up lines meant to be spoken or sung aloud or ritualistic actions performed in time of need. In tight spots, Catholics might recite a Hail Mary or two, touch a pendant or rosary beads, or cross themselves.[1] Looking disaster in the face, others might follow their lead. "Now, I'm not even Catholic," admitted Bob Johnson of the 340th Bomb Group, "but I said a Hail Mary" when an unfamiliar VIP from the RAF sitting across the flight deck from him in the copilot's seat seemed on the brink of crashing their B-25 on takeoff.[2] Harold Buell of VB-2 was Protestant but was observed by the ship's Catholic chaplain aboard the USS *Hornet* always making the Sign of the Cross before taxiing his SB2C Helldiver into position for launching.[3] All sorts could say the Lord's Prayer.[4] Among bomber crews, calling out Psalm 23 proved quite popular, especially in dangerous situations, as, on occasion, did airborne hymn-singing.[5]

American clergy, for their part, might go beyond their formal duties in promoting the idea that such rituals had a protective effect. Chaplain Constantine E. Zielinski altered Psalm 23 to make it more flier-friendly—"though I fly through treacherous storms and darkness" rather than "though I walk through the valley of death," for example—while with the enthusiastic support of combat crews both Catholic and Protestant clergy ministering to the USAAF might engage in the practice of blessing or even christening bomber aircraft.[6]

Though an aeronautical version of the nineteenth-century hymn *Eternal Father, strong to save*—better known as *For those in peril on the sea*—had been written for the Royal Flying Corps back in 1915 and was still in use a quarter-century on, there is no evidence of the blessing or christening of planes in the World War II Royal Air Force.[7] This did not mean, however, that individual RAF clergymen might not find themselves at the center of other de facto rituals. On bomber bases in the United Kingdom padres sometimes were seen to cycle 'round the dispersal points and offer words of encouragement—"Everything OK? Godspeed," for instance—which struck at least one crewman as ritualistic in nature.[8] A Halifax crew with 434 Squadron felt distinctly uneasy during their last operational sortie because for some reason the chaplain had failed to make it to the dispersal point before it was time to start taxiing.[9] Moreover, on at least one occasion a Bomber Command chaplain developed his own ritual, as Doug Johnston, signals leader with 427 Squadron, recalled:

> The padre participated in the pre takeoff and debriefing exercises. He played a little game with the boys. He would hand out half a stick of gum to anyone who wanted it and tell them they could pick up the other half on their return. I would kid him about it saying he was encouraging superstition among a group who were already superstitious enough. He refuted that with asserting that it wasn't superstition at all—it was faith. The boys were clinging to something tangible even if it was only half a stick of gum. They had faith they would return for the other half.

For many Halifax crews operating from Leeming in the summer of 1944 this ritual became indispensable. Other fliers "would not think of taking off without their piece of gum," Johnston later wrote, adding, "nor would I."[10]

That it was the chaplain doing this mattered, since beyond prayers and blessings he was thought to possess through his vocation a greater-than-average link to the supernatural world. It was probably no accident that as B-29 crews prepared for the first combat mission of the 40th Bomb Group in June 1944, one crew member came up to Father Bartholomew Adler and handed him his wallet: "Keep this for me, Padre," he explained, the implication being that he would pick it up at debriefing. Adler noted that the man had never done that before. After briefing, this Catholic chaplain noted that one crew after another called out as they prepared to go out to the flight line, "Well, so long, Padre, we'll be seeing you." This sort of thing was not by any means unique to the 40th.[11]

The vast majority of aircrew rituals and incantations, however, lacked any religious overtones at all—though they sometimes might rank high in the lexicon of common superstition. "Our flying gear was in individual wooden boxes, stored in a tent on the flight line," wrote P-47 pilot Bob Brulle of the 366th Fighter Group: "After getting out my flying gear for a mission, I habitually closed my equipment box and knocked on the wood door twice."[12]

More generally, particular words or, more commonly, actions, or a se-ries of them in a highly specific order, could seem essential in order to avoid an aerial catastrophe. B-17 bombardier Weston Jayne of the 351st Bomb Group always laid out his shoes and long underwear in the same specific pattern before missions: "I was superstitious a little bit," he con-ceded.[13] Once aboard a B-17, navigator Frank Guest of the 379th Bomb Group always took care to observe the ritual of placing his cap on the same spot atop a particular piece of navigational equipment before de-parture.[14]

Certain repetitive actions or words were clearly meant to reassure the men concerned that they were going to be coming back to base in one piece. "I wasn't really superstitious but I started to develop rituals that I kept up throughout my combat tour," explained B-17 copilot George Kesselring of the 91st Bomb Group. "I wouldn't leave my room before a mission without stopping to look into the mirror and reassuring myself that I was there, that I was fine and that I was going to be okay."[15] Before leaving his quarters for a mission "I patted the blanket on the foot of my bed for good luck," wrote Beirne Lay, commander of the 487th Bomb Group.[16] The ground crew chief looking after the 397th Bomb Group B-17 flown by Hershell Streit gave the pilot before the first mission a penny that he asked be returned to him when the plane got back; it did, and thereafter pilot and crew chief always repeated this action.[17] In the 485th Bomb Group it became common for B-24 crews to search for and pick up a pebble from the edge of the hardstand before they set out on missions and to replace the pebble carefully where they had found it on their return. They also took to leaving a valued pen or their wallet with a friend, "under the assumption that one would get back to reclaim it that evening," radioman Edwin Koch remembered.[18] John Steinbeck, report-ing for the *New York Herald Tribune*, noticed that many enlisted USAAF bomber crewmen would leave their bunks unmade before missions as a sign that they would be back to slip between the covers.[19]

This sort of thing also happened in the RAF. "Some men had to make sure that they had left some task unfinished," remembered Jim Auton, a bomb aimer with 178 Squadron, "such as a book half read or a letter half written."[20] Gilbert McElroy, an air gunner in 625 Squadron, always planted the palms of both hands firmly on the ground as a signal of his intent to return to terra firma in one piece before climbing aboard his Lancaster and making his way to the rear turret.[21]

Phrases might accompany actions. "When we took off," recalled Arthur Aldridge, an RAF air gunner flying Beaufort torpedo-bombers over the English Channel, "I always used to blow a kiss to England—'see ya later.'"[22] At Scampton, a heavy-bomber base, Edna Skeen, a WAAF map clerk, became aware that many navigators picking up charts from her prior to sorties said "see you tonight" before they left as an affirmation that they would be returning from the operation. "This became a ritual," she added.[23]

Bob Morgan, captain of the *Memphis Belle*, a B-17 with the 91st Bomb Group, developed a "little ritual" for the crew "after we'd been on a few missions and seen the losses start to skyrocket." He would gather the men together in a huddle next to the aircraft before they boarded and have them recite a pledge: "If only one plane comes back today, it's gonna be ours."[24] His was not the only American bomber crew to develop this kind of team-building activity. "Before boarding the plane we gathered in a circle," remembered Les Triplett, a B-29 radar operator in the 504th Bomb Group: "We stacked hands much like ball players before a game," adding that "we never flew a mission without first going through this ritual."[25]

Sometimes, though less commonly, the necessary action took place after rather than before flying took place. Alex Ingram, a ball gunner with the 94th Bomb Group, noticed that after rough trips crew members would "fall on their knees and kiss the ground." This became, he noted, "a ritual."[26] For a skipper in the 389th Bomb Group it became of vital importance over time to perform a particular set of actions accompanied by a certain local youngster after each mission. "We started a tradition on that first day and it carried on," remembered English schoolboy David Hastings of being allowed through the boundary fence after being spotted observing the return and shutdown of the B-24 *Pugnacious Princess*

Pat one day: "Al [Dexter] would put his arm around my right shoulder and walk me all the way around the Pat, looking at any battle damage and talking about what had happened." Dexter's wife dreaded the effect on her husband's morale if the boy for some reason failed to appear when the ship arrived at its hardstand after a mission.[27]

A performance of more obviously supernatural intent was observed of a Halifax skipper, Geoff Maddern. "He has 'Nickel,' the ops room cat, on his lap, stroking her, drawing luck from her," wrote his navigator. "She has become part of his departure routine."[28] A more collective supernatural ritual was witnessed by a Bomber Command station chaplain, who explained what he had seen to the station medical officer:

> Watching from a short distance away the crew of an aircraft about to take off on an operational flight, he noticed what he thought was the crew forming a "Magic Circle" round the aircraft. He was not sure that what he saw was in fact this, but on subsequent nights he saw, without letting them know, the same crew and again and again before each trip, certainly without being conscious of what they were doing, arranging themselves in a circle almost equally spaced [around their plane].[29]

Other crews took to circling their bomber once or even twice in single file.[30]

Sometimes the power of a talisman was associated with a specific action. Klaus "Heinie" Adam, flying Typhoons with 609 Squadron, always turned the signet ring his parents had given him and that he wore on all operations three times before takeoff.[31] Al Kotler, a B-17 radioman with the 99th Bomb Group, did something similar with his lucky air-cadet ring: "Every time we got on the plane, before I put my gloves on, I would rub it."[32] It was essential for Nathan Lazenby, an air gunner with 189 Squadron, to move his cigarette case from his rear trouser pocket to his left breast pocket before his Lancaster left the ground.[33] As described in a letter to his wife, the ritual followed by P-47 pilot Quentin Aanenson of the 466th Fighter Group was as follows: "As I'm climbing into the cockpit, I whistle the first bar of the Air Corps Song."[34]

In certain cases an entire bomber crew was required to participate. In 467 Squadron one of the ground crew was permanently tasked with rubbing a lucky rabbit's tail behind the ear of each aircrew member of one Lancaster before they boarded, while in 50 Squadron everyone in a certain Lanc crew touched the lucky photograph of the navigator's fi-ancée before assuming their pretakeoff positions in the aircraft.[35] In a particular 103 Squadron crew everyone had to rub the belly of a little devil painted on the Lancaster's tail assembly, and after climbing aboard the navigator had to rub an actual horseshoe held over his map table.[36] Those flying *Miss Irish*, a B-17 with the 100th Bomb Group, were all required to perform rituals designed to support the shamrock painted on the ship's nose.[37] A crew with 178 Squadron took to touching the Charteris-style stick-figure "Saint" painted on their Halifax.[38]

Tactile rituals, though, were not always connected with lucky charms. John Gee, flying a Lancaster for 153 Squadron, always gave his plane "an affectionate pat" after each operation as he climbed out the main hatch, as did at least one B-17 gunner.[39] More than one Lancaster crewman pat-ted the big 4,000-pound "cookie" blast bomb in the bomb bay before clambering inside the aircraft.[40] An air gunner in 429 Squadron always touched the prop blades before boarding and implored them to keep turning once started.[41]

Sometimes saliva was deemed a necessary part of the ritual. Ivor Turley, flying as rear gunner with 218 Squadron, remembered how the mid-upper gunner on his Lancaster crew, Joe "Mac" Thompson, before boarding knelt and kissed the ground, exclaiming "Tat-ta love, shan't be long."[42] In 460 Squadron, an entire Lancaster crew took to kissing the palm of one hand and then pressing it to the fuselage by the entrance door, incanting "Good luck, girl" as they climbed in.[43] "Before we clam-bered into the aircraft," Halifax navigator Robert Kensett of 158 Squadron later wrote of his first operation, "Min [Menno 'Min' Barsch, the pilot] . . . for luck walked under the bomb bays, which were still open, and inspected the bomb load consisting of fifteen 500-pound bombs. Min walked up to the bomb in the centre of the bay, licked the fingers of his right hand, and slapped the bomb." Kensett noted that the aircraft captain "carried out this ritual on all subsequent ops, and we always waited until he had performed this action before getting on board."[44] With the en-thusiastic approval of the rest of the crew, Lancaster rear gunner Danny Driscoll of 550 Squadron always spat on one of the aircraft tail fins for luck before they took off on operations.[45] Bob Gates, an Australian pilot from 467 Squadron, habitually smooched the piece of kangaroo foot he wore around his neck before releasing the brakes of his Lancaster.[46] Geoff Maddern and Doug Richards, respectively the pilot and flight engineer of a Lancaster crew in 103 Squadron, upon the successful completion of each operation took care to kiss the behind of the toy rabbit mascot that hung above the instrument panel.[47]

Americans might engage in similar rituals. After helping the ground crew prep the engines by pulling 'round the props, B-17 copilot Truman Smith of the 385th Bomb Group discovered that his pilot, Ernest "Moon" Baumann, had something extra in mind:

> With the job finished and leaning against the [propeller] blade to catch our breath, Moon said, "Kiss it."
> "Whaaat?"
> "Kiss the goddamned prop," he said and gave it a great big kiss.
> I stared at him as if he'd lost his mind and he stared back.
> "KISS THE GODDAMNED PROP!"
> He'd never ordered me to do anything before, but this was a command. He was serious and I was dumbfounded. I guess he felt he owed me some kind of explanation, so he said, "It's for good luck. Kiss the goddamned prop." I did and he walked away.

"I mean, you never really know about these things," Smith reflected, "and there was no reason to invite any bad luck."[48] As well as whistling a particular tune, Quentin Aanenson always kissed the ring given to him by his wife once he had climbed into the cockpit.[49] B-17 copilot Bill Marvin, owner of a wooden Indian mascot in the 91st Bomb Group, insisted that before boarding the rest of his crew lick a thumb and rub it "across his butt three times."[50] John Godfrey of the 4th Fighter Group always licked his finger before patting the engine cowling of his plane.[51]

It was another bodily fluid, though, that featured in an action very common in the RAF but practiced also in the USAAF: urinating against an aircraft tire before an operation or mission began.[52] So common did this become in the RAF that corrosion problems led to oft-ignored requests and orders for it to cease.[53]

This was sometimes explained away in terms of a "nervous pee"— men responding to their body's natural reaction in the face of imminent danger.[54] It was also presented as a "practical gesture" before a lengthy flight.[55] Onboard toilet facilities tended to be either primitive or nonexistent in wartime aircraft, and at far-flung dispersal points the landing gear might be the only convenient bit of cover from the elements and public view.[56] There were, though, often alternatives: pilots and crews might pee at the edge of the hardstand, say, or arrange to carry bottles or tins in case they were caught short.[57] Moreover, many of the aircrew who always performed this action admitted that it was a ritual designed to bring good fortune.[58] "To pee [before heading out on a long operation] was vital," wrote Lancaster pilot Peter Russell of 625 Squadron; "to do so on the wheel was for luck."[59]

Naval aviators might also develop rituals. "I went through a regular routine before each mission," remembered VF-13 pilot John Robbins with reference to his preparations before taking off from the deck of the USS *Franklin* in an F6F. "I took a silver dollar and put it in my leg pocket. Then I tied a red handkerchief around my neck and put my baseball cap in the record rack in our ready room. When I did, nothing could touch me with a ten-foot pole. Or at least I *thought* that anyway." He understood this was all superstition, but he did it nonetheless: "A guy has to use everything to get through a mission."[60]

This sort of thing often arose from faulty *post hoc ergo propter hoc* logic of a kind that would generate a great deal of ritualistic behavior.[61] In seeking to make sense of and adapt to the external world, the human brain has evolved in such a way that it constantly seeks to detect patterns in perceived events. This form of natural learning is generally a good thing but can on occasion cause problems, because if one event happens after another event it does not, necessarily, mean that the first actually produced the second.[62] A number of famous experiments in the behavioral sciences have underlined the extent to which the brain can draw false inferences and detect cause-and-effect relationships where none exist.[63] Having survived their initial forays into hostile skies, fliers might conclude that what they had done and the order in which they had done it had led fate to smile on them—and that therefore it was vitally important to not deviate from the established pattern even in small matters: "if you'd done it last night and come back and then if you didn't do it tonight," as 101 Squadron Lancaster pilot Ken Gray explained, "my God you might not come back—so you did all these things."[64]

This line of thinking could influence behavior almost every waking moment but was of particular importance when preparing to fly. Certain gramophone tunes might be played, songs sung, or games played beforehand.[65] At briefings, B-24 pilot Richard Feldman made a point of always writing down the estimated time of arrival back at the base of the 459th Bomb Group in southern Italy and carrying the piece of paper about his person on each and every trip.[66] As men donned their flying clothing, they often took care to dress in exactly the same order as before.[67] Wearing the same parachute each trip could become important.[68] "You always put your parachute on in a certain way, carry your helmet under your left arm, begin to do all these idiotic things," commented B-17 pilot Robert Parke.[69] Pilots with the 354th Fighter Group would always climb into the cockpit from the left side of their P-47s or P-51s.[70] Lancaster crews in 83 Squadron made sure that they sat in exactly the same seats on the motor transport taking them to their dispersal points.[71] The order in which crew members boarded aircraft might matter as well. "I had to be the first to enter the plane through the nose hatch," remembered B-17 navigator David McCarthy of the 381st Bomb Group.[72] "It was funny to see the great lengths they would go to stop anyone inadvertently getting out of sequence," wrote Wellington pilot Maurice Lihou of his crewmates in 37 Squadron: "If this did happen, they would get into a flap trying to put it right."[73]

Other preflight actions were more personal. "I would survive," thought B-17 navigator Elmer Bendiner of the 379th Bomb Group, "but only if I followed my private ritual, only if I went out and found a poppy to put in my buttonhole." This was vital because "I had worn poppies before and survived."[74] Ron Smith, rear gunner in a 626 Squadron Lancaster crew, always saluted from his turret the ground staff who regularly gathered and waved to the bombers during their takeoff "in the superstitious belief that if I forgot the gesture, we should not return."[75] The necessary preflight actions could also become somewhat complicated: "I wore my wristwatch on my right wrist on all even days and on my left wrist on all odd days," one B-24 navigator admitted.[76]

Rituals might also arise during the flight itself. David McCarthy always stood behind the pilot and copilot during takeoff, and once their B-17 was airborne he "put my arms around their necks and hugged them."[77] One RAF wireless operator, flying Stirlings with 218 Squadron, was known to chew only a single stick of gum—issued in quantity to RAF crews in order to help keep the Eustachian tubes clear—throughout each operation and drink coffee from the thermos provided only after the aircraft was back over England.[78] They also might develop in connection with the successful completion of a sortie. "As we touched down," remembered Eric Silbert, a Lancaster wireless operator with 7 Squadron, "Reg [Perry, the navigator] would turn to me and put up the number of fingers indicating whether it was the second raid, the twelfth raid, or what have you. I would return the gesture." As this was a Pathfinder squadron, there was a second navigator aboard, George "Mungo" Parkes, who "joined in the superstition by putting his hands over his head, boxer fashion, which meant another one completed."[79] Harley Tuck, a radioman in the 447th Bomb Group, remembered that at the end of each mission various members of his B-17 crew would habitually say to each other: "Well, our name wasn't on that machine gun," or "We made it again!"[80] A B-17 air gunner with the 92nd Bomb Group, Fred Koger, came to realize that his "ritual" habit of immediately recording each mission in his logbook after landing had become a "fixation."[81]

Sometimes particular phrases as well as (or apart from) gestures were considered important. The mid-upper gunner of a 214 Squadron Stirling had a ritual involving both words and actions as he fastened his parachute harness. "As he bent and pulled the crotch straps in place," wrote his skipper, Murray Peden, "he always pulled them too tight and exclaimed in soprano tones: 'Oooooo, my goodneth'; then, as he slacked off and clicked the ends home in the quick-release box, he dropped his voice an octave below normal to give a hearty bass 'Ah, that's better.'"[82] Flying as a Lancaster bomb aimer with 100 Squadron, Peter Bond took to whistling the song *Taking a Chance on Love*—"I made sure I whistled that every time"—while putting on his flying kit, changing "love" to "life" in his head.[83]

"At first," wrote Irving Schreiber, a B-17 navigator with the 487th Bomb Group, "I wasn't aware that I was doing it, but I soon realized that before we left on mission, I managed to get into conversation with someone who was not flying that day. The conversation always ended with me saying, 'Well, I'll see you later.' That was my insurance policy that I would come back."[84] Such interactive premission rituals also appeared in the RAF. Brian Stoker, a Lancaster navigator, remembered that on his second tour, with 35 Squadron, a civilian sweeper in the crew room one day had touched his cap and wished him good luck as he was leaving. "After that, I found myself going out of my way so that I could see this old chap, who I knew by now would wish me luck," Stoker admitted: "I had taken him on board as a necessary good omen, and I seriously didn't wish to go out to the aircraft without his good wishes."[85]

Robert Boydston, who flew with the 364th Fighter Group, recalled that in the truck taking aircrew out to their P-38s and, later in 1944, P-51s, one particular pilot would always incant, "We could get our butts shot off doing this!"[86] In a 156 Squadron Lancaster crew, the two gunners would always engage in the following bit of repartee at the hardstand before they boarded the aircraft. "Arthur, my boy," Australian rear gunner Bill Love would ask the Birmingham-born mid-upper gunner, Arthur Irwin, "what sort of mood will the Reaper be in this fine evening?" Irwin would gloomily reply in a strong Brummie accent: "Billy, I fear they'll be blud on the moon tonight!"[87] Just before takeoff, B-17 radioman Ben Smith of the 303rd Bomb Group habitually called out over the interphone: "I have a premonition of disaster!" In retrospect he thought this was tempting fate, but it became so much a part of missions that his captain insisted he say it the one time he forgot so that the plane could start to roll.[88] "Our pilot always said over the interphone, 'Tallyho, boys,'" a B-24 crew member in the 453rd Bomb Group recalled, "and we were on our way."[89]

To the combat flier, though, voicing or doing the same thing time after time might not always seem enough to appease "whoever it was that controlled his destiny," as an observant Halifax pilot put it.[90] Certain phrases, actions, numbers, and even people perceived as potentially dangerous had to be shunned in order to avoid improving the odds against survival.

CHAPTER FIVE

JINXES AND JONAHS

In the minds of many fliers, bad luck needed to be avoided just as assiduously as good fortune needed to be cultivated.[1] Through a combination of fears about tempting fate, *post hoc ergo propter hoc* reasoning, limited understanding of the laws of probability, along with traditional superstitions and—in one specific context—more than a hint of misogyny, there arose a small host of things that were thought to actively attract disaster.

There were various actions or spoken phrases that some men thought brought bad fortune on operational sorties. In the face of directions from his skipper to stop dumping his parachute and other equipment in the aisle of the flight deck after boarding, a B-29 copilot in the 73rd Bomb Wing argued that to do so would create a jinx: "It's been that way on every mission and it's no time to start [something new] now."[2] In the 93rd Bomb Group a B-24 pilot argued that it was courting bad luck to change the name of an inherited ship, and when later ordered by the commander of the 451st Group to paint over the skull-and-crossbones artwork on the nose of their B-24 in order to avoid providing ammunition to enemy "air gangster" propaganda claims, many of the crew of *The Jolly Roger* feared that after fourteen successful missions their luck would thereby be erased.[3] A navigator was furious with the nose gunner of another crew in the same bombardment group after he lit three cigarettes for two other crew members and himself during a delay before boarding, thus breaking the three-on-a-match taboo.[4] According to one Wellington pilot, writing a letter to a loved one just in case one did not return "was considered among bomber crews to be the ultimate jinx."[5] Volunteering for an operational task in the Fleet Air Arm was thought to be "very unlucky," indeed "asking for trouble," according to Swordfish pilot Charles Lamb: "If we are told to do something, no matter what, that's okay; but volunteer—never."[6] And within Bomber Command's 75 Squadron it was even considered dangerous to wish anyone good luck before setting out.[7]

The 100th Bomb Group and 359th Fighter Group, among others, shared the superstition that saying goodbye before takeoff was inviting a final reckoning with the Grim Reaper.[8] In other units, making any reference to what one would do upon returning from an operation or mission was believed to lengthen the odds against survival for that particular sortie.[9] Members of Air Group 15 aboard the USS *Essex* took care to avoid uttering the words "when I get back" before launches.[10]

Ellis Woodward, a B-17 pilot with the 479th Bomb Group, disliked fliers who used gallows humor to assuage their fears after briefings about how the enemy was going to blow the group from the sky. "I was superstitious," he admitted, "and thought that if you talked negatively about something happening, it just might increase the possibility of it happening."[11] George Webster, a B-17 radio operator with the 92nd Bomb Group, was worried that blurting out "I really hope this is the last one" about a mission late in his tour would have adverse consequences.[12] During a Berlin raid on the night of March 27–28, 1943, a 207 Squadron wireless operator chose not to wish the tail gunner, whose birthday began after midnight, many happy returns.[13] Why? "Fate or luck or providence might hear us and rap our knuckles for being certain of their favours," argued Halifax bomb aimer Geoff Dawson of 158 Squadron.[14]

A similar desire to keep in the good books of Lady Luck—"we didn't want to offend her"—lay behind the decision by some US crews not to decorate the nose of their bombers once they had racked up a number of successful missions in anonymous machines.[15] It also explains the deep unease felt by other crewmembers when B-17 tail gunner Gene "Wing Ding" Carson of the 388th Bomb Group took to whistling the first few bars of Chopin's Funeral March each time their bomber left behind the English coastline. Only when one of the crew was killed did he cease this practice: "It seemed to be inappropriate."[16] Another B-17 tail gunner, Arnold Willis of the 303rd Bomb Group, chose from the start not to write down the details of rough missions in his logbook on returning to base: "That would be tempting fate."[17]

The same sort of fears might deter fliers from posing in front of their aircraft for a photo snapshot during a tour of operations.[18] "Most of the crews considered it to be tempting fate and refused to be photographed,"

Wellington pilot Edward Coates of 115 Squadron wrote, echoing the recorded sentiments of others in RAF Bomber Command.[19] Inevitably, *post hoc ergo propter hoc* also came into the equation once an aircraft was lost whose crew had dared to have their picture taken. "Having noticed that those crews who posed for photos in front of aircraft inevitably got into trouble we had refused to get one taken ourselves," recalled Lancaster pilot Bob Petty of 49 Squadron, adding tongue in check that, "Our refusal to be photographed as a crew was a statistically determined response, owing nothing at all to superstition."[20]

This was not a phobia confined to British bomber crews. Stan Turner, a Canadian who flew Hurricanes with 242 Squadron, considered it "bad luck" to pose for newspaper photographers.[21] American fliers might also feel that being photographed in front of their planes before a mission brought on ill fortune.[22] According to Dave Toomey of the 3rd Photo-Reconnaissance Group, a fellow P-38 pilot "wasn't too keen about having his picture taken." The one day he allowed himself to be photographed just before he took off, he was badly shot up. "After that, if someone ever took a picture of him, he wouldn't fly that day. I made the mistake of snapping his picture once, and he saw me do it and he really came at me. It took two guys to hold him back. He was rabid."[23]

The role of *post hoc ergo propter hoc* reasoning in relation to photographs is illustrated by the behavior of the crew of the B-17 *Sack Rabbit* from the 487th Bomb Group. The crew billeted in the hut next to theirs had been on leave in Scotland, where all ten men had dressed up in Highland garb to have their picture taken—up till then a common practice. "About a week later," recalled navigator Irving Schreiber, "they were shot down." Making the cause-effect connection, the members of the *Sack Rabbit* crew, when they themselves were sent on leave to Scotland a couple of weeks after that, each came to the conclusion that such photos were a jinx: "Not one member of our crew came back with a photo of himself dressed in Scottish regalia."[24]

Nor was this sort of thinking confined to those who flew from land. John Hoare, a Fleet Air Arm observer, thought it "an ill omen" when the aircrews aboard the escort carrier HMS *Thane* had a group photograph taken, because he recalled 828 Squadron doing the same thing shortly before being "demolished" in an ill-fated strike launched from HMS *Victorious* some years earlier.[25] It was widely believed among US naval aviators, doubtless through similar *post hoc ergo propter hoc* reasoning following a particular incident, that having one's photograph taken from a carrier deck during landing would result in a crash.[26]

A run of bad luck could easily leave the impression that particular units, aircraft, or indeed people were somehow dogged by ill fortune. Thus, if possible, they were shunned in order to prevent "contagion."

In the Eighth Air Force, heavy losses suffered by one particular heavy bombardment group led to it famously being dubbed "The Bloody 100th"; but it was not alone in being seen as an unlucky outfit.[27] At various times the number of aircraft lost in the 44th, 96th, and 492nd Groups led them to be considered jinxed by others.[28] Furthermore: "It was an article of faith that every bomb group had a 'hard luck' squadron," reflected B-17 radio operator Ben Smith of the 303rd Bomb Group based at Molesworth. "As long as I was there, the 358th Squadron was the eightball bunch."[29] On the island of Saipan, the loss of eight crews from the 878th Squadron meant that it became "known around the [499th] group as the hard luck squadron," according to a B-29 pilot in the outfit.[30] Evidence that unit jinxes were taken seriously includes an incident in which, despite the real risk of being picked off by enemy fighters, a delayed B-17 from the 385th Bomb Group chose to fly on alone into enemy territory seeking its own formation rather than joining up with that of the 100th.[31]

RAF Bomber Command also had its share of units that at times seemed to be cursed. "This is [a] real jinx squadron," wrote Halifax pilot Geoff Maddern shortly after joining 103 Squadron at Elsham Wolds.[32] 51 Squadron, another Halifax unit, also developed an unlucky reputation in the middle war years, "to the point where we would sooner have got posted to any other squadron but 51," remembered Canadian air gunner Robert Masters.[33] 12 Squadron, equipped with Lancasters, was also thought of as a "chop squadron."[34] While learning his trade at an Operational Training Unit, bomber pilot John Rowland was warned that he should "stay away from 12 Squadron where the losses were horrendous."[35] Over time comparative squadron attrition tended to fluctuate, with bad patches matched by better times. Yet as second-tour Halifax pilot Jerrold Morris noted of the supposedly ill-starred 419 Squadron, "Once a squadron picked up a reputation for bad luck it tended to stick."[36]

Particular fighter units, too, might find themselves under a cloud for a time. Losses in the first month of combat for a P-51 squadron of the 357th Fighter Group, for instance, led one pilot to note that "there seems to be a jinx on [the] 362nd."[37]

Individual planes might also seem to be bringers of ill fortune for those manning them. "Every squadron had a jinx aeroplane," asserted pilot Jack "Benny" Goodman, who flew with a number of RAF Bomber Command units: "Anything awful that was going to happen would happen to that aeroplane."[38] In 103 Squadron, a crew had had such bad experiences aboard a particular Halifax that they insisted on taking another plane despite the latter's engine problems.[39] "We would be flying 'old 579,'" anxious B-24 navigator Wright Lee of the 445th Bomb Group wrote in his diary, "somewhat of a jinxed ship, or so the other boys told us."[40] *Tinker Toy*, a B-17 with the 381st Bomb Group, developed a reputation as ill-fated because she always seemed to sustain battle damage during missions, and gunners in particular were not keen to be assigned to fly missions in her.[41] The reputation of *Bad Penny* in the 91st Bomb Group became such that nobody wanted to be assigned to this particular B-17.[42] The successive loss of no less than three B-29s dubbed *Filthy Fay* in the 498th Bomb Group in early 1945 made it obvious to at least one observer on Saipan that "powers unseen" were at work.[43]

In reality the problems of apparently jinxed aircraft were due either to poor manufacturing and iffy maintenance or entirely random encounters with the enemy.[44] But this did not stop airmen from thinking that a plane was cursed.[45] Indeed, adverse experiences in an RAF machine with a particular identification letter could produce an aversion to flying any other plane emblazoned with the same letter.[46]

Sometimes only subterfuge would persuade fliers that a jinxed plane was safe. In the 309th Fighter Group there was at one time a Spitfire that possessed an engine that always seemed to malfunction in flight despite repeated efforts to fix it. By the time a representative from Rolls-Royce announced that he had solved the problem, pilots were convinced that it was cursed. The only way the group commander, Sandy McCorkle, managed to get it back into operational service was by having it sent away and then returned as a supposedly different plane thanks to new identification markings.[47] The same sleight of hand was practiced in the RAF: "This was essential because of the superstitious nature of many aircrew," an engineering officer explained.[48]

Even if a plane was not considered ill-fated, those inside might be. The men who normally flew a B-17 in the 493rd Bomb Group called *Heavy Evy* considered her to be their lucky ship after she emerged from a string of missions with hardly a scratch; yet she was lost when a different, clearly ill-starred, group of fliers took her aloft for the first time over enemy territory while the "owners" were on a 48-hour pass.[49] Crews without obvious skill weaknesses might suffer a succession of minor or major problems, perhaps culminating in the loss of their lives.[50] Accidents and other difficulties early in the tour could generate fears among observers and the men concerned that they belonged to a "jinx crew" destined for destruction.[51]

On occasion, an individual flier might be regarded as a Jonah.[52] Joining 102 Squadron, Doug Mourton was assigned as a wireless operator and air gunner to a Whitley crew. On his first operational trips something went badly wrong each time, leading the skipper to conclude that "you are a bloody jinx."[53] Peter Russell, a Lancaster pilot in 625 Squadron, was made distinctly uneasy about flying with a flight engineer who had bailed out from two crashing machines: Was he therefore "a jinx?"[54]

Individuals in the USAAF might also apparently acquire the mark of Cain. Within a B-24 crew with the 392nd Bomb Group a tail gunner took note that when they flew with their regular flight engineer "we got banged around pretty good" but that when he was absent "we didn't have it quite so rough."[55] Flying ground-attack missions with the 366th Fighter Group, Robert Brulle recalled a fellow P-47 pilot who "had the dubious distinction of having the most shot-up aircraft. It seemed that on every mission he would come home all shot up, some [of the planes he flew] even ending up classed as junk. Those pilots assigned an aircraft dreaded him flying their aircraft [in their place] since it was almost sure to be hit."[56]

This sort of thing could make life difficult for the men concerned. The unlucky pilot in the 366th mentioned above seriously wondered if he was being struck more often than anyone else in the group because he was Jewish.[57] Alan Peart, an RNZAF Spitfire pilot transferring in stages by air from North Africa to India with 81 Squadron, had so many problems en route that he decided that he was temporarily jinxed and insisted on using ground transport for the final leg of the journey.[58] Ed Smith, a B-17 navigator with the 2nd Bomb Group, flew with a dozen different crews but gradually became aware that each one of them was being shot down after he moved on: "I began to think of myself as a jinx."[59] In the 44th Bomb Group, William Weatherwax was known as "the hard luck kid," and "nobody wanted to fly with him because he always got shot up." According to a radio operator in the group, if any of his own crew were out of action, anyone not already assigned "would report to sick call if they thought they had to fly with Weatherwax."[60] Guy Weddell, a B-17 gunner in the 388th Bomb Group, was thought to be "cursed" after a series of missions in which planes had been damaged and crew members killed: "Why in the hell would anyone want to fly with you?" asked fellow air gunner "Wing Ding" Carson.[61] "About the saddest case I know was a pilot who thought he was bad luck for everybody," stated Haley Aycock, commander of the 324th Squadron of the 91st Bomb Group, "because every time he went out somebody else on his ship got killed." This pilot had to stop flying as a result of his jinx status.[62]

In some RAF Bomber Command squadrons, faulty *post hoc ergo proctor hoc* reasoning could consign an entire class of neophyte fliers to the Jonah category. To worry about being sent aloft with strangers rather than the men with whom one had trained was logical in light of the need, especially during an emergency, for smooth crew coordination.[63] There was no such defense of the superstition that it was bad luck to have to carry a "second dickey"—a newly minted bomber pilot—on an operation, since the man concerned was there strictly for orientation purposes and had no role to play beyond observation. Nonetheless the "jinx tag was strong," remembered Lancaster pilot Royan Yule of his own ride after being posted to 626 Squadron; "so many crews carrying 'second dickeys' were lost, that to the superstitious members of any crew it was an extra dread."[64] Halifax pilot Ken Blyth was made aware of this on his own orientation trip with 40 Squadron: "The fact that they had a spare pilot in case anything happened to their pilot was offset by their superstition that my coming along was ominous," he observed. "Crews hated taking along a second dickie," Blyth later wrote.[65] Frank Broome, a rear gunner in 626 Squadron, concurred: "It was unfortunately a very popular belief."[66]

An extra man could also provoke prejudice among American heavy-bomber crews. Unlike in RAF Bomber Command, combat orientation flights for new pilots did not involve adding to the total number of men aboard, since USAAF bombers carried two pilots—rather than one as in the RAF from 1942 onward—and the green flier could simply replace the copilot of an experienced crew for what would hopefully be a "milk run." Yet sometimes crews were ordered to take a photographer or newspaperman along, which was thought by some to bring bad luck.[67]

Partly this was a practical matter. "One thing I didn't need during a bombing run was for some guy to be crashing around the plane with a camera in one hand and his oxygen bottle in the other, bumping into my gunners and asking my navigator for a closeup," B-17 pilot Bob Morgan of the 91st Bomb Group argued.[68] An eleventh man would also mean taking on unnecessary extra weight on a long trip.[69] But superstition was also at work. As a stranger the passenger was an unknown quantity and might turn out to be a jinx.[70] It was widely known that the B-24 in which *New York Times* reporter Robert Post was sent aloft for the first time had been hit by fighters and exploded in the air, killing him and eight others.[71]

It was not just those who flew that might be considered harbingers of death, though. The women with whom fliers came in contact could also sometimes find themselves treated as pariahs. This involved a mixture of *post hoc ergo propter hoc* logic leavened by a certain amount of misogyny insofar as the females concerned were both desired and feared.[72] Aircrew wives were not an issue for the USAAF in Europe, given that they were for the most part back in the United States. For the RAF in the United Kingdom, however, especially Bomber Command, they were often seen as a problem, since their presence was said to divert husbands from the all-consuming business of war. Married life on or near an operational station was a distraction, dangerously dividing the loyalties of the husband between his wife and his crew.[73] This was why a number of station and group commanders banned wives from living in RAF accommodation and tried to prevent them from moving into nearby villages.[74]

It was also part of the reason some married fliers actually thought it bad luck to have their wives live nearby.[75] Single men, indeed, might regard those with wives as a positive danger to a crew. According to Halifax pilot Russell McKay of 420 Squadron, it was uncanny how many men who chose to marry were killed shortly thereafter.[76] "We didn't know," a Halifax flight engineer with 427 Squadron commented on the marriage of his crew's bomb aimer, adding that if they had "we would never have flown with him."[77] According to air gunner Peter James, in each of the three bomber squadrons he was attached to "they were the blokes you never flew with."[78]

As for girlfriends, they too might be considered potential or actual jinxes. American airmen, to be sure, often pursued carnal and other social relations with members of the opposite sex with great enthusiasm and considerable success when stationed in England.[79] Yet there also existed concerns that either fleeting or longer-term relationships might cause a flier to become dangerously distracted or even mark him for death.[80] In the United States prior to the war, after all, aviators had thought it unlucky to allow a woman into an aircraft.[81] Now, in the context of a life-and-death existence, she might turn out to be a femme fatale.

In the 31st Fighter Group, it was noticed that two successive pilots with whom a particular "Jinx Woman" had been involved had been killed, and a third became worried that he was next to die.[82] A similar situation existed in the 339th Fighter Group, where an especially attractive female living in nearby Cambridge acquired the nickname "Kiss of Death" because "every pilot who'd known this girl had gone down on a mission soon thereafter."[83] Those manning bombers could be as susceptible as those flying fighters. "At a Saturday night 'free for all' at the [Officers] Club, there was a woman named Kaye," Stan Peterson, a B-17 navigator with the 96th Bomb Group based at Snetterton in East Anglia, later related. "The word got out that at least six men had romanced her and they all went MIA [missing in action], POW [prisoner of war] or worse." He and the crew bombardier, Howie "Doc" Jornod, noticed that their co-pilot, Curt Mosier, seemed interested in her and warned him to beware. Mosier, however, was not deterred and, "flirting with fate," made a date with Kaye. Two days later, Mosier was killed by a piece of flak over Saarbrucken, confirming Peterson's opinion that Kaye was indeed deadly.[84]

The same sort of superstition could arise among British crews. It was noted at Mildenhall that no less than three men who had sequentially taken out the attractive barmaid of a local pub had perished. Thenceforth she was known as the "Chop Blonde."[85] A Halifax crew with 78 Squadron, based at Middleton St. George, were unhappy with a liaison their rear gunner had struck up in nearby Darlington with a young woman whose previous air-gunner boyfriends had all been killed in action. She was considered so great a jinx that they successfully plotted to break up the relationship.[86]

The problem was much greater in RAF Bomber Command, however, than in the USAAF Eighth Air Force due to the presence or absence of women on base. Service personnel on American stations, barring a few American Red Cross welfare representatives, were exclusively male.[87] On RAF stations, however, large numbers of women enrolled in the WAAF were by the middle war years serving as everything from cooks and waitresses to clerks and telephone operators.

In terms of superstition this could be a positive thing in that individual parachute packers, dispersal drivers, and the WAAFs who stood with other station personnel to wave to crews as their planes accelerated down the runway could be considered to embody good luck.[88] There was a flip side to the coin, however.

The superstition that having a woman in or near a plane brought bad luck existed in the United Kingdom as well as in the United States. "They just wouldn't let a WAAF come onto the hard-standing on the night of an operation," Lancaster pilot Lawrence Pilgrim of 44 Squadron remembered of a particular ground crew at Waddington. "If a WAAF driver came out with a message for the pilot," he explained, "one of them would take the note from her and deliver it himself. They believed we wouldn't be coming back if a WAAF set foot on our hard-standing."[89] Sometimes individual WAAFs might gain a reputation as a "jinx" and be told "Buzz off!" if in the course of duty they approached an aircraft.[90]

The most common reason for servicewomen to be treated as pariahs had to do with their private lives. "Any innocent member of the WAAF who happened to have two successive boyfriends who failed to return from operations would be labelled a chop girl and shunned," an observer at Marham noted.[91] It was the same story on many other bomber stations.[92] A pretty WAAF working in the ops room at Pocklington, for example, "was going out with a pilot, and he went missing," Halifax navigator Harry Hughes of 102 Squadron recalled, "so she went out with another pilot, and he went missing; and then she went out with a navigator and he went missing." She was now considered a chop girl, and "nobody would have anything to do with her."[93] At Methwold, a 218 Squadron bomb aimer was worried that his Lancaster crew would be shot down because the wireless operator had danced a few times with a cookhouse WAAF known to be "a notorious chop-girl."[94] One 50 Squadron pilot was apparently convinced that his Lancaster exploded over Germany one night because the "jinx" WAAF at Skellingthorpe had spoken a few words to him in the mess before he could escape and had waved to his aircraft from the end of the runway during takeoff.[95] Those ignorant enough to risk going out with a WAAF chop girl might find themselves confronted by other members of their crew with a demand that they drop her or be dropped themselves.[96] Some aircrew decided that it was simply too risky to get involved with a servicewoman on station in case she turned out to be jinxed.[97] Not surprisingly, the WAAFs concerned could find all this highly distressing.[98]

This phenomenon was, however, only one of a number of primal fears associated with death through association. A replacement B-29 crew with the 468th Bomb Group were deeply disturbed when detailed for a mission to a target where those whose place they had taken had been killed.[99] Within the 307th Bomb Group, one B-24 navigator concluded that carrying a borrowed pistol was a death warrant after two officers who had done so were killed.[100] In the 5th Fighter Group, a pair of pajamas worn by a P-38 pilot who was shot down were considered jinxed after the three men who successively inherited them were also lost.[101] Wearing a dead man's flying kit was often considered particularly dangerous. Lancaster bomb aimer Miles Tripp of 218 Squadron owned a fur-lined leather jacket that had been taken off the body of a drowned Coastal Command flier. "Because of its morbid associations I wore it only on motor-bike journeys" and never aloft. When the mid-upper gunner in his crew, Paul Songest, not knowing its history, asked to borrow this jacket as they were preparing to head out, Tripp felt he could not admit to being superstitious; but "I didn't like the idea of him wearing a dead man's gear" and once aboard "wished I hadn't lent Paul the jacket."[102] Nothing untoward happened, but fears concerning dead men's clothing were difficult to overcome.[103]

The billets, beds, furniture, and pets of the departed could also provoke unease. "Well, sir, I have to tell you this is a very unlucky room," newly minted bomber pilot Stanley Mansbridge was told by his batman (valet) on arrival at an Operational Training Unit; "we've had three, three dead 'uns in this room."[104] Hurricane pilot Desmond Scott, quartered at one point in a bungalow outside Martlesham Heath, shared a room with a succession of pilots who were all killed in short order. Prior to the arrival of a longer-lived roommate, "I was beginning to feel the room had a jinx on it and [I] was about to move into a small cubicle below the stairs."[105] B-24 crews of the 514th Bomb Squadron, 376th Bomb Group, operating from a base near San Pangrazio in Italy in the last years of the war, began to notice that the succession of men who occupied a particular tent were shot down. "Finally, after several crews had disappeared in this manner," nose gunner "Mac" MacKenzie wrote, "the billeting personnel stopped assigning new crews to this tent."[106] Where dead men had lain their heads might be a more specific jinx. Newly billeted at the 92nd Bomb Group base at Podington, air gunner Bill Stewart selected a bunk near the stove, until one of the other occupants mentioned that this was the bed of a flight engineer who had received a mortal wound to the head a few days before. "With no further words I selected another bunk,"

Stewart recalled, "farther away from the heat of the stove."[107] At Binbrook, the base of 460 Squadron, it seemed that the men occupying particular bunks always got the chop: "Nothing would have made us sleep in those beds," observed Lancaster navigator Arthur Hoyle.[108] Stan Peterson, observing that the navigator who sat ahead of him one day at a briefing for the 96th Bomb Group at Snetterton failed to return, took what he considered appropriate action: "I never sat in that chair!"[109] Members of a B-24 crew in the 392nd Bomb Group became quite agitated when a spaniel that had been the mascot of a crew that had been shot down suddenly became friendly with them. "Get that damned dog out of here!" the tail gunner shouted: "I'll kill that damned dog!"[110]

Pets aside, the actions of specific birds and animals could also generate fear, especially among Americans prone to superstition even before they joined up. "There were guys in the barracks [at Thorpe Abbotts] who, when they heard an owl cry, would shoot it," related 100th Group B-17 waist gunner Alexander Nazemetz, "because they figured that meant disaster, the next day."[111] Coming as they did from a nation where about 20 percent of the population believed that black cats were bad luck, it is no surprise to find that ebony felines seemed to pose a great danger.[112] Eddie Picardo, a B-24 tail gunner with the 44th Bomb Group, recalled how Bill Stern, a radio operator on another crew, reacted to a sudden encounter while they made their way on foot to the mess hall at Shipham:

> While we were walking, a black cat appeared. Bill wouldn't let that cat cross his path. He said, "Come on. Let's walk around it." He wanted me to go with him into a large field to get around that cat. "You're crazy," I told him. "I'm going to get my breakfast." I was just finishing breakfast when he came in huffing and puffing. "I got around that cat," he said, "so I'm going to be all right today."[113]

He was in fact killed that afternoon, but Stern was not alone in fearing that a black cat crossing his path meant certain doom. John McCrary, a public relations officer scheduled to fly with the 91st Bomb Group as an observer the next day, had an encounter at Bassingbourne the night before:

> A black kitten—not a cat, but a kitten—walked across the road. Then it wasn't satisfied to walk across after I growled at it . . . frightened, it

doubled back and circled me. Remember, it was a kitten—had much time to scatter its bad luck around. I stalked the kitten—not to kill it, just to catch it. I took it inside and examined it in the light. It wasn't grey, or black and white. It was all black. All bad luck. 100%.

McCrary was sufficiently spooked to allow himself to be talked out of flying the next day, which turned out to be the right decision in view of the fact that the B-17 he was due to accompany was shot down.[114]

As if all this were not enough, combat aircrew might fear the impact of particular letters of the alphabet, numbers, and combinations thereof. Numerology, it turned out, was high on the list of fliers' superstitions.

CHAPTER SIX
NUMBERS AND SYMBOLS

Given the stresses they were under, it is not surprising that fliers succumbed to numerological and other symbolic superstitions already fairly common in the English-speaking world. In the United States, where transatlantic visitors thought the population more superstitious than in the United Kingdom, fears concerning calendrical coincidences such as Friday the 13th cost businesses what *Life* magazine described just before the war as an "inexcusable sum of time and money."[1] The British, though, were pretty superstitious about numbers and the calendar too. Almost a quarter of those responding to a survey in the United Kingdom shortly after the war believed that particular numbers could be lucky or unlucky, while 17 percent believed that particular days affected one's fortunes.[2]

Individuals might draw positive significance from numerical coincidences. Spitfire pilot E. A. W. Smith, for instance, was especially happy to be posted to 127 Squadron because "127 coincides with the last three digits of my serial number, 1333127."[3] Seven, a numeral widely considered lucky in western society, might have positive associations for fliers. Among USAAF bomber crews the seventh mission might be thought of as "our lucky seventh."[4] The skipper of a 425 Squadron Halifax apparently thought—wrongly, as it happened—that as it was the crew's seventh operation, they would survive a particularly difficult night trip to Germany.[5] Naval aviator Will Fletcher, about to launch from the USS *Intrepid* during the Battle of Leyte Gulf, took comfort from the fact that he had been assigned the seventh TBF Avenger in the VT-8 inventory.[6] Others might go for eleven, a symbol of strength in the tarot system.[7] In the 345th Bomb Group, meanwhile, an officer flying B-25s thought it highly significant that "every mission we've flown with six or eight ships, for the past two weeks [in early 1945], we haven't lost an airplane."[8]

By necessity or through experience, there was even some triskaideka-philes (those who give positive meaning to the number 13).[9] Don Berkus, a B-24 pilot with the 13th Air Force in the Southwest Pacific, convinced himself that thirteen was an inherently positive number:

> Our country started with 13 colonies; 13 signers of the Declaration of Independence; 13 stripes on our flag. Look at a dollar bill. There are 13 steps on the pyramid, 13 letters in Latin above the pyramid, 13 letters in "E Pluribus Unum," 13 stars above the Eagle, 13 plumes of feathers on each span of the Eagle's wings, 13 bars on that shield, 13 leaves on the Olive branch and 13 fruits. If you look closely, there are 13 arrows in the claw of the eagle.[10]

When a new B-17 crew arrived at the 100th Bomb Group in England, part of the 13th Air Wing, on October 13, 1944, and were designated Crew 13 and assigned aircraft number 413, they chose to view all this as a good rather than a bad omen.[11] Positive associations might also generate a certain degree of triskaidekaphilia. Because of the frequency with which the number cropped up in the personal and professional lives of a B-17 crew with the 390th Bomb Group, they decided to embrace rather than reject the option of being designated Crew 13 in the 569th Bomb Squadron.[12] "I got my first Zero that day, October 13 [1942]," noted F4F pilot Joe Foss, who flew from Guadalcanal with VMF-121, "flying the Number 13 Grumman I'd brought in from the carrier four days before."[13]

Unlucky numbers, though, seem to have been uppermost in the thoughts of superstitious aviators. Air force personnel often subscribed to the belief that bad luck happens in threes and either were happy that the worst was over or anxious that worse was to come.[14] Donald Stones, a Hurricane pilot in 79 Squadron, after first losing his lucky red scarf and then making a wheels-up landing, was among the latter: "I wondered what 'number three' was cooking up for me." The next day he was shot down.[15] "In the Air Corps the superstition prevailed that accidents occurred in threes," observed B-24 pilot James Mahoney of the 467th Bomb Group, adding that "deep down, even amongst the most intelligent, there was at least an uneasy feeling after two accidents in quick succession, and a sense of relief after the third."[16] Associations with "the number of the beast" could make six a problem too. Dick Johnson, a B-17 pilot in the 303rd Bomb Group, was unhappy to be assigned to a B-17 with the serial number 43–3766 stenciled on the tail: "Two sixes and two threes."[17] Sometimes, presumably because of a bad experience, the number 7 became a jinx to be avoided.[18]

The numeral that raised the most widespread concern among fliers, as it did in western society generally, was of course thirteen, "the unluckiest number of all," as one B-17 navigator put it.[19] In the spring of 1941 the commander of Torpedo Five decided that the reason he had misjudged a landing aboard the USS *Yorktown* so badly (his plane slid over the side and he nearly drowned) was because this particular TBD torpedo-bomber was the thirteenth in the squadron inventory.[20] In VMSB-132, USMC crews routinely refused to fly or aborted missions from Guadalcanal aboard an SBD dive-bomber with the dreaded number painted on it until the engineering officer repainted the three into an eight.[21] After almost getting killed in a dogfight on his first mission with the 325th Fighter Group in May 1943, Herky Green exchanged the P-40 he had flown for another because the first had thirteen stenciled on the fuselage.[22]

The trouble for triskaidekaphobes was that the number 13 could appear with distressing frequency. Though at least one US aircraft manufacturer avoided it in assigning serial numbers, the number could still crop up in call signs and formation positions.[23] The officers' mess at Leeming contained a room No. 13 that "most aircrew wouldn't use because it was unlucky," according to Halifax navigator W. A. Wilson of 427 Squadron.[24] The inevitable march of time meant that fliers might face a sortie into the wild blue on an unlucky day each month. Other dates might be dreaded— B-17 gunner George Watt of the 388th Bomb Group, for instance, did not want to tempt fate on his thirtieth birthday because "I've always said if I live to thirty, I'll live to a ripe old age"—but the thirteenth came up every month and could not be avoided indefinitely.[25] B-17 pilot Richard Bushong, on the final mission of his tour with the 390th Bomb Group, was unhappy—"maybe I was a little superstitious"—to be flying on April 13, 1944.[26] Made aware by another Spitfire pilot how often he had got into trouble on the thirteenth day, Hugh Godefroy of 401 Squadron was afraid as he took off on March 13, 1942, that "this was 'it.'"[27]

If one flew on the thirteenth day of the month and that day happened to be Friday, then trouble would inevitably follow. B-24 pilot George Gaines of the 781st Bomb Group thought this was why he became a prisoner of war: "On Friday the 13th [of October 1944], we were shot down over Blechhammer."[28] In the Fleet Air Arm, it was commonly considered very bad luck to join a new carrier on such a particularly inauspicious day.[29]

One thirteen was bad enough; but they could appear in clusters.[30] B-17 radio operator Roger Armstrong was concerned that his first combat mission was from the thirteenth base he had been posted to and on September 13, 1944.[31] "I should have known that taking off in an aircraft with the last two numbers 13 (42–30213) and on the thirteenth of the month [in November 1943] was not going to bring the best of luck to my crew," reflected B-17 pilot Bob Simmons of an abortive mission in which they had to take to their parachutes due to an engine problem.[32] Ken McGlashan, flying Hurricanes with 96 Squadron, noted that thirteen was the total of both the serial-number numerals of the aircraft he was flying and the date on which he was shot down over Dunkirk.[33] "It was our thirteenth sortie," flight engineer Stan Bridgman of 463 Squadron reflected on the night his Lancaster was shot down. "We had dropped thirteen bombs (one had hung up), my Service number (1393508) began with thirteen and the numerals of 463 Squadron added up to thirteen."[34] Walt Byrne, a B-17 waist gunner with the 390th Bomb Group, felt particularly aggrieved because not only was he due to fly a combat mission on November 13, 1944, but in a ship—*Phyllis Marie*—with a serial number on its tail that ended in thirteen.[35] A couple of months later, John Godley of the FAA was distinctly worried to find himself leading thirteen Swordfish into the air after being appointed commanding officer of 835 Squadron on January 13, 1945.[36]

Undoubtedly the most common aspect of triskaidekaphobia concerned fears about the thirteenth combat mission or operational sortie in a tour. "Not just another Op for us," Lancaster flight engineer Gordon Colquhoun of 467 noted of a raid on Rennes on the night of June 8, 1944, "the dreaded thirteenth!"[37] Inevitably some planes would be lost on their thirteenth trip; and time and again in diaries, memoirs, and interviews, fliers mentioned worries about the outcome for them.[38] "Unable to sleep, the longer I laid in bed thinking about #13 being the one we wouldn't complete, the more convinced I became," wrote B-17 pilot Truman Smith of the 385th Bomb Group.[39] "I had imagined something awful would happen," admitted B-17 flight engineer Sam Honeycutt on his crew's safe return from their thirteenth mission in December 1943, "and that we would be shot down."[40] For others a bad outcome was confirmation that the number was indeed a jinx. "I felt something inauspicious looming over us like a dark cloud," remembered B-17 pilot Charles

Alling of his crew's thirteenth mission in January 1945, in which they nearly died.[41] Marion Carl, flying F4Fs, noted that the day he was shot down by a Zero "I was flying my thirteenth mission at Guadalcanal, in my old number thirteen Wildcat, and had just made my thirteenth kill."[42] When nothing happened, as was more common, fliers often expressed relief rather than skepticism. "Sure was glad to get by that 13th mission OK," P-47 pilot Jack Pitts of the 371st Fighter Group noted in his diary in mid-October 1944.[43] Needless to say, having to fly the thirteenth trip on the thirteenth of the month generated even more stress.[44]

So great was the anxiety over this hurdle that many crews chose to try to counter its implications of doom by calling it something else. In the RAF it might be talked of and listed in logbooks as "12A." "All Lancaster aircrew preferred to think of the thirteenth Operation as their No 12A," wrote a 44 Squadron pilot.[45] In the USAAF, "12-B" seems to have been more common.[46] "We never flew Mission #13," stated Richard Bushong. "We flew Mission #12 and Mission #12B," he explained, "but never Mission #13."[47] Calling it "12 1/2" was a further option pursued by some, while pilot Anthony Alberco of the 92nd Bomb Group pursued yet another possibility. "This was my first mission," he recorded after his initial combat operation, "but I am counting it as my 13th."[48]

Identification letters on aircraft could also seem problematic.[49] After a series of mishaps flying a Spitfire with 54 Squadron, Al Deere wondered if "the letter 'B' (the flight letter of the aircraft I always flew) has something unlucky about it."[50] David Cox of 72 Squadron concluded that a particular letter was a jinx for him after being shot down in two different Spitfires so labeled: "And I never did fly on any other occasion on operations" in any plane "with the letter L on it."[51] In 103 Squadron, Lancasters with "M" on the fuselage gained a bad reputation at one stage because they always seemed to be attacked by night fighters and shot down.[52] Laurie Simpson, a Halifax pilot with 460 Squadron, was very conscious that he had crashed twice, each time in an aircraft lettered "K."[53] Archie Bain, a radio operator with 75 Squadron, had a terrifying experience in an aircraft labeled "P" in another unit, and he was so horrified when the crew were given a new Lancaster with "P" painted on it that his skipper was worried he would refuse to fly.[54] In 630 Squadron, a succession of mechanical problems afflicted a Lancaster with the letter "G" painted on it that culminated in a fatal crash landing. "The squadron refused to code an aircraft G-George for the rest of the war," flight engineer Edwin Watson recalled.[55]

Post hoc ergo propter hoc reasoning might not always be the root cause of such superstition. Navigator Don "Fizz" Feesey, for example, became nervous about flying in an old Lancaster suddenly rechristened "E-Easy." Why? "The identification letters of 166 Squadron were AS and painted in large letters on the side [to the left and right of the fuselage roundels] were the letters AS E. I found myself humming 'The Death of Ase' from Grieg's Peer Gynt Suite No.1."[56]

Those strongly influenced by numerology might turn letters into numbers, sometimes with worrying results. Archie Bain, who seemed to his crewmates particularly frightened during a raid on the Rhein-Preussen synthetic oil refinery, may have worked out that the target contained thirteen letters.[57] Walt Byrne certainly did so with major consequences for his morale when he heard "Bremen, Germany" in a mission briefing.[58]

Names might contain other forms of hidden meaning. John Ellis, a Hurricane pilot in 85 Squadron during the Battle of Britain, had decided that if he was going to be killed it would be over the sea, because the syllables of his middle name—Mortimer—sounded something more or less like "Death at Sea" in French.[59]

Even the artwork painted on the fuselage might become a representation of bad luck. Al Deere originally had a kiwi painted below his Spitfire cockpit but, after several mishaps, decided that it, rather than the letter "B," was responsible for his misfortune and at the urging of a friend had it removed when he joined 602 Squadron.[60] Another ace, Clayton Gross of the 354th Fighter Group, initially had *Lil' Pigeon* painted on his fighter, but after several crashes "I decided it was NOT a very lucky name!"[61] One day the crew of a B-24 with the 446th Bomb Group agreed to paint a red-and-white shark's mouth on the nose. "Our ground crew were not happy with this," recorded pilot Bill Turner. "They said it was bad luck; that there had been a plane in the [705th] Squadron painted in such a fashion before and it had been shot down." The fliers dismissed this, but in the wake of being forced to bail out and taken prisoner shortly thereafter Turner reflected that "we should have listened but we didn't."[62]

As noted in chapter three, naming a ship for luck and having that title displayed on the forward fuselage was popular in the USAAF. There were some, though, who felt that it was bad luck to name a plane after a living person, and others for whom naming or decorating the nose at all seemed a dangerous practice. In the 305th Bomb Group one B-17 crew, presented with a brand-new aircraft, asked their ground crew chief to select a name. The crew chief, however, explained that every plane he named got shot down; hence it was decided not to paint a special name on the nose and stick with *F for Freddie* as a call sign.[63] A crew from the 487th Bomb Group eventually named their aluminum-finish B-17 *Elliot's Idiots* but decided that it would be bad to spell this out on the nose. "Why not?" asked radio operator Joe Gaffney rhetorically: "Because we had completed half the required 25 missions with no paint. Superstition had taken over, and we trusted to good luck."[64] In other words, painting on the name would alter the balance of fortune in favor of the bad. Others, though, claimed that not painting on a name was a simple matter of prudence. "We never painted the name of our Fort," bombardier Ted Hallock of the 306th Bomb Group noted of his crew's B-17, "because the Forts with names seemed to get shot up more than the ones without."[65] Given the distances, angles, and speeds involved, it is impossible that enemy flak gunners on the ground, and extremely unlikely that enemy fighter pilots in the air, would have been able to see whether or not a B-17 sported a particular name; so this was yet again a case of *post hoc ergo propter hoc* generating a superstition. The same probably held true for those who thought that particular bomb groups were being singled out for hostile attention because the Germans could identify group markings on the tail.[66]

The presence or absence of distinctive paint schemes or even camouflage might also be thought to bring ill fortune. The crew of a B-17 with the 381st Bomb Group decided to have the engine cowlings painted red as a mark of distinction. The pilot, however, after several rough missions, ordered the paint job scraped away: "I want all that damn red paint off the airplane before you hit the sack tonight."[67] There might seem to be solid logic at work here. "If the Krauts see a fancy painting on a P-47's nose," Bud Fortier of the 355th Fighter Group explained to a friend of his decision to forgo one, "they figure the pilot must be a big wheel," while "a guy with no artwork on his nose must be just a peon—not worth shooting at."[68] The distances and angles at which dogfighting occurred, though, did not generally allow an attacking fighter to see much in the way of artwork on an enemy fighter unless it involved the entire nose or tail of the aircraft being distinctive; and flak gunners were either too far below or the aircraft moving too swiftly to allow for this level of identification most of the time.[69]

There might be more than a hint of magical thinking involved in drawing conclusions about the presence or absence of overall camouflage paintwork. In the wake of the USAAF decision to deliver new planes to various active theaters without camouflage late in the war, there were those who were worried about standing out. A flight commander in the 305th Bomb Group warned his pilots to "stay away from those new silver airplanes, stay with the old khaki camouflaged ones."[70] This perhaps made some sense in terms of not attracting the attention of German fighters. Thus a fresh crew for the 2nd Bomb Group, on having to exchange the shiny new B-17 in which they had arrived for an older model, were told "we were better off," because an unpainted bomber "would stick out like a sore thumb" and enemy pilots "would want to see what it could do."[71] But flak fired skyward from over four or five miles below, where the planes appeared as mere dots, was another matter. The first aluminum-finish B-24s to arrive went to the 466th Bomb Group. On a subsequent mission, the 458th Bomb Group, flying in formation ahead of the 466th, noted that the only ship to be shot down behind them was an aluminum-finish B-24. "For a considerable time thereafter," related navigator Jackson Granholm, "a number of crews tried to avoid flying in unpainted bombers." This was, he recognized, out of superstition rather than rational analysis, since there was no logical cause-and-effect connection between being downed by flak and lack of paint.[72]

Last but not least, certainly for those affected, was the matter of hearing or, worse yet, "seeing things." Dreams while asleep and other premonitions are discussed in chapter seven; but it is worth noting that a small number of fliers experienced hallucinations while on operations that they were initially uncertain how to interpret. Were they good or bad omens?

Sometimes the experience might be strictly aural. Spitfire pilot Alan Peart was startled one day while flying a patrol over North Africa to hear through his headphones, quite suddenly and distinctly, a harp solo. "I was greatly alarmed," he admitted; and it did not help that fellow members of 81 Squadron teasingly argued that "it is an omen" and "your time has come."[73]

Visual hallucinations, though, were often worse.

Bill Garrioch, a Wellington pilot with 115 Squadron, had one such experience in the wake of a German night-fighter attack. It began with his navigator asking if the plane was on fire. "Bob's sudden announcement on the intercom must have paralyzed my senses if only for a fleeting instant," Garrioch recalled, "because as I was looking through the cockpit window, superimposed on space, just outside the windscreen was a very clear picture of my grandfather and a great uncle looking directly at me." Both these relations had been dead for roughly seven years, and he was understandably frightened by what he had briefly experienced.[74] Another Wellington pilot, Maurice Lihou of 37 Squadron, while descending through thick cloud, thought he saw the smiling face of his wife beyond the cockpit. "It's impossible," he thought, "I'm seeing things." But he was understandably worried.[75]

Nick Knilans, an American pilot flying Lancasters with 619 Squadron, had a particularly vivid vision as he was climbing to cruising altitude one evening. "The upper sky before me was still somewhat lighted. A figure of a woman several thousand feet high slowly emerged into my startled view." He realized that he was seeing the face of a young women he had loved who had caught pneumonia and suddenly died some years earlier. "She had a slight smile on her lips as I flew towards her. The vision slowly melted into the darkening sky around us." Knilans was "a bit uneasy" over this vision, being uncertain "if she had appeared to reassure me that she would keep me from harm or if she was welcoming me into her world of the hereafter."[76]

Flight engineer Gordon Colquhoun of 467 Squadron for a second or two thought he saw a khaki-clad soldier at briefing one afternoon and then again waving at his Lancaster as it took off; but the figure vanished when he looked directly at it. He was not sure what this portended, but the soldier appeared a third time inside the aircraft that night at a critical moment over the target and prevented him from jumping just as the skipper rescinded a bailout order.[77] An RAF tail gunner, Thomas Quinlan of 103 Squadron, while his Lancaster was attempting to evade flares being dropped by an enemy aircraft, had an odd encounter. "There appeared to be a figure outside my turret," he related. "No matter what I did [in terms of moving his turret and his guns] he stayed with us." This was "a queer sensation" that he could not understand.[78]

There are a number of explanations for such visions that do not involve the supernatural. Among the general causes was a combination of fatigue and stress: the sort of thing that caused a senior Spitfire pilot from 242 Squadron to almost shoot down a Spitfire from 81 Squadron while hallucinating that he was chasing an enemy plane, or that drove a B-26 pilot with the 344th Bomb Group to try to swerve to avoid an oncoming aircraft that, as his copilot confirmed, was simply not there.[79]

There were also more specific factors. Garrioch was likely stunned by a cannon shell that had exploded a second before in the radio compartment.[80] 467 Squadron had been operating pretty much continuously and suffering serious losses in the week or so leading up to Colquhoun's hallucinations, the third of which occurred during a chaotic in-flight emergency in which he banged his head so severely that, just after he had his vision, he passed out. When he came to shortly thereafter, it was the bomb aimer, not the phantom soldier, he saw and felt pulling him away from the open emergency hatch.[81]

In the case of Lihou and Quinlan, they were both under extreme pressure at the time, the one lost in clouds and the other aware that the dangling flares could mean a fighter attack any second. Their hallucinatory experiences were perhaps akin to those of Fred Slevar, a Canadian flying as mid-upper gunner on Halifaxes with 427 Squadron. During a particularly harrowing bomb run one night he "saw" his parents about to receive a telegram announcing their son's death. "No! No! The telegram is not right," he told himself, and he was "hysterically relieved" that the crew and plane emerged unscathed and that he had not experienced an omen of doom.[82] To take another case, when Philip Fletcher was attempting to land at base and saw the runway suddenly change into a housing estate, causing him to pull up and go around again, he was trying to wrestle a damaged Halifax to the ground without crashing.[83]

As for Nick Knilans, he was either suffering from cumulative operational stress—he noted that the only other time he had experienced something similar was when he had seen angels in the sky as a child during the burial of his elder brother—or from oxygen deprivation (hypoxia).[84] "A man is breathing oxygen from a tube and his eyes and ears are working in the reduced [atmospheric] pressure," noted John Steinbeck of the USAAF bomber crews he met in England. "It is little wonder, then, that he sometimes sees things that are not there. . . . If you happen to see little visions now and then, why, that's bound to happen."[85]

Learning from an engineering officer that atmospheric conditions might have made it possible for his VHF set to pick up a fragment of radio broadcast involving a harp solo, Alan Peart concluded that "the agony of waiting expectantly for my imminent demise had been quite unnecessary."[86] Bill Garrioch logically deduced that the apparitions he had seen were the result of the cannon shell exploding in the radio compartment, while Gordon Colquhoun admitted his sights of the phantom soldier had been "illusions."[87]

Nonetheless it was often difficult for the fliers involved not to think in supernatural terms and believe that they had encountered the spirit world.[88] The face of his wife that Maurice Lihou saw appeared to be nodding in the direction he ought to fly through the clouds in order to find his base, and he arrived safely.[89] Nick Knilans, though unsure of what it symbolized, seems to have concluded that what he had witnessed was some sort of ghost.[90] And after a conversation with his father who indicated that he had dreamed that he was with his son on the night the latter had sensed another presence in his turret, Thomas Quinlan appears to have decided that somehow or other his father's spirit had been with him that night, presumably to reassure him.[91]

Visions or sounds of this kind, though, were essentially an anomaly. Relatively speaking, more common, and infinitely more disturbing, was the feeling—sometimes overwhelmingly strong—of impending catastrophe before taking to the skies.

CHAPTER SEVEN

PREMONITIONS OF DISASTER

Doctors and others might dismiss resorting to charms, rituals, or even entreaties to an omniscient and omnipotent deity, along with belief in jinxes and hoodoos, as a return to the magical thinking of childhood. But for those who experienced them, premonitions were somehow "darker, more mysterious," involving as they commonly did a sudden and overwhelming sense of imminent catastrophe that proved much more difficult to explain in such terms.[1] They came unbidden, sometimes while asleep but often when awake, either to the fliers concerned or to observers—and seemed uncomfortably prescient. The goal of this chapter is to give a sense of the feeling of being marked and to explain how it was that flying personnel suddenly became, in their own minds, clairvoyant.

Cases of apparent precognition began to appear among RAF fliers soon after sustained aerial fighting began. Paul Richey, flying Hurricanes with 1 Squadron in May 1940, suddenly became "continually troubled" by something that proclaimed itself as a premonition of disaster prior to being shot down.[2] Later that summer, air gunner Mike Henry noted two cases of Blenheim aircrew members of 110 Squadron who seemed to have had an accurate premonition of death in the hours before they took off and failed to return. In the first instance a fellow gunner, normally cheerful and chatty, "didn't utter a word" on the bus taking crews to their aircraft dispersal points and was subsequently killed in a crash landing. The second case involved a navigator who, after squadron briefing, "persisted in going the rounds telling everybody that he wasn't coming home that night." He did indeed not return.[3] "I had an uneasy feeling that something was going to happen," Roger Hall recalled of an evening in late 1940 in which he felt uncharacteristically "unsettled and restless" before taking off on patrol as pilot of a 255 Squadron Defiant.[4] Desmond Scott, flying fighters with 3 Squadron in 1941, recalled waking up while on leave from a dream in which a friend was shot down in a burning Hurricane only to later discover that this fellow New Zealander had been killed in a manner consistent with his nightmare.[5]

The rapid expansion of Bomber Command and its night operations in 1942 brought forth more instances of foreknowledge that were memorable enough to be recalled and recorded decades later. At the end of May that year, Bob Horsley, a wireless operator/air gunner in a crew flying with 50 Squadron, "had the strongest premonition that we would be shot down." That night the Manchester he was flying in was hit so badly by antiaircraft fire over Cologne that the crew were forced to bail out before it crashed.[6] Three months later George Moreton, a Wellington navigator, after being briefed for a raid on Bremen, found that while changing into his flying clothing "I had the odd experience of knowing I was not coming back." His aircraft was hit by flak and forced to crash-land in enemy territory. Like Horsley, Moreton had taken solace from the belief—later borne out by events—that while his bomber would not survive the operation, he would escape serious injury.[7] Not so Lancaster rear gunner Roy Gadsen, who told his crew, before a raid on Osnabrück in early October 1942, that he was not going to last the night. Their aircraft was brought down by a fighter, and while the other six crew members successfully bailed out, Gadsen was killed in the attack.[8]

It was not just the men of Bomber Command who were experiencing unsettling thoughts about the immediate future by the middle of the war. In the Fleet Air Arm, fighter pilot Hank Adlam told himself just before takeoff from a carrier deck: "This flight is going to be your last."[9] The fliers of RAF Fighter Command also continued to be subject to occasional deathly premonitions. Spitfire pilot Bill Norris became "firmly convinced that he would be making his final flight the next day"—and so it came to be.[10]

American fliers also began experiencing premonitions after the USAAF commenced operations over the Continent. One morning in the first week of January 1943, Bert W. Humphreys, a B-17 pilot with the 91st Bomb Group, recorded in his diary how, after having "spent a very restless night" full of "wild dreams and nightmares," he awoke "with [a] premonition that disaster was close on my heels." Sure enough, the mission for the day turned out to be a rough one in which his B-17 was hit badly by flak and fighters, two other crew members were wounded, and the plane barely made it back to England.[11] Two months later, Pete

Edris experienced "a funny feeling" that he would not be returning from a mission with the 306th Bomb Group and was indeed forced to bail out later that day when the B-17 he was flying was shot down.[12] In the first week of April 1943, B-17 radio operator Jack Luehrs of the 305th Bomb Group, due to fly on a mission to a target outside Paris, "had the feeling that this was going to be my last raid." He left a note asking that his cash savings be forwarded to his father in Oregon before leaving his billet, and he was duly shot down.[13] Several months after that, public relations officer John R. McCrary, scheduled to fly with the crew of a B-17 of the 91st Bomb Group, was horrified to find that everyone involved, including himself, felt very strongly that they would not survive the upcoming mission—"They knew it. And I knew it"—and was very glad to be ordered off the plane before takeoff and spared the apparently predestined shooting down over Germany of *Our Gang*, which failed to return that day.[14] "Your ship won't make it back today," waist gunner Vance Van Hooser of the 94th Bomb Group told the crew chief of the B-17 he was due to board at Bury St. Edmunds for a strike against a synthetic rubber plant near Frankfurt on October 4; "I have a feeling that my time has come." Later that day he was very badly wounded and his ship had to make an emergency landing near the English coast.[15] Less than a week later B-17 navigator James F. Goff discovered the night before a scheduled mission that a bombardier he knew, Robert "Catfish" Wing, also with the 95th Bomb Group, was certain that he would die the following day. Goff tried to convince him otherwise, but "his feelings of impending death were very strong" and Wing did indeed perish on October 9, 1943.[16] A few days later a B-17 gunner with the 96th Bomb Group, Jack Novey, was disconcerted to hear a gunner on another crew state that "he knew he wasn't going to make it" as they dressed for another mission to Germany.[17] On the morning of the last day of the year, according to flight engineer Ray T. Matheny of the 379th Bomb Group, the tail gunner of his B-17 had a "vague premonition" that he was about to suffer injury and was indeed wounded during the subsequent mission.[18]

Those on RAF stations, meanwhile, continued to observe or experience frightening premonitions of doom. One evening in February 1943, an entire seven-man Halifax crew from 102 Squadron, usually highly extrovert and confident in their behavior as they prepared to board, appeared very different to ground-crew member Norman Noble:

This particular night they got off their transport and climbed into the aircraft without saying a word to anyone or to each other at all. I pulled away the starter battery trolley after the engines had fired, went upstairs with the "700" [clearance form] and waited until the skipper ran up the engines and did all the necessary checks. He throttled back the engines and then just sat there staring into space. I put the 700 in front of him open for the first signature, but he still didn't move. I gave him a pencil, thinking that he probably hadn't one. He signed and gave me the form back. I had to repeat the procedure twice more for the other signatures required. I gave him a pat on the shoulder. "See you in the morning," and left him still staring. I don't think he heard me. But all the rest of the crew were the same, not a word, not a sound, and all sat staring, completely lifeless. It was an atmosphere I have never forgotten.

Noble observed that "I was the last person to see that crew alive."[19]

Nineteen forty-four, when the efforts of the USAAF, USN, and RAF were at their height, would prove a bumper year for instances of apparent precognition that were later remembered. William R. Cubbins, a B-24 pilot with the 450th Bomb Group, wrote of another pilot in his squadron early in the year "who was convinced that the mission [scheduled for the following day] would be his last, and that he would die," a premonition of death that came true the next morning.[20] Around the same time, Robert Long, a gunner with the 392nd Bomb Group, recalled that he and the rest of his crew were "really down . . . down in the dumps" on the morning prior to the mission on which their B-24 was knocked out of the sky by an enemy fighter.[21] Louis H. Breitenbach, a B-17 flight engineer with the 303rd Bomb Group, was so certain his ship would be shot down on a particular mission that after the briefing he took off his diamond ring and placed it in his footlocker so that it would not be melted down in the subsequent crash.[22] "I had a feeling about this one," remembered B-24 flight engineer Charles Bistline of the April mission on which he had to bail out: "Not just being scared, I was always scared. This was different." So much so that he handed over his wallet to the crew chief with instructions to send the money to his mother.[23] Al Bibbens, a B-17 gunner shot down the following month, later concluded that he must have had an unconscious premonition that something was going to happen that day, since the night before he had written and left behind a note concerning the future of the crew's pet puppy.[24]

The second half of 1944 was no better. In the third week of June, radio operator Thomas Wilcox, flying B-26s with the 344th Bomb Group based at Stansted, encountered a friend on another crew who, anticipating the next day's mission, suddenly announced to his barrack-mates, "Fellows, this is my last mission. I won't be back." He could not be dissuaded that this was the case, and he was indeed killed while trying to bail out after a flak hit the following morning.[25] At the start of September, P-47 pilot Johnny B. Corbitt had an uneasy feeling that the day's mission would go wrong and ended up having to bail out.[26] Less than a week later, part-way through the showing of a Hollywood mystery in the camp theater at Ridgewell, B-17 bombardier Bill Sederwall of the 381st Bomb Group suddenly became distressed: "I became highly agitated and had to leave. I had a premonition that something was going to happen on tomorrow's mission." The next day his plane was badly damaged by flak and had to make an emergency landing in Belgium.[27] About a month after that, navigator Jackson Granholm of the 458th Bomb Group encountered a B-24 pilot who—accurately, as it transpired—foresaw his imminent end: "They're gonna get me . . . they're gonna shoot me down."[28] On the morning of November 21, at Molesworth airfield in England, bombardier Carl Ulrich of the 303rd Bomb Group revealed to his best friend, Jim O'Leary, a pilot on another crew, that he had experienced a dream on four occasions in which his B-17 was shot down. O'Leary subsequently took these dreams to be prophetic, since Ulrich was killed later that day.[29]

A sense of imminent doom could invade men's thoughts in the China–Burma–India Theater as well in 1944. "For some unknown reason," B-24 pilot Elmer E. Haynes of the 308th Bomb Group confided to his diary on October 24, "a premonition of disaster kept invading my thoughts."[30] The next mission from their base in China was indeed a dicey one.[31] "For some unexplained reason I had a bad feeling about that mission," B-29 navigator John Misterly of the 444th Bomb Group remembered of the hours leading up to a strike against Singapore from India on November 5: "I was very uneasy."[32] Looking back, he thought that he had experienced an accurate sixth-sense premonition that he would be wounded.[33]

In the Pacific, meanwhile, naval aviators might also experience the future. "For at least a month before I was shot down [on October 25, flying from the USS *Kadashan*]," wrote FM-2 pilot Doy Duncan, "I dreamed of a crash almost every night," adding that "I never had it again after I was shot down."[34] Keith Gardner was struck by the way in which a fellow TBF replacement pilot, F. H. Bissell, seemed completely certain on Christmas Day that he would not make it home—and by the fact that Bissell did indeed fail to return from a patrol launched from the USS *Essex*.[35]

This sort of thing peaked in the RAF also in 1944. Briefed for a raid on Berlin in January, a Halifax pilot from 102 Squadron, Laurie Underwood, suddenly found that "I had a premonition that I would not be coming back at least for some time." So strong was the feeling that he sat down at once and wrote a farewell letter to his fiancée, asking her to await his eventual return. As he predicted, his bomber was shot down over the German capital that night. Underwood, having earlier made sure his parachute was clipped on properly, successfully bailed out and became a prisoner of war.[36] The same month, James Kyle, a Typhoon fighter-bomber pilot, had such a strong premonition of doom one day about a particular operation—"Something was wrong. I didn't want to go"—that he refused to fly. This was entirely out of character but, apparently, justified by the subsequent loss of three out of four aircraft.[37] Eleven months later, Joe Herman, an Australian pilot from 466 Squadron, had a fleeting but equally accurate premonition soon after getting airborne that he would be away for some time: his Halifax was shot down that night, and like Underwood he found himself a POW until the end of the war.[38] There were also those in 1944 flying for the RAF whose premonitions convinced them they were going to die. In the early spring, Lancaster pilot Ralph Edwards of 7 Squadron based at Oakington had a disturbing encounter with a senior air gunner of another crew, "normally a cheerful person, very gregarious," who was now convinced he was about to be killed. "He kept repeating to me, 'We shall get the chop tonight! I know we shall! We shall get the chop tonight!'" This overwhelming premonition of death proved to be correct.[39]

Even in the final stages of the war, fliers might have disturbing hunches or nightmares. "I felt something inauspicious looming over us like a dark cloud," Charles Alling, a B-17 pilot with the 34th Bomb Group, remembered of a premonition of disaster he had felt on the morning of January 20, 1945, being borne out by a near-miss with another bomber while climbing toward the rally point.[40] B-24 radioman R. J. Hammer, upon waking on the morning of February 21, 1945, accurately warned another crew that the day's mission would be Vienna, one of the most heavily defended targets in the Third Reich.[41] Flying with the 357th Fighter Group, Chuck Yeager found himself one morning the next month in the cockpit of his P-51 "with a real premonition that I was taking my last ride." Luckily, the mission was aborted just before he started to taxi out onto the runway.[42] On May 7, bombardier Tony Braidic of the 95th Bomb Group declined to fly a final extra mission with his B-17 crew as a result of what he later thought was "an unconscious premonition" that—as turned out to be the case—they would not return.[43]

British and Commonwealth fliers also suffered uneasy presentiments in 1945. In the crew room at Metheringham on the evening of January 7, Bill Winter found fellow wireless operator Harry Stunell, normally a cheerful soul, very uneasy. "I've got a strange feeling about this bloody Munich job," Stunell confided, adding "I don't feel happy at all." He was right to be worried, insofar as his Lancaster collided with another bomber over the target and was forced to make a crash-landing in France. Only the rear gunner and wireless operator survived.[44] Just over two weeks later, on the other side of the globe, Corsair pilot Ben Heffer was astonished when a fellow Kiwi in 1833 Squadron aboard HMS *Illustrious* calmly announced as crews were preparing for a strike against the Japanese that "I won't be coming back this time"—and so it proved.[45]

Subsequently comparing notes in a POW camp, the survivors of a 100 Squadron radio countermeasures Liberator shot down by a night fighter on the night of February 20–21 during an operation to Dortmund all confessed that they had felt a strong sense at dispersal that their aircraft would not be returning to base at Oulton.[46] On April 4, Lancaster crews of 153 Squadron at Scampton were briefed to drop sea mines that night in the Kattegat. Wing Commander F. S. Powley, commanding the squadron, was due to fly. But as he admitted to fellow pilot John Gee, he had experienced a nasty "premonition" about the operation. "If I had the guts I would take myself off the Order of Battle," he explained, "but if I did I would never again be able to look the Squadron in the face." His aircraft, *U-Uncle*, failed to return the next morning.[47] These, it should be noted, are only a sample of the known instances of premonition among Allied wartime aircrew.[48]

Such presentiments, moreover, did not have to be confided or made obvious in order for at least some observers on the ground to feel they possessed a sixth sense. Working behind the bar of the officers' mess at West Malling in the latter part of 1942, a certain member of the Women's

Auxiliary Air Force named Nina would agree to read the palms of Mosquito crews from 85 Squadron. In two instances within a few months of each other she had suddenly closed a flier's hand and refused to say more, and in both cases the man had been killed aloft within the next few nights.[49] In late May 1944, an American officer, after reading the palms of a number of P-40 pilots from the 27th Fighter Group, privately admitted that despite what he had told one of them, "he saw only death" in the palm of a man who would die the next month.[50]

"Once I had the eerie experience of dancing [in a local village hall near Waddington] with a quiet, pleasant Scottish sergeant pilot," WAAF member Pip Beck recalled, "and suddenly knowing he was 'for the chop.' I knew it with a certainty. I wondered if he had any suspicion of it himself. Sure enough, on his next op he didn't come back."[51] This form of sixth sense was by no means confined to women. Michael Bentine, then an intelligence officer at Wickenby, the base from which Lancasters from Nos. 12 and 626 squadrons were operating against Berlin in the winter of 1943–1944, discovered that, through what he termed "clairvoyance," he knew ahead of time which men were for the chop. "To put it simply," he later wrote, "I could tell which members of the aircrews would die that night."[52] Fliers themselves might develop an uncanny sense about the future of others. "You would sit in a lorry with maybe two or three crews going out to the aircraft," remembered Bomber Command special operator Leslie Temple, "and you could look into the face of certain individuals, and you got a feeling 'they're not coming back.'"[53]

Little wonder that some Allied airmen should conclude that it was indeed possible to sense someone's fate before it happened.[54] Yet there are plenty of recorded aircrew premonitions of equal or even greater strength that did *not* come to pass; and scientific studies over the years have failed consistently to demonstrate precognition as a human sixth sense.[55] What, then, was causing fliers to experience these intimations of doom?

It should be kept in mind that some premonitions about the future were soundly rooted in the material circumstances of the present. A sense of deep unease could be generated by awareness, not necessarily conscious, of material circumstances lengthening the odds against survival on a particular sortie. If a plane had a history of mechanical problems or was an unknown quantity, for instance, it was not all that irrational to develop "a premonition" about that mission or operation.[56] When waist gunner Vance Van Hooser suddenly announced to the crew chief that his B-17 was not coming back from that day's mission, he was likely influenced by the fact that his crew had been given a substitute aircraft to fly that day—the oldest plane in the group.[57] Similarly, the bad "feeling" experienced by Charles Bistline on the one hand and John Misterly on the other was likely connected to the fact that their announced targets, respectively Ploesti and Singapore, were known to be very heavily defended.[58]

There were plenty of other logical reasons to be worried about the outcome of a sortie. Graham Welsh, a Wellington navigator in 9 Squadron, found himself suddenly quite "apprehensive" about a scheduled operation one night in April 1942, but he soon realized that this was due to justified concerns that the pilot plus other members of the crew were so tired that they were likely to crash (a view subsequently endorsed by the station medical officer, who pulled them from the battle order).[59] B-24 pilot Dick Lewis, flying with the 493rd Bomb Group, "got the premonition that all wasn't going to go as planned" on August 13, 1944, as the result of an unsettlingly vague mission briefing.[60] Chuck Yeager had his pretakeoff premonition of death on a day when the weather "was terrible . . . rain squalls and turbulent winds": if the mission had not been aborted because of storms, he might very well never have returned alive.[61] The vague feeling of incipient disaster felt by B-17 pilot Charles Alling on January 20, 1945, was mostly because of the fact that he would be "flying in the snowfall with poor visibility."[62]

For those not flying single-seat fighters, there was also the matter of with whom one flew. Fliers usually disliked having to go into combat with men they did not know.[63] This was entirely reasonable, insofar as a combat crew was a team, and coordination between strangers more difficult to achieve, leading to decreased efficiency in the air in general and combat in particular: "an invitation to the Grim Reaper, always on the lookout for deviants," as one Australian navigator put it.[64] If someone had suddenly to be replaced, little wonder that those involved might develop a sense that the end was nigh.[65] It was likely no coincidence that Pete Edris experienced the feeling that he was not coming back from a particular mission on the day he was flying as copilot with an unfamiliar crew; or that George Webster had to force himself into boarding a B-17 with an inexperienced crew after having a strong presentiment that he was doomed.[66]

More generally, those who felt worrying premonitions were invariably men under stress. From takeoff to landing, pilots or other crew members had to try to remain completely alert in order to do their jobs and avoid disaster. Uninsulated and unpressurised cockpits and cabins were often deafeningly noisy and inadequately heated for higher altitudes. For pilots in particular, flying in bad weather and above all maneuvering in combat was both physically and mentally demanding. In periods of intense activity, fliers might not get enough proper rest between sorties. Most significant of all in terms of operational strain, they were constantly aware that the enemy was doing his level best to kill them, and at times with considerable chance of success. The cumulative effect, both physically and psychologically, was inescapable. As the author of a study of aviation medicine based on wartime experience concluded, nobody could fly combat operations or missions over time "without signs of strain beginning to make themselves evident."[67]

Fliers who experienced premonitions, which could range from a vague sense of unease to frighteningly specific dreams about the morrow, were almost invariably approaching exhaustion in mind and body.[68] Paul Richey, for example, experienced his premonition of doom after nine days of more or less continuous dogfighting over France in May 1940, by which time, as he admitted, his "nerves and morale" were under great strain.[69] By the time Roger Hall experienced his premonition that December, he had been flying combat sorties more or less continuously for over six months.[70] His fellow fighter pilot Desmond Scott recalled in reference to his nightmare of disaster the following year that "I had been flying myself almost to a standstill at about that time."[71]

Premonitory experiences, in other words, were commonly a product of combat fatigue brought on by repeated sorties against an often deadly foe, as some of the more perceptive fliers recognized. When his friend announced that he would not be returning from the next day's mission, for example, Thomas Wilcox observed that "it was only because we had been on several tough missions that he thought that way."[72] After B-24 navigator Ray Parker of the 445th Bomb Group had experienced the "edgy ominous feeling" that he was going to be shot down just before it happened in early 1944, he had wondered: "Is it a premonition? It's probably just a recognition that the odds are against my finishing my tour of duty."[73] Dwight M. Curo, a B-17 navigator with the 303rd Bomb

Group, who developed a sense of "forbading [*sic*] and presentiment" after a briefing in the summer of 1943, was surely right in putting this down to "nerve strain" in the wake of the disastrous Schweinfurt-Regensburg raid that he had flown two days earlier.[74]

As for dreams, research suggests that they are a way the brain processes and sorts important waking experience, and that nightmares are not always successful efforts to cope with stressful or indeed traumatic events.[75] Though a fair number of aircrew experienced what one RAF physician described as "terrifying dreams of air battle experiences," only a minority remembered the specific content after waking.[76] Studies indicate that those suffering from nightmares that they can recall are more prone to believe that what they have experienced asleep will come to pass if it has not already.[77] Moreover, on closer examination certain dreams turn out not to mirror future events as closely as they might seem at first glance. Doy Duncan, for instance, admitted that in his repeated nightmares of disaster "it wasn't always me who would crash. Sometimes it was, but sometimes it was someone else. Sometimes I didn't even know who it was."[78]

It is also worth noting that, though there were exceptions,[79] many of those fliers already invested in magical thinking often found it harder than others to rationalize premonitions as being manifestations of stress. When John McCrary developed the overwhelming feeling that he would perish if he flew with the crew of *Our Gang* on the Schweinfurt-Regensburg mission, it was in the wake of crossing paths with a black cat.[80] Both the B-17 flight engineer from the 303rd Bomb Group and the B-24 crew from the 445th Bomb Group who had experienced bad premonitions about a particular mission were all worried because it was to be their thirteenth trip—obviously unlucky.[81] "My thirteenth mission superstition?" Bill Sederwall asked himself of his sudden mid-movie sense of impending doom. His answer: "Maybe!"[82] The danger, of course, was that doom-laden premonitions could turn into self-fulfilling prophecies, since the fliers concerned might more easily give way to fatalism and stop fighting as hard as they could to survive in the air. This was likely the fate of the crew Norman Noble observed and the sort of thing that worried RAF bomber leader Leonard Cheshire.[83]

What, though, of those who thought they possessed a sixth sense concerning the deathly fate of others? Even if a premonition of death was not confided to anyone, observers could often ascertain a high level of fatigue and stress through visual means. Those who believed they could tell if someone they knew was going to die were in fact "reading" speech, faces, and body language in the manner of professional psychics.[84] USAAF doctors noted that combat stress could often manifest itself through "coarse tremors."[85] What British fliers referred to as "the twitch"—jerky body movements, facial tics, stammering, staring, rapidly blinking or hollowed eyes—was a result of operational exhaustion.[86] WAAF member Joan Beech, for instance, had an accurate premonition that a Lancaster wireless operator she knew from 97 Squadron in 1943 was to die one particular night after seeing his "jerky hands" and "panic and disaster in his eyes."[87] The two men whom the WAAF at West Malling had apparently identified as for the chop both had "troubled eyes."[88] Tellingly, Michael Bentine, in discussing his apparently supernatural ability to discern who was about to die, wrote: "Their faces have the look of death."[89]

Fliers themselves made accurate predictions about the fate of their fellows in which observational experience rather than a sixth sense was cited as justification.[90] One morning in late October 1942, for example, Stirling rear gunner Bill Jackson found himself in conversation with Tony Wheldon (the veteran assistant gunnery leader in 218 Squadron) around the tea wagon discussing a mid-upper gunner by the name of Jimmy White due to fly operationally that night:

> "White's for the chop tonight," he [Wheldon] said quietly, nodding towards Jimmy's shaking glass [tea mug]. I gasped at the callousness of the remark.
> "Christ, Tony, don't say things like that. Jimmy's always a little nervous but he's great once he takes off."
> "Seen it a hundred times, Jacko. Wait and see. You'll learn."

White and the rest of his crew were indeed shot down over enemy territory some hours later.[91]

Such haunted souls, though, were not always marked for death. The more perceptive among Allied medical and intelligence officers, squadron commanders, and station chaplains could see the physical manifestations of operational fatigue and, when possible, used that knowledge to pull men off flying temporarily or permanently before they met their end through impaired airmanship or an outright refusal to carry on.[92]

In retrospect it is not surprising that the sense of imminent doom emerged among fliers amid the stresses and strains of high-stakes combat operations. While a glimpse of the apparent future might occasionally be experienced in time of peace, it was no accident that the feeling of being marked for death emerged strongly in the context of wartime flying. The phenomenon had first occurred in World War I and would emerge again in the conflicts of the second half of the century, but on a scale dwarfed by the exponentially larger World War II.[93] For those who experienced premonitions of doom, unless they were able to use reason to overcome fear, the sky could indeed seem fated.

CONCLUSION

In light of widespread references to charms, rituals, and other forms of magical thinking in memoirs, diaries, and interviews, it is all too easy to assume that superstition among wartime fliers was pretty much universal.[1] However, assessing the relative extent and degree of superstitious thought and action among combat aviators is problematic. On the one hand, those susceptible to magical thinking tended to argue in retrospect that it was ubiquitous and powerful. On the other, there were plenty of former fliers for whom it apparently mattered little and who thought it of limited importance overall. These contradictory generalizations need to be viewed with care.

Some veterans thought they were far from alone carrying talismans and engaging in other forms of magical thinking. "All aircrew tended to be highly superstitious," wrote one senior pilot in RAF Bomber Command, echoing almost word for word the sentiments of others in British and Commonwealth squadrons.[2] It was the same in the USAAF. "When you flew combat," stated B-17 radio operator Alvin Kotler of the 99th Bomb Group, "you were either religious, or you were superstitious."[3] This kind of observation was by no means unique to bomber crews or always ex post facto. P-47 pilot Quentin Aanenson, for instance, wrote in a letter to his wife in July 1944 that virtually "every pilot I know over here has some sort of good luck charm, or ritual he goes through before a mission."[4]

Yet this was not a universal opinion. "You hear about people wearing the same underwear or the same hat," commented former B-17 radioman John Smith as a prelude to emphasizing that "I didn't know anyone who did that."[5] At the time, canny war correspondent Ernie Pyle noticed that he only occasionally encountered magical thinking while staying with various USAAF units: "Superstition was rare even among the pilots."[6]

There is evidence to support this observation—for instance, "I didn't feel at all superstitious about this being the 13th mission," B-17 flight engineer Andy Anzanos of the 390th Bomb Group noted in his diary after landing—and not just for the army air forces.[7] "I was never a superstitious person," asserted F6F pilot John Galvin of VF-8, and therefore he did not consider it "portentous" to be flying on April Fool's Day, even though that was the date he was shot down.[8] "Not being superstitious," Kenneth Walsh, an F4U pilot with VMF-124 explained, he had no problem regularly assuming the thirteenth slot in bomber-escort formations.[9] Indeed, there are a goodly number of detailed and revealing first-person accounts in which the issue of superstition does not appear even tangentially.[10] Furthermore, when asked in interviews on both sides of the Atlantic if they had carried lucky charms or engaged in rituals, plenty of veterans replied firmly in the negative.[11] Like air gunner Arthur Batten, who flew Stirlings with 190 Squadron, many of them seem to have thought that "having your bloody bunny rabbit with you would make no bloody difference" as to whether you lived or died.[12]

Moreover, there were instances of both individuals and entire crews who consciously chose to challenge what they regarded as illogical and possibly dangerous beliefs. "I always figured that war wasn't really God's business," B-17 tail gunner Arnold Willis explained of his decision not to pray for divine intercession on his behalf.[13] Robert Brown, flying Mustangs with 268 Squadron, also assumed that the Almighty was not out to protect him personally more than any other pilot.[14] After all, as B-17 flight engineer John Comer heard himself thinking, "German pilots rising up to meet you are asking the same thing."[15] When he discovered that the tail gunner was praying rather than watching for fighters during missions, a B-17 captain in the 390th Bomb Group who did not believe in the power of prayer threatened to kick him and anyone else off the crew who was not fully attending to their duties.[16] John Matthews, an observer (navigator/bomb aimer) on Wellingtons with 57 Squadron, along with the two gunners, refused point-blank to fly with a particular pilot because they were convinced his tendency to rely on the power of prayer made him a menace to all:

> I didn't tell the wingco [wing commander] this but the pilot we objected to was a Geordie whose father was a Methodist priest in Newcastle. The pilot, a sergeant, was a man of God and we had heard from

people who had flown with him that during the most dangerous parts of the flight, when he should have been taking evasive action, he never did. He always told his crew: "God will look after us." Well, nobody was going to believe that. If you were attacked by a fighter he kept going straight and level. He would not corkscrew because God was on their side.

Luckily the wingco himself needed a crew that night and gave the pilot a different set of substitutes. "Perhaps God was on the side of the Germans when they later shot down the God-fearing pilot and his unfortunate crew," Matthews drily reflected.[17]

What applied to religious supplication might also be the case for lucky charms, bad omens, premonitions, and other superstitions. "I was anti-superstition," stated bomber pilot Trevor Timperley, who flew Wellingtons with 166 Squadron and subsequently Lancasters with 156 Squadron, explaining that if a crew member somehow forgot his lucky item and was convinced he was for the chop, then he would not focus on the job at hand and might thereby make his premonition a self-fulfilling prophecy.[18] Leonard Cheshire, who commanded 76 Squadron and later 617 Squadron, thought the same about those flying bombers who thought they were doomed to die.[19] "I realized that if I was going to let that sort of thing rule my life here," P-39 pilot Ted Park wrote of his decision not to refuse the flight suit of a man recently killed in the 35th Fighter Group on New Guinea, "I might as well just go out and crash on takeoff."[20]

Fliers might even choose to try to expose the absurdity of magical thinking by acting in a contrary manner. This could involve individuals, crews, or even entire units.

When William Behrns of the 80th Fighter Group learned that other pilots in the 459th Squadron were refusing to fly a P-38 numbered 113 because of triskaidekaphobia, he insisted on taking the ship himself. "I have always believed the best way to defeat a superstition was to go straight at it," he later explained, "and that is what I did."[21] In 100 Squadron, there was a magical belief among Lancaster crews surrounding a recording in the officers' mess of "Java Jive (I Like Coffee, I Like Tea)" sung by the Ink Spots. Bomb aimer Geoffrey Willatt remembered that the navigator on his crew, Dickie Fairweather from British Honduras, "knew there was a superstition that anyone putting on that record would be shot down that night," but one evening before ops "he played it with a large grin saying, 'What nonsense,' and of course, we came safely back from Nürnberg that night."[22] Even more daringly, Lancaster bomb aimer John Walsh of 619 Squadron chose to wear the Irvin jacket and trousers of someone who had been killed: "I shall be the best dressed chap in the Squadron and the least superstitious."[23]

One 158 Squadron crew decided, on receiving a new Halifax III with "F" on the fuselage on a particularly inauspicious day, to call their plane *Friday the Thirteenth*. "Besides reflecting the delivery date," bomb aimer Sandy Slack recalled, "we deliberately set out to defy convention, plastering the fuselage with every bad luck symbol we could bring to mind; we even had a ladder painted over the entrance door!" *Friday the Thirteenth* went on to complete 128 operational sorties and to survive the war.[24] In the USAAF, several B-17s and a B-24 were dubbed *Friday the 13th*, presumably for similar reasons.[25] Other American crews chose to defy Lady Luck by giving their ships names like *SNAFU* and even *13th Jinx*. In the 95th Bomb Group, *Hāārd Luck* was a B-17 whose nose was not only adorned with these words but also with the traditional seminude calendar girl: though her brassiere in this case consisted of the halves of an eight ball. *Hāārd Luck*, though eventually shot down, survived well beyond the average length of time a heavy bomber was in operation.[26]

Meanwhile, members of the 13th Squadron to be formed in the RAAF, a light bomber unit created in wartime when official badges were not being issued, developed and adopted an unofficial crest designed to underline their collective dismissal of magical thinking. The Latin motto was *Fratres Diaboli*—the Devil's brothers—while the four heraldic quarters featured a figure walking under a ladder, a cracked mirror, a calendar open to Friday the 13th, and a match lighting three cigarettes.[27]

There were also fliers who overcame, through experience, an initial belief in a particular charm or omen. Tony Rieck, for instance, was far from happy to be flying his first strafing operation as a Beaufighter pilot with 177 Squadron in Burma on Friday, October 13, 1944. But he escaped all harm and noted decades later than "I have never been superstitious about Friday the 13th since."[28]

Superstition, then, was clearly not universal. Its prevalence should at the same time not be underestimated. The number of American heavy bombers with names obviously designed to bring good luck, after all, outnumbered those designed to challenge superstitions by at least a factor of ten.[29]

Not mentioning charms and rituals in retrospect, it should be kept in mind, does not mean they were not present at the time. In his best-selling and otherwise revealing war memoir, Spitfire pilot Geoffrey Wellum gives no hint that he carried a talisman.[30] When questioned, however, he happily recalled a stuffed Eeyore donkey given to him by his girlfriend as a good-luck token: "I never flew without him."[31] P-51 ace Kit Carson of the 357th Fighter Group seems not to have grasped the ritualistic nature of his dressing routine before combat. "I always wore a tie or scarf, sometimes both," he later wrote, adding: "don't know why."[32] Furthermore, at least some of those who claimed not to be affected did in fact engage in magical thinking.[33] Fighter pilot Herky Green, for instance, wrote in his memoirs that "I was totally without superstition" yet made a point after his first mission of switching from a P-40 of the 325th Fighter Group with the number 13 on the fuselage to one labeled 11.[34] Later in the war Richard Greene, a B-17 waist gunner in the 398th Bomb Group, carried a copy of the New Testament, given to him by his brother, in his shirt pocket on every mission and argued that this was "not a good luck charm" but rather a sign of his faith in the power of the Lord.[35] B-17 navigator Dan Kalish of the 388th Bomb Group claimed that he did not believe in luck; but when presented with a tour-expired crewman's special hat and admonished that without it he would go down in flames, he found himself too afraid not to wear it on every subsequent trip to Germany.[36] "I never performed any ritual nor did I have a talisman," wrote B-24 bombardier Al Altvater of the 451st Bomb Group confidently, while adding that "I did take my camera wherever I went, particularly on missions."[37]

Embarrassment could mean that a personal charm or repetitive action was kept secret. "I recently discovered that Min had always kept a little cloth rabbit in one of his pockets," Halifax navigator Robert Kensett of 158 Squadron wrote over fifty years after the war of his Canadian pilot, Menno "Min" Bartsch, "which we did not know about."[38] The same desire to avoid potential ridicule from crewmates could also affect the degree of openness concerning unlucky numbers. "Who me? No, I'm not superstitious," Daniel Becker, a B-17 pilot in the 95th Bomb Group, wrote in his diary regarding his secret fears about mission thirteen, adding: "it's just that—oh well."[39]

Nor should the strength of feeling thereby generated be undervalued. Looking back, some fliers seemed a bit embarrassed by their own or their comrades' wartime habits and sought to downplay them. "I don't think

I paid much attention," observed a B-17 radio operator.[40] "It didn't mean a lot, really," commented one Lancaster gunner.[41] "It was always a bit of joke," wrote a senior RAF pilot. At the time, though, as even the latter had to admit, superstitions "were taken very seriously."[42]

Just how much magical beliefs could matter is illustrated by cases where a talisman or ritual was somehow forgotten. Reactions among American, British, and Commonwealth fliers could be quite dramatic.

Don Collumbell, an Australian navigator with 10 Squadron, recalled that the rear gunner in his crew "had a sheepskin jacket and he would not go without that sheepskin jacket even if we had to turn the bus back when it took us out to the aircraft to go back and get it."[43] This was by no means an isolated case. A rag doll carried by the wireless operator had become indispensable to a Lancaster crew with 218 Squadron. One evening, on the way out to dispersal, it was discovered that the doll had been left behind—and the entire crew rushed back to find it.[44] A Lancaster crew with 550 Squadron came to place great faith in the rear gunner, Danny Driscoll, spitting on a rudder fin before they boarded. On one occasion they were about to turn onto the runway from the perimeter track when the skipper, Gordon Markes, checked with Driscoll over the intercom to confirm that this ritual had been carried out. "Danny replied that he had forgotten," recalled the bomb aimer, Vernon Wilkes. The pilot "slammed on the brakes and told him to get out and do it." This took some time, not least because of the slipstream from the four idling propellers. "Flying control couldn't understand why our Lancaster was holding up the whole squadron take-off and was frantically flashing green lights at us." Eventually Markes was forced to begin to move, the rear gunner having to run alongside and be hauled in the rear door by the mid-upper gunner, Len Buckell.[45] An air gunner in 405 Squadron was so upset on discovering that the talismanic brassieres with which he had adorned his turret had been removed that he flagged down a passing crew truck and pleaded—successfully—for the WAAF driver to divest herself of the required item of clothing.[46] Other fliers, such as Typhoon pilot Klaus Adam or P-47 pilot Bob Brulle, admitted to distinct uneasiness when they accidentally flew without their charms or forgot to perform rituals.[47]

In the 485th Bomb Group, the chaplain normally said a prayer for safekeeping at the end of mission briefings. "One day the chaplain didn't show up," recalled B-24 radio operator Edwin Koch, "and close to 100 men refused to leave the room until he had been found . . . and had said his customary prayers for the men."[48] Edward Tracy, a pilot in the 384th Bomb Group, a staunch Methodist, became forcibly aware one day of how "as much superstition as real interest in the Word of God" was associated with the copy of the Bible he usually had his radio operator read Psalm 91 from when he brought along a different item:

> When I gave my New Testament to the radio operator he almost went berserk. We were at the hardstand where our B-17 was sitting awaiting the signal from the tower, and without permission, he raced on a bicycle for over a mile to where I was billeted. He entered the officers quarters—a no no—rummaged through my stuff and found my Bible and raced back to the hardstand where we were yet awaiting takeoff orders. We could have gotten into a peck of trouble, but he chanced it rather than taking off without my Bible![49]

B-24 pilot Pete Riegel of the 487th Bomb Group remembered the day one of his crew thought he had forgotten his St. Christopher medal. It had been given to him by a pair of aunts back in Nebraska, and "he believed that as long as he wore the medal he would return home safely." Finding himself without this vital talisman, he "insisted that we abort the mission." Riegel decided that there was no way they could turn around for this reason, but the crew member was very insistent and threatened to bail out if his pleas were not heeded. The crisis was resolved when the man discovered that the item he had misplaced was in fact still about his person rather than back at base.[50]

Even being shot down might not dent a flier's overall faith in lucky items. Len Bradfield, a Lancaster bomb aimer with 49 Squadron who was forced to bail out over Germany in August 1943, admitted that once on the ground he had "chucked my lucky golliwog away." This, though, was because "I thought it had failed me" rather than because he now understood that that such objects had no supernatural usefulness.[51]

The observations of various journalists and physicians confirm that magical thinking was deep-rooted.[52] Superstition, moreover, could thrive because those in leadership positions did nothing to stop it. There were two likely reasons for this benign attitude.

The first was that some of them were susceptible to magical thinking themselves—and thus likely to be sympathetic. At the formation level, for instance, the station commander at Grimsby, an RAF airfield serving two Lancaster squadrons toward the end of the war, always peed on the starboard main tire before he flew on operations. "It brings good luck," he explained.[53] In the Eighth Air Force there were people like Frank Armstrong, who led two USAAF heavy bomber groups and then an entire wing, yet sheepishly admitted that "I was superstitious" in repeatedly engaging in a B-17 boarding ritual.[54]

At command level there were also superstitious men. USN carrier admiral William "Bull" Halsey, for instance, was so appalled to be put in charge of Task Force 13 and an operation due to commence on February 13, 1942, that he managed to get Pacific Fleet headquarters to change both the number and the date.[55] Tactical airpower advocate Elwood R. "Pete" Queseda, in charge of the fighter-bombers of the USAAF Ninth Air Force, was known to have resorted before the war to urinating on the tail of his aircraft to improve his luck.[56] His nominal boss in 1944, the head of the Allied Expeditionary Air Forces, Trafford Leigh-Mallory, came from the RAF but was if anything even more prone to superstition, having blocked the demolition of a country house to make way for an airfield because he believed it was inhabited by a ghost.[57] In the Southwest Pacific Theater the commander of the Fifth Air Force, George C. Kenney, always carried a pair of lucky dice.[58] Ira Eaker, who led the Eighth Air Force from England between 1942 and 1944, thought it bad luck to have his photograph taken before flying.[59] Carl A. "Tooey" Spaatz, who commanded all US strategic air forces in Europe in 1944–1945, believed that having a pair of kittens with him could improve his odds at poker.[60] Magical thinking, indeed, might reach all the way to the top. In the RAF, the Chief of Air Staff at the start of the war, Sir Cyril Newall, had personally intervened to make sure a new air gunner brevet had twelve feathers rather than the proposed thirteen.[61] Henry H. "Hap" Arnold, commanding all US Army air forces in World War II, was superstitious about naming aircraft after living people.[62]

The second reason a benign official attitude toward superstition prevailed was because even among those admirals, generals, and air marshals who were not themselves affected—or even, like RAF Bomber Command chief Butch Harris or US Eighth Army Air Force commander Jimmy Doolittle, men who personally opposed magical thinking—there were those who thought it would be bad for fliers' morale for the authorities to try and challenge firmly held beliefs about matters of life and death.[63] In the RAF this became directly evident in the reaction to what might be termed bomber crews' "home remedies" to the problem posed by searchlights and radar-directed flak at night, while in the USAAF it manifested itself in relation to preferences in body armor.

In attempts to maximize the chances of survival over Germany, RAF bomber crews might, through applying *post hoc ergo propter hoc* logic, develop unorthodox countermeasures. In the early stages of the bomber offensive someone came up with the idea that empty beer bottles dropped from an aircraft would whistle downward and thereby confuse the sound locators helping direct the searchlights or make the locator crews think they were being bombed. In reality any whistling sound would have been drowned out in the ears of the sound-locator operators by the noise of the engines, but there were enough instances of searchlights moving away or being turned off when this was tried for at least some bomber crews to deduce cause and effect.[64] Even as it became clear over the months and years that radar was the real threat and that the official RAF countermeasure introduced in 1943—dropping large numbers of strips of paper covered with reflective aluminum—was effective, the beer-bottle idea did not disappear entirely. One Lancaster crew from 103 Squadron, for example, attached these strips, known as "Window," to bottles and threw them out when caught in searchlights: "as they fell," the rear gunner insisted, "the flak and searchlights followed them."[65] The wireless operator was also convinced that he could hear a click on his radio that indicated the plane was being tracked by radar as an immediate prelude to successively closer bursts of antiaircraft fire. After the pilot took evasive action and a flak burst was thereby "avoided," the entire crew became convinced they had discovered the key to countering radar-directed flak and spread the good word.[66] In actual fact German Würzburg gun-laying radar operated at a frequency much too high to be picked up by the RAF's standard R.1155 receiver set.[67]

A more common alternative antiradar technique involved the Identification Friend or Foe (IFF) transponder installed on British aircraft. This was designed to allow ground radars in the United Kingdom to distinguish between friendly and hostile planes by sending specific interrogation signals designed to elicit the correct electronic responses from an aircraft with the transponder aboard. Bomber crews, however, became convinced that if they were caught in a cone of searchlights, having the wireless operator toggle the IFF switch would generate radio interference sufficient to confuse the radar operators directing the beams of light and allow them to make their escape.[68] So common was this belief that in the autumn of 1941 a study by the Operational Research Section at Bomber Command Headquarters was commissioned. The resulting report indicated that there was in fact no correlation between evading a searchlight cone and use of the IFF switch.[69]

Reactions among senior officers to this sort of thing are instructive. Concerning the beer-bottle technique, the commander of 5 Group within Bomber Command in 1941–1942, John Slessor, admitted that he did not think the concept was a sound one. "I found it extremely hard to believe there was anything in this," he later wrote. Yet he instructed an Operational Research Section representative "on no account to pour scorn on the idea," his reason being that "even if there was nothing whatever in it, the boys thought there was, and it gave them a warm feeling." Thus, at least until Slessor left the group in the spring of 1942, "the beer bottle remained a highly-regarded piece of operational equipment."[70] As for the IFF switch, even in the wake of the Operational Research Section report there was a reluctance among the air marshals at High Wycombe to disseminate the truth. "Bomber Command argued that it was a good thing to let the pilots go on using I.F.F.," as indignant scientist R. V. Jones remembered, "because it would encourage them to press home attacks over defended areas when they might otherwise be inclined to turn tail if caught by searchlights."[71] Only when it was proven conclusively in 1944 that the Germans, as a means of pinpointing an aircraft's location, had learned to send signals that switched-on IFF sets responded to were orders issued to keep the transponders switched off over enemy territory.[72]

In the USAAF, official unwillingness to challenge strongly held beliefs among bomber crews was evident in the matter of flak suits. Introduced in 1943 to reduce the number of shrapnel wounds resulting from close flak bursts, this form of body armor—overlapping high-tensile steel plates sewn into a strong fabric vest—was designed to protect the vital organs in the torso. American fliers, however, often preferred to either sit or stand on their flak suits rather than actually wear them over their shoulders, more worried about their reproductive organs than anything else and convinced that since flak was fired from below most shrapnel must come through the underside of the ship. Flight surgeons compiled data that showed that in fact most flak came through the sides of the fuselage rather than the bottom and that men who chose not to wear flak suits over their torsos were in reality running a much higher risk of injury. Yet despite the protests of the aeromedical establishment, the headquarters of the Eighth Air Force defended such actions: "It is doubtful whether crew members should be ordered not to place suits on the otherwise unprotected floor." Popular wisdom, in other words, trumped scientific evidence.[73]

Air commanders seem to have intuited that any belief that buttressed morale, and thereby performance, ought not to be discouraged as long as this seemed to outweigh any potential harm it might do. This is vividly illustrated in an incident that took place at Leaconfield on the evening of March 15, 1944, as Dudley Forsyth, commanding 466 Squadron, RAAF, came 'round the Halifax dispersal points to chat prior to that night's operation. Andy Wiseman, a German-Jewish bomb aimer, recalled what happened when the CO arrived at his aircraft.

> As he and the rest of the crew exchanged pleasantries, Forsyth noted that I seemed to be in a strange mood and asked me what was wrong. Jean [Wiseman's girlfriend] had knitted me a golly, and I used to take it with me as a good luck token. By mistake I had left it in my locker, and in my haste to don my flying gear had forgotten to bring it with me. The anxiety must have shown in my face. Without hesitating, Forsyth spun the wheel of his jeep and raced away, returning a few minutes later with my talisman. Now at last we could get on with the war.[74]

In the Royal Navy, it is worth noting, Captain Denis Boyd, commanding the aircraft carrier HMS *Illustrious*, made it clear in 1941 that "I can understand that outlook" with reference to the Fleet Air Arm superstition against volunteering but being perfectly happy to be assigned.[75]

There were also indulgent unit commanders in the USAAF and USN. A number of bomber group commanders in the Eighth Air Force, for instance, allowed the development of unofficial completion-of-tour ceremonies that included the men concerned being presented with impressive-looking certificates indicating that the fickle finger of fate had allowed them to join "The Lucky Bastard[s] Club."[76] When the first five of seven P-47 pilots inhabiting a tent in Corsica were sequentially killed in action, leaving their beds empty one after the other around the tent, the CO of the 79th Fighter Group in the autumn of 1944 granted the request of the remaining two not to have replacement pilots take the place of the departed in order to stop the cycle of deadly fate. As Kenneth Thompson recalled, "the brass honored our feelings on this."[77] Many months earlier Tom Blackburn, on assuming command of VF-17, specifically allowed his F4F pilots to carry "personal totems" aloft.[78]

At unit level, chaplains, as noted earlier, sometimes encouraged overtly magical thinking in order to keep up the men's spirits. Physicians, meanwhile, were being instructed to keep an eye out for various visible signs of operational fatigue and to help avoid psychological casualties through the imposition of enforced rest.[79] Superstitious behavior might sometimes be viewed as a de facto symptom of combat stress; but since charms and rituals generally did not seem to impede fliers in the performance of their duties—unlike, say, radical mood shifts, an inability to sleep, or uncontrollable tremors—medical officers and flight surgeons generally did not try and make superstitious fliers "see reason."[80]

Recent research suggests that a benign laissez-faire approach by those who ministered to body and soul as well as commanders at various levels was actually of value in operational terms. Studies indicate that believing a particular item or action is lucky actually does, more often than not, translate into better end results.[81] Additionally, while the reality and extent of divine intervention as a result of personal supplication remains impervious to scientific analysis, psychological studies nonetheless indicate that individual prayer definitely does help bolster self-control of the sort that operational aircrew clearly needed.[82]

What can be said with absolute certainty is that the risks and stresses involved in operational flying during World War II greatly increased the number of otherwise rational men who succumbed to magical thinking. What was more, this was the case just as much among commissioned officers as it was among noncommissioned officers, and—with some variation in the popularity of certain beliefs—superstitious faith seems to have transcended both nationality and service branch in the English-speaking world.[83] Accounts, however, suggest an anomaly unconnected to rank, citizenship, or service. Though both bomber crews and fighter pilots could be intensely superstitious, magical thinking seems to have been less prevalent among the latter than among the former.[84] This was likely because fighter pilots had greater agency than bomber crews, more of a sense of being masters of their own fate, able to radically alter course, speed, attitude, and altitude as the need arose in a way simply not true for those piloting or performing other needed functions aboard bombers. "They could control their situation," B-17 pilot Bill Healy put in reference to the "Little Friends" who flew escort missions for the 94th Bomb Group: "We couldn't."[85] Based on his observations and those of others, a Fifteenth Air Force neuropsychiatrist discovered that, because of their role, fighter-escort pilots were significantly less subject to anxiety than the bomber crews they shepherded.[86] As P-51 pilot Clayton Gross of the 354th Fighter Group put it, "You were the boss! You had the best seat; the only one and you controlled what you did in the air."[87]

It is worth reiterating that magical thinking among combat fliers was not confined to World War II and pointing out that, even in time of peace, the risks might be such as to encourage supernatural belief.[88] In the first half of the twentieth century fatal accidents were far more common than they are in civil aviation today, while in the second half flying military jets became—as it remains—a high-risk peacetime profession.[89] "It is a bit if a superstition," Mike Child of the Red Arrows RAF aerobatic team admitted in an interview in 2012, "but pilots generally try to keep flying with the same pair of gloves because they bring good luck!"[90]

The experience of being deliberately shot at in time of war, however, raises the stakes enormously. "It had been the closest I had ever come to losing my life," remembered an American bomber pilot of the first night of the 1991 Gulf War air campaign. "Within a few brief minutes my cavalier 'can't hurt me' attitude had been shattered . . . my mind was no longer a slave to the self-image I had created over the years, an image of calculated toughness, the sense of being bulletproof."[91] And no air campaign prior to, during, or since World War II has matched the size and scope of the fight against the Axis. As losses mounted, physicians noted how in England anxiety grew among USAAF bomber crews and superstition surged in RAF Bomber Command.[92] "Life on the razor's edge made fertile soil for superstition to grow in," as Ben Smith, a B-17 radio operator with the 303rd Bomb Group, rightly observed.[93]

This book has been an attempt to explore a major phenomenon in the life of wartime combat fliers in greater depth than has been possible thus far.[94] It is not, however, by any means intended as the last word. The place of magical thinking in other professions where skill cannot fully substitute for luck—notably sports—continues to be subject to academic research and interpretation, and there is plenty of room for further exploration and debate about wartime fliers and their superstitions.[95] Hopefully, though, readers will now have a greater sense of just how varied and deeply felt superstitious beliefs were to many of the tens of thousands of young men, including "the bravest and most competent," who flew combat in World War II.[96]

Though some of them might remain convinced into old age that their lives had been saved by an entreaty, talisman, or ritual, in reality the only positive effect related to their sense of agency, of exerting some control over their fate beyond what skill could provide.[97] That, however, was enough to keep a lot of young men flying against the foe. In this sense superstition really did work for those who believed.

TOUR LENGTH

How long pilots and other aircrew should have to fly against the enemy, either in terms of hours or operational sorties, was a subject that occupied a good deal of attention in the RAF, USAAF, and also the USN, though less so in the RN. The resulting official decisions, designed to maximize the usefulness of trained fliers while allowing them a sense that despite combat losses they might survive, produced directives that varied over time and place.

In the RAF, fighter pilots were expected to complete about 200 operational flying hours before being taken off operations for a lengthy period. Day bomber crews by 1942 were being officially rested after 20 operations, while starting in May 1943 night bomber crews were expected to complete 30 operational trips for a first tour, plus 20 for an obligatory second tour after an extended rest from operations.[1] After a brief period in late April 1944 when journeys to targets in western France were only to count for one-third of those to Germany, the first tour was extended to 35 in May, then rolled back to 30 in August after the heavy bombers were released from ground support duties, and then extended once again to 36 in February 1945 and finally to 50 in April as loss rates continued to decline.[2] Operating from North Africa and Italy rather than England, bomber crews might face a total of 40 operational sorties;[3] while in the Far East in late 1944 aircrew tours were reduced from 300 to 200 flying hours.[4]

In the USAAF, the individual force commanders determined how long men would fly. During the desperate efforts to stem the Japanese tide in 1942–1943, this could in practice mean more than 60 missions in what became the Fifth Air Force.[5] In the Eighth Air Force based in England, the policy from March 1943 was that fighter pilots were supposed to complete at least 200 hours flying combat missions while bomber crews needed to have flown at least 25 combat missions.[6] This was raised to 30 missions for bomber crews and 300 hours for fighter pilots at the end of March 1944 as loss rates declined, and later in the year tours were extended still further.[7] In the Ninth Air Force, fighter pilots flew between 200 and 300 combat hours, and for bomber crews 300 combat hours or 50 missions were needed; while in the Fifteenth Air Force, operating from North Africa and Italy, a minimum of 300 hours for fighter pilots and 50 missions for bomber crews was required (though heavy bomber crews received double credit for tough targets such as Munich, Ploesti, and Vienna).[8] In the war with Japan, by 1943–1944 a tour for Fifth Air Force bomber crews in the Southwest Pacific was about 40 missions,[9] and in the Tenth and Fourteenth air forces in China–Burma–India about 400 hours by 1944.[10] In 1945 the tour for Twentieth Air Force crews was extended from 30 to 35 missions,[11] the same total crews in the Thirteenth Air Force were expected to fly.[12]

In the USN, carrier air groups were eventually expected to serve up to a maximum of nine months before being rotated home. In early March 1944, this was reduced to six months.[13] The RN, meanwhile, continued to move Fleet Air Arm aircrew around from one operational squadron to another for up to several years at a time, such that a pilot might, with only brief periods of leave, serve more or less continuously aboard carriers for eighteen or more months before it was thought necessary to provide a rest from frontline duty.[14]

Needless to say, fliers were often not happy if they found themselves in operational units when tours were extended. "Twenty-five [missions] had seemed like a million to us," remembered Byron Cook, a B-17 waist gunner with the 388th Bomb Group. "Thirty was almost too staggering to contemplate."[15] Eric Cropper, a Lancaster navigator with 103 Squadron, remembered how crews were "incredulous" when it was announced in April 1944 that it would take three trips over France to count for a single operation: "I can recall the slightly sick feeling with which this was received."[16] When B-29 crew tours were extended in mid-1945 to 35 missions, there was, according to one pilot, "a near riot on Saipan."[17]

AIRCRAFT TYPES

The following list is designed to give readers unfamiliar with the aircraft of World War II a sense of the crew size and function of various planes mentioned in the text:

A-36 APACHE—ground-attack fighter and dive-bomber, single engine, one pilot.

B-17 FLYING FORTRESS—heavy bomber, four engines, crew of ten: pilot, copilot, bombardier or togglier, navigator, flight engineer/top-turret gunner, radio operator, two waist gunners (eventually reduced to one), ball-turret gunner, tail gunner.

B-24 LIBERATOR—heavy bomber, four engines, crew of ten: pilot, copilot, bombardier or togglier, navigator, flight engineer/top-turret gunner, radio operator, two waist gunners (eventually reduced to one), ball-turret gunner, tail gunner.

B-25 MITCHELL—medium bomber, two engines, crew of six: pilot, copilot, bombardier/navigator, flight engineer/top-turret gunner, radio operator/waist gunner, tail gunner.

B-26 MARAUDER—medium bomber, two engines, crew of six: pilot, copilot, radio operator, navigator, bomb aimer/nose gunner, dorsal gunner.

B-29 SUPERFORTRESS—very heavy bomber, four engines, crew of eleven: pilot, copilot, bombardier, flight engineer, navigator, radio operator, radar observer, right gunner, left gunner, central fire control/top turret, tail gunner.

BEAUFORT—torpedo-bomber, two engines, crew of four: pilot, navigator/bomb aimer, wireless operator, rear gunner.

BLENHEIM—light bomber, two engines, crew of three: pilot, navigator/bombardier, radio operator/gunner.

BOSTON—British designation for A-20 HAVOC twin-engine light bomber, crew of three: pilot, navigator/bombardier, radio operator/gunner.

DEFIANT—fighter, single engine, crew of two: pilot, gunner.

F4F WILDCAT—fighter, single engine, single pilot.

F4U CORSAIR—fighter, single engine, single pilot.

F6F HELLCAT—fighter, single engine, single pilot.

FM2—late-model F4F.

HALIFAX—heavy bomber, four engines, crew of seven: pilot, flight engineer, bomb aimer, navigator, radio operator, mid-upper gunner, tail gunner.

HAMPDEN—medium bomber, two engines, crew of four: pilot, navigator/bomb aimer, radio operator/dorsal gunner, ventral gunner.

HURRICANE—fighter, single engine, single pilot.

LANCASTER—heavy bomber, four engines, crew of seven: pilot, flight engineer, bomb aimer, navigator, radio operator, mid-upper gunner, tail gunner.

MANCHESTER—heavy bomber, two engines, crew of seven: pilot, flight engineer, bomb aimer, navigator, radio operator, mid-upper gunner, tail gunner.

MOSQUITO—light bomber/night fighter, two engines, crew of two: pilot, navigator.

P-38 LIGHTNING—fighter, two engines, single pilot.

P-39 AIRACOBRA—fighter, single engine, single pilot.

P-40 WARHAWK—fighter/fighter-bomber, single engine, single pilot.

P-47 THUNDERBOLT—fighter/fighter-bomber, single engine, single pilot.

P-51 MUSTANG—fighter, single engine, single pilot.

PB4Y-2 PRIVATEER—patrol bomber, four engines, crew of eleven: two pilots, navigator, bombardier, two radio operators, five gunners.

SB2C HELLDIVER—dive-bomber, single engine, crew of two: pilot, radio operator/gunner.

SBD DAUNTLESS—dive-bomber, single engine, crew of two: pilot, gunner.

SPITFIRE—fighter, single engine, single pilot.

STIRLING—heavy bomber, four engines, crew of seven: two pilots, flight engineer, navigator/bomb aimer, radio operator/front gunner, mid-upper gunner, rear gunner.

SWORDFISH—torpedo-bomber, single engine, crew of three: pilot, observer, radio operator/gunner.

TBD DEVASTATOR—torpedo-bomber, single engine, crew of three: pilot, navigator, radioman/gunner.

TBF AVENGER—torpedo-bomber, single engine, crew of three: pilot, turret gunner, radioman/bombardier/ventral gunner.

TYPHOON—fighter-bomber, single engine, single pilot.

WELLINGTON—medium bomber, two engines, crew of six: pilot, copilot, navigator/bomb aimer, radio operator, nose gunner, rear gunner.

WHITLEY—medium bomber, two engines, crew of five: pilot, second pilot/navigator, radio operator, bomb aimer/nose gunner, rear gunner.

APPENDIX III

AIR ORGANIZATION

The relative significance of Allied air units during World War II for aircrew could vary according to nation and service. For readers unfamiliar with the relevant structural models adopted, a brief outline in relation to the USAAF, USN, and USMC, the RAF plus the air forces of the dominions, and the Fleet Air Arm of the RN may be helpful.

The fighting portion of the USAAF was organized into a growing list of numbered air forces, most of them based abroad like the Eighth Air Force in England, the Fifteenth Air Force in Italy, the Thirteenth Air Force in the Southwest Pacific, and the Twentieth Air Force in the Marianas. Each air force was divided into numerically identified functional commands, divisions, and wings, with aircraft organized into individual squadrons. However, the primary USAAF air unit for both combat and administrative purposes was the three-squadron group. A bombardment group, identified by number and bombload—"(VH)" for very heavy, "(H)" for heavy, "(M)" for medium, and "(L)" for light—could range in size from well under fifty to upward of a hundred multiengine planes, with a larger number of aircrews to take account of illness, injury, losses, and the need for rest. An army air force fighter or fighter-bomber group—"(F)"—might incorporate seventy-five or more single- or twin-engine planes, the number of assigned pilots again exceeding the number of designated ships. It was the individual group that tended to form the locus of aircrew identity, except in the Pacific, where the component squadrons were often spread out rather than concentrated on a single airfield.

Aviators of the USN and USMC, meanwhile, while organized into air groups and wings flying a range of different aircraft types, tended to owe their allegiance both afloat and ashore to their individual squadrons. These were composed of anywhere from a half-dozen to three dozen single- or multiengine aircraft of the same type. Each squadron was numbered, with preceding code letters to identify function: "V" meant heavier-than-air, to distinguish aircraft from airships; "F" meant fighter, "B" meant bomber, "BF" meant fighter-bomber, "T" meant torpedo, "P" meant patrol, and "C" meant composite. "M" was added to the mix in the case of the Marines.

The fighting units of the RAF, in combination with those of the dominion air forces, were mostly organized according to role—Fighter Command, Bomber Command, and Coastal Command—while operating from Great Britain, with Army Co-operation Command eventually becoming a Tactical Air Force in its own right. Overseas there were a succession of mixed-use regional air forces mostly divided, like the home commands, into numbered groups and wings. The primary RAF fighting unit, however, and the one with which aircrew readily identified, was the numbered squadron. Depending on the period of the war and aircraft type, RAF squadrons were normally made up of between a dozen and about two dozen aircraft plus reserves, with extra pilots and crews attached. Though air wings and subsequently carrier air groups were eventually organized in the wartime Royal Navy, the standard FAA naval air unit operating off the deck or from land bases during World War II was also the squadron. In the RN this typically meant roughly twelve British or American planes, usually of the same type. As in other forces, the aircrew complement in a numbered FAA naval air squadron in theory if not always in practice would be in excess of aircraft strength.

NOTES

LIST OF ACRONYMS

AFHRA—Air Force Historical Research Agency, Maxwell AFB, AL

AWM—Australian War Memorial, Canberra

CAPS—Combat Aircrews' Preservation Society

CSWS—Center for the Study of War and Society, University of Tennessee, Knoxville

EAA—Experimental Aircraft Association

ECU—East Carolina University

FAA—Fleet Air Arm

IWM—Imperial War Museum, Lambeth

LC—Peter Liddle Collection, University of Leeds

NMMEAF—National Museum of the Mighty Eighth Air Force, Pooler, GA

RAAF—Royal Australian Air Force

RAF—Royal Air Force

RAFBCA–RAF Bomber Command Association

RAFM—Royal Air Force Museum, Hendon

RCAF—Royal Canadian Air Force

RN—Royal Navy

RNZAF—Royal New Zealand Air Force

ROHA—Rutgers Oral History Archives

SAAF—South African Air Force

TMP—The Memory Project, Toronto

TNA—The National Archives, Kew

UNT—University of North Texas

USAAF—United States Army Air Forces

USMC—United States Marine Corps

USN—United States Navy

UVic—University of Victoria, BC

VHP—Veterans History Project, Library of Congress

WAAF—Women's Auxiliary Air Force

INTRODUCTION

1. See, e.g., *Canberra Times*, May 31, 1927, 4; Kenneth Brown Collings, "Pilots Are Superstitious," *Flying and Popular Aviation*, October 1941, 24–28, 86; Mike

Klesius, "One More for the Checklist," *Air & Space Magazine*, September 2010, airspacemag.com, accessed December 10, 2014; Charles Platt, *Popular Superstitions* (London: Herbert Jenkins, 1925), 205; Bill Wallrich, "Superstition and the Air Force," *Western Folklore* 19 (1960): 11–16; Barrett Tillman, "Omens, Augurs, Jinxes and Other Aviation Superstitions," *Air Progress*, April 1971, 27–29; Helen Paul White, "Airmen Slaves to Pet Superstitions," *The Sun* [Baltimore], November 28, 1926, 4; Mark Wilkins, "Luck and Death: WWI Pilots and Their Superstitions," *Air & Space Magazine*, March 20, 2014, airspacemag.com, accessed December 7, 2014.

2. There is no mention of aircrew superstition, for instance, in the excellent book by Mark K. Wells, *Courage and Air Warfare: The Allied Aircrew Experience in the Second World War* (London: Frank Cass, 1995). Scholars who do mention aircrew superstition—albeit in the latter three cases necessarily in passing—include: Vanessa Ann Chambers, "Fighting Chance: Popular Belief and British Society, 1900–1951," PhD diss., University of London, 2007, 75–87; Mark Connelly, *Reaching for the Stars: A New History of Bomber Command* (London: I. B. Tauris, 2001), 91; Martin Francis, *The Flyer: British Culture and the Royal Air Force, 1939–1945* (Oxford: Oxford University Press, 2008), 109, 124–125; and Paul Fussell, *Wartime: Understanding and Behavior in the Second World War* (New York: Oxford University Press, 1989), 49. For popular historians and aircrew superstition, see e.g. Patrick Bishop, *Bomber Boys: Fighting Back 1940–1945* (London: HarperPress, 2007), 162–163; Martin W. Bowman, *Echoes of England: The 8th Air Force in World War II* (Stroud, UK: Tempus, 2006), 153–156; Spencer Dunmore and William Carter, *Reap the Whirlwind: The Untold Story of 6 Group, Canada's Bomber Force of World War II* (Toronto: McClelland & Stewart, 1991), 190–192; John C. McManus, *Deadly Sky: The American Combat Airman in World War II* (Novato, CA: Presidio, 2000), 312–315; Andrew R. B. Simpson, *'Ops': Victory at All Costs: On Operations over Hitler's Reich with the Crews of Bomber Command, Their War—Their Words* (Pulborough, UK: Tattered Flag, 2012), 105–108; James Taylor and Martin Davidson, *Bomber Crew* (London: Hodder & Stoughton, 2004), 137–139.

3. See e.g. Conrad C. Crane, *American Airpower Strategy in World War II: Bombs, Cities, Civilians, and Oil* (Lawrence: University Press of Kansas, 2016); Robert S. Ehlers Jr., *The Mediterranean Air War: Airpower and Allied Victory in World War II* (Lawrence: University Press of Kansas, 2015); Richard Overy, *The Bombing War: Europe 1939–1945* (London: Allen Lane, 2013); Peter Preston-Hough, *Commanding Far Eastern Skies: A Critical Analysis of the Royal Air Force Air Superiority Campaign in India, Burma, and Malaya, 1941–1945* (Solihull, UK: Helion, 2015); Christopher M. Rein, *The North African Air Campaign: U.S. Army Air Forces from*

El Alamein to Salerno (Lawrence: University Press of Kansas, 2012); Herman S. Wolk, *Cataclysm: General Hap Arnold and the Defeat of Japan* (Denton: University of North Texas Press, 2010).

4. See Roy R. Grinker and John P. Spiegel, *Men under Stress* (Philadelphia: Blakiston, 1945), 131; D. Stafford-Clark, "Morale and Flying Experience: Results of a Wartime Study," *Journal of Mental Science* 95 (1949): 16.

5. Francis, *The Flyer*, 124; see also Connelly, *Reaching for the Stars*, 91.

6. See e.g. Tim Cook, "Grave Beliefs: Stories of the Supernatural and the Uncanny among Canada's Great War Trench Soldiers," *Journal of Military History* 77 (2013): 521–542; Paul Fussell, *The Great War and Modern Memory* (New York: Oxford University Press, 1975), 124–125; Christopher M. Hamner, *Enduring Battle: American Soldiers in Three Wars, 1776–1945* (Lawrence: University Press of Kansas, 2011), 87–88; Lee Kennett, *G.I.: The American Soldier in World War II* (New York: Scribner's, 1987), 144; Peter S. Kindsvatter, *American Soldiers: Ground Combat in the World Wars, Korea, and Vietnam* (Lawrence: University Press of Kansas, 2003), 116–117; Michael Snape, *God and the British Soldier: Religion and the British Army in the First and Second World Wars* (London: Routledge, 2005), 33–38; Samuel A. Stouffer et al., *The American Soldier: Combat and Its Aftermath* (Princeton: Princeton University Press, 1949), 184–185, 188; Alexander Watson, *Enduring the Great War: Combat, Morale, and Collapse in the German and British Armies, 1914–1918* (Cambridge: Cambridge University Press, 2008), 92–100.

7. For superstitions among Soviet fliers, see e.g. Artem Drabkin, *Barbarossa and the Retreat from Moscow: Recollections of Fighter Pilots on the Eastern Front* (Barnsley, UK: Pen & Sword Military, 2007), 19, 47, 92, 115; Andrew L. Jenks, *The Cosmonaut Who Couldn't Stop Smiling: The Life and Legend of Yuri Gagarin* (DeKalb: Northern Illinois University Press, 2012), 132–133; Anna Timofeeva-Ogorova, *Over Fields of Fire: Flying the Sturmovik in Action on the Eastern Front, 1942–45*, ed. Sergey Anisomov, trans. Vladimir Kroupnik (Solihull, UK: Helion, 2010), 28. For superstitions within the German and Japanese air forces, see e.g. Gunther Bloemertz, *Heaven Next Stop* (London: Kimber, 1953), 31–33; Colin D. Heaton and Anne-Marie Lewis, *The Star of Africa: The Story of Hans Marseille, the Rogue Luftwaffe Ace Who Dominated the WWII Skies* (Minneapolis: Zenith, 2012), 35; ibid., *The German Aces Speak: World War II Through the Eyes of Four of the Luftwaffe's Most Important Commanders* (Minneapolis: Zenith, 2011), 40–41, 152–153; Dan King, *The Last Zero Fighter: Firsthand Accounts from WWII Japanese Naval Pilots* (Irvine, CA: Pacific, 2012), 58, 66, 135, 272; Emiko Ohnuki-Tierney, *Kamikaze Diaries* (Chicago: University of Chicago Press, 2010), 166; Saburo Sakia with Martin Caiden and Fred Saito, *Samurai!* (New York: Ballantine, 1958),

57; Raymond F. Toliver and Trevor J. Constable, *The Blond Knight of Germany: A Biography of Erich Hartmann* (Blue Ridge Summit, PA: Aero, 1970), 65 footnote; Kuwahara Yasuo and Gordon T. Allred, *Kamikaze*, 7th ed. (Clearfield, UT: American Legacy Media, 2007), 206.

8. For superstition in Afghanistan, see e.g. Alex Duncan, *Sweating the Metal* (London: Hodder & Stoughton, 2011), 58; Ade Orchard with James Barrington, *Joint Force Harrier* (London: Michael Joseph, 2008), 187. For the Gulf War, see e.g. Sherman Baldwin, *Ironclaw: A Navy Carrier Pilot's Gulf War Experience* (New York: William Morrow, 1996), 198; Pablo Mason, *Pablo's War* (London: Bloomsbury, 1992), 3–4, 84; William L. Smallwood, *Warthog: Flying the A-10 in the Gulf War* (Washington, DC: Brassey's, 1993) 82; see also Michael Napier, *Tornado over the Tigris: Recollections of a Fast Jet Pilot* (Barnsley, UK: Pen & Sword Aviation, 2015), 235. For the Falklands, see e.g. David H. S. Morgan, *Hostile Skies: The Falklands Conflict Through the Eyes of a Sea Harrier Pilot* (London: Weidenfeld & Nicolson, 2006), 29, 64, 71, 88, 290; N. Ward interview, 12820/1, IWM. For Vietnam, see e.g. Randy Cunningham with Jeff Ethell, *Fox Two: The Story of America's First Ace in Vietnam* (Meza, AZ: Champlin Fighter Museum, 1984), 38; Ross C. Detwiler, *The Great Muckrock and Rosie* (Bloomington, IN: Abbott, 2013), 155; Jack Foisie, "U.S. Pilots Fly Modern Jets but Cling to Superstitions," *Western Folklore* 30 (1971), 140; Ed Rasimus, *When Thunder Rolled: An F-105 Pilot over North Vietnam* (Washington, DC: Smithsonian, 2003), 43, 97, 185–186, 191–194, 205. For Korea, see e.g. Bud Farrell, *"No Sweat": B-29 Aircraft # 44–70134, 93rd Bomb Squadron, 19th Bomb Group, Korean War 1952–53* (Bloomington, IN: 1st Books, 2004), 279; Arthur L. Haarmeyer, *Into the Land of Darkness: A Bombardier-Navigator's Story* (Sacramento, CA: Haarmeyer, 2013), 82–83, 86, 89, 92, 115–118; Charles W. Hinton, *Korea: A Short Time in a Small War; A Combat Story in the B-26 in the Korean War* (Satellite Beach, FL: Hinton, 2014), 21, 60, 84. For World War I, see e.g. Paul Bewsher, *"Green Balls": The Adventures of a Night-Bomber* (Edinburgh: Blackwood, 1919), 80; A. R. Kingsford, *Night of the Raiders* (London: Greenhill, 1988), 115; W. J. Harvey [Night-Hawk], *Rover of the Night Sky* (London: Greenhill, 1984), 54; David S. Ingalls, *Hero of the Angry Sky: The World War I Diaries and Letters of David S. Ingalls, America's First Naval Ace*, ed. Geoffrey L. Rossano (Athens: Ohio University Press, 2013), 221, 269; Arthur Gould Lee, *Open Cockpit* (London: Grub Street, 2012), 136; Joshua Levine, *On a Wing and a Prayer* (London: Collins, 2008), 314; Edwin C. Parsons, *I Flew with the Lafayette Escadrille* (New York: Arno, 1972), 102; Raymond Laurence Rimell, *The Airship VC: The Life of Captain William Leefe Robinson* (Bourne End, UK: Aston, 1989), 31; E. M. Roberts, *A Flying Fighter: An American above*

the Lines in France (London: Greenhill, 1988), 260; Elliott White Springs, *War Birds: Diary of an Unknown Airman* (New York: Grosset & Dunlap, 1926), 276; Humphrey Wynn, *Darkness Shall Cover Me: Night Bombing over the Western Front 1918* (Shrewsbury, UK: Airlife, 1989), 83–84; V. M. Yeates, *Winged Victory* (London: Cape, 1961), 169.

9. Office of Statistical Control, *Army Air Forces Statistical Digest: World War II* (Washington, DC: Office of Statistical Control, 1945), 18; Harold E. Hartney, *Wings over France*, ed. Stanley M. Ulanoff (Folkestone, UK: Bailey and Swifen, 1974), 233.

10. Office of the Chief of Naval Operations, *United States Naval Aviation, 1910–1970* (Washington, DC: Department of the Navy, 1970), 365.

11. Michael Clodfelter, *Warfare and Armed Conflicts: A Statistical Reference, Vol. II, 1900–1999* (Jefferson, NC: McFarland, 1992), 887–888; Walter J. Boyne Jr., *Beyond the Wild Blue*, 2nd ed. (New York: Thomas Dunne, 2007), 161.

12. Michael Armitage, *The Royal Air Force* (London: Brockhampton, 1995), 277; Clodfelter, *Warfare and Armed Conflicts*, 779, 888.

13. See e.g. *British Naval Aviation: The First 100 Years*, ed. Tim Benbow (London: Ashgate, 2011).

14. Connelly, *Reaching for the Stars*, 91.

15. See John Comer, *Combat Crew* (New York: William Morrow, 1988), 101; Bill Hancock in Pat Cunningham, *Fighter! Fighter! Corkscrew Port!* (Barnsley, UK: Pen & Sword Aviation, 2012), 67; Roald Dahl, *The Gremlins* (New York: Random House, 1943); Charles Demoulin, *Firebirds! Flying the Typhoon in Action* (Shrewsbury, UK: Airlife, 1987), 125; Ted Fahrenwald, *Wot a Way to Run a War! The World War II Exploits and Escapades of a Pilot in the 352nd Fighter Group* (Havertown, PA: Casemate, 2014), 9–10; Reginald J. Lane interview, UVic, uvic.ca, accessed August 13, 2014; John R. Lester, *Frontline Airline* (Manhattan, KS: Sunflower University Press, 1994), 103–106; Marion E. Carl, *Pushing the Envelope* (Annapolis, MD: Naval Institute Press, 1994), 74, 76; Russell McKay, *One of the Many* (Burnstown, ON: GSPH, 1989), 69; William George Pearce, *The Wing Is Clipped* (Margate, QLD: Slipstream, 2000), 53; C. F. Rawnsley with Robert Wright, *Night Fighter* (London: Collins, 1957), 103, 190; Harold C. Rosser and Robert Bantas in *The 390th Bomb Group in Action: An Anthology*, vol. 1, ed. Wilbert H. Richarz, Richard H. Perry, and William J. Robinson (Tucson, AZ: 390th Memorial Museum Foundation, 1983), 111–114; C. Wade Rodgers, *There's No Future in It* (Orford, TAS: Rodgers, 1988), 76; Jack Rodgers, *Navigator's Log* (Braunton, UK: Merlin, 1985), 80; Harold C. Rosser, *No Hurrahs for Me* (Sevierville, TN: Covenant House, 1994), 94; P. W. Rowling, *The Rest of My Life With 50 Squadron,*

comp. Noella Lang (Northbridge, WA: Access, 1997), 101; Robert H. Tays Jr., *Country Boy Combat Bomber Pilot*, 53, 2010.0132.0001, NMMEAF; Colin Watt in Alan White, *The King's Thunderbolts* (Lincoln, UK: Tucann, 2007), 94; Arthur White, *Bread and Butter Bomber Boys* (Upton on Severn, UK: Square One, 1995), 89, 145–146; Ernest L. H. Williams ['H. W.'], *Sh! Gremlins!* (London: Crowther, 1942); see also Tim Hamilton, *The Life and Times of Pilot Officer Prune: Being the Official Story of Tee Emm* (London: HMSO, 1991), 69.

16. "Superstition," *Oxford English Dictionary* 17 (1989): 242. On the origin of the term, see Chambers, "Fighting Chance," 64–65; see also Stuart Vyse, *Believing in Magic*, updated ed. (New York: Oxford University Press, 2014), 25.

17. See Richard L. Gorsuch, "On the Limits of Scientific Investigation: Miracles and Intercessory Prayer," in *Miracles: God, Science, and Psychology in the Paranormal*, vol. 1, *Religious and Spiritual Events*, ed. J. Harold Ellens (Westport, CT: Praeger, 2008), 284; but see also Ken S. Masters, Glen I. Spielmans, and Jason T. Goodson, "Are There Demonstrable Effects of Distant Intercessory Prayer? A Meta-Analytic Review," *Annals of Behavioral Medicine* 32 (2006): 21–26; Leanne Roberts, Irshad Ahmed, and Andrew Davidson, "Intercessory Prayer for the Alleviation of Ill Health," Cochrane Library, accessed November 5, 2015, onlinelibrary.wiley.com. On problems with studies, see e.g. Richard P. Sloan and Rajasekhar Ramakrishnan, "Science, Medicine, and Intercessory Prayer," *Perspectives in Biology and Medicine* 49 (2006): 504–514.

18. For the record, the author is agnostic leaning toward atheism.

19. See Lysann Damisch, Barbara Stoberock, and Thomas Mussweiler, "Keep Your Fingers Crossed! How Superstition Improves Performance," *Psychological Science* 21 (2010): 1014–1020; Malte Faise et al., "Personal Prayer Counteracts Self-control Depletion," *Consciousness and Cognition* 29 (2014): 90–95. See also Richard Wiseman and Caroline Watt, "Measuring Superstitious Belief: Why Lucky Charms Matter," *Personality and Individual Differences* 37 (2004): 1534.

20. See e.g. Grinker and Spiegel, *Men under Stress*, 131; Stafford-Clark, "Morale and Flying Experience," 16.

21. See e.g. Sydney Brandon, "LMF in Bomber Command 1939–45: Diagnosis or Denouncement?" in *150 Years of British Psychiatry*, vol. 2, *The Aftermath*, ed. Hugh Freeman and German E. Berrios (London: Athlone, 1996), 119–129; Edgar Jones, "'LMF': The Use of Psychiatric Stigma in the Royal Air Force during the Second World War," *Journal of Military History* 70 (2006): 439–458; John McCarthy, "Aircrew and 'Lack of Moral Fibre' in the Second World War," *War & Society* 2 (1984): 87–101; Wells, *Courage and Air Warfare*, passim.

CHAPTER I: MEN AGAINST ODDS

1. Mass-Observation, *Puzzled People: A Study in Popular Attitudes to Religion, Ethics, Progress and Politics in a London Borough* (London: Gollancz, 1948), 53–59; Mass-Observation, FR 975, Report on Superstition, November 26, 1941; see also Geoffrey Gorer, *Exploring English Character* (London: Cresset, 1955), 265.

2. Gallup Survey 376-K, Question 14a, August 16–21, 1946 and Gallup Survey 390-K, Question 6b, February 19, 1947, in George H. Gallup, *The Gallup Poll: Public Opinion 1935–1971*, vol. 1, *1935–1948* (New York: Random House, 1972), 609, 634; Gallup Survey GO 122013, January 17–20, 1991, in George Gallup Jr., *The Gallup Poll: Public Opinion 1991* (Wilmington, DE: Scholarly Resources, 1993), 34; see also "The Rabbit's Foot Survives the Advance of Science," *Saturday Evening Post*, April 10, 1948, 156.

3. On wartime fliers as the best and brightest, see *The Navy's Air War: A Mission Completed*, ed. A. R. Buchanan (New York: Harper, 1946), 308–309; Tom Blackburn, *The Jolly Rogers: The Story of Tom Blackburn and Navy Fighting Squadron VF-17* (New York: Orion, 1989), 5; *The Army Air Forces in World War II*, vol. 6, *Men and Planes*, ed. Wesley Frank Craven and James Lea Cate (Washington, DC: Office of Air Force History, 1983), 430, 435–436, 540–541, 549; Alan D. English, *The Cream of the Crop: Canadian Aircrew, 1939–1945* (Montreal/Kingston: McGill-Queen's University Press, 1996), 28; Allan Stephens, *The Royal Australian Air Force* (Melbourne: Oxford University Press, 2001), 68; John Terraine, *The Right of the Line: The Role of the RAF in World War Two* (Barnsley, UK: Pen & Sword Aviation, 2010), 549, 682; see also Andrew Maitland, *Through the Bombsight* (London: Kimber, 1986), 9; Robert A. Winston, *Fighting Squadron* (New York: Holiday, 1946), 22. On superstition and educational attainment, see Naci Mocan and Luiza Ogorelova, "Compulsory Schooling Laws and the Formation of Beliefs: Education, Religion and Superstition," Working Paper 20557, National Bureau of Economic Research, October 2014, accessed November 5, 2015, nber.org/papers/w20557; Jocen Musch and Katja Ehrenberg, "Probability Misjudgment, Cognitive Ability, and Belief in the Paranormal," *British Journal of Psychology* 93 (2002): 169–177.

4. See George J. Dudycha, "The Superstitious Beliefs of College Students," *Journal of Abnormal Psychology* 27 (1933), 459, 461; Eugene E. Levitt, "Superstitions: Twenty-Five Years Ago and Today," *American Journal of Psychology* 65 (1952): 445. On Friday the 13th as the most popular superstition—though the 1933 study was misread—see Nathaniel Lachenmeyer, *13: The Story of the World's Most Popular Superstition* (New York: Thunder's Mouth, 2004), 92.

NOTES TO PAGE 5 : 119

5. D. Stafford-Clark, "Morale and Flying Experience: Results of a Wartime Study," *Journal of Mental Science* 95 (1949): 16.

6. Mark K. Wells, *Courage and Air Warfare: The Allied Aircrew Experience in the Second World War* (London: Frank Cass, 1997), 133 n. 26.

7. Anthony J. Mireless, *Fatal Army Air Forces Aviation Accidents in the United States, 1941–1945*, vol. 1 (Jefferson, NC: McFarland, 2006), xi.

8. Doy Duncan, *Abandoned at Leyte: The World War II Memories of Dr. Doy Duncan, Wildcat Pilot* (Fayetteville, AR: Phoenix, 2002), 13; John F. Smith, *Hellcats over the Philippine Deep* (Manhattan, KS: Sunflower University Press, 1995), 18; see also e.g. Laurie Jones, *A Pilot's Story: Of Flying in War and Peace* (Wahroonga, NSW: L. R., 1996), 26; Robert R. Rea, *Wings of Gold: An Account of Naval Aviation in World War II*, ed. Wesley Phillips Newton and Robert R. Rea (Tuscaloosa: University of Alabama Press, 1987), 33.

9. Clayton E. Fisher, *Hooked: Tales and Adventures of a Tailhook Warrior* (Denver, CO: Outskirts, 2009), 145.

10. Rebecca Cameron, *Training to Fly: Military Flight Training, 1907–1945* (Washington, DC: Air Force History and Museums, 1999), 396; see e.g. John Boeman, *Morotai: A Memoir of War* (Garden City, NY: Doubleday, 1981), 36; William H. Bowen, *The Boy from Altheimer: From the Depression to the Boardroom* (Fayetteville: University of Arkansas Press, 2006), 29–30; Bryan Cox, *Too Young to Die: The Story of a New Zealand Fighter Pilot in the Pacific War* (Ames: Iowa State University Press, 1989), 59; Thomas G. Dye, *Private to WWII Pilot* (Victoria, BC: Trafford, 2004), 14–15; James M. Davis, *In Hostile Skies: An American B-24 Pilot in World War II*, ed. David L. Snead (Denton: University of North Texas Press, 2006), 29–30; Gerald M. French, *Liberal Lady I-IV: Reflections of a Military Pilot* (Seattle: BookSurge, 2007), 9–10; Norman Hanson, *Carrier Pilot: An Unforgettable True Story of Wartime Flying* (Cambridge, UK: Patrick Stephens, 1979), 107; Richard B. Lewis, *Angel on My Wing: An Odyssey of Flying Combat with the 493rd Bomb Group, 8th Air Force in 1944* (Jacksonville Beach, FL: High Pitched Hum, 2009), 47; James Sanders, *Of Wind and Water: A Kiwi Pilot in Coastal Command* (Shrewsbury, UK: Airlife, 1989), 25; James W. Vernon, *The Hostile Sky: A Hellcat Flier in World War II* (Annapolis, MD: Naval Institute Press, 2003), 71, 103; Geoffrey Wellum, *First Light* (London: Viking, 2002), 71–73; David Zellmer, *The Spectator: A World War II Bomber Pilot's Journal of the Artist as Warrior* (Westport, CT: Praeger, 1999), 4–5.

11. Eric S. Rickman in Malcolm Smith, *Voices in Flight: The Fleet Air Arm; Recollections from Formation to Cold War* (Barnsley, UK: Pen & Sword Aviation, 2013), 115.

12. Mae Mills Link and Hubert A. Coleman, *Medical Support of the Army Air Forces in World War II* (Washington, DC: Office of the Surgeon General, USAF, 1955), 691–692; see e.g. Warren P. Conrad diary, June 25, 1944, 2016.0201.0001, NMMEAF; James R. Hedtke, *The Freckleton, England, Air Disaster: The B-24 Crash That Killed 38 Preschoolers and 23 Adults, August 23, 1944* (Jefferson, NC: McFarland, 2014).

13. S. C. Rexford-Welch, *The Royal Air Force Medical Services*, vol. 2, *Commands* (London: HMSO, 1955), 75.

14. Aviation Personnel Fatalities in World War II, Naval History and Heritage Command, accessed November 27, 2015, history.navy.mil; Robert Sherrod, *History of Marine Corps Aviation in World War II* (San Rafael, CA: Presidio, 1980), 430; Royal, Indian, & Dominion Navy Casualties—Index, Naval-History.Net, accessed December 5, 2015, naval-history.net; see also Duncan, *Abandoned at Leyte*, 13; Smith, *Hellcats over the Philippine Deep*, 18.

15. Terraine, *Right of the Line*, 682; Link and Coleman, *Medical Support*, 707.

16. Aviation Personnel Fatalities in World War II, Naval History and Heritage Command, accessed November 27, 2015, history.navy.mil; Sherrod, *History of Marine Corps Aviation*, 430.

17. See appendix I.

18. Patrick Bishop, *Bomber Boys: Fighting Back 1940–1945* (London: HarperPress, 2007), xxvi; Wells, *Courage and Air Warfare*, 45.

19. Samuel A. Stouffer et al., *The American Soldier: Combat and Its Aftermath* (Princeton: Princeton University Press, 1949), 407.

20. Arthur Harris, *Bomber Offensive* (London: Collins, 1947), 267.

21. Wells, *Courage and Air Warfare*, 26.

22. Earl Snyder, *General Leemy's Flying Circus: A Navigator's Story of the 20th Air Force in World War II* (New York: Exposition, 1955), 102.

23. James D. Billo in James A. Oleson, *In Their Own Words: True Stories and Adventures of the American Fighter Ace* (New York: iUniverse, 2007), 34.

24. 828 Squadron lost five aircraft flying from HMS *Victorious* against Norway one day in July 1941, and Torpedo Squadron 8 operating from the USS *Hornet* lost all fifteen planes in as many minutes during the Battle of Midway in early June 1942.

25. Andy Rooney, *My War* (New York: Times Books, 1995), 78; see also John Matt, *Crewdog: A Saga of a Young American* (Hamilton, VA: Waterford, 1992), 119.

26. Freeman Dyson, *Disturbing the Universe* (New York: Basic, 1979), 22–23. Efforts might also be made to shield men from the scale of the losses in training accidents. See e.g. Ted Nelson, *A Survivor's Tale: The True Life of a Wireless Opera-*

tor/Air Gunner from Enlistment to Demobilisation in 1946 (Cowbit, UK: Old Forge, 2009), 19.

27. See e.g. Tony Bird, *A Bird over Berlin* (Bognor, UK: Woodfield, 2000), 44; Ray Carré, *Maximum Effort* (Burbank, CA: National Literary Guild, 1984), 103–104; Warren G. Helm, *Big War, Little People* (El Paso, TX: Helm, 2000), 160; Frank Musgrove, *Dresden and the Heavy Bombers* (Barnsley, UK: Pen & Sword Aviation, 2005), 14; Ralph L. Peterson, *Fly a Big Tin Bird: 379th Bombardment Group* (Victoria, BC: Trafford, 2000), 71; Donald W. Smith, The Flying Experiences of the Crew of the Flying Fortress "Queen of the Ball," 13, 2009.0059.0001, NMMEAF.

28. James B. Morehead, *In My Sights: The Memoir of a P-40 Ace* (Novato, CA: Presidio, 1998), 65; see also e.g. Franklin Hook, *Pinky: The Story of North Dakota's First Aerial Combat Ace Flying on Guadalcanal* (Hot Springs, SD: Fall River, 2014), 103.

29. Robert S. Nielsen, *With the Stars Above* (Olympia, WA: JENN, 1984), 672; see e.g. Jack Hardie, *From Timaru to Stalag VIIB: A New Zealand Pilot's Wartime Story* (Wellington, NZ: Steele Roberts, 2009), 35; Russell Margerison, *Boys at War* (Bolton, UK: Ross Anderson, 1986), 29; F. F. Rainsford, *Memoirs of an Accidental Airman* (London: Harmsworth, 1986), 84; Jack Rodgers, *Navigator's Log: Of a Tour in Bomber Command* (Braunton, UK: Merlin, 1985), 51.

30. Samuel P. Fleming as told to Ed Y. Hall, *Flying with the "Hell's Angels": Memoirs of a B-17 Flying Fortress Navigator* (Spartanburg, SC: Honoribus, 1992), 49; see Donald W. Hastings, David G. Wright, Bernard C. Glueck, *Psychiatric Experiences of the Eighth Air Force: First Year of Combat* (New York: Josiah Macy Jr., 1944), 4; see also e.g. Cedric Colby Cole, Crew 33 and Flak Magnet, 458th Bomb Group, accessed October 24, 2014, 458bg.com/crew33flakmagnet.htm; Donald R. Currier, *50 Mission Crush* (Shippensburg, PA: Burd Street, 1992), 123; Neal B. Dillon, *A Dying Breed: The True Story of a World War II Air Combat Crew's Courage, Camaraderie, Faith, and Spirit* (Grants Pass, OR: Hellgate, 2000), 130; Robert B. Kilmer interview TS, 77, OH 1433, UNT; Keith B. Lamb, 35 Times: Experiences as a B-17 Bomber Pilot during World War II, 49, 2010.0196.0001, NMMEAF; Robert G. Ritter interview, AFC/2001/001/64532, VHP; Harry E. Slater, *Lingering Contrails of the Big Square A: A History of the 94th Bomb Group (H), 1942–1945* (Hadley, PA: Slater, 1980), 38; Ben Smith Jr., *Chick's Crew: A Tale of the Eighth Air Force*, 2nd ed. (Tallahassee, FL: Rose, 1983), 47; Brian Stoker, *If the Flak Doesn't Get You the Fighters Will* (Hailsham, UK: J&KH, 1995), 29.

31. George Webster, *The Savage Sky: Life and Death in a Bomber over Germany in 1944* (Mechanicsburg, PA: Stackpole, 2007), 127; see also e.g. Earl Benham

memoir, 38, 2010.0213.0001, NMMEAF; William H. Couch Sr., *My Story: A World War II Remembrance*, 2, 2009.0414.0001, NMMEAF; A. B. Feuer, *General Chennault's Secret Weapon: The B-24 in China: Based on the Diary and Notes of Captain Elmer E. Haynes* (Westport, CT: Praeger, 1992), 53; Harry X. Ford, *Mud, Wings, and Wire: A Memoir* (Lost Altos, CA: Enthusiast, 2006), 140–145.

32. Bill Grierson, *We Band of Brothers* (Hailsham, UK: J&KH, 1997), 110; see e.g. Bob Curtis, *What Did You Do in the War Grandpa? The Wartime Experiences of Bob Curtis, RAAF 1941–1945* (Frenchs Forest, NSW: Curtis, 1995), 50; Richard Dyson interview TS, RAF, 033, LC; Lloyd Henderson interview, TMP, accessed October 21, 2013, thememoryproject.com/stories.

33. William Thomas Wright, *My Three Years in the Army Air Forces in World War II: December 9, 1942 to December 8, 1945* (Raleigh, NC: Lulu, 2014), 70.

34. Marvin Bledsoe, *Thunderbolt: Memoirs of a World War II Fighter Pilot* (New York: Van Norstrand Reinhold, 1982), 71; see also e.g. Quentin Aanenson, A Fighter Pilot's Story, 11, 2012.0055.0001, NMMEAF; Richard "Dick" Wiessner, *The Real World of War*, ed. Ruth Welsh (Edina, MN: Beaver's Pond, 2015), 142.

35. E. E. Barringer, *"Alone on a Wide, Wide Sea": The Story of 835 Naval Air Squadron in the Second World War* (London: Leo Cooper, 1995), 105.

36. Dennis Scranton, *Crew One: A World War II Memoir of VPB-108* (Bennington, VT: Merriam, 2001), 134.

37. See e.g. John Bushby, *Gunner's Moon* (London: Ian Allan, 1972), 106; Gene T. Carson, *Wing Ding* (Bloomington, IN: Xlibris, 2000), 104–105; Paul Marable in *The 305th Bomb Group in Action: An Anthology*, ed. John V. Craven (Burleson, TX: 305th Bombardment Group [H] Memorial Association, 1990), 205; William C. Crawford in *Hell's Angels Newsletter*, vol. 1, *Silver Anniversary Collection, 1976–2001*, ed. Eddie Deerfield (Palm Harbor, FL: 303rd Bomb Group Association, 2002), 576; Jack Currie, *Lancaster Target* (London: Goodhall, 1981), 93; Ralph Edwards, *In the Thick of It* (Upton, UK: Images, 1994), 126; Clem R. Haulman in *Voices of My Comrades: America's Reserve Officers Remember World War II*, ed. Carol Adele Kelly (New York: Fordham University Press, 2007), 221; Maitland, *Through the Bombsight*, 55, 70; Chester Marshall, *Sky Giants over Japan: A Diary of a B-29 Combat Crew in WWII* (Winona, MN: Apollo, 1984), 179; Fred Moritz interview, TMP, accessed October 21, 2013, thememoryproject.com/stories; Ray Parker, *Down in Flames: A True Story* (Minneapolis: Mill City, 2009), 62; Van R. Parker, *Dear Folks* (Memphis, TN: Global, 1989), 221; Peterson, *Fly a Big Tin Bird*, 71; John W. Walcott, *One Fighter Pilot's War* (Bloomington, IN: iUniverse, 2015), 78.

38. Curtis E. LeMay with MacKinlay Kantor, *Mission with LeMay* (Garden City, NY: Doubleday, 1965), 278.

39. Arthur Harris introduction to Guy Gibson, *Enemy Coast Ahead—Uncensored: The Real Guy Gibson* (Manchester, UK: Crécy, 2003), 10; see also Harris, *Bomber Offensive*, 267.

40. Wellum, *First Light*, 169; see also e.g. Bledsoe, *Thunderbolt*, 187.

41. Perry Bauchman, *Spitfire Pilot* (Hantsport, NS: Lancelot, 1996), 127; see also e.g. William B. Colgan, *Allied Strafing in World War II: A Cockpit View of Air to Ground Battle* (Jefferson, NC: McFarland, 2010), 82; Desmond Scott, *Typhoon Pilot* (London: Leo Cooper, 1982), 75. On not discovering friendly fighter losses until after the fight was over in high-altitude aerial combat, see e.g. Richard E. Turner, *Big Friend, Little Friend: Memoirs of a World War II Fighter Pilot* (Meza, AZ: Champlin Fighter Museum, 1983).

42. Dillon, *Dying Breed*, 131; see also e.g. Carson, *Wing Ding*, 84; John A. Clark, *An Eighth Air Force Combat Diary: A First-Person, Contemporaneous Account of Combat Missions Flown with the 100th Bomb Group, England, 1944–1945* (Ann Arbor, MI: Proctor, 2001), 59; Eugene Fletcher, *The Lucky Bastard Club: A B-17 Pilot in Training and in Combat, 1943–45* (Seattle: University of Washington Press, 1992), 312: Byron Lane, *Byron's War: I Never Will Be Young Again* (Central Point, OR: Hellgate, 1997), 195.

43. Kenneth D. Jones memoir, 36, NMMEAF; see also Paul Katz in *Memories from the Out House Mouse: The Personal Diaries of One B-17 Crew* (Victoria, BC: Trafford, 2002), 116; Bud Klint in Brian O'Neill, *Half a Wing, Three Engines and a Prayer: B-17s over Germany*, special ed. (New York: McGraw-Hill, 1999), 63. On the effect of direct hits, see also e.g. Theodore Michael Banta, *Vignettes of a B-17 Combat Crew* (New York: Banta, 1997), 81; Kenneth Clarke, *The Trip Back: World War II as Seen from the Belly of a B-17* (Austin, TX: World Library, 2004), 194; Carl Fyler, *Staying Alive: A B-17 Pilot's Experiences Flying Unescorted Bomber Missions by 8th Air Force Elements during World War II* (Leavenworth, KS: J. H. Johnston, 1995), 56; Robert B. Kilmer interview TS, 56, OH 1433, UNT; John Muirhead, *Those Who Fall* (New York: Random House, 1986), 56; William F. Somers, *Fortress Fighters: Autobiography of a B-17 Aerial Gunner* (Tempe, AZ: Somers, 2000), 77; Charles N. Stevens, *An Innocent at Polebrook: A Memoir of an 8th Air Force Bombardier* (Bloomington, IN: 1st Books, 2004), 35.

44. On observed collisions, see e.g. Webster, *Savage Sky*, 68. On seeing "friendly" bombs hitting bombers, see e.g. Wilbur Richardson, *Aluminum Castles: WWII from a Gunner's View* (Chino Hills, CA: Cantemos, 2012), 35.

45. Vincent F. Fagan, *Liberator Pilot: The Cottontails' Battle for Oil* (Carlsbad,

CA: California Aero, 1992), 17; see e.g. Clark, *Eighth Air Force Combat Diary*, 39; Paul Marable in Craven, *305th Bomb Group in Action*, 206; Kenneth Drinnon, *Wings of Tru Love: A WWII B-17 Ball-Turret Gunner Memoir* (Bloomington, IN: Xlibris, 2011), 60; Jackson Granholm, *The Day We Bombed Switzerland: Flying with the US Eighth Army Air Force in World War II* (Shrewsbury, UK: Airlife, 2000), 50; Keith W. Mason, *My War in Italy: On the Ground and in Flight with the 15th Air Force* (Columbia: University of Missouri Press, 2016), 171.

46. Jim O'Leary in *Hell's Angels Newsletter*, vol. 1, *Silver Anniversary Collection, 1976–2001*, ed. Eddie Deerfield (Palm Harbor, FL: 303rd Bomb Group [H] Association, 2002), 34.

47. Carré, *Maximum Effort*, 72; Webster, *Savage Sky*, 104, 145; see also e.g. Andy Anzanos, *My Combat Diary: With Eighth Air Force B-17s, 390th Bomb Group*, rev. ed. (Raleigh, NC: lulu.com, 2009), 28; Donald Fleming interview TS, 35, OH 1505, UNT; James H. Keefe III, *Two Gold Coins and a Prayer: The Epic Journey of a World War II Bomber Pilot and POW* (Fall City, WA: Appell, 2010), 77; James J. Mahoney and Brian H. Mahoney, *Reluctant Witness: Memoirs from the Last Year of the European Air War, 1944–45* (Victoria, BC: Trafford, 2001), 182; Jack Novey, *The Cold Blue Sky: A B-17 Gunner in World War II*, ed. Fryar Calhoun (Charlottesville, VA: Howell, 1997), 43–44; Keith C. Schuyler, *Elusive Horizons* (Cranbury, NJ: A. S. Barnes, 1969), 138.

48. John S. Sloan, *The Route as Briefed: The History of the 92nd Bomb Group, USAAF, 1942–1945* (Cleveland: Argus, 1946), 48–49. The flight engineer was losing so much blood the decision was taken to drop him over Germany by parachute in the hope that enemy medical staff could save his life.

49. John J. Shiver, *I Always Wanted to Fly: Memoirs of a World War II Flight Engineer/Gunner* (Atmore, AL: Shiver, 2012), 139; see also e.g. Currier, *50 Mission Crush*, 120; Bert Stiles, *Serenade to the Big Bird* (Carthage, TX: Howland Associates, 1999), 44–45; Moritz Thomsen, *My Two Wars* (South Royalton, VT: Steerforth, 1996), 197.

50. See e.g. Frank J. Condreras, *The Lady from Hell: Memories of a WWII B-17 Top Turret Gunner* (Charleston, SC: BookSurge, 2005), 150; O'Neill, *Half a Wing*, 340–346.

51. Ray T. Matheny, *Rite of Passage: A Teenager's Chronicle of Combat and Captivity in Nazi Germany* (Clearfield, UT: American Legacy Media, 2009), 151.

52. James M. Davis, *In Hostile Skies: An American B-24 Pilot in World War II*, ed. David L. Snead (Denton: University of North Texas Press, 2006), 102 n. 14.

53. Novey, *Cold Blue Sky*, 134.

54. Alvin E. Kotler as told to Jack Flynn, *We Came to Fight a War: The Story of*

a B-17 Radio Gunner and His Pilot (Bennington, VT: Merriam, 2012), 87; see also e.g. Harold L. Jones interview TS, 91, OH 1336, UNT; Keith M. Turnham, *Death Denied* (San Diego: Fairdale, 2007), 113.

55. Kevin Herbert, *Maximum Effort: The B-29's against Japan* (Manhattan, KS: Sunflower University Press, 1983), 48.

56. Peter Russell, *Flying in Defiance of the Reich: A Lancaster Pilot's Rites of Passage* (Barnsley, UK: Pen & Sword Aviation, 2007), 159–160. On witnessing sudden massive explosions in Bomber Command, see e.g. John Harding, *The Dancin' Navigator* (Guelph, ON: Asterisk, 1988), 61; Doug Mourton, *Lucky Doug: Memoirs of the RAF 1937–1946 and After* (Edinburgh: Pentland, 1999), 97; David H. Pearce, *Dark Skies and Dead Reckoning* (Moe, VIC: Pearce, 2000), 84. On seeing bombers hit by night fighters or flak catching fire and plunging to earth, see e.g. Denys Braithwaite, *Target for Tonight: Flying Long-range Reconnaissance and Pathfinder Missions in World War II* (Barnsley, UK: Pen & Sword Aviation, 2005), 102; Jack Mossop, *A Pathfinder's Story: The Life and Death of Jack Mossop* (Barnsley, UK: Pen & Sword Aviation, 2007), 118, 120, 133, 143, 135; Murray Peden, *A Thousand Shall Fall: A Pilot for 214* (Stittsville, ON: Canada's Wings, 1979), 250; Les Perkins in *Flight into Yesterday*, comp. L. W. Perkins (Victoria, BC: Trafford, 2002), 157.

57. Arthur Eyeton-Jones, *Day Bomber* (Stroud, UK: Sutton, 1998), 35; see also e.g. James Campbell, *Maximum Effort* (London: Alison & Busby, 1957), 174; Mary Thomas, *Behind Enemy Lines: A Memoir of James Moffat* (Belleville, ON: Epic, 2001), 39; Harold J. Wright, *Pathfinder Squadron* (London: Kimber, 1987), 150.

58. On keeping mangled aircraft secluded, see e.g. John Beede, *They Hosed Them Out* (London: Tandem, 1971), 59; Thomas, *Behind Enemy Lines*, 42. On removing body parts, see also e.g. B. W. Martin, *Memoirs of an Engineer Officer in Bomber Command* (Hailsham, UK: J&KH, 1998), 24–25; George Moreton, *Doctor in Chains* (London: Corgi, 1980), 50–51.

59. See Doug Harvey in *The Valour and the Horror: Death by Moonlight*, dir. Brian McKenna (Gala Films, 1992).

60. Stanislaw Jósefiak in Pat Cunningham, *Bomb on the Red Markers* (Newbury, UK: Countryside, 2010), 71; Ian S. Currie, *The White Crows* (London: Minerva, 1996), 105; see also e.g. Henry Archer and Edward Pine, *To Perish Never* (London: Cassell, 1954), 140; Dave McIntosh, *Terror in the Starboard Seat* (Don Mills, ON: GSPH, 1980), 118–119.

61. Beede, *They Hosed Them Out*, 77.

62. Ross A. Pearson, *Australians at War in the Air*, vol. 1 (Kenthurst, NSW: Kangaroo, 1995), 101.

63. See e.g. Richard G. Byers, *Attack* (Sandy, UT: Aardvark, 1984), 234; H. L. Hogan, *My Battle: An R.A.A.F. Pilot's Experiences during the Air War, 1939–1945* (Palm Beach, NSW: Hogan, 1991), 51; Harlo Jones, *Bomber Pilot: A Canadian Youth's War* (St. Catherines, ON: Vanwell, 2001), 180; Linda Audrey Kantor, *Emil's Story: Memoir of a World War II Bomber Pilot* (Lexington, KY: CreateSpace, 2012), 95; Ernest Millington, *Was That Really Me?* (Palo Alto, CA: Fultus, 2006), 79; Mel Rolf, *To Hell and Back* (London: Grub Street, 1998), 161–168; Arthur C. Smith, *Halifax Crew: The Story of a Wartime Bomber Crew* (Stevenage, UK: Carlton, 1983), 22; John C. Walter, *My War: The True Experiences of a U.S. Army Air Force Pilot in World War II* (Bloomington, IN: AuthorHouse, 2004), 148.

64. On overt combat refusals, see e.g. courts martial cases, AIR 18/13–15, TNA; Don Bowling, *"Follow P-D-I": My Experiences as an AAF B-25 Pilot during World War II* (Lomita, CA: Cambria, 2009), 67–69; Harold L. Buell, *Dauntless Helldivers: A Dive-Bomber Pilot's Epic Story of the Carrier Battles* (New York: Orion, 1991), 273–274; Ted Cachart, *Ted the Lad: A Schoolboy Who Went to War* (Derby, UK: JoTe, 2007), 66; Hugh Constant Godefroy, *Lucky Thirteen* (Stittsville, ON: Canada's Wings, 1983), 242–243; Herbert, *Maximum Effort*, 86; Douglas A. Robinson, *Life Is a Great Adventure* (London: Janus, 1997), 29; Thomsen, *My Two Wars*, 179; John Wainwright, *Tail-End Charlie* (London: Macmillan, 1978), 180.

65. See e.g. Bledsoe, *Thunderbolt*, 130–131; Alan C. Deere, *Nine Lives*, 2nd ed. (Canterbury, UK: Wingham, 1991), 101–102, 107; Doug Johnston, *From Air Gunner to Prisoner of War* (Toronto: Laing McDowell, 1994), 169–175; George G. Loving, *Woodbine Red Leader: A P-51 Mustang Ace in the Mediterranean Theater* (New York: Presidio, 2003), 188; Leonard Herman with Rob Morris, *Combat Bombardier: Memoirs of Two Combat Tours in the Skies over Europe in World War Two* (Bloomington, IN: Xlibris, 2007), 35; Royan Yule, *On a Wing and a Prayer* (Derby, UK: Derby Books, 2012), 63.

66. Dwight S. Mears, "The Catch-22 Effect: The Lasting Stigma of Wartime Cowardice in the U.S. Army Air Forces," *Journal of Military History* 77 (2013): 1025–1054; Catherine J. Prince, *Shot from the Sky: American POWs in Switzerland* (Annapolis, MD: Naval Institute Press, 2003); Rolph Wegmann and Bo Widfeldt, *Making for Sweden, Part 1: The Royal Air Force* (Walton-on-Thames, UK: Air Research, 1997), 7, 287; see also e.g. N. J. Crisp, *Yesterday's Gone* (London: Macdonald, 1983), 196, 210; Charles S. Hudson and Ross N. Olney, *Combat, He Wrote . . .* (Coalinga, CA: Airborne, 1994), 93–94; Richard Riley Johnson, *Twenty Five Milk Runs (And a Few Others): To Hell's Angels and Back* (Victoria, BC: Trafford, 2004), 113. On the comparatively miniscule numbers who were unable to cope, see Wells, *Courage and Air Warfare*, 212.

67. On not calculating odds, see e.g. Dan Conway, *The Trenches in the Sky: What It Was Like Flying in RAF Bomber and Transport Commands in World War II* (Carlisle, WA: Hesperian, 1995), 144, 167. On the ability to distance oneself emotionally, see e.g. Beede, *They Hosed Them Out*, 60; Elmer Bendiner, *The Fall of Fortresses: A Personal Account of the Most Daring—and Deadly—American Air Battles of World War II* (New York: Putnam's, 1980), 192; Currier, *50 Mission Crush*, 74; Hyman A. Enzer, *The Most Exciting Year of Our Lives: Memoir of a World War II B-24 Co-Pilot* (Bloomington, IN: CreateSpace, 2012), 41; Matt, *Crewdog*, 130–131; John Watson, *Johnny Kinsman* (London: Cassell, 1955), 129.

68. Clarence E. "Bud" Anderson, with Joseph P. Hamelin, *To Fly and Fight: Memoirs of a Triple Ace* (New York: St. Martin's, 1990), 121; see also e.g. Fred F. Ohr interview, AFC/2001/001/86287, VHP; Melvyn Paisley with Vicki Paisley, *Ace! Autobiography of a Fighter Pilot, World War II* (Boston: Branden, 1992), 198; Micael Renaut, *Terror by Night: A Bomber Pilot's Story* (London: Kimber, 1982), 80; Gordon Thorburn, *Bombers First and Last* (London: Robson, 2006), 182.

69. See e.g. John Comer, *Combat Crew: A True Story of Flying and Fighting in World War II* (New York: William Morrow, 1988), 108–109; S. H. Johnson, *It's Never Dark above the Clouds* (Trigg, WA: Johnson, 1994), 168–169; Ron Smith, *Rear Gunner Pathfinders* (Manchester, UK: Crécy, 1987), 40.

70. James Kyle, *A Typhoon Tale* (Bognor, UK: New Horizon, 1984), 120; see also e.g. Frank Broome, *Dead Before Dawn: A Heavy Bomber Tail-gunner in World War II* (Barnsley, UK: Pen & Sword Aviation, 2008), 250; Comer, *Combat Crew*, 109.

71. John Wellham, *With Naval Wings: The Autobiography of a Fleet Air Arm Pilot in World War II* (Staplehurst, UK: Spellmount, 2003), 22.

72. C. Wade Rodgers, *There's No Future in It* (Orford, TAS: Rodgers, 1988), 56; see also e.g. John Mathews in Mel Rolf, *Flying into Hell: The Bomber Command Offensive as Seen Through the Experiences of Twenty Crews* (London: Grub Street, 2001), 39.

73. Robert L. Scott Jr., *God Is My Co-Pilot* (New York: Scribner's, 1943), xiii.

74. Herschel H. Green, *Herky: Memoirs of a Checkertail Ace* (Atglen, PA: Schiffer, 1996), 63; see e.g. John R. Johnson, *Un-Armed, Un-Armored and Un-Afraid: A World War II C-46 Troop Carrier Remembers* (Bennington, VT: Merriam, 2014), 144.

75. See e.g. George M. Blackburn in *Missions Remembered: The Men of the Middle Tennessee WWII Fighter Pilots Association*, ed. John K. Breast (Brentwood, TN: JM Productions, 1995), 8–9; Buell, *Dauntless Helldivers*, 225–226; Dye, *Private to WWII Pilot*, preface; Vincent Fox in *B-17s over Berlin: Personal Stories from the 95th*

Bomb Group (H), ed. Ian L. Hawkins (Washington, DC: Brassey's, 1990), 176; Charles O'Sullivan in Oleson, *In Their Own Words*, 30; Harley H. Tuck Sr., with Ann I. Clizer, *Angel on My Shoulder: I've Joined the Lucky Bastard Club* (Bloomington, IN: AuthorHouse, 2015), 39.

76. Dean M. Bloyd, *Flak at 12 O'Clock: A Teenage Kansas Farm Boy's Experiences That Led to His Becoming a B-17 Co-Pilot in the 8th Air Force during the Final Months of World War II* (San Jose, CA: Writers Club, 2001), 87; see e.g. Dan Culler, *Black Hole of Wauwilermoos* (Tucson, AZ: Ghost River Images, 1995), 155; William R. Dunn, *Fighter Pilot: The First American Ace of World War II* (Lexington: University Press of Kentucky, 1982), 53; Jim Everhart interview, CAPS, accessed August 22, 2015, combataircrew.org; Howard M. Peterson in *Gentlemen From Hell: Men of the 487th Bomb Group*, ed. C. C. Neal (Paducah, KY: Turner, 2005), 132; Calvin E. Rains Sr., *The Story of One Navy Fighter Pilot* (Bloomington, IN: AuthorHouse, 2006), 118; Shiver, *I Always Wanted to Fly*, 202; Snyder, *General Leemy's Flying Circus*, 121; William S. Whitlow interview TS, 3, CAPS, accessed August 22, 2015, combataircrew.org; Winston, *Fighting Squadron*, 17.

77. See Norman A. Levy, *Personality Disturbances in Combat Fliers* (New York: Josiah Macy Jr., 1945), 9.

78. Beirne Lay Jr., *Presumed Dead: The Survival of a Bomb Group Commander* (New York: Dodd, Mead, 1980), 1; see also Wayne Livesay in John C. McManus, *Deadly Sky: The American Combat Airman in World War II* (Novato, CA: Presidio, 2000), 315; Jay A. Stout, *Hell's Angels: The True Story of the 303rd Bomb Group in World War II* (New York: Berkley Caliber, 2015), 99.

79. David John Evans interview, 13348/3, IWM; see also Don Charlwood interview TS, 9, S00568, AWM.

80. George Bury, *Wellingtons of 115 Squadron over Europe* (Swindon, UK: Air Force Publishing Services, 1994), 24.

81. Robert Allison, *One Man's War* (Seattle: CreateSpace, 2012), 196.

82. John H. Truluck Jr., *And So It Was: Memories of a World War II Fighter Pilot* (Walterboro, SC: Press and Standard, 1989), 99; see also e.g. Bob Schimanski in *Forever Remembered: The Fliers of World War II*, ed. Irv Broughton (Spokane: Eastern Washington University Press, 2001), 376; Francis Gabreski as told to Carl Molesworth, *Gabby: A Fighter Pilot's Life* (New York: Orion, 1991), 216; Robin Olds with Christina Olds and Ed Rasimus, *Fighter Pilot: The Memoirs of Legendary Ace Robin Olds* (New York: St. Martin's, 2010), 86; Jim Cannon in Paul M. Sailer, *The Oranges Are Sweet: Major Don M. Beerbower and the 353rd Fighter Squadron, November 1942 to August 1944* (Wadena, MN: Loden, 2011), 152, 252.

83. Roscoe Brown in Stuart Leuthner and Oliver Jensen, *High Honor: Recollec-*

tions by Men and Women of World War II Aviation (Washington, DC: Smithsonian, 1989), 245; see also e.g. Clarence Anderson in Oleson, *In Their Own Words*, 85.

84. Richard Stouffer interview, EAA, accessed October 11, 2014, eaavideo.org; John L. Stewart, *The Forbidden Diary: A B-24 Navigator Remembers* (New York: McGraw-Hill, 1988), 69; see also e.g. George Snook in Elizabeth Cassen, *The Last Voices: World War II Veterans of the Air War Speak More Than Half a Century Later* (Seattle: CreateSpace, 2014), 25; Ed Domski interview, EAA, accessed October 24, 2014, eaavideo.org; Enzer, *Most Exciting Year*, 41–44; Kotler, *We Came to Fight a War*, 47; Harold Mann interview, AFC/2001/001/09871, VHP; William J. Peters interview, AFC/2001/001/64353, VHP; Jesse Richard Pitts, *Return to Base: Memoirs of a B-17 Copilot, Kimbolton, England, 1943–1944* (Charlottesville, VA: Howell, 2004), 166; Stanley Pytko interview, EAA, accessed October 24, 2014, eaavideo.org.

85. Frank Dennis in Andrew R. B. Simpson, *'Ops': Victory at All Costs: On Operations over Hitler's Reich with the Crews of Bomber Command, Their War—Their Words* (Pulborough, UK: Tattered Flag, 2012), 137; see also e.g. Hanson, *Carrier Pilot*, 107; Billy Strachen in Robert N. Murray, *Lest We Forget: The Experiences of World War II Westindian Ex-Service Personnel* (Nottingham, UK: Westindian Combined Ex-Servicemen's Association, 1996), 75; Leslie Temple in *Into the Wind*, dir. Steven Hatton (Electric Egg, 2011); Robert Willis Petty in Pat Cunningham, *Fighter! Fighter! Corkscrew Port!* (Barnsley, UK: Pen & Sword Aviation, 2012), 223; Stoker, *If The Flak Doesn't Get You*, 41.

86. Charles E. Wedell in James P. Busha, *The Fight in the Clouds: The Extraordinary Combat Experiences of P-51 Mustang Pilots during World War II* (Minneapolis: Zenith, 2014), 29; see also e.g. Donald L. Seesenguth interview, AFC/2001/001/20002, VHP.

87. Meron Naydler, *Young Man, You'll Never Die!* (Barnsley, UK: Pen & Sword Aviation, 2005), 116; see also e.g. Neville Duke in collaboration with Alan W. Mitchell, *Test Pilot* (London: Grub Street, 1992), 37.

88. Bob Nelson, 398th Bomb Group, accessed November 1, 2014, 398th.org; see also e.g. Paul Arbon in *388th Anthology*, vol. 1, *Tales of the 388th Bombardment Group*, ed. Janet Pack and Richard Singer (San Jose, CA: Writers Club, 2001), 67; Richard G. Byers, *Attack* (Sandy, UT: Aardvark, 1984), 26, 29; Edward J. Drake interview TS, 107, OH 1468, UNT; Norman C. Johnson Jr. interview TS, 5, Oral History Collection, NMMEAF; Johnson, *Twenty Five Milk Runs*, 179, 205; Robert Raimer in Leuthner and Jensen, *High Honor*, 187; Matt, *Crewdog*, 131; Bradford P. Wilson, *Everyday P.O.W.: A Rural California Boy's Story of Going to War* (Pollock Pines, CA: Storyteller, 2010), 109; Robert Whitcomb in Irv Broughton, *Hanger*

Talk: Interviews with Fliers, 1920s-1990s (Cheney: Eastern Washington University Press, 1998), 214.

89. Laurence Deane, *A Pathfinder's War and Peace* (Braunton, UK: Merlin, 1993), 47; see also e.g. Laurie Brown in W. R. Chorley, *To See the Dawn Breaking: 76 Squadron Operations* (Ottery St. Mary, UK: Chorley, 1981), 83; D. R. Field, Boy, Blitz and Bomber, 83, 1943, IWM; Kenneth Douglas Gray interview TS, 46, S00539, AWM; Robert G. Ladbury interview, UVic, accessed August 3, 2014, uvic.ca; Reginald J. Lane interview, UVic, accessed August 13, 2014, uvic.ca; E. F. Lovejoy, *Better Born Lucky Than Rich: The Diary of an Ordinary Airman* (Braunton, UK: Merlin, 1986), 74; Les Morrison, *Of Luck and War: From Squeegee Kid to Bomber Pilot in World War II* (Burnstown, ON: GSPH, 1999), 84; Arthur Madelaine in Rolfe, *Flying into Hell*, 47; Ross Pearson, *Australians at War*, 99; Bob Porter, *The Long Return* (Burnaby, BC: Porter, 1997), 26; Tom Sawyer, *Only Owls and Bloody Fools Fly at Night* (London: Kimber, 1982), 136–137; Eric Silbert, *Dinkum Mishpochah* (Perth, WA: Artlook, 1981), 174; Sydney Percival Smith and David Scott Smith, *Lifting the Silence* (Toronto: Dundurn, 2010), 103.

90. Robert Morgan with Ron Powers, *The Man Who Flew the* Memphis Belle*: Memoir of a WWII Bomber Pilot* (New York: Dutton, 2001), 133; see also e.g. Wilbur T. Mahoney Jr. interview, AFC/2001/001/05932, VHP; Joseph Rutter, *Wreaking Havoc: A Year in an A-20* (College Station: Texas A&M University Press, 2004), 110; Stuart J. Wright, *An Emotional Gauntlet: From Life in Peacetime America to the War in European Skies* (Madison: University of Wisconsin Press, 2004), 253.

91. Des Andrews in *Into the Wind*, dir. Steven Hatton (Electric Egg, 2011); see also e.g. Harry Yates, *Luck and a Lancaster: Chance and Survival in World War II* (Shrewsbury, UK: Airlife, 1999), 105.

92. Ray T. Matheny, *Rite of Passage: A Teenager's Chronicle of Combat and Captivity in Nazi Germany* (Clearfield, UT: American Legacy Media, 2009), 119; see also e.g. Fagan, *Liberator Pilot*, viii, x; Byron Lane, *Byron's War: I Never Will Be Young Again* (Central Point, OR: Hellgate, 1997), 211; Emmett G. MacKenzie, *Ten Men, a "Flying Boxcar," and a War: A Journal of B-24 Crew 323, 1944 to 1945* (New York: iUniverse, 2005), 104–105; Pitts, *Return to Base*, 166.

93. Kenneth S. Tucker and Wanda Tucker Goodwin, *Last Roll Call* (Southport, FL: Priority, 2009), 80.

94. A. Les Bartlett interview, tape 1577, RAF 006, LC; see also e.g. John Costigan interview, 13573/4, IWM; George "Johnny" Johnson, *The Last British Dambuster* (London: Ebury, 2014), 120.

95. Maitland, *Through the Bombsight*, 55; see also e.g. Denis Hornsey, Here Today, Bomb Tomorrow: The Saga of a Bomber Pilot, 333–334, 4559, IWM; Ron

Mayhill, *Bombs on Target: A Compelling Eye-Witness Account of Bomber Command Operations* (Sparkford, UK: Patrick Stephens, 1991), 56; Jack E. Thompson, *Bomber Crew* (Victoria, BC: Trafford, 2005), 60.

96. See e.g. J. H. Brook, *No Bacon and Eggs Tonight* (Southport, UK: Creativelines, 2002), 43; T. E. Done, *All Our Mates* (Candelo, NSW: Widgeram, 1995), 80; Granholm, *Day We Bombed Switzerland*, 79; Russell, *Flying in Defiance*, 86.

97. Hank Nelson, *Chased by the Sun: Courageous Australians in Bomber Command in World War II* (Sydney: ABC, 2002), 195; Wells, *Courage and Air Warfare*, 46.

98. Hal Turell, 445th Bomb Group, accessed October 31, 2014, 445bg.org /gotha.html.

99. Cedric Colby Cole, Crew 33 and Flak Magnet, 2, 458th Bombardment Group, accessed October 24, 2014, 458bg.com/crew33flakmagnet.htm; see also e.g. Myron Morgan in Dillon, *A Dying Breed*, 130.

100. James O'Connor in Pack and Singer, *388th Anthology*, Vol. 1, 260.

101. James Moffat in *The Valour and the Horror: Death by Moonlight*, dir. Brian McKenna (Gala Films, 1992).

102. Geoff D. Copeman, *Right-Hand Man: A Flight Engineer's Story* (Baldock, UK: Euro Slug, 1996), 74.

103. K. B. McGlashan, *Down to Earth: A Fighter Pilot's Experiences of Surviving Dunkirk, the Battle of Britain, Dieppe and D-Day* (London: Grub Street, 2007), 160.

104. Thompson, *Bomber Crew*, 44; see also e.g. Campbell Muirhead diary, July 20, 1944, *Diary of a Bomb Aimer: Training in America and Flying with 12 Squadron in WWII*, ed. Philip Swan (Barnsley, UK: Pen & Sword Aviation, 2009), 130; Stoker, *If The Flak Doesn't Get You*, 86; Tom Wingham, *Halifax Down! On the Run from the Gestapo, 1944* (London: Grub Street, 2009), 70; Yates, *Luck and a Lancaster*, 123.

105. Herbert Hatch, *An Ace and His Angel: Memoirs of a World War II Fighter Pilot* (Paducah, KY: Turner, 2000), 8; see also e.g. Olds, *Fighter Pilot*, 86.

106. Donald E. Smith in Valarie Evans, *We That Are Left . . . Remember: New Brunswickers in the Air Force* (St. John, NB: 250 RCAF [Saint John] Wing Air Force Association of Canada, 2002), 406; see also e.g. Michael J. Lasprogato interview TS, 14, CAPS, accessed August 22, 2015, combataircrew.org.

107. Charles N. Stevens, *An Innocent at Polebrook: A Memoir of an 8th Air Force Bombardier* (Bloomington, IN: 1st Books, 2004), 116–117; see also e.g. Novey, *Cold Blue Sky*, 55; Jack W. Seagraves interview TS, 96, OH 1434, UNT.

108. Miles Tripp, *The Eighth Passenger: A Flight of Recollection and Discovery*

(London: Macmillan, 1969), 97; see also e.g. Joseph J. Geraldi interview, AFC /2001/001/91299, VHP; Ray L. Silver, *Last of the Gladiators: A World War II Bomber Navigator's Story* (Shrewsbury, UK: Airlife, 1995), 38.

109. Richard K. Curtis, *Dumb But Lucky! Confessions of a P-51 Fighter Pilot in World War II* (New York: Ballantine, 2005), 171; see also e.g. Olds, *Fighter Pilot,* 86; Paisley, *Ace!,* 198.

110. Bill Albertson, *I Flew With Hell's Angels: Thirty-Six Combat Missions in a B-17 "Flying Fortress," 1944–1945* (Westminster, MD: Heritage, 2005), 25; see also e.g. James W. Hill in Craven, *305th Bomb Group in Action,* 153; Lloyd Krueger, *Come Fly With Me: Experiences of an Airman in World War II* (Dubuque, IA: Shepherd, 1990), 142; Earl Wilde interview TS, 75, OH 1419, UNT.

111. Joe Foss as told to Walter Simmons, *Joe Foss, Flying Marine: The Story of His Flying Circus* (Washington, DC: Zenger, 1979), 88–89.

112. Charles Moutenot in Leuthner and Jensen, *High Honor,* 55.

113. Roger Coverley in John Nichol, *The Red Line* (London: Collins, 2013), 42; see also e.g. Grierson, *We Band of Brothers,* 230.

114. Johnston, *From Air Gunner to Prisoner of War,* 88, 168; see also e.g. Jim Auton, *RAF Liberator over the Eastern Front: A Bomb Aimer's Second World War* (Barnsley, UK: Pen & Sword Aviation, 2008), 93; Les Munro in James Holland, *Dam Busters: The Race to Smash the Dams, 1943* (London: Bantam, 2012), 200; Hornsey, Here Today, Bomb Tomorrow, 163, 4559, IWM; Ray L. Silver, *Last of the Gladiators: A World War II Bomber Navigator's Story* (Shrewsbury, UK: Airlife, 1995), 38; Harold J. Wright, *Pathfinder Squadron* (London: Kimber, 1987), 223.

115. Byers, *Attack,* 207; see also e.g. Richard L. Alexander, *They Called Me Dixie* (Hemet, CA: Typographics, 1988), 90; C. E. "Bud" Anderson in Busha, *Fight in the Clouds,* 54; Campbell, *Maximum Effort,* 55; Clark, *Eighth Air Force Combat Diary,* 188; Comer, *Combat Crew,* 58–59; Harding, *Dancin' Navigator,* 50; J. N. Hockaday, One Little Man Went to War, 264, 4183, IWM; Frank Halm in McManus, *Deadly Sky,* 316; John Misterly Jr., *Over and Under* (New York: Carlton, 1987), 156; Smith, *Rear Gunner Pathfinders,* 92.

116. Mayhill, *Bombs on Target,* 120; Brown, *On the Edge,* 77; see also e.g. Howard Muncho in Broughton, *Forever Remembered,* 539; Lovejoy, *Better Born Lucky,* 76.

117. Pitts, *Return to Base,* 163; see also e.g. Parker, *Dear Folks,* 221.

118. Ted McGindle *Pimpernel Squadron: An Anecdotal History of 462 Squadron R.A.A.F., August 1944–May 1945* (Beechworth, VIC: McGindle, 2000), 23.

119. Bill Williams, *Five Miles High and Forty Below: Fifty Missions of a B-17 Bomber Crew, June–August 1944* (Bonanza, OR: CP Media, 2009), 51; see also e.g.

Eric Cropper, *Back Bearings: A Navigator's Tale, 1942–1974* (Barnsley, UK: Pen & Sword Aviation, 2010), 50; Deane, *Pathfinder's War,* 37.

120. John "Ted" Crosbie in Oleson, *In Their Own Words,* 19.

121. Peter Bone in Martin W. Bowman, *RAF Bomber Command: Reflections of War,* vol. 5, *Armageddon* (Barnsley, UK: Pen & Sword Aviation, 2013), 94; Warren Ellis in Evans, *We That Are Left,* 156; Robert B. Park in Leuthner and Jensen, *High Honor,* 138–139; Jack Singer, *Grandpa's War in Bomber Command* (Ottawa: War Amps, 2012), ix; see also e.g. Howard Gee, Premonitions, RAFBCA, accessed April 26, 2014, rafbombercommand.com; Peterson, *Fly a Big Tin Bird,* 71; Stiles, *Serenade to the Big Bird,* 60–61, 92; Wingham, *Halifax Down,* 87; Wright, *Pathfinder Squadron,* 278. On skill over luck, see e.g. Fagan, *Liberator Pilot,* x; Pitts, *Return to Base,* 90; Robert H. Sherwood, *Certified Brave* (Victoria, BC: Trafford, 2004), 7; Stoker, *If the Flak Doesn't Get You,* 67, 86; Williams, *Five Miles High,* 51.

122. Melvin W. McGuire and Robert Hadley, *Bloody Skies: A 15th AAF Combat Crew: How They Lived and Died* (Las Cruces, NM: Yucca Tree, 1993), 309.

123. McGlashan, *Down to Earth,* 160.

124. Vernon, *Hostile Sky,* 115.

125. See e.g. Albertson, *I Flew with Hell's Angels,* 145; William R. Cubbins, *The War of the Cottontails: A Bomber Pilot with the Fifteenth Air Force against Nazi Germany* (Chapel Hill, NC: Algonquin, 1989), 35; Curtis, *Dumb But Lucky!,* 172; Terry Goodwin in Peter W. Fydenchuk, *Immigrants of War: Americans Serving with the Royal Air Force and Royal Canadian Air Force during World War II* (Crediton, ON: WPF, 2006), 227; David A. McCarthy, *Fear No More: A B-17 Navigator's Journey* (Pittsburgh: Cottage Wordsmiths, 1991), 109; Eddie Wheeler, *Just to Get a Bed!* (Worcester, UK: Square One, 1990), 107.

126. Robert S. Capps, *Flying Colt: Liberator Pilot in Italy: Diary and History, World War II* (Alexandria, VA: Manor House, 1997), 141.

127. See Janet Goodall, "Superstition and Human Agency," *Implicit Religion* 13 (2010): 307–318; Eric J. Hammerman and Carey K. Morewedge, "Reliance on Luck: Which Achievement Goals Elicit Superstitious Behavior," *Personality and Social Psychology Bulletin* 41 (2015): 323–335; Giora Keinan, "The Effect of Stress and Desire for Control on Superstitious Behavior," *Personality and Social Psychology Bulletin* 28 (2002): 102–108; Giora Keinan, "Effects of Stress and Tolerance of Ambiguity on Magical Thinking," *Journal of Personality and Social Psychology* 67 (1994): 48–55; Vernon R. Padgett and Dale O. Jorgenson, "Superstition and Economic Threat: Germany, 1918–1940," *Personality and Social Psychology Bulletin* 8 (1982): 736–741.

128. Robert Grilley, *Return from Berlin: The Eye of a Navigator* (Madison: University of Wisconsin Press, 2003), 156.

129. On "lady luck," see e.g. Jim Davis, *Winged Victory: The Story of a Bomber Command Air Gunner* (London: Leach, 1997), 29, 51, 53–54, 67; Philip Gray, *Ghosts of Targets Past*, ed. E. J. Coulter (London: Grub Street, 1995), 155; Roland Hammersley, *Into Battle with 57 Squadron* (Bovington, UK: Hammersley, 1992), 116; Marshall, *Sky Giants*, 61; Muirhead, *Those Who Fall*, 122; Douglas Sample interview, TMP, accessed October 21, 2014, thememoryproject.com; Keith C. Schuyler, *Elusive Horizons* (Cranbury, NJ: Barnes, 1969), 145; Smith, *Chick's Crew*, 135.

130. Roy R. Grinker and John P. Spiegel, *Men under Stress* (Philadelphia: Blakiston, 1945), 131; see also Laurance D. Shaffer et al., "Surveys of Experiences of Returned Personnel," in *Army Air Forces Aviation Psychology Program Research Reports: Psychological Problems of Redistribution: Report No. 14*, ed. Frederic Wickert (Washington, DC: US Government Printing Office, 1947), 132.

CHAPTER 2: ASKING FOR MIRACLES

1. For "Command Pilot," see e.g. Willis W. Marshall Jr. memoir, 35, 2010.0229.0001, NMMEAF; Robert Morgan with Ron Powers, *The Man Who Flew the* Memphis Belle*: Memoir of a WWII Bomber Pilot* (New York: Dutton, 1991), 145. For "Man Upstairs," see e.g. Dean M. Bloyd, *Flak at 12 O'Clock: A Teenage Kansas Farm Boy's Experiences That Led to His Becoming a B-17 Co-Pilot in the 8th Air Force during the Final Months of World War II* (San Jose, CA: Writers Club, 2001), 87; William C. Crawford in *Hell's Angels Newsletter*, vol. 1, *Silver Anniversary Collection, 1976–2001*, ed. Eddie Deerfield (Palm Harbor, FL: 303rd Bomb Group [H] Association, 2002), 541; Jim Everhart interview TS, 19, CAPS, accessed August 22, 2015, combataircrew.org. Doubtless influenced by the bestselling memoir of CBI theater fighter pilot Robert L. Scott Jr., *God Is My Co-Pilot* (New York: Scribner's, 1943), single-seat fliers might also refer to the Almighty as "copilot." See e.g. Norman W. Achen in Michael Snape, *God and Uncle Sam: Religion and America's Armed Forces in World War II* (Woodfield, UK: Boydell, 2015), 323.

2. See Donald F. Crosby, *Battlefield Chaplains: Catholic Priests in World War II* (Lawrence: University Press of Kansas, 1994), 229. No FAA memoirs mention ready-room prayers. On public-address system prayers, see Clifford M. Drury, *The History of the Chaplain Corps, United States Navy*, vol. 2, *1939–1949* (Washington, DC, 1949), 191, 198–199; Gordon Taylor, *The Sea Chaplains: A History of the Chaplains of the Royal Navy* (Oxford: Oxford Illustrated, 1978), 401–402.

3. Snape, *God and Uncle Sam*, 993–994; see e.g. Kenneth T. Brown, *Marauder Man: World War II in the Crucial but Little-Known B-26 Marauder* (Pacifica, CA: Pacifica, 2001), 125; Donald E. Casey, *To Fight for My Country, Sir! Memoirs of a 19 Year Old B-17 Navigator Shot Down in Nazi Germany and Imprisoned in the WWII "Great Escape" Camp* (Chicago: CreateSpace, 2009), 70; Charles Hudson, Missions with Charlie, 1, 2, 8, 91st Bomb Group, accessed October 23, 2014, 91st bombgroup.com; L. W. "Mac" McFarland, Raid on Berlin, 9, 447th Bomb Group, accessed October 23, 2014, 447bg.com; John McGlauchlin interview, EAA, accessed October 11, 2014, eaavideo.org; Eddie S. Picardo, *Tales of a Tail Gunner: A Memoir of Seattle and World War II* (Seattle: Hara, 1996), 155; Moritz Thomsen, *My Two Wars* (South Royalton, VT: Steerforth, 1996), 246; Frederick D. Worthen, *Against All Odds: Shot Down over Occupied Territory in World War II* (Santa Barbara, CA: Narrative, 2001), 46; Stuart J. Wright, *An Emotional Gauntlet: From Life in Peacetime America to the War in European Skies* (Madison: University of Wisconsin Press, 2004), 255.

4. Jeffrey Ethell and Alfred Price, *Target Berlin: Mission 250; 6 March 1944* (London: Brassey's, 1981), 34; see e.g. Julius Altvater, *Off We Go . . . Down in Flame* (Victoria, BC: Trafford, 2002), 102; James Good Brown, *The Mighty Men of the 381st: Heroes All,* 2nd ed. (Salt Lake City: Publishers Press, 1986), 40; Dan Culler, *Black Hole of Wauwilermoos* (Tucson, AZ: Ghost River Images, 1995), 124; Donald R. Currier, *50 Mission Crush* (Shippensburg, PA: Burd Street, 1992), 63; Richard Fogg and Janet Fogg, *Fogg in the Cockpit: Howard Fogg, Master Railroad Artist, World War II Fighter Pilot; Wartime Diaries, October 1943 to September 1944* (Philadelphia: Casemate, 2011), 87, 142, 314; Robert Grilley, *Return from Berlin: The Eye of a Navigator* (Madison: University of Wisconsin Press, 2003), 28; David S. Kahne, The Kraut Krusher, 37, 2008.0631.0001, NMMEAF; Philip Kaplan and Jack Currie, *Round the Clock: The Experience of the Allied Bomber Crews Who Flew by Day and Night from England in the Second World War* (London: Cassell, 1993), 31; Albert F. Pishioneri, *Me, Mom, and World War II* (Bloomington, IN: AuthorHouse, 2008), 266, 419; Wilmer A. Plate, *The Storm Clouds of War: Reflections of a WWII Bomber Pilot* (Portsmouth, NH: Vilnius, 2014), 104; Van R. Porter, *Dear Folks* (Memphis, TN: Global, 1989), 225; Gene Wink, *Born to Fly* (Bloomington, IN: AuthorHouse, 2006), 72.

5. Steve Bruce, *God Is Dead: Secularization in the West* (Oxford: Blackwell, 2002), 67; Geoffrey Gorer, *English Character* (London: Cresset, 1955), 237; see also John Wolffe, *God and Greater Britain: Religion and National Life in Britain and Ireland, 1843–1945* (London: Routledge, 1994), 255.

6. Mass-Observation, *Puzzled People: A Study in Popular Attitudes to Religion, Ethics, Progress and Politics in a London Borough* (London: Gollancz, 1948), 157.

7. John Knaresborough, *R.A.F. Chaplains Look Ahead: Report of Some R.A.F. Chaplains' Conferences, 1944* (London: SPCK, 1945), 7.

8. George H. Gallup, *The Gallup Poll: Public Opinion, 1935–1971*, vol. 1, *1935–1948* (New York: Random House, 1972), 473; Edwin S. Gaustad, "America's Institutions of Faith: A Statistical Postscript," in *Religion in America*, ed. William G. McLoughlin and Robert M. Bellah (Boston: Houghton Mifflin, 1968), 122.

9. Daniel Jorgensen, *The Service of Chaplains to Army Air Units, 1917–1946* (Washington, DC: Office, Chief of Air Force Chaplains, 1961), 279, 284–287; see Timothy J. Cathcart, "On Angels' Wings: The Religious Origins of the US Air Force," in *The Martial Imagination: Cultural Aspects of American Warfare*, ed. Jimmy L. Bryan Jr. (College Station: Texas A&M University Press, 2013), 163–180.

10. Jorgensen, *Service of Chaplains*, 134. On relative Catholic enthusiasm for denominational services in the USAAF, see Jorgensen, *Service of Chaplains*, 278. On Catholic chaplains giving communion and absolution before missions, see e.g. B. Edward Schlesinger memoir, 30, 2010.0206.0001, NMMEAF; Walter H. Lohse interview TS, 4, Oral History Collection, NMMEAF. In England, Catholic membership between 1931 and 1951 seems to have increased somewhat even as other denominational membership declined. Wolffe, *God and Greater Britain*, 69–70.

11. See e.g. Don Charlwood interview TS, 40, S00568, AWM; Laurie Godfrey interview, 27799/2, IWM; Knaresborough, *R.A.F. Chaplains*, vii, 20; Notes for Commissioned and Officiating Chaplains, 1939, RAF Chaplains—History 1918–1945, accessed July 24, 2015, raf.mod.uk/chaplains/aboutus/history1918.cfm.

12. John L. Stewart, *The Forbidden Diary: A B-24 Navigator Remembers* (New York: McGraw-Hill, 1998), 39; see also e.g. Ben Smith Jr., *Chick's Crew: A Tale of the Eighth Air Force*, 2nd ed. (Tallahassee, FL: Rose, 1983), 121. For three chaplains on an 8th air force bomber station, see e.g. James H. May, My War, 17, 2010.0233.0001, NMMEAF; James Rossman, Heaven Can Wait, 1, 2008.0584 .0001, NMMEAF.

13. Arnold Willis interview, EAA, accessed October 10, 2014, eaavideo.org; see also e.g. Bernd T. Jule memoir, 50, 2010.0205.0001, NMMEAF.

14. Richard Riley Johnson, *Twenty-Five Milk Runs (And a Few Others): To Hell's Angels and Back* (Victoria, BC: Trafford, 2004), 178.

15. Les Rentmeester in Ethell and Price, *Target Berlin*, 34; see e.g. Philip Ardery, *Bomber Pilot: A Memoir of World War II* (Lexington: University Press of

Kentucky, 1978), 99; Peter Seniawsky in Travis L. Ayers, *The Bomber Boys: Heroes Who Flew the B-17s in World War II* (New York: NAL Caliber, 2009), 83; David Schelhamer in Brian D. O'Neill, *Half a Wing, Three Engines and a Prayer: B-17s over Germany*, special ed. (New York: McGraw-Hill, 1999), 128; John C. Donovan in Ken Stone, *Triumphant We Fly: A 381st Bomb Group Anthology, 1943–1945* (Paducah, KY: Turner, 1994), 73; Robert H. Tays Jr., Country Boy Combat Bomber Pilot, 32, 2010.0132.0001, NMMEAF.

16. Frank Speer, *One Down, One Dead: The Personal Adventures of Two Fourth Fighter Group Combat Pilots as They Face the Luftwaffe over Germany* (Bloomington, IN: Xlibris, 2003), 31. On post-briefing blessings in fighter groups, see also e.g. Peter Hahn, Winging It in WWII, f. 20, 2009.8268.0001, NMMEAF.

17. Harold D. Weekley and James B. Zasas, *The Last of the Combat B-17 Drivers* (Carthage, NC: Flying Fortress International, 2007), 173; see also e.g. Theodore Michael Banta, *Vignettes of a B-17 Combat Crew* (New York: Banta, 1997), 79; Gary A. Best, *Belle of the Brawl: Letters Home from a B-17 Bombardier* (Portland, OR: Inkwater, 2010), 180; James H. Keeffe III, *Two Gold Coins and a Prayer: The Epic Journey of a World War II Bomber Pilot and POW* (Fall City, WA: Appell, 2010), 64. On "spiritual insurance," see Jorgensen, *Service of Chaplains*, 193. On a spike in attendance and rituals once combat began, see e.g. Stanley H. Samuelson in Elizabeth Cassen, *The Last Voices: World War II Veterans of the Air War Speak More Than Half a Century Later* (Seattle: CreateSpace, 2014), 91; Kevin Herbert, *Maximum Effort: The B-29's against Japan* (Manhattan, KS: Sunflower University Press, 1983), 43–44; John R. Lester, *Frontline Airline: Troop Carrier Pilot in World War II* (Manhattan, KS: Sunflower University Press, 1994), 86–89; Harry E. Trask, *Harry's War: A Memoir of World War II by a Navigator in a B-29 in the Pacific Theater* (Brockton, PA: One Tiny Pizza, 2004), 110; Harley H. Tuck Sr., with Ann I. Clizer, *Angel on My Shoulder: I've Joined the Lucky Bastard Club* (Bloomington, IN: AuthorHouse, 2015), 32. As in other contexts, Catholic rituals seem to have been particularly popular. See e.g. Robert L. Sandstedt, *My B-29 Story* (St. Louis, MO: Sandstedt, 2003), 379.

18. Randall L. Rasmussen, *Hell's Belle: From a B-17 to Stalag 17B* (Santa Fe, NM: Sunstone, 2003), 27; see also e.g. Ardery, *Bomber Pilot*, 92; John J. Briol, *Dead Engine Kids: World War II Diary of John J. Briol, B-17 Ball Turret Gunner, with Comments from Notes of Other Crew Members*, ed. John F. Welch (Rapid City, SD: Silver Wings Association, 1993), 25, 40, 45, 74, 80, 146; James O'Conner in *388th Anthology*, vol. 1, *Tales of the 388th Bombardment Group (H) 1942–45*, ed. Janet Pack and Richard Singer (San Jose, CA: Writers Club, 2001), 243; William S. Whitlow interview TS, 5, CAPS, accessed August 22, 2015, combataircrew.org.

19. John Harding, *The Dancin' Navigator* (Guelph, ON: Asterisk, 1988), 49; see also e.g. Ken Trent, *Bomb Doors Open: From East End Boy to Lancaster Bomber Pilot with 617 "Dambusters" Squadron* (St. Mary, UK: Seeker, 2016), 156.

20. See, though, Sydney Smith and David Scott Smith, *Lifting the Silence* (Toronto: Dundurn, 2010), 80.

21. Gregory Brown and Basil Spiller, *Halifax Navigator: An Oral and Extended History of Flying Officer Basil Spiller's Years at War* (Howrah, TAS: CreateSpace, 2013), 117, 154; see also e.g. Bob Pierson in John Nicol and Tony Rennell, *Tail-End Charlies: The Last Battles of the Bomber War, 1944–45* (London: Viking, 2004), 137; Russell McKay, *One of the Many* (Burnstown, ON: GSPH, 1989), 68.

22. P. Hamilton Pollock, *Wings on the Cross: A Padre with the R.A.F.* (Dublin: Clanmore and Reynolds, 1954), 72, 75.

23. See e.g. Spencer Dunmore and William Carter, *Reap the Whirlwind: The Untold Story of 6 Group, Canada's Bomber Force of World War II* (Toronto: McClelland & Stewart, 1991), 190; Laurie Godfrey interview, 27799/2, IWM; McKay, *One of the Many*, 24, 27; Bob Porter, *The Long Return* (Burnaby, BC: Porter, 1997), 44; Lance Buttler in Kevin Wilson, *Bomber Boys: The RAF Offensive of 1943* (London: Weidenfeld & Nicolson, 2005), 382; see also, though, John Walsh, Happy Landings, 29, 12812, IWM.

24. Will Iredale, *The Kamikaze Hunters: Fighting for the Pacific, 1945* (London: Macmillan, 2015), 159.

25. See e.g. Warren G. Helm, *Big War, Little People* (El Paso, TX: Helm, 2009), 114; Elmer Brown in O'Neill, *Half a Wing*, 44; Leo Richer, *I Flew the Lancaster Bomber* (Windermere, BC: Richer, 1998), 4; Jesse Richard Pitts, *Return to Base: Memoirs of a B-17 Copilot, Kimbolton, England, 1943–1944* (Charlottesville, VA: Howell, 2004), 159.

26. Melvin W. McGuire and Robert Hadley, *Bloody Skies: A 15th AAF Combat Crew: How They Lived and Died* (Las Cruces, NM: Yucca Tree, 1993), 311; see also e.g. Keith W. Mason, *My War in Italy: On the Ground and in Flight with the 15th Air Force* (Columbia: University of Missouri Press, 2016), 212.

27. Harry Lomas, *One Wing High—the Navigator's Story* (Shrewsbury, UK: Airlife, 1995), 156.

28. William James Hunter, *From Coastal Command to Captivity* (Barnsley, UK: Leo Cooper, 2003), 50.

29. Smith and Smith, *Lifting the Silence*, 80.

30. Peter Jacobs with Les Bartlett, *Bomb Aimer over Berlin: The Wartime Memoirs of Les Bartlett* (Barnsley, UK: Pen & Sword Aviation, 2007), 99; see also A. Les Bartlett diary, November 22, 1943, RAF 006, LC.

31. Ronnie Waite, *Death or Decoration* (Cowden, UK: Newton, 1991), 98; see also e.g. Denis Hornsey, Here Today, Bomb Tomorrow: The Saga of a Bomber Command Pilot, 163, 4559, IWM; Harry Le Marchant, Superstitions, RAFBCA, accessed April 26, 2014, rafbombercommand.com; Bob Pierson in Nicol and Rennell, *Tail-End Charlies*, 137.

32. Richard Kelly interview, TMP, accessed October 21, 2013, thememory project.com.

33. William H. Dowden Jr. interview, AFC/2001/001/90085, VHP; see e.g. Forrest S. Clark interview TS, 15, Oral History Collection, NMMEAF; Helm, *Big War*, 116–117; Jack Keller interview TS, 3, Oral History Collection, NMMEAF; Ralph E. Simester journal, 11, 2010.011.0001, NMMEAF; Frank A. Wiswall interview TS, 64, ROHA, accessed September 26, 2015, oralhistory.rutgers.edu.

34. Leonard Herman with Rob Morris, *Combat Bombardier: Memoirs of Two Combat Tours in the Skies over Europe in World War Two* (Bloomington, IN: Xlibris, 2007), 52; see also e.g. Plate, *Storm Clouds*, 105.

35. William P. Maher, *Fated to Survive: 401st Bombardment Group (H), Eighth Air Force: Memoirs of a B-17 Flying Fortress Pilot/Prisoner of War*, ed. Ed Y. Hall (Spartanburg, SC: Honoribus, 1992), 34; see also e.g. Bert W. Humphries, Times of Our Lives (An Autobiography), 24, 91st Bomb Group, accessed October 23, 2014, 91stbombgroup.com.

36. John J. Shiver, *I Always Wanted to Fly: Memoirs of a World War II Flight Engineer/Gunner* (Atmore, AL: Shiver, 2012), 202; see also e.g. Charles M. Olson diary entry, May 30, 1944, 2010.0210.0001, NMMEAF.

37. Jackson Granholm, *The Day We Bombed Switzerland: Flying with the US Eighth Army Air Force in World War II* (Shrewsbury, UK: Airlife, 2000), 78; see also e.g. Russell Meyne, One Mo' Time, 41, 2010.0128.0001, NMMEAF.

38. Thomas C. Wilcox, *One Man's Destiny* (Mogadore, OH: Telecraft, 1991), 97.

39. Currier, *50 Mission Crush*, 140. On individual prayers made while on the ground by bomber crew members, see also e.g. Walter Wooten in Patricia Chapman Meder, *The True Story of Catch-22: The Real Men and Missions of Joseph Heller's 340th Bomb Group in World War II* (Philadelphia: Casemate, 2012), 54; Ben West, Bombing the Breisach Bridge, 2, 320th Bomb Group, accessed October 31, 2014, 320thbg.org/breisach_bridge_1.html.

40. Keith B. Lamb, 35 Times: My Experiences as a B-17 Bomber Pilot during World War II, 49, 2010.0196.0001, NMMEAF.

41. Michael J. Donahue, Individual Fear, 28, 2009–0321.0073, NMMEAF.

42. Richard K. Curtis, *Dumb But Lucky! Confessions of a P-51 Fighter Pilot in World War II* (New York: Ballantine, 2005), 175.

43. Al Zlaten, *By the Grace of God: Or It Ain't All Luck* (Longmont, CO: Zlaten, 2000), 54.

44. Hal Shook, *Fighter Pilot Jazz: Role of the P-47 and Spirited Guys in Winning the Air-Ground War in Normandy, 1944* (Huntington, WV: Humanomics, 2005), 175; see also e.g. John M. Foster, *Hell in the Heavens: The True Combat Adventures of a Marine Fighter Pilot in World War Two* (Washington, DC: Zenger, 1981), 155.

45. Marvin Bledsoe, *Thunderbolt: Memoirs of a World War II Fighter Pilot* (New York: Van Norstrand Reinhold, 1982), 46. On the devout, see e.g. William B. Colgan, *World War II Fighter-Bomber Pilot*, 3rd ed. (Westminster, MD: Heritage, 2008), 28; Francis "Gabby" Gabreski in *Forever Remembered: The Fliers of World War II*, ed. Irv Broughton (Spokane: Eastern Washington University Press, 2001), 28; James Kyle, *A Typhoon Tale* (Bognor, UK: New Horizon, 1984), 124; Steve N. Pisanos, *The Flying Greek: An Immigrant Fighter Ace's WWII Odyssey with the RAF, USAAF, and French Resistance* (Washington, DC: Potomac, 2008), 203.

46. Craig Harris in *Fait Accompli III: A Historical Anthology of the 457th Bomb Group (H): The Fireball Outfit*, ed. Craig Harris, comp. James L. Bass (Nashville, TN: JM, 2000), 202; see also John C. McManus, *Deadly Sky: The American Combat Airman in World War II* (Novato, CA: Presidio, 2000), 309; Shiver, *I Always Wanted to Fly*, 166.

47. David E. Lundy interview TS, 9, Oral History Collection, NMMEAF.

48. Anthony B. Tabor in Stone, *Triumphant We Fly*, 116.

49. William J. Fili, *Passage to Valhalla: The Human Side of Aerial Combat over Nazi Occupied Europe* (Media, PA: Filcon, 1991), 78.

50. Paul Katz in *Memories from the Out House Mouse: The Personal Diaries of One B-17 Crew*, ed. G. R. Harvey (Victoria, BC: Trafford, 2002), 35; see also e.g. Kenith N. Gillespie interview, AFC/2001/001/80981, VHP.

51. Herbert, *Maximum Effort*, 48.

52. Levin Beasley, World War II Happened and I Went Along for the Ride, 40, 2009.0269.0001, NMMEAF.

53. McKay, *One of the Many*, 108.

54. Eddie Wheeler, *Just to Get a Bed!* (Worcester, UK: Square One, 1990), 108; see also e.g. David H. Pearce, *Dark Skies and Dead Reckoning* (Moe, VIC: Pearce, 2000), 112.

55. Bob Schimanski in Broughton, *Forever Remembered*, 376.

56. John T. Godfrey, *The Look of Eagles* (New York: Random House, 1958), 85; see also e.g. Kenneth Lane Glemby as told to Norman Auslander, *"Flyboy": Memoirs of a P-47 Pilot* (Seattle: CreateSpace, 2015), 22.

57. Harold C. Rosser, *No Hurrahs for Me* (Sevierville, TN: Covenant House, 1994), 232.

58. Mark A. Savage, *"Those Were the Days": Aviation Adventures of World War II* (Dublin, OH: Markas, 1993), 37.

59. Carl H. Moore, *Flying the B-26 Marauder over Europe: Memoir of a World War II Navigator*, 2nd ed. (Jefferson, NC: McFarland, 2013), 68; see also e.g. Richard C. Baynes, *Replacement Crew: The Training and Combat Experience of a Typical 8th Air Force Replacement Crew in 1944* (Irvine, CA: Baynes, 1993), 56–57; Alan Cook, The Story of Umbriago, 4, 447th Bomb Group, accessed October 23, 2014, 447bg.com; John Comer, *Combat Crew: A True Story of Flying and Fighting in World War II* (New York: William Morrow, 1988), 44; Kenneth C. Drinnon, *Wings of Tru Love: A WWII B17 Ball-Turret Gunner Memoir* (Bloomington, IN: Xlibris, 2011), 63; Ray Hann interview TS, 4, CAPS, accessed August 22, 2015, combataircrew.org; Ivo de Jong, *Mission 376: Battle over the Reich, May 28, 1944* (Mechanicsburg, PA: Stackpole, 2003), 181; L. W. McFarland, Raid on Berlin, 9, 447th Bomb Group, accessed October 23, 2014, 447bg.com.

60. Stewart, *Forbidden Diary*, 104; see also e.g. Jack D. Rude interview TS, 10, Oral History Collection, NMMEAF; Jack Young in Erik Dyreborg, *The Lucky Ones: Airmen of the Mighty Eighth* (San Jose, CA: Writers Club, 2002), 267.

61. Gordon Bennett Robertson Jr., *Bringing the Thunder: The Missions of a World War II B-29 Pilot in the Pacific* (Mechanicsburg, PA: Stackpole, 2006), 205; see also e.g. Allen T. Stein, *Into the Wild Blue Yonder: My Life in the Air Force* (College Station: Texas A&M University Press, 2005), 37.

62. Bruce Muirhead in Pack and Singer, *388th Anthology*, vol. 2, *Tales of the 388th Bombardment Group (H) 1942–45*, ed. Janet Pack and Richard Singer (San Jose, CA: Writer's Club, 2001), 35; see also e.g. G. M. Etherington narrative, 2, Memories, December 14, 1944, 40th Bomb Group Association, accessed January 19, 2015, 40thbombgroup.org; see also e.g. Anthony Alberco and Kenneth Carey interview TS, 24, Oral History Collection, NMMEAF; Forrest S. Clark interview TS, 15–16, Oral History Collection, NMMEAF.

63. Bob Hutton and Andy Rooney, *Air Gunner* (New York: Farrar & Rinehart, 1944), 83; see Anthony Kellett, *Combat Motivation: The Behavior of Soldiers in Battle* (Boston: Kluwer, 1982), 195. An official survey of over 4,000 tour-expired USAAF aircrew in 1944–1945 found that 58 percent of the officers and 67 percent of the enlisted men had used prayer to help them cope. Laurance D. Shaffer et al., "Surveys of Experiences of Returned Personnel," in *Army Air Forces Aviation Psychology Research Reports: Psychological Problems of Redistribution: Re-*

port No. 14, ed. Frederic Wickert (Washington, DC: US Government Printing Office, 1947), 132.

CHAPTER 3: TALISMANS AND MASCOTS

1. Ian Gleed, *Arise to Conquer* (New York: Random House, 1942), 59; see also e.g. George Henry Albert Bilton interview, 13444/2, IWM; Edward Gordon, So You Want to Be a Flyer—An Air Gunner's Story—Part 3 Chapters 11 to 12a, BBC WW2 People's War, accessed January 19, 2013, bbc.co.uk/history/ww2peoples war/stories/46/a4104046.shtml; Thomas Clifford Iveson interview, 18020/3, IWM; Gordon Mellor interview, 28650/12, IWM; Leo Richer, *I Flew the Lancaster Bomber* (Windermere, BC: Richer, 1998), 4.

2. Ben Smith Jr., *Chick's Crew: A Tale of the Eighth Air Force*, 2nd ed. (Tallahassee, FL: Rose, 1983), 135; see also e.g. Raymond M. Castellane in Ernest Gaillard Jr., *Flight Surgeon: Complete and Unabridged Combat Medical Diary, US Eighth Army Air Force, 381st Bomb Group, 242nd Medical Dispensary, Station 167, Ridgewell, Essex, England, 1943–1944*, ed. William N. Gaillard (Bloomington, IN: 1st Books, 2005), 82; Thomas P. Reynolds, *Belle of the Brawl: A Biographical Memoir of Walter Malone Baskin* (Paducah, KY: Turner, 1996), 53.

3. Sydney Percival Smith and David Scott Smith, *Lifting the Silence* (Toronto: Dundurn, 2010), 80.

4. Keith C. Schuyler *Elusive Horizons* (Cranbury, NJ: A. S. Barnes, 1969), 153–154; see also e.g. Forrest S. Clark interview TS, 17, ROHA, accessed September 26, 2015, oralhistory.rutgers.edu.

5. Bill Wallrich, "Superstition and the Air Force," *Western Folklore* 19 (1960), 12; see e.g. Charles J. Fletcher, *Quest for Survival* (Aurora, CO: Glenbridge, 2002), 75–77; John Muirhead, *Those Who Fall* (New York: Random House, 1986), 123.

6. E. J. Johnson, *Hann's Crew* (Paducah, KY: Turner, 2000), 32.

7. Sidney Munns, *As Luck Would Have It: Reminiscences of a Retired RAF Observer/Navigator* (Northampton, UK: Friday File, 1992), 18–19.

8. Jack Pitts, *P-47 Pilot: Scared, Bored, and Deadly* (San Antonio, TX: Pitts, 1997), 194.

9. Bill Jackson, *Three Stripes and Four Brownings* (North Battleford, SK: Turner-Warwick, 1990), 124; see Hank Nelson, *Chased by the Sun: Courageous Australians in Bomber Command in World War II* (Sydney: ABC, 2002), 141.

10. John R. McCrary and David E. Scherman, *First of the Many: A Journal of Action with the Men of the Eighth Air Force* (New York: Simon & Schuster, 1944), 43.

11. Van R. Parker, *Dear Folks* (Memphis, TN: Global, 1989), 226; see ibid., 245; see also e.g. Carl Frey Constein, *Born to Fly the Hump: A WWII Memoir* (Bloomington, IN: 1st Books, 2001), 37.

12. Robert L. Gushwa, *The Best and the Worst of Times: The United States Army Chaplaincy, 1920–1945* (Washington, DC: Office of the Chief of Chaplains, Department of the Army, 1977), 170.

13. *Hell's Angels Newsletter*, vol. 1, *Silver Anniversary Collection, 1976–2001*, ed. Eddie Deerfield (Palm Harbor, FL: 303rd Bomb Group [H] Association, 2002), 504; see Wayne E. Dorsett interview TS, 11, Oral History Collection, NMMEAF; Gushwa, *Best and Worst of Times*, 168–169; Harry E. Slater, *Lingering Contrails of the Big Square A: A History of the 94th Bomb Group (H), 1942–1945* (Hadley, PA: Slater, 1980), 117.

14. Kenneth C. Drinnon, *Wings of Tru Love: A WWII B17 Ball-Turret Gunner Memoir* (Bloomington, IN: Xlibris, 2011), 75; see also e.g. Anthony Alberco and Kenneth Carey interview TS, 24, Oral History Collection, NMMEAF.

15. John J. Briol, *Dead Engine Kids: World War II Diary of John J. Briol, B-17 Ball-Turret Gunner, with Comments from Notes of Other Crew Members*, ed. John F. Welch (Rapid City, SD: Silver Wings Association, 1993), 40.

16. Smith, *Chick's Crew*, 121; see Gushwa, *Best and Worst of Times*, 179; see also e.g. R. E. Peppy Blount, *We Band of Brothers* (Austin, TX: Eakin, 1984), 164; Dennis R. Okerstrom, *The Final Missions of* Bottoms Up: *A World War II Pilot's Story* (Columbia: University of Missouri Press, 2011), 104.

17. Ted Peck in Pat Cunningham, *Fighter! Fighter! Corkscrew Port!* (Barnsley, UK: Pen & Sword Aviation, 2012), 128.

18. John Marsden in Pat Cunningham, *The Fear in the Sky: Vivid Memories of Operational Aircrew in World War II* (Barnsley, UK: Pen & Sword Aviation, 2012), 150; see also e.g. Dan Brennan in Irv Broughton, *Hanger Talk: Interviews With Fliers, 1920s–1990s* (Cheney: Eastern Washington University Press, 1998), 148; William Dives, *A Bundu Boy in Bomber Command: Memoirs of a Royal Air Force Lancaster Pilot* (Victoria, BC: Trafford, 2003), 260; Les Hood in Sean Feast, *Master Bombers: The Experiences of a Pathfinder Squadron at War 1944–1945* (London: Grub Street, 2008), 26; W. E. "Bill" Goodman, *Of Stirlings and Stalags: An Air-Gunner's Tale* (London: PublishNation, 2013), 81; Peter Jacobs with Les Bartlett, *Bomb Aimer over Berlin: The Wartime Memoirs of Les Bartlett* (Barnsley, UK: Pen & Sword Aviation, 2007), 99; Maurice G. Lihou, *Out of the Italian Night: Wellington Bomber Operations, 1944–45* (Shrewsbury, UK: Airlife, 2000), 29; Sam Lipfriend interview, 31462/4, IWM; Tom Sawyer, *Only Owls and Bloody Fools Fly at Night* (London: Kimber, 1982), 55; C. J. Sheddan with Norman Franks, *Tempest*

Pilot (London: Grub Street, 1993), 40; P. Hamilton Pollock, *Wings on the Cross: A Padre with the R.A.F.* (Dublin: Clanmore and Reynolds, 1954), 77; John Wainwright, *Tail-End Charlie* (London: Macmillan, 1978), 94.

19. Norman Fortier, *An Ace of the Eighth: An American Fighter Pilot's Air War in Europe* (New York: Presidio, 2003), 184; see Smith, *Chick's Crew*, 135; see also e.g. Blount, *We Band of Brothers*, 164; Bob Hanson in *Hanger Talk*, 205; Jack D. Rude interview TS, 10, Oral History Collection, NMMEAF; Allen T. Stein, *Into the Wild Blue Yonder: My Life in the Air Force* (College Station: Texas A&M University Press, 2005), xi, 7; James W. Vernon, *The Hostile Sky: A Hellcat Flier in World War II* (Annapolis, MD: Naval Institute Press, 2003), 158.

20. E. A. W. Smith, *Spitfire Diary: The Boys of One-Two-Seven* (London: Kimber, 1988), 31; see also e.g. J. Norman Ashton, *Only Birds and Fools: Flight Engineer, Avro Lancaster, World War II* (Shrewsbury, UK: Airlife, 2000), 24; Gordon James Hurley, *Corkscrew Starboard* (York, UK: Field House, 2009), 84.

21. Robert S. Nielsen, *With the Stars Above* (Olympia, WA: JENN, 1984), 554, 593 n. 32; see also e.g. Frederick William Brown, Get Fell In!, 49, RAF 017, LC; Ian Campbell in *Aircrew Memories* (Victoria, BC: Victoria Publishing, 1999), 127; Ian Darling, *Amazing Airmen: Canadians Flying in the Second World War* (Toronto: Dundurn, 2009), 179.

22. See e.g. Max Lambert, *Night after Night: New Zealanders in Bomber Command* (Auckland: HarperCollins, 2005), 255; Muirhead, *Those Who Fall*, 123.

23. Ted Fahrenwald, *Wot a Way to Run a War! The World War II Exploits and Escapades of a Pilot in the 352nd Fighter Group* (Havertown, PA: Casemate, 2014), 141.

24. Mike Henry, *Air Gunner* (London: Foulis, 1964), 50.

25. Reynolds, *Belle of the Brawl*, 53–54.

26. Harry B. Crosby, *A Wing and a Prayer: The "Bloody 100th" Bomb Group of the U.S. Eighth Air Force in Action over Europe in World War II* (San Jose, CA: iUniverse, 2000), 34; see also Laurie Woods, *Flying into the Mouth of Hell* (Loftus, NSW: Australian Military History Publications, 2003), 216.

27. Vern Kling interview, 398th Bomb Group, accessed November 1, 2014, 398th.org. On the buckeye as a good-luck piece, see Claudia De Lys, *A Treasury of American Superstitions* (New York: Philosophical Library, 1958), 113, 115.

28. Linda Piper, Mystery behind Pilot's Death, May 29, 2008, This is Local London, accessed October 3, 2015, thisislocallondon.co.uk; Mel Rolfe, *Hell on Earth: Dramatic First Hand Experiences of Bomber Command at War* (London: Grub Street, 1999), 79.

29. On silver dollars, see Wallrich, "Superstition and the Air Force," 11–12. On lucky coins, see also e.g. Charles Furey, *Going Back: A Navy Airman in the*

Pacific War (Annapolis, MD: Naval Institute Press, 1997), 157; Robert J. Goebel, *Mustang Ace: Memoirs of a P-51 Fighter Pilot* (Pacifica, CA: Pacifica, 1991), 109; Leonard M. Nealis interview TS, 14, Oral History Collection, NMMEAF; Jack D. Rude interview TS, 10, Oral History Collection, NMMEAF; Roger L. Sandstedt, *My B-29 Story* (St. Louis, MO: Sandstedt, 2003), 397.

30. Sawyer, *Only Owls and Bloody Fools*, 55.

31. John Kilbracken, *Bring Back My Stringbag: Swordfish Pilot at War, 1940–45*, rev. ed. (London: Leo Cooper, 1996), 80.

32. Donald R. Schneck and Ralph H. Schneck, *Letters from a World War II Hoosier Pilot* (West Lafayette, IN: Purdue University Press, 2013), 101 n. 7.

33. Rollo Kingsford-Smith, *I Wouldn't Have Missed It for Quids* (Exeter, NSW: Kingsford-Smith, 1999), 69.

34. Desmond Scott, *Fighter Pilot* (London: Leo Cooper, 1980), 43; see Murray Peden, *A Thousand Shall Fall: A Pilot for 214* (Stittsville, ON: Canada's Wings, 1979), 414.

35. Colin Dudley in *Recollections and Reminiscences: Some Reminiscences and Recollections of W.W.2: A Collection of Stories Written by Members of the Aircrew Association of South Australia*, ed. E. W. Davies (Hyde Park, SA: Aircrew Association of South Australia, 1997), 103.

36. Harry McLean in Mel Rolfe, *To Hell and Back* (London: Grub Street, 1998), 148; Miles Tripp, *The Eighth Passenger: A Flight of Recollection and Discovery* (London: Macmillan, 1969), 30; Geoff King interview, 28657/6, IWM; T. W. Fox, *My Life with Bomber-Command during the 2nd World War*, 12, 7811, IWM; Ashton, *Only Birds and Fools*, 24, 72; see also e.g. R. L. Austen, *High Adventure—Navigator at War* (Chichester, UK: Barry Rose, 1989), 40; James Campbell, *Maximum Effort* (London: Alison & Busby, 1957), 16–17.

37. Robert H. Tays in Martin W. Bowman, *Echoes of England: The 8th Air Force in World War II* (Stroud, UK: Tempus, 2006), 156.

38. Melvin McGuire and Robert Hadley, *Bloody Skies: A 15th AAF Combat Crew: How They Lived and Died* (Las Cruces, CA: Yucca Tree, 1993), 309.

39. James Lee Hutchinson, *The Boys in the B-17* (Bloomington, IN: Author-House, 2011), 23; see also e.g. Johnnie B. Corbitt in *Missions Remembered: The Men of the Middle Tennessee WWII Fighter Pilots Association*, ed. John K. Breast (Brentwood, TN: JM Productions, 1995), 23; Albert L. Beuhler in *The 390th Bomb Group in Action: An Anthology*, vol. 1, ed. Wilbert H. Richarz and Richard H. Perry (Tucson, AZ: 390th Memorial Museum Foundation, 1983), 241.

40. See James A. Goodson, *A Tumult in the Clouds* (New York: St. Martin's, 1983), 114, 118.

41. William (Paul) Thayer in James A. Oleson, *In Their Own Words: True Stories and Adventures of the American Fighter Ace* (New York: iUniverse, 2007), 62.

42. Bryan Cox, *Too Young to Die: The Story of a New Zealand Fighter Pilot in the Pacific War* (Ames: Iowa State University Press, 1989), 134.

43. Scott, *Typhoon Pilot*, 43; see also e.g. Gordon Thorburn, *Bombers First and Last* (London: Robson, 2006), 95.

44. Hugh Russell in Martin W. Bowman, *RAF Bomber Command at War: Reflections of War*, vol. 1, *Cover of Darkness* (Barnsley, UK: Pen & Sword Aviation, 2011), 105.

45. Hamilton Mero interview, 398th Bomb Group Association, accessed October 31, 2014, 398th.org; see Bob Hutton and Andy Rooney, *Air Gunner* (New York: Farrar & Rinehart, 1944), 163; see also e.g. Wayne E. Dorsett interview TS, 11, Oral History Collection, NMMEAF.

46. The lucky charm of one bomber pilot and his crew was, rather unusually, a large iron kettle. Ken Trent, *Bomb Doors Open: From East End Boy to Lancaster Bomber Pilot with 617 "Dambusters" Squadron* (St. Mary, UK: Seeker, 2016), 106.

47. Jimmy Corbin, *Last of the Ten Fighter Boys* (Stroud, UK: Sutton, 2007), 97, 104.

48. Dave McCausland in Max Arthur, *Lost Voices of the Royal Air Force* (London: Hodder, 2005), 167.

49. See e.g. Smith, *Chick's Crew*, 135. On lucky caps, see also e.g. Kevin Herbert, *Maximum Effort: The B-29's against Japan* (Manhattan, KS: Sunflower University Press, 1983), 43; Robert Rosenthal interview, 100th Bomb Group, accessed November 30, 2014, 100thbg.com; John Misterly Jr., *Over and Under* (New York: Carlton, 1987), 234; Sandstedt, *My B-29 Story*, 397; Earl Snyder, *General Leemy's Flying Circus: A Navigator's Story of the 20th Air Force in World War II* (New York: Exposition, 1955), 161.

50. Snyder, *General Leemy's Flying Circus*, 159; Bowman, *Echoes of England*, 156. On lucky shoes, see e.g. Robert V. Brulle, *Angels Zero: P-47 Close Air Support in Europe* (Washington, DC: Smithsonian, 2000), 132; Marion Carl, *Pushing the Envelope: The Career of Fighter Ace and Test Pilot Marion Carl* (Annapolis, MD: Naval Institute Press, 1994), 93. On lucky socks, see e.g. Robin Olds with Christina Olds and Ed Rasimus, *Fighter Pilot: The Memoirs of Legendary Ace Robin Olds* (New York: St. Martin's, 2010), 325; John Talbot Smith interview TS, 59, ROHA, accessed September 26, 2015, oralhistory.rutgers.edu.

51. Marc Eliot, *Jimmy Stewart: A Biography* (New York: Harmony, 2006), 179.

52. Goodson, *Tumult*, 114.

53. Stanley A. Peterson, *"The Saint": Stories by the Navigator of a B-17* (Lexing-

ton, KY: CreateSpace, 2014), ch. 8, p. 1; Gene T. Carson, *Wing Ding* (Blooming-ton, IN: Xlibris, 2000), 111; see also e.g. Julius Altvater, *Off We Go . . . Down in Flame* (Victoria, BC: Trafford, 2002), 102.

54. Robert E. Wannop, *Chocks Away* (Worcester, UK: Square One, 1989), 42.

55. On lucky neckwear, see e.g. Edward Gordon, So You Want to Be a Flyer—An Air Gunner's Story—Part 3 Chapters 11 to 12a, Ch. 11, BBC WW2 People's War, accessed January 19, 2013, bbc.co.uk/history/ww2peopleswar/stories/46/a4104046.shtml; Henry, *Air Gunner*, 50; Harry Lomas, *One Wing High: Halifax Bomber—The Navigator's Story* (Shrewsbury, UK: Airlife, 1995), 167; Thomas G. Quinlan, *Corkscrew to Safety: A Tail-Gunner's Tour with 103 Squadron RAF, 1944/5* (Bognor, UK: Woodfield, 2011), 147; Mel Rolfe, *Gunning for the Enemy: Wallace McIntosh* (London: Grub Street, 2003), 80; Donald Stones, *A Pilot's Passion: The Story of 'Dimsie,'* ed. Adrian Burt (London: Burt, 2014), 56; Geoff Taylor, *Piece of Cake* (London: Corgi, 1980), 25; Thorburn, *Bombers First and Last*, 166; Tripp, *Eighth Passenger*, 30. On lucky service hats, see e.g. T. P. M. Cooper-Slipper in Air-crew Association, *Aircrew Memories: The Collected World War II and Later Memo-ries of Members of the Aircrew Association, Vancouver Island Branch, Victoria, B.C.* (Victoria, BC: Victoria Publishing, 1999), 25; Thorburn, *Bombers First and Last*, 30; Tripp, *Eighth Passenger*, 30.

56. Nelson, *Chased by the Sun*, 141.

57. Frank Tolley in Kevin Wilson, *Journey's End: Bomber Command's Battle from Arnhem to Dresden and Beyond* (London: Weidenfeld & Nicolson, 2010), 243.

58. J. Douglas Harvey, *Boys, Bombs and Brussels Sprouts: A Knees-Up, Wheels-Up Chronicle of WWII* (Toronto: McClelland & Stewart, 1981), 53.

59. Geoff King interview, 28657/6, IWM.

60. Harry J. Task in *The 305th Bomb Group in Action: An Anthology*, ed. John V. Craven (Burleson, TX: 305th Bombardment Group [H] Memorial Association, 1990), 103; see also e.g. Edward L. Jessup interview TS, 8, Oral History Collec-tion, NMMEAF.

61. James Calvin Stivender Jr. interview, AFC/2001/001/82621, VHP.

62. S. H. Johnson, *It's Never Dark above the Clouds* (Trigg, WA: Johnson, 1994), 58.

63. Peden, *Thousand Shall Fall*, 414; see e.g. Dave Maltby in Harry Humphries, *Living with Heroes: The Story of the Dam Busters* (Norwich, UK: Erskine, 2003), 34.

64. Lomas, *One Wing High*, 167; see also e.g. Nelson, *Chased by the Sun*, 141.

65. John C. Walter, *My War: The True Experiences of a U.S. Army Air Force Pilot in World War II* (Bloomington, IN: AuthorHouse, 2004), 123; Rolfe, *Hell and Back*, 18; see also e.g. Gordon Redfeldt memoir, 2, 2010.0097.0003, NMMEAF.

66. See e.g. Howard Muncho in *Forever Remembered: The Fliers of World War II*, ed. Irv Broughton (Spokane: Eastern Washington University Press, 2001), 538; Roy R. Fisher Jr., with Susan Fisher Anderson, *The Lucky Bastard Club: Letters to My Bride from the Left Seat* (Bloomington, IN: AuthorHouse, 2002), 111; Bill Frankhouser, *World War II Odyssey: Pennsylvania Dutch Farm Boy Becomes 8th Air Force Navigator* (Bedford, VA: Hamilton's, 1997), 87; Tom Schoolcraft in Fiske Hanley, *History of the 504th Bomb Group (VH) in World War II* (Enfield, CT: 504th Bomb Group Association, 1992), 258; Fred Koger, *Countdown!* (Chapel Hill, NC: Algonquin, 1990), 33; Mike Quering in C. C. Neal, *Gentlemen from Hell: Men of the 487th Bomb Group* (Paducah, KY: Turner, 2005), 217; Irving Schreiber, *The War Years: My Participation in the Second World War* (Rockville, MD: Schreiber, 2012), 171; Arnold Willis interview, EAA, accessed October 10, 2014, eaavideo.org; William Zauner interview, EAA, accessed October 10, 2014, eaavideo.org; see also Wallrich, "Superstition and the Air Force," 14.

67. Walter, *My War*, 123.

68. Jack Novey, *The Cold Blue Sky: A B-17 Gunner in World War II*, ed. Fryar Calhoun (Charlottesville, VA: Howell, 1997), 4.

69. Bert Stiles, *Serenade to the Big Bird* (Carthage, TX: Howland Associates, 1999), 28.

70. Jack R. Myers, *Shot at and Missed: Recollections of a World War II Bombardier* (Norman: University of Oklahoma Press, 2004), 101.

71. David McCarthy, *Fear No More: A B-17 Navigator's Journey* (Pittsburgh: Cottage Wordsmiths, 1991), 145; see also e.g. Warren Alden Blower interview, AFC/2001/001/20709, VHP; Les Hansen in William F. Somers, *Fortress Fighters: An Autobiography of a B-17 Aerial Gunner* (Tempe, AZ: Somers, 2000), 45.

72. George Moffat in Michael Thixton, George E. Moffat, John J. O'Neill, *Bombs Away: By Pathfinders of the Eighth Air Force* (Trumbull, CT: FNP, 1998), 56.

73. William Zauner interview, EAA, accessed October 10, 2014, eaavideo.org.

74. Johnnie Houlton, *Spitfire Strikes: A New Zealand Fighter Pilot's Story* (London: John Murray, 1985), 25; Ian McLachlan and Russell J. Zorn, *Eighth Air Force Bomber Stories: Eye-Witness Accounts from American Airmen and British Civilians of the Perils of War* (Sparkford, UK: Patrick Stephens, 1991), 112.

75. William Carigan, *Ad Lib: Flying the B-24 Liberator in World War II* (Manhattan, KS: Sunflower University Press, 1988), 12.

76. Geoff D. Copeman, *Right-Hand Man: A Flight Engineer's Story* (Baldock, UK: Euro Slug, 1996), 36.

77. Stuffed rabbits might have seemed the next best thing to an actual rabbit's foot, while golliwogs may have been favored in the RAF because black people

were thought to carry luck. See Paul Fussell, *Wartime: Understanding and Behavior in the Second World War* (New York: Oxford University Press, 1989), 49. For golliwogs, see also e.g. A. Les Bartlett diary, November 10, 1943, RAF 006, LC; Arthur William Doubleday in Martin W. Bowman, *Scramble: Memories of the RAF in the Second World War* (Stroud, UK: Tempus, 2006), 95; John Pennington in Alan White, *The King's Thunderbolts: No. 44 (Rhodesia) Squadron Royal Air Force: An Operational Record and Roll of Honour, 1917–1982* (London: Tucann, 2007), 112. For stuffed rabbits, see e.g. Don Charlwood interview TS, 23, S00568, AWM; Gordon James Hurley, *Corkscrew Port* (York, UK: Field House, 2009), 233; Russell Margerison, *Boys at War* (Bolton, UK: Ross Anderson, 1986), 42.

78. On teddy bears, see e.g. Stephen Beaumont in Bill Howard, *What the RAF Airman Took to War* (Oxford: Shire, 2015), 83; Geoff King interview, 28657/6, IWM; Alfie Martin, *Bale Out! Escaping Occupied France with the Resistance* (Newtonards, NI: Colourpoint, 2005), 28. On teddies in the FAA, see Roy Hawkes in Will Iredale, *The Kamikaze Hunters: Fighting for the Pacific, 1945* (London: Macmillan, 2015), 191. On Koalas, see e.g. T. E. Done, *All Our Mates* (Candelo, NSW: Widgeram, 1995), 85. On stuffed pandas, see e.g. Peden, *Thousand Shall Fall*, 414; R. C. Rivaz, *Tail Gunner* (Stroud, UK: Sutton, 1996), 13. On stuffed penguins, see e.g. Austen, *High Adventure*, 61.

79. Bob Pierson in Nichol and Rennell, *Tail-End Charlies*, 137.

80. Leroy W. Newby, *Target Ploesti: View From a Bombsight* (Novato, CA: Presidio, 1983), 136, 4, 22, 25, 179, 207; see also e.g. Gregory J. Matenkoski, *Lucky Penny's Tail: The True Story of Edmund Survilla, Tail Gunner 453rd Bomb Group, January 1944 to June 1945* (Lexington, KY: Matenkoski, 2010), 17, 182; Leonard M. Nealis interview TS, 14, Oral History Collection, NMMEAF.

81. Ashton, *Only Birds and Fools*, 18, 21–22, 29, 59, 96.

82. See e.g. Lomas, *One Wing High*, 128, 167; Rolfe, *Gunning for the Enemy*, 80.

83. Robert E. Vickers Jr. interview TS, 17, Oral History Collection, NMMEAF.

84. Richard L. Feldman in Rade Petrovi Kent, *Is It Just Poor Memory . . . Or Just One More Treason?* (Lausanne: L'Age d'Homme, 1998), 17.

85. Chester Marshall, *Sky Giants over Japan: A Diary of a B-29 Combat Crew in WWII* (Winona, MN: Apollo, 1984), 19.

86. Robert A, Mann, *The B-29 Superfortress: A Comprehensive Registry of the Planes and Their Missions* (Jefferson, NC: McFarland, 2005), 93.

87. Wallace R. Foreman, *B-17 Nose Art Directory* (North Branch, MN: Phalanx, 1996), 40–41; ibid., *B-24 Nose Art Directory* (North Branch, MN: Phalanx, 1996), 43–44; Mann, *B-29*, 93; see e.g. Matenkoski, *Lucky Penny's Tail*, 18–19. See also

Samuel Russ Harris Jr., *B-29s over Japan: A Group Commander's Diary* (Jefferson, NC: McFarland, 2011), 253; Hanley, *History of the 504th Bomb Group (VH)*, 111; Misterly, *Over and Under*, 201.

88. Foreman, *B-17 Nose Art*, 9, 13, 14; Foreman, *B-24 Nose Art*, 11, 16; Mann, *B-29*, 89.

89. Foreman, *B-17 Nose Art*, 29; Foreman, *B-24 Nose Art*, 32.

90. Edward F. Logan Jr., *"Jump, Damn It, Jump!": Memoir of a Downed B-17 Pilot in World War II* (Jefferson, NC: McFarland, 2006), 97.

91. Robert S. Johnson with Martin Caidin, *Thunderbolt!* (New York: Rinehart, 1958), 275; Clayton Kelly Gross, *Live Bait: WWII Memories of an Undefeated Fighter Ace* (Portland, OR: Inkwater, 2006), 129.

92. Brooke Hindle, *Lucky Lady and the Navy Mystique: The* Chenango *in WW II* (New York: Vantage, 1991), 98.

93. See Caitlin McWilliams, "Camaraderie, Morale and Material Culture: Reflections on the Nose Art of No. 6 Group, Royal Canadian Air Force," *Canadian Military History* 19 (2010): 24.

94. Clarence Simonsen, *RAF and RCAF Aircraft Nose Art in World War II* (Ottringham, UK: Hikoki, 2001), 121–122, 130, 204.

95. N. J. N. Hockaday, One Little Man Went to War, 153, 42183, IWM.

96. George Johnson, *The Last British Dambuster* (London: Ebury, 2014), 5; J. T. Maddock narrative, 64, 5807, IWM.

97. Tim Vigors, *Life's Too Short to Cry: The Compelling Memoir of a Battle of Britain Ace* (London: Grub Street, 2006), 180.

98. Alan C. Deere, *Nine Lives*, 2nd ed. (Canterbury, UK: Wingham, 1991), 61, 73, 163.

99. Rolfe, *Hell on Earth*, 134. Conversely, the accidental death of the black Labrador belonging to the commander of 617 Squadron prior to the start of the famous dams raid of May 1943 was considered such "a very bad omen" that Guy Gibson left strict instructions for the dog to be buried at about the time the attack was due to begin, presumably in order to placate the canine gods. Humphries, *Living With Heroes*, 9, 34. On a donkey mascot, see Novey, *Cold Blue Sky*, 79. On a crow mascot, see Johnson, *Thunderbolt!*, picture section.

100. John T. Godfrey, *The Look of Eagles* (New York: Random House, 1958), 47, 147. On other canine mascots, see e.g. James Edwin Armstrong, *Escape! An American Airman's Escape from Hitler's Fortress Europe* (Spartanburg, SC: Honoribus, 2002), 38.

101. Thomas Lancashire and Stuart Burbridge, *A Trenchard Brat at War* (Oxford: ISIS, 2010), 87–88.

102. Matenkoski, *Lucky Penny's Tail*, 17, 109; Donald E. Casey, *To Fight For My Country, Sir! Memoirs of a 19 Year Old B-17 Navigator Shot Down in Nazi Germany and Imprisoned in the WWII "Great Escape" Camp* (Chicago: CreateSpace, 2009), 109; see also e.g. Furey, *Going Back*, 135.

103. Harley E. Cannon in Deerfield, *Hell's Angels Newsletter*, vol. 1, 188–189; see also e.g. Hutton and Rooney, *Air Gunner*, 11; Benjamin "Benny" Randolph biography, James F. Justin Museum, accessed September 26, 2015, justinmuseum .com; Rowan T. Thomas, *Born in Battle: Round the World Adventures with the 513th Bombardment Squadron* (Philadelphia: Winston, 1944), 264.

104. Damien Lewis, *The Dog Who Could Fly: The Incredible True Story of a WWII Airman and the Four-Legged Hero Who Flew at His Side* (New York: Atria, 2013).

105. Ross H. Hamilton in *Flight into Yesterday*, comp. L. W. Perry (Victoria, BC: Trafford, 2002), 94.

106. Virginia C. McPartland, *Brothers at Daybreak: World War II B-24 Crew Beats the Odds over Pacific Waters* (Los Gatos, CA: Robertson, 2013), 34.

107. Rolfe, *Hell on Earth*, 136. This is interesting as it runs counter to the standard superstition of redheads as bad news.

108. James Good Brown, *The Mighty Men of the 381st: Heroes All*, 2nd ed. (Salt Lake City: Publishers Press, 1986), 276.

109. A. B. Feuer, *General Chennault's Secret Weapon: The B-24 in China; Based on the Diary and Notes of Captain Elmer E. Haynes* (Westport, CT: Praeger, 1992), 124.

110. Albert F. Pishioneri, *Me, Mom, and World War II* (Bloomington, IN: AuthorHouse, 2008), 334; see also e.g. Novey, *Cold Blue Sky*, 138.

111. Edward Ah Tye interview, AFC/2001/001/93410, VHP; see also e.g. Casey Hasey, *My Bombsight View of WWII* (Bloomington, IN: AuthorHouse, 2011), 145–146, 172.

112. Arthur Aldridge with Mark Ryan, *The Last Torpedo Flyers* (London: Simon & Schuster, 2013), 121.

113. Harley H. Tuck Sr., with Ann I. Clizer, *Angel on My Shoulder: I've Joined the Lucky Bastard Club* (Bloomington, IN: AuthorHouse, 2015), 29.

114. Margerison, *Boys at War*, 42; Ted Hitchcock interview, 30005/4, IWM.

115. Pishioneri, *Me, Mom, and World War II*, 290–291.

116. Stephen E. Ambrose, *The Wild Blue: The Men And Boys Who Flew the B-24s over Germany* (New York: Simon & Schuster, 2001), 173.

117. Schuyler, *Elusive Horizons*, 152–154.

118. Lihou, *Out of the Italian Night*, 29; Lambert, *Night after Night*, 255.

119. Linda Audrey Kantor, *Emil's Story: Memoir of a World War II Bomber Pilot* (Lexington, KY: CreateSpace, 2012), 124; see also e.g. Edwin E. Koch, "G.I. Lore:

Lore of the Fifteenth Air Force," *New York Folklore Quarterly* 9 (1953), 60; McLachlan and Zorn, *Eighth Air Force Bomber Stories*, 76.

120. See e.g. Douglas Ross Arrowsmith interview, 30080/4, IWM; McGuire and Hadley, *Bloody Skies*, 309; Harlo Jones, *Bomber Pilot: A Canadian Youth's War* (St. Catherines, ON: Vanwell, 2001), 171–172; Marshall, *Sky Giants*, 15; Bob Pierson in Nichol and Rennell, *Tail-End Charlies*, 6; Okerstrom, *Final Mission*, 104; Snyder, *General Leemy's Flying Circus*, 160; Gerald Walls interview, UVic, accessed August 4, 2014, uvic.ca.

121. Wainwright, *Tail-End Charlie*, 94.

122. See e.g. Richard C. Baynes, *Replacement Crew: The Training and Combat Experience of a Typical 8th Air Force Replacement Crew in 1944* (Irvine, CA: Baynes, 1993), 65; Geoffrey Hall and Gilbert Haworth in Bowman, *RAF Bomber Command: Reflections of War*, vol. 2, *Live to Die Another Day*, 165, 194; Grace Hall in *We, Also, Were There: A Collection of Recollections of Wartime Women of Bomber Command*, ed. Grace Hall (Braunton, UK: Merlin, 1985), 54, 56; G. Eric Harrison interview, 30002/6, IWM; Harry Le Marchant, Superstitions, RAFBCA, accessed April 26, 2014, rafbombercommand.com; Geoffrey Wellum in William Little, *The Psychic Tourist: A Voyage into the Curious World of Predicting the Future* (London: Icon, 2010), 274; Quinlan, *Corkscrew to Safety*, 147. On snapshots, see e.g. Koch, "G.I. Lore," 60; McGuire and Hadley, *Bloody Skies*, 309; Okerstrom, *Final Mission*, 104; see also e.g. Don Charlwood, *Journeys into Night* (Hawthorn, VIC: Hudson, 1991), 179; Taylor, *Piece of Cake*, 31. On scarves, see e.g. Copeman, *Right-Hand Man*, 36; Ted Peck in Cunningham, *Fighter! Fighter!*, 128; H. H. Spiller, *Ticket to Freedom* (London: Kimber, 1988), 23; Tripp, *Eighth Passenger*, 44; Robert Young Ulrich interview, 27058/6, IWM. On lingerie, see e.g. Gilbert Howarth in Bowman, *RAF Bomber Command: Reflections of War*, vol. 2, *Live to Die Another Day*, 194; Ted Peck in Cunningham, *Fighter! Fighter!*, 128; John Gee, RAFBCA, accessed April 26, 2013, rafbombercommand.com; Rex Kimblin, *How Lucky I Was: 35 Missions in a Lancaster Bomber* (Toowong, QLD: Chambers, 2012), 181; Tripp, *Eighth Passenger*, 76; Wallrich, "Superstition and the Air Force," 12.

123. Robert Fritsch in *The Fight in the Clouds: The Extraordinary Combat Experiences of P-51 Mustang Pilots during World War II*, ed. James P. Busha (Minneapolis: Zenith, 2014), 77.

124. Robert C. Kensett, *A Walk in the Valley* (Burnstown, ON: GSPH, 2003), 53; Ken Lee in Steve Darlow, *Five of the Few: Survivors of the Battle of Britain and the Blitz Tell Their Story* (London: Grub Street, 2006), 23.

125. Bennie E. Hatfield interview, AFC/2001/001/20378, VHP.

126. Harry Yates in Nichol and Rennell, *Tail-End Charlies*, 84.

127. Schneck, *Letters from a World War II Hoosier Pilot*, 101 n. 7.

128. Warren Ellis in Valarie Evans, *We That Are Left . . . Remember: New Brunswickers in the Air Force* (St. John, NB: 250 RCAF [Saint John] Wing Air Force Association of Canada, 2002), 156.

129. Quinlan, *Corkscrew to Safety*, 147.

130. Tripp, *Eighth Passenger*, 30.

131. Jacobs with Bartlett, *Bomb Aimer over Berlin*, 99.

132. Barrett Tillman, *Clash of the Carriers: The True Story of the Marianas Turkey Shoot of World War II* (New York: NAL Caliber, 2005), 214; J. Bryan III and Philip Reed, *Mission Beyond Darkness* (New York: Duell, Sloan and Pearce, 1945), 44.

133. Schneck, *Letters from a World War II Hoosier Pilot*, 101 n. 7.

CHAPTER 4: INCANTATIONS AND RITUALS

1. On Hail Mary, see e.g. John Zima in Roger A. Freeman, *The American Airman in Europe* (Osceola, WI: Motorbooks, 1991), 84; Clayton Kelly Gross, *Live Bait: Memories of an Undefeated Fighter Ace* (Portland, OR: Inkwater, 2006), 188; Alvin E. Kotler as told to Jack Flynn, *We Came to Fight a War: The Story of a B-17 Radio Gunner and His Pilot* (Bennington, VT: Merriam, 2012), 58; Victor Tenger interview, 29957/8, IWM; John Welch in *Dead Engine Kids: World War II Diary of John J. Briol, B-17 Ball Turret Gunner, with Comments from Notes of Other Crew Members*, ed. John F. Welch (Rapid City, SD: Silver Wings Association, 1993), 51. On rosary beads and crossing, see e.g. Anthony Teta and Bob Valliere in Travis L. Ayers, *The Bomber Boys: Heroes Who Flew the B-17s in World War II* (New York: NAL Caliber, 2009), 43, 238, 242; Perry D. Luckett and Charles L. Byler, *Tempered Steel: The Three Wars of Triple Air Force Cross Winner Jim Kasler* (Dulles, VA: Potomac, 2005), 12. On touching rosary beads while saying a Hail Mary, see e.g. Wes Mansir in Joanne Pfannenstiel Emerick, *Courage Before Every Danger, Honor Before All Men: The History of the 31st Bombardment Squadron (H) in World War II . . . In Their Own Words* (Colby, KS: Leroy, 2010), 247.

2. Robert M. Johnson in *Voices of My Comrades: America's Reserve Officers Remember World War II*, ed. Carol Adele Kelly (New York: Fordham University Press, 2007), 162.

3. Harold L. Buell, *Dauntless Helldivers: A Dive-Bomber Pilot's Epic Story of the Carrier Battles* (New York: Orion, 1991), 224.

4. See e.g. Paul Ross in Elizabeth Cassen, *The Last Voices: World War II Veterans of the Air War Speak More Than Half a Century Later* (Seattle: CreateSpace, 2014), 114; G. M. Etherington memories re 14 December 1944, 40th Bomb Group Association, accessed January 19, 2015, 40thbombgroup.org; Robert Gadbois, *Hell-*

cat Tales: A U.S. Navy Fighter Pilot in World War II (Bennington, VT: Merriam, 2005), 90; Doug Johnston, *From Air Gunner to Prisoner of War* (Toronto: Laing McDowell, 1994), 79; Tony Redding, *Flying for Freedom: Life and Death in Bomber Command* (Bristol, UK: Cerberus, 2005), 119.

5. See e.g. Charles Alling, *A Mighty Fortress: Lead Bomber over Europe* (Havertown, PA: Casemate, 2012), 47; Don Charlwood, *Journeys into Night* (Hawthorn, VIC: Hudson, 1991), 185; William C. Crawford in *Hell's Angels Newsletter*, vol. 2, *Silver Anniversary Collection, 1976–2001*, ed. Eddie Deerfield (Palm Harbor, FL: 303rd Bomb Group [H] Association, 2002), 687; Marvel Domke, 446th Bomb Group, accessed October 24, 2014, 446bg.com; Colby LeNeve in James Lee Hutchinson, *The Boys in the B-17* (Bloomington, IN: AuthorHouse, 2011), 123; Bill McCrea, *A Chequer-Board of Nights* (Longton, UK: Compaid, 2003), 113; F. A. Taylor in Martin Middlebrook, *The Nuremberg Raid* (London: Penguin, 1986), 158; Don Keohane in *The 390th Bomb Group in Action: An Anthology*, vol. 1, ed. Wilbert H. Richarz, Richard H. Perry, and William J. Robinson (Tucson, AZ: 390th Memorial Museum Foundation, 1983), 48–49; Jack Spark [Halifax wireless operator, 102 Squadron] in Ian McLachlan, *Eighth Air Force Bomber Stories: A New Selection* (Stroud, UK: Sutton, 2004), 62; Charles N. Stevens, *An Innocent at Polebrook: A Memoir of an 8th Air Force Bombardier* (Bloomington, IN: 1st Books, 2004), 34; see also James T. Hammond, *Tom's War: Flying with the U.S. Eighth Army Air Force in Europe, 1944* (Lincoln, NE: iUniverse, 2007), 30.

6. Daniel B. Jorgensen, *The Service of Chaplains to Army Air Units, 1917–1946* (Washington, DC: Office, Chief of Air Force Chaplains, 1961), 193–194, 289; see e.g. Owen T. Brennan memoir, 6, 2009.0265.0001, NMMEAF; Chester Marshall, *Sky Giants over Japan: A Diary of a B-29 Combat Crew in WWII* (Winona, MN: Apollo, 1984), 55.

7. See e.g. *Flight into Yesterday*, comp. L. W. Perkins (Victoria, BC: Trafford, 2002), vi. On the origins of *For those in peril in the air*, see *The Spectator*, October 30, 1915, 16; Rupert Christiansen, "The Story behind the Hymn," *Telegraph*, September 22, 2007, accessed September 20, 2016, telegraph.co.uk/culture/music/3668061/The-story-behind-the-hymn.html.

8. Laurie Godfrey interview, 27799/2, IWM; Bob Pierson in John Nichol and Tony Rennell, *Tail-End Charlies: The Last Battles of the Bomber War, 1944–45* (London: Viking, 2004), 137.

9. Spencer Dunmore and William Carter, *Reap the Whirlwind: The Untold Story of 6 Group, Canada's Bomber Force of World War II* (Toronto: McClelland & Stewart, 1991), 190.

10. Johnston, *From Air Gunner to Prisoner of War*, 204.

11. Father Bartholomew Adler, Memories *re* 5 June 1944, 40th Bomb Group Association, accessed January 19, 2015, 40thbombgroup.org; see also e.g. James Good Brown, *The Mighty Men of the 381st: Heroes All*, 2nd ed. (Salt Lake City: Publishers Press, 1986), 179–180, 443.

12. Robert V. Brulle, *Angels Zero: P-47 Close Air Support in Europe* (Washington, DC: Smithsonian, 2000), 132.

13. Weston O. Jayne interview TS, 7, Oral History Collection, NMMEAF.

14. Frank J. Guest interview TS, 11, Oral History Collection, NMMEAF.

15. Jay A. Stout, *Unsung Eagles: True Stories of America's Citizen Airmen in the Skies of World War II* (Philadelphia: Casemate, 2013), 236.

16. Beirne Lay Jr., *Presumed Dead: The Survival of a Bomb Group Commander* (New York: Dodd, Mead, 1980), 22.

17. Jesse Richard Pitts, *Return to Base: Memoirs of a B-17 Copilot, Kimbolton, England, 1943–1944* (Charlottesville, VA: Howell, 2004), 75.

18. Edwin E. Koch, "G.I. Lore: Lore of the Fifteenth Air Force," *New York Folklore Quarterly* (1953), 60; see e.g. Edward J. Giering, *B-17 Bomber Crew Diary*, ed. Abigail T. Siddall (Manhattan, KS: Sunflower University Press, 1985), 55; Carol Edgemon Hipperson, *The Belly Gunner* (Brookfield, CT: Twenty-First Century, 1991), 58.

19. John Steinbeck, *Once There Was a War* (New York: Viking, 1958), 31; see also e.g. Robert Capen interview, AFC/2001/001/09225, VHP.

20. Jim Auton, *RAF Liberator over the Eastern Front: A Bomb Aimer's Second World War and Cold War Story* (Barnsley, UK: Pen & Sword Aviation, 2008), 92. On not making up one's bed, see e.g. Doug Penny in Dunmore and Carter, *Reap the Whirlwind*, 191–192.

21. Russell Margerison, *Boys at War* (Bolton, UK: Ross Anderson, 1986), 42.

22. Bill Carroll in Arthur Aldridge with Mark Ryan, *The Last Torpedo Flyers* (London: Simon & Schuster, 2013), 121.

23. Edna Skeen in *We, Also, Were There: A Collection of Recollections of Wartime Women of Bomber Command*, ed. Grace Hall (Braunton, UK: Merlin, 1985), 53.

24. Robert Morgan with Ron Powers, *The Man Who Flew the* Memphis Belle: *Memoir of a WWII Bomber Pilot* (New York: Dutton, 2001), 207, 134–135; see also e.g. Keith W. Mason, *My War in Italy: On the Ground and in Flight with the 15th Air Force* (Columbia: University of Missouri Press, 2016), 212; D. A. Lande, *From Somewhere in England* (Osceola, WI: Motorbooks, 1990), 32.

25. Les Triplett in Fiske Hanley, *History of the 504th Bomb Group (VH) in World War II* (Enfield, CT: 504th Bomb Group Association, 1992), 276; see also e.g. Van R. Parker, *Dear Folks* (Memphis, TN: Global, 1989), 219.

26. Alexander Ingram interview TS, 12, Oral History Collection, NMMEAF.

27. David Hastings interview TS, 3, Oral History Collection, NMMEAF.

28. Don Charlwood, *Journeys into Night* (Hawthorn, VIC: Hudson, 1991), 178.

29. Victor Tempest, *Near the Sun: The Impressions of a Medical Officer of Bomber Command* (Brighton, UK: Crabtree, 1946), 34–35.

30. Ron Mayhill, *Bombs on Target: A Compelling Eyewitness Account of Bomber Command Operations* (Sparkford, UK: Patrick Stephens, 1991), 46; Maurice Flower in James Taylor and Martin Davidson, *Bomber Crew* (London: Hodder & Stoughton, 2004), 137.

31. Ken Adam, chapter 21, Web of Stories, accessed February 25, 2014, webof stories.com; see James Holland, *Twenty-One: Coming of Age in the Second World War* (London: HarperCollins, 2006), 182.

32. Alvin E. Kotler as told to Jack Flynn, *We Came to Fight a War: The Story of a B-17 Radio Gunner and His Pilot* (Bennington, VT: Merriam, 2012), 58.

33. Nathan Lazenby, Lads Together, 9, X003–2966, RAFM.

34. Quentin Aanenson, A Fighter Pilot's Story, 5, 2012.0055.0001, NMMEAF.

35. Arnold Ralph Easton interview, 12562/1, IWM; John Taylor interview, 30416/7, IWM.

36. Charlwood, *Journeys into Night*, 198.

37. Ian McLachlan and Russell J. Zorn, *Eighth Air Force Bomber Stories: Eye-Witness Accounts from American Airmen and British Civilians of the Perils of War* (Sparkford, UK: Patrick Stephens, 1991), 55.

38. Arthur Minnet in Pat Cunningham, *The Fear in the Sky: Vivid Memories of Operational Aircrew in World War II* (Barnsley, UK: Pen & Sword Aviation, 2012), 198.

39. John W. Gee, *Wingspan: The Recollections of a Bomber Pilot* (Wellesbourne, UK: Self-Publishing Association, 1988), 165; see Randall L. Rasmussen, *Hell's Belle: From a B-17 to Stalag 17B* (Santa Fe, NM: Sunstone, 2003), 40; see also Grover C. Hall, *1000 Destroyed: The Life and Times of the 4th Fighter Group* (Fallbrook, CA: Aero, 1978), 72.

40. See e.g. Geoff D. Copeman, *Right-Hand Man: A Flight Engineer's Story* (Baldock, UK: Euro Slug, 1996), 37; Walter Clapham, *Night Be My Witness* (London: Jonathan Cape, 1952), 195.

41. Al Avant in Dunmore and Carter, *Reap the Whirlwind*, 191.

42. Ivor Turley in Martin W. Bowman, *RAF Bomber Command: Reflections of War*, vol. 5, *Armageddon* (Barnsley, UK: Pen & Sword Aviation, 2013), 42.

43. Dave Fellows in *Bomber Command*, dir. Mai Liddell (ITV, 2012).

44. Robert C. Kensett, *A Walk in the Valley* (Burnstown, ON: GSPH, 2003), 58.

45. See Vernon T. Wilkes quoted in Vanessa Chambers, "Fighting Chance: War, Popular Belief and British Society, 1900–1951," PhD diss., University of London, 2007, 79–80; Roger A. Freeman, *The British Airman* (London: Arms & Armour, 1989), 89.

46. Mel Rolfe, *Hell on Earth: Dramatic First Hand Accounts of Bomber Command at War* (London: Grub Street, 1999), 79.

47. Don Charlwood, *No Moon Tonight* (Manchester, UK: Crécy, 2000), 172; Don Charlwood interview TS, 23, S00568, AWM.

48. Truman Smith, *The Wrong Stuff: The Adventures and Misadventures of an 8th Air Force Aviator* (Norman: University of Oklahoma Press, 2002), 58–59.

49. Quentin Aanenson, A Fighter Pilot's Story, 5, 2012.0055.0001, NMMEAF.

50. William Zauner interview, EAA, accessed October 10, 2014, eaa.org.

51. Hall, *1000 Destroyed*, 206–207.

52. See e.g. Douglas Ross Arrowsmith interview, 30080/4, IWM; George Bilton interview, 13444/2, IWM; Jack Currie, *Lancaster Target: The Story of a Crew Who Flew from Wickenby* (London: Goodhall, 1981), 156; John Golley, *The Day of the Typhoon: Flying with the RAF Tankbusters in Normandy* (Wellingborough, UK: Patrick Stephens, 1986), 42; J. Douglas Harvey, *Boys, Bombs and Brussels Sprouts: A Knees-Up, Wheels-Up Chronicle of WWII* (Toronto: McClelland & Stewart, 1981), 53; Maurice G. Lihou, *Out of the Italian Night: Wellington Bomber Operations 1944–45* (Shrewsbury, UK: Airlife, 2000), 28; Gerald W. Johnson with John C. McClure and Charlotte S. McClure, *Called to Command: A World War II Fighter Ace's Adventurous Journey* (Paducah, KY: Turner, 1996), 32; R. C. Pointer, Target Koln 2 Feb 1943, A2051335, BBC WW2 People's War, accessed January 19, 2013, bbc.co.uk/history/ww2peopleswar/stories/35/a2051335.shtml; Fred Rochlin, *Old Man in a Baseball Cap: A Memoir of World War II* (New York: HarperCollins, 1999), 48; Walter R. Thompson, *Lancaster to Berlin* (Southside, UK: Goodall, 1997), 105; Gerald Walls interview, UVic, accessed August 4, 2015, uvic.ca.

53. See Bill Bailey, *Alone I Fly* (Barnsley, UK: Pen & Sword Aviation, 2009), 21; Derek Lovell in Stephen Darlow, *Victory Fighters: The Veterans' Story: Winning the Battle for Supremacy in the Skies over Western Europe, 1941–1945* (London: Grub Street, 2005), 203; K. B. McGlashan, *Down to Earth: A Fighter Pilot's Experiences of Surviving Dunkirk, the Battle of Britain, Dieppe and D-Day* (London: Grub Street, 2007), 48; Doug Booth in Wayne Ralph, *Aces, Warriors and Wingmen: Firsthand Accounts of Canada's Fighter Pilots in the Second World War* (Mississauga, ON: Wiley, 2005), 106; Ken Rees with Karen Arrandale, *Lie in the Dark and Listen: The Remarkable Exploits of a WWII Bomber Pilot and Great Escaper* (London: Grub Street, 2004), 51; Gordon Thorburn, *Bombers First and Last* (London: Robson,

2006), 96; Graham White, *"The Long Road to the Sky": Night Fighter over Germany* (Barnsley, UK: Pen & Sword Aviation, 2006), 98.

54. On the "nervous pee," see e.g. Frederick William Brown, Get Fell In!, 49, RAF 017, LC; Neal B. Dillon, *A Dying Breed: The True Story of a World War II Air Combat Crew's Courage, Camaraderie, Faith, and Spirit* (Grants Pass, OR: Hellgate, 2000), 59; David Hutchens, Schweinfurt and the Hutchens Crew, 1, 381st Bomb Group, accessed October 31, 2014, 381st.org; George G. Loving, *Woodbine Red Leader: A P-51 Mustang Ace in the Mediterranean Theater* (New York: Presidio, 2003), 187; Les Morrison, *Of Luck and War: From Squeegee Kid to Bomber Pilot in World War II* (Burnstown, ON: GSPH, 1999), 83; Jack Watts, *Nickels and Nightingales* (Burnstown, ON: GSPH, 1995), 122.

55. Ron Mayhill, *Bombs on Target: A Compelling Eye-Witness Account of Bomber Command Operations* (Sparkford, UK: Patrick Stephens, 1991), 46.

56. On the desire to avoid the primitive toilet facilities with which heavy bombers were equipped, see e.g. Ron James in Theo Boiten, *Nachtjagd: The Night Fighter versus Bomber War over the Third Reich, 1939–1945* (Marlborough, UK: Crowood, 1997), 111; James Arthur Davies, *A Leap in the Dark: A Welsh Airman's Adventures in Occupied Europe* (London: Leo Cooper, 1994), 20; George Johnson, *The Last British Dambuster* (London: Ebury, 2014), 20; Francis McGovern interview, 17825/2, IWM; J. Ralph Wood, My Lucky Number Was 77, 12, B4311, RAFM. On using the wheel assembly as a convenient cover, see e.g. Stanley Tomlinson in Freeman, *British Airman*, 82; Francis McGovern interview, 17825/4, IWM; Stuart J. Wright, *An Emotional Gauntlet: From Life in Peacetime America to the War in European Skies* (Madison: University of Wisconsin Press, 2004), 253; Royan Yule, *On a Wing and a Prayer* (Derby, UK: Derby Books, 2012), 108.

57. On urinating away from the aircraft, see e.g. R. L. Austen, *High Adventure—Navigator at War* (Chichester, UK: Barry Rose, 1989), 74; Dean M. Bloyd, *Flak at 12 O'Clock: A Teenage Kansas Farm Boy's Experiences That Led to His Becoming a B-17 Co-Pilot in the 8th Air Force during the Final Months of World War II* (San Jose, CA: Writers Club, 2001), 91; Gene T. Carson, *Wing Ding* (Bloomington, IN: Xlibris, 2000), 60; Jones, *Bomber Pilot*, 171; Earle M. Nelson, *If Winter Comes* (Lovely Banks, VIC: Nelson, 1989), 42; Arthur Carlton Smith in Geoffrey P. Jones, *Raider: The Halifax and Its Flyers* (London: Kimber, 1978), 159; Campbell Muirhead, *Diary of a Bomb Aimer: Training in America and Flying with 12 Squadron in WWII*, ed. Philip Swan (Barnsley, UK: Pen & Sword Aviation, 2009), 151; Robert L. Sandstedt, *My B-29 Story* (St. Louis, MO: Sandstedt, 2003), 352; Arthur C. Smith, *Halifax Crew: The Story of a Wartime Bomber Crew* (Stevenage, UK: Carlton, 1983), 18; Kenneth S. Tucker and Wanda Tucker Goodwin, *Last Roll*

Call (Southport, FL: Priority, 2009), 90; Arthur White, *Bread and Butter Bomber Boys* (Upton on Severn, UK: Square One, 1995), 90. On carrying pee tins or bottles, see e.g. Gee, *Wingspan*, 64; Bill Grierson, *We Band of Brothers* (Hailsham, UK: J&KH, 1997), 101; Edward B. Schlesinger memoir, 31, 2010.0206.0001, NMMEAF; Watts, *Nickels and Nightingales*, 132.

58. See e.g. Charlwood, *Journeys into Night*, 183; George Harsh, *Lonesome Road* (New York: Norton, 1971), 145; Gordon James Hurley, *Corkscrew Starboard* (York, UK: Field House, 2009), 84; Peter Jacobs with Les Bartlett, *Bomb Aimer over Berlin: The Wartime Memoirs of Les Bartlett* (Barnsley, UK: Pen & Sword Aviation, 2007), 99; H. J. Spiller, *Ticket to Freedom* (London: Kimber, 1988), 25; Geoffrey Williams, *Flying Backwards: Memoirs of a Rear Gunner* (Loftus, NSW: Publishing Services, 2001), 25.

59. Peter Russell, *Flying in Defiance of the Reich: A Lancaster Pilot's Rites of Passage* (Barnsley, UK: Pen & Sword Aviation, 2007), 157; see also e.g. Kenneth Lane Glemby as told to Norman Auslander, *"Flyboy": Memoirs of a P-47 Pilot* (Seattle: CreateSpace, 2015), 25; Sidney Munns, *As Luck Would Have It: Reminiscences of a Retired RAF Observer/Navigator* (Northampton, UK: Friday File, 1992), 37; Wallace McIntosh in Mel Rolfe, *Gunning for the Enemy: Wallace McIntosh* (London: Grub Street, 2001), 46; Ken Trent, *Bomb Doors Open: From East End Boy to Lancaster Bomber Pilot with 617 "Dambusters" Squadron* (St. Mary, UK: Seeker, 2016), 107; Ronnie Waite, *Death or Decoration* (Cowden, UK: Newton, 1991), 101.

60. John Robbins in Joseph A. Springer, *Inferno: The Life and Death Struggle of the USS* Franklin *in World War II* (Minneapolis: Zenith, 2011), 148.

61. See e.g. Ben Cecil interview, 30621/2, IWM; Alfred Watson interview, 23198/10, IWM.

62. See e.g. Bruce M. Hood, *The Science of Superstition: How the Developing Brain Creates Supernatural Beliefs* (New York: HarperOne, 2009), 9–14; Michael Shermer, *The Believing Brain* (New York: Times Books, 2011), 60.

63. See B. F. Skinner, "Superstition in the Pigeon," *Journal of Experimental Psychology* 38 (1948): 168–172; Kiochi Ono, "Superstitious Behavior in Humans," *Journal of the Experimental Analysis of Behavior* 47 (1987): 261–271.

64. Kenneth Douglas Gray interview TS, 28, S00539, AWM; see also John H. Biddle interview, AFC/2001/001/19930, VHP; Margerison, *Boys at War*, 42; Wright, *An Emotional Gauntlet*, 253.

65. See e.g. Martin W. Bowman, *RAF Bomber Command: Reflections of War*, vol. 3, *Battleground Berlin* (Barnsley, UK: Pen & Sword Aviation, 2012), 106: Martin W. Bowman, *Scramble: Memories of the RAF in the Second World War* (Stroud, UK: Tempus, 2006), 90; Dan Brennan in Irv Broughton, *Hanger Talk: Inter-*

views with Fliers, 1920s–1990s (Cheney: Eastern Washington University Press, 1998), 148; George Ellis Parkinson in Cunningham, *Fear in the Sky*, 50; Kenneth Douglas Gray interview TS, 29, S00539, AWM; Max Hastings, *Bomber Command* (London: Michael Joseph, 1979), 160; Jacobs and Bartlett, *Bomb Aimer over Berlin*, 98–99.

66. Richard L. Feldman in Rade Patrovi Kent, *Is It Just Poor Memory . . . Or Just One More Treason?* (Lausanne: L'Age d'Homme, 1998), 17.

67. See e.g. Leslie E. Traughber in *Missions Remembered: The Men of the Middle Tennessee WWII Fighter Pilots Association*, ed. John K. Breast (Brentwood, TN: JM Productions, 1995), 132; Harvey, *Boys, Bombs*, 53; William James Kelbrick interview, 17729/4, IWM; Margerison, *Boys at War*, 42; Rochlin, *Old Man in a Baseball Cap*, 48; Barrett Tillman, *Clash of the Carriers: The True Story of the Marianas Turkey Shoot of World War II* (New York: NAL Caliber, 2005), 214.

68. Len Greenham in Jones, *Raider*, 199.

69. Robert B. Parke in Stuart Leuthner and Oliver Jensen, *High Honor: Recollections by Men and Women of World War II Aviation* (Washington, DC: Smithsonian, 1989), 139.

70. Bill Crump in *Forever Remembered: The Fliers of World War II*, ed. Irv Broughton (Spokane: Eastern Washington University Press, 2001), 568.

71. Thompson, *Lancaster to Berlin*, 104.

72. David A. McCarthy, *Fear No More: A B-17 Navigator's Journey* (Pittsburgh: Cottage Wordsmiths, 1991), 145.

73. Lihou, *Out of the Italian Night*, 28; see also e.g. Rolfe, *Hell on Earth*, 161; Dunmore and Carter, *Reap the Whirlwind*, 191.

74. Elmer Bendiner, *The Fall of Fortresses: A Personal Account of the Most Daring—and Deadly—American Air Battles of World War II* (New York: Putnam's, 1980), 11.

75. Ron Smith, *Rear Gunner Pathfinders* (Manchester, UK: Crécy, 1987), 22.

76. Rochlin, *Old Man in a Baseball Cap*, 484–489.

77. McCarthy, *Fear No More*, 145–146.

78. Jack Dickenson, *The Time of My Life, 1940–1945: Life with 218 and 623 Squadrons* (Preston, UK: Compaid, 1999), 95.

79. Eric Silbert, *Dinkum Mishpochah* (Perth, WA: Artlook, 1981), 171.

80. Harley H. Tuck with Ann I. Clizer, *Angel on My Shoulder: I've Joined the Lucky Bastard Club* (Bloomington, IN: AuthorHouse, 2015), 37.

81. Fred Koger, *Countdown!* (Chapel Hill, NC: Algonquin, 1990), 33.

82. Murray Peden, *A Thousand Shall Fall: A Pilot for 214* (Stittsville, ON: Canada's Wings, 1979), 414.

83. Peter Bond in *Into the Wind*, dir. Steven Hatton (Electric Egg, 2011).

84. Irving Schreiber, *The War Years: My Participation in the Second World War* (Rockville, MD: Schreiber, 2012), 171–172.

85. Brian Stoker, *If the Flak Doesn't Get You the Fighters Will* (Hailsham, UK: J&KH, 1995), 105.

86. Robert W. Boydston interview, AFC/2001/001/55643, VHP.

87. S. H. Johnson, *It's Never Dark above the Clouds* (Trigg, WA: Johnson, 1994), 71–72.

88. Ben Smith Jr., *Chick's Crew: A Tale of the Eighth Air Force*, 2nd ed. (Tallahassee, FL: Rose, 1983), 117.

89. Lloyd Nelson in Lande, *From Somewhere in England*, 32.

90. Tom Sawyer, *Only Owls and Bloody Fools Fly at Night* (London: Kimber, 1982), 55.

CHAPTER 5: JINXES AND JONAHS

1. See John Comer, *Combat Crew: A True Story of Flying and Fighting in World War II* (New York: Murrow, 1988), 95.

2. Earl Snyder, *General Leemy's Flying Circus: A Navigator's Story of the 20th Air Force in World War II* (New York: Exposition, 1955), 160.

3. Alfred Asch with David Asch, *The Whole Nine Yards . . . and Then Some* (Franklin, TN: Don Wise, 2013), 144; William C. Atkinson, *The Jolly Roger: An Airman's Tale of Survival in World War II* (Indianapolis: Dog Ear, 2015), 130; see also e.g. Snyder, *General Leemy's Flying Circus*, 160.

4. William J. Fili, *Passage to Valhalla: The Human Side of Aerial Combat over Nazi Occupied Europe* (Media, PA: Filcon, 1991), 125.

5. Maurice G. Lihou, *Out of the Italian Night: Wellington Bomber Operations 1944–45* (Shrewsbury, UK: Airlife, 2000), 112; see e.g. Mike Henry, *Air Gunner* (London: Foulis, 1964), 50; though see also Terence O'Brien, *Chasing after Danger: A Combat Pilot's War over Europe and the Far East, 1939–42* (London: Collins, 1990), 69.

6. Charles Lamb, *To War in a Stringbag* (Garden City, NY: Doubleday, 1980), 114–115.

7. N. J. N. Hockaday, One Little Man Went to War, 160, 4183, IWM.

8. See Harry H. Crosby, *A Wing and a Prayer: The "Bloody 100th" Bomb Group of the U.S. Eighth Air Force in Action over Europe in World War II* (San Jose, CA: iUniverse, 2000), 135; Richard Fogg and Janet Fogg, *Fogg in the Cockpit: Howard Fogg, Master Railroad Artist, World War II Fighter Pilot: Wartime Diaries, October 1943 to September 1944* (Philadelphia: Casemate, 2011), 315; see also John Nichol

and Tony Rennell, *Tail-End Charlies: The Last Battles of the Bomber War, 1944–45* (London: Viking, 2004), 6.

9. See e.g. E. A. W. Smith, *Spitfire Diary: The Boys of One-Two-Seven* (London: Kimber, 1988), 92; Archie Hall in *We, Also, Were There: A Collection of Recollections of Wartime Women of Bomber Command*, ed. Grace Hall (Braunton, UK: Merlin, 1985), 33.

10. Morris Markey, *Well Done! An Aircraft Carrier in Battle Action* (New York: Appleton-Century, 1945), 45.

11. Ellis M. Woodward, *Flying School: Combat Hell* (Baltimore: American Literary Press, 1998), 126–127.

12. George Webster, *The Savage Sky: Life and Death in a Bomber over Germany in 1944* (Mechanicsburg, PA: Stackpole, 2007), 219.

13. Mel Rolfe, *Gunning for the Enemy: Wallace McIntosh* (London: Grub Street, 2003), 54.

14. See e.g. Geoffrey P. Dawson, Wartime Memoirs, 37, 16764, IWM.

15. Keith C. Schuyler, *Elusive Horizons* (Cranbury, NJ: Barnes, 1969), 145; see e.g. Robert B. Parke in Stuart Leuthner and Oliver Jensen, *High Honor: Recollections by Men and Women of World War II Aviation* (Washington, DC: Smithsonian, 1989), 139–140; Joe Gaffney in C. C. Neal, *Gentlemen from Hell: Men of the 487th Bomb Group* (Paducah, KY: Turner, 2005), 83–84; Irving Schreiber, *The War Years: My Participation in the Second World War* (Rockville, MD: Schreiber, 2012), 172–173. It might also be thought that a more anonymous appearance might make enemy fighters less likely to be attracted to a particular plane. See e.g. Comer, *Combat Crew*, 90; Stuart J. Wright, *An Emotional Gauntlet: From Life in Peacetime America to the War in European Skies* (Madison: University of Wisconsin Press, 2004), 254.

16. Gene Carson, *Wing Ding* (Bloomington, IN: Xlibris, 2000), 64, 84, 113.

17. Arnold Willis interview, EAA, accessed October 10, 2014, eaavideo.org.

18. This was a common superstition in the prewar aviation community: see Kenneth Brown Collings, "Pilots Are Superstitious," *Flying and Popular Aviation*, October 1941, 25–26.

19. Edward Coates, *Lone Evader: The Escape from France of RAAF Sergeant Pilot Ted Coates, 1942–1943* (Loftus, NSW: Australian Military History Publications, 1995), 2; see also e.g. Pip Beck, *Keeping Watch: A WAAF in Bomber Command* (Manchester, UK: Crécy, 2004), 119–120; Spencer Dunmore and William Carter, *Reap the Whirlwind: The Untold Story of 6 Group, Canada's Bomber Force of World War II* (Toronto: McClelland & Stewart, 1991), 192; Doug Hudson interview, UVic, accessed August 3, 2014, uvic.ca; Doug Johnston, *From Air Gunner to*

Prisoner of War (Toronto: Laing McDowell, 1994), 210; Rex Kimblin, *How Lucky I Was: 35 Missions in a Lancaster Bomber* (Toowong, QLD: Chambers, 2012), 224.

20. Robert Willis Petty in Pat Cunningham, *Fighter! Fighter! Corkscrew Port!* (Barnsley, UK: Pen & Sword Aviation, 2012), 227; see also e.g. Steve Masters in Stephen Darlow, *D-Day Bombers: The Veterans' Story: RAF Bomber Command and the U.S. Eighth Air Force Support to the Normandy Invasion 1944* (London: Grub Street, 2004), 192–193.

21. Mere Handful of Pilots Alive, AP, October 13, 1945, Aces of WW2, accessed October 12, 2015, acesofww2.com/Canada/aces/turner.htm.

22. See Grover C. Hall, *1000 Destroyed: The Life and Times of the 4th Fighter Group* (Fallbrook, CA: Aero, 1978), 75; Barrett Tillman, "Omens, Augurs, Jinxes and Other Aviation Superstitions," *Air Progress*, April 1971, 27.

23. Dave Toomey in Mike Klesius, "One More for the Checklist," 2, *Air & Space Magazine*, accessed October 12, 2014, airspacemag.com.

24. Schreiber, *War Years*, 172.

25. John Hoare, *Tumult in the Clouds: A Story of the Fleet Air Arm* (London: Michael Joseph, 1976), 194.

26. Brooke Hindle, *Lucky Lady and the Navy Mystique: The Chenango in WW II* (New York: Vantage, 1991), 154.

27. See e.g. Bob Vallerie in Travis L. Ayers, *The Bomber Boys: Heroes Who Flew the B-17s in World War II* (New York: NAL Caliber, 2009), 236. The legend—entirely fictitious—was that a B-17 from the group under attack one day from fighters had lowered its landing gear, a sign of surrender, but had then gone on to shoot down the escorting German planes, causing the enemy subsequently to seek out bombers with the group's tail markings for special attention. See e.g. Warren G. Hall, *Big War, Little People* (El Paso, TX: Helm, 2009), 119; Jim Capraro in *388th Anthology*, vol. 1, *Tales of the 388th Bombardment Group (H) 1942–45*, ed. Janet Pack and Richard Singer (San Jose, CA: Writer's Club, 2001), 56–57; Charles M. Stevens, *An Innocent at Polebrook: A Memoir of an 8th Air Force Bombardier* (Bloomington, IN: 1st Books, 2004), 112. The exact same legend was spread concerning one Liberator with the 450th Bomb Group in Italy and another with the 492nd Bomb Group in England. See Vincent F. Fagan, *Liberator Pilot: The Cottontails' Battle for Oil* (Carlsbad, CA: California Aero, 1992), 27–28; Gerald M. French, *Liberal Lady I-IV: Reflections of a Military Pilot* (Seattle: BookSurge, 2007), 28–29; Robert H. Tays Jr., Country Boy Combat Bomber Pilot, 29, 2010.0132.0001, NMMEAF.

28. See John W. McClane in Martin W. Bowman, *Echoes of England: The 8th Air Force in World War II* (Stroud, UK: Tempus, 2006), 154; James J. Mahoney and Brian H. Mahoney, *Reluctant Witness: Memoirs from the Last Year of the Eu-*

ropean Airwar, 1944–45 (Victoria, BC: Trafford, 2001), 240–241; John J. Taylor interview TS, 6, Oral History Collection, NMMEAF.

29. Ben Smith Jr., *Chick's Crew: A Tale of the Eighth Air Force*, 2nd ed. (Tallahassee, FL: Rose, 1983), 135; see also Bob Hutton and Andy Rooney, *Air Gunner* (New York: Farrar & Rinehart, 1944), 84–85.

30. Chester Marshall, *Sky Giants over Japan: A Diary of a B-29 Combat Crew in WWII* (Winona, MN: Apollo, 1984), 179.

31. Bob Valliere in Ayers, *Bomber Boys*, 241.

32. Geoff Maddern in Don Charlwood, *Journeys into Night* (Hawthorn, VIC: Hudson, 1991), 119; see also John Harding, *The Dancin' Navigator* (Guelph, ON: Asterisk, 1988), 26.

33. Robert L. Masters interview, UVic, accessed July 14, 2014, uvic.ca.

34. Campbell Muirhead, *Diary of a Bomb Aimer: Training in America and Flying with 12 Squadron in WWII*, ed. Philip Swan (Barnsley, UK: Pen & Sword Aviation, 2009), 41.

35. John Rowland, *Return Flights in War and Peace* (Barnsley, UK: Pen & Sword Aviation, 2011), 89.

36. Jerrold Morris, *Canadian Artists and Airmen, 1940–45: A Wartime Memoir* (Toronto: Morris Gallery, 1974), 189.

37. Fletcher Adams diary, February 26, 1944, in Joey Maddox, *Bleeding Sky: The Story of Captain Fletcher E. Adams and the 357th Fighter Group* (Bloomington, IN: Xlibris, 2009), 191.

38. Jack Goodman in Steve Darlow, *Five of the Many: Survivors of the Bomber Command Offensive from the Battle of Britain to Victory Tell Their Stories* (Oxford: ISIS, 2009), 100; see also e.g. H. E. Bates, *Something in the Air: Comprising* The Greatest People in the World *and* How Sleep the Brave (London: Cape, 1944), 56.

39. Charlwood, *Journeys into Night*, 167.

40. Wright Lee, *Not as Briefed: Memoirs of a B-24 Navigator/Prisoner of War, 1943–1945* (Spartanburg, SC: Honoribus, 1995), 83.

41. See James Good Brown, *The Mighty Men of the 381st: Heroes All*, 2nd ed. (Salt Lake City: Publishers Press, 1986), 188; Comer, *Combat Crew*, 95, 107, 132; see also e.g. James M. Davis, *In Hostile Skies: An American B-24 Pilot in World War II*, ed. David L. Snead (Denton: University of North Texas Press, 2006), 112; Bradford P. Wilson, *Everyday P.O.W.: A Rural California Boy's Story of Going to War* (Pollock Pines, CA: Storyteller, 2010), 98, 109.

42. Red Cliburn in John R. McCrary and David E. Scherman, *First of the Many: A Journal of Action with the Men of the Eighth Air Force* (New York: Simon & Schuster, 1944), 20.

43. Kevin Herbert, *Maximum Effort: The B-29's against Japan* (Manhattan, KS: Sunflower University Press, 1983), 51.

44. See Bill Wallrich, "Superstition and the Air Force," *Western Folklore* 19 (1960), 15.

45. See e.g. Robert E. Wannop, *Chocks Away* (Worcester, UK: Square One, 1989), 82.

46. See e.g. Max Hastings, *Bomber Command* (London: Michael Joseph, 1979), 211; Thomas G. Quinlan, *Corkscrew to Safety: A Tail-Gunner's Tour with 103 Squadron RAF 1944/5* (Bognor, UK: Woodfield, 2011), 34, 99; Edwin Watson in Kevin Wilson, *Journey's End: Bomber Command's Battle from Arnhem to Dresden and Beyond* (London: Weidenfeld & Nicolson, 2010), 244; Harry Yates, *Luck and a Lancaster: Chance and Survival in World War II* (Shrewsbury, UK: Airlife, 1999), 9–10, 12, 82, 102–103, 105, 112, 113.

47. George L. Loving, *Woodbine Red Leader: A P-51 Mustang Ace in the Mediterranean Theater* (New York: Presidio, 2003), 118; see also e.g. Theodore Michael Banta, *Vignettes of a B-17 Combat Crew* (New York: Banta, 1997), 71–76.

48. B. W. Martin, *War Memoirs of an Engineer Officer in Bomber Command* (Hailsham, UK: J&KH, 1998), 66–67.

49. Wayne E. Dorsett interview TS, 11, Oral History Collection, NMMEAF.

50. See e.g. Kimblin, *How Lucky I Was*, 197–198.

51. See e.g. John W. Carson narrative, James F. Justin Museum, accessed September 26, 2015, justinmuseum.com; Crosby, *Wing and a Prayer*, 35; Emmett G. MacKenzie, *Ten Men, a "Flying Boxcar," and a War: A Journal of B-24 Crew 323, 1944 to 1945* (New York: iUniverse, 2005), 29–31.

52. See Brian Johnson and H. I. Cozens, *Bombers: The Weapon of Total War* (London: Thames Metheun, 1984), 226; Tim Hamilton, *The Life and Times of Pilot Officer Prune: Being the Official Story of Tee Emm* (London: HMSO, 1991), 77–78.

53. Doug Mourton, *Lucky Doug: Memoirs of the RAF 1937–1946 and After* (Edinburgh: Pentland, 1999), 81.

54. Peter Russell, *Flying in Defiance of the Reich: A Lancaster Pilot's Rites of Passage* (Barnsley, UK: Pen & Sword Aviation, 2007), 135.

55. James M. Ross, "Our Turn Next," ch. 2, f. 7, B24.NET, accessed October 24, 2014, b24.net/stories/ross.htm#tour; see also e.g. Harry D. George and Harry D. George Jr., *Georgio Italiano: An American B-24 Pilot's Unlikely Tuscan Adventure* (Victoria, BC: Trafford, 2000), 117; Onan A. Hill in *Voices of My Comrades: America's Reserve Officers Remember World War II*, ed. Carol Adele Kelly (New York: Fordham University Press, 2007), 339.

56. Robert V. Brulle, *Angels Zero: P-47 Close Air Support in Europe* (Washington, DC: Smithsonian, 2000), 54.

57. Ibid.

58. Alan McGregor Peart, *From North Africa to the Arakan: The Engrossing Memoir of a Spitfire Ace* (London: Grub Street, 2008), 139.

59. Charles Richards, *The Second Was First* (Bend, OR: Maverick, 1999), 324; see also e.g. Walter F. Hughes, *A Bomber Pilot in WWII: From Farm Boy to Pilot: 35 Missions in a B-24 Liberator Bomber* (Fremont, CA: Hughes, 1994), 56; Leslie Mann, *And Some Fell on Stony Ground: A Day in the Life of an RAF Bomber Pilot* (London: Icon, 2014), 28.

60. Forrest S. Clark in Bowman, *Echoes of England*, 154.

61. Carson, *Wing Ding*, 149–152.

62. Haley Aycock in McCrary and Sherman, *First of the Many*, 27.

63. See e.g. S. H. Johnson, *It's Never Dark above the Clouds* (Trigg, WA: Johnson, 1994), 157; Douglas A. Robinson, *Life Is a Great Adventure* (London: Janus, 1997), 44; Tom Sawyer, *Only Owls and Bloody Fools Fly at Night* (London: Kimber, 1982), 19; Richard Stowers, *Wellingtons over the Med: A Kiwi Pilot's Story from the Mediterranean* (Hamilton, NZ: Stowers, 2012), 68.

64. Royan Yule, *On a Wing and a Prayer* (Derby, UK: Derby Books, 2012), 57.

65. Kenneth K. Blyth, *Cradle Crew: Royal Canadian Air Force World War II* (Manhattan, KS: Sunflower University Press, 1997), 92.

66. Frank Broome, *Dead Before Dawn: A Heavy Bomber Tail-gunner in World War II* (Barnsley, UK: Pen & Sword Aviation, 2008), 271; see also, with reference to second dickeys in 75 Squadron, N. J. N. Hockaday, One Little Man Went to War, 147, 4183, IWM.

67. Wallrich, "Superstition and the Air Force," 14. See also, though, Sid Golden, Just Three Came Back, 2, 388th Bomb Group, accessed November 8, 2014, 388thbg.org.

68. Robert Morgan with Ron Powers, *The Man Who Flew the* Memphis Belle (New York: Dutton, 2001), 174–175.

69. See James F. Goodrich in Charles W. Richards, *The Second Was First: The Lives and Times of the Second Bombardment Group (Heavy) during World War II* (Bend, OR: Maverick, 1999), 407.

70. He might, for example, be named Smith, which to B-17 pilot Bob McCallum always meant bad luck. McCrary and Scherman, *First of the Many*, 55.

71. Walter Cronkite, *A Reporter's Life* (New York: Knopf, 1996), 98–99; Morgan, *Man Who Flew the* Memphis Belle, 173.

72. See David D. Gilmore, *Misogyny: The Male Malady* (Philadelphia: Univer-

sity of Pennsylvania Press, 2001), 222–223; Jack Holland, *Misogyny: The World's Oldest Prejudice* (London: Robinson, 2006), 5, 276.

73. See e.g. Guy Gibson, *Enemy Coast Ahead—Uncensored: The Real Guy Gibson* (Manchester, UK: Crécy, 2003), 160–161. As evidence of this, some fliers pointed to men whose wives apparently drove them toward refusing to carry on flying: see William James Kelbrick interview, 17729/4, IWM; H. Nick Knilans, A Yank in the RCAF, 61, B2445, RAFM; Nathan Lazenby, Lads Together, 7, X003–2966, RAFM; Charlie Kaye in Mel Rolfe, *Flying into Hell: The Bomber Command Offensive as Seen Through the Eyes of Twenty Crews* (London: Grub Street, 2001), 136. See also courts martial cases, AIR 18/19, 18/23, TNA.

74. See Brian Frow, Memoirs of a Bomber Baron, 51, X002–5619, RAFM; Gibson, *Enemy Coast Ahead*, 161; Robert G. Ladbury interview, UVic, accessed August 3, 2014, uvic.ca; Jack Rodgers, *Navigator's Log: Of a Tour in Bomber Command* (Braunton, UK: Merlin, 1985), 57; Victor Tempest, *Near the Sun: The Impressions of a Medical Officer of Bomber Command* (Brighton, UK: Crabtree, 1946), 46.

75. See e.g. Walter Clapham, *Night Be My Witness* (London: Cape, 1952), 240. It might also be thought that living near the station put unnecessary stress on wives since it would be obvious when their husbands were placing themselves in harm's way. See e.g. Henry Archer and Edward Pine, *To Perish Never* (London: Cassell, 1954), 110; Eddie Wheeler, *Just to Get a Bed!* (Worcester, UK: Square One, 1990), 101.

76. Russell McKay, *One of the Many* (Burnstown, ON: GSPH, 1989), 48–9; see also e.g. John Walsh, Happy Landings, 31, 12812, IWM.

77. Stan Selfe in Darlow, *D-Day Bombers*, 121.

78. Peter James interview, 13573/3, IWM; see also e.g. Bill Higgs in Andrew R. B. Simpson, *'Ops': Victory at All Costs: On Operations over Hitler's Reich with the Crews of Bomber Command, Their War—Their Words* (Pulborough, UK: Tattered Flag, 2012), 105.

79. Roy R. Grinker and John P. Spiegel, *Men under Stress* (Philadelphia: Blakiston, 1945), 132; see e.g. Carson, *Wing Ding, passim*; Jack Novey, *The Cold Blue Sky: A B-17 Gunner in World War II*, ed. Fryar Calhoun (Charlottesville, VA: Howell, 1997), 93–101.

80. On the dangers of distraction see e.g. Ray Carré, *Maximum Effort* (Burbank, CA: National Literary Guild, 1984), 92 ff. On being apparently marked for death through a sexual liaison, see e.g. Hughes, *Bomber Pilot in WWII*, 46 ff.

81. Wallrich, "Superstition and the Air Force," 14.

82. Robert J. Goebel, *Mustang Ace: Memoirs of a P-51 Fighter Pilot* (Pacifica, CA: Pacifica, 1991), 161.

83. John L. Sutton in *339th Fighter Group*, ed. G. P. Harry (Paducah, KY: Turner, 1991), 87.

84. Stanley A. Peterson, *"The Saint": Stories by the Navigator of a B-17* (Lexington, KY: CreateSpace, 2014), chapter 8, ff. 1–4.

85. Bernard Dye in Roger A. Freeman, *The British Airman* (London: Arms & Armour, 1989), 89.

86. Ronnie Waite, *Death or Decoration* (Cowden, UK: Newton, 1991), 95–97; see also Johnston, *From Air Gunner to Prisoner of War*, 103–105.

87. See e.g. Gordon W. Weir, Navigating Through World War II: A Memoir of the War Years, 39, 2010.0179.0001, NMMEAF.

88. On lucky WAAF drivers, see e.g. R. L. Austen, *High Adventure—Navigator at War* (Chichester, UK: Barry Rose, 1989), 183; Charlwood, *Journeys into Night*, 180; Quinlan, *Corkscrew to Safety*, 123; Mel Rolfe, *To Hell and Back* (London: Grub Street, 1998), 102; Charlie Churchill in Alan White, *The King's Thunderbolts: No. 44 (Rhodesia) Squadron Royal Air Force* (Lincoln, UK: Tucann, 2007), 85. On a lucky parachute packer, see e.g. Bill McCrea, *A Chequer-Board of Nights* (Longton, UK: Compaid, 2003), 100. On WAAFs waving off the planes as talismanic, see e.g. Rolfe, *Gunning for the Enemy*, 50; Russell, *Flying in Defiance*, 181.

89. Lawrence Pilgrim in Philip Kaplan and Jack Currie, *Round the Clock: The Experience of the Allied Bomber Crews Who Flew by Day and Night from England in the Second World War* (London: Cassell, 1993), 149.

90. Earle M. Nelson, *If Winter Comes* (Lovely Banks, VIC: Nelson, 1989), 43.

91. Unidentified diarist, 115 Squadron, in Martin W. Bowman, *Scramble: Memories of the RAF in the Second World War* (Stroud, UK: Tempus, 2006), 84.

92. See e.g. Fred Mills in Thomas G. Docherty, *No. 7 Bomber Squadron RAF in World War II* (Barnsley, UK: Pen & Sword Aviation, 2007), 77; Tom Burnard in Mel Rolfe, *Hell on Earth: Dramatic First Hand Accounts of Bomber Command at War* (London: Grub Street, 1999), 133–134.

93. Henry Hughes in *Bomber Command*, dir. Maia Liddell (ITV, 2012).

94. Miles Tripp, *The Eighth Passenger: A Flight of Recollection and Discovery* (London: Macmillan, 1969), 145.

95. D. G. Gray in Martin Middlebrook, *The Nuremberg Raid* (London: Penguin, 1986), 113, 264.

96. Jack Currie, *Lancaster Target: The Story of a Crew Who Flew from Wickenby* (London: Goodhall, 1981), 107–108; Gordon Colquhoun, *How Many for Breakfast?* (Seaton, UK: Motoprint, 1997), 92; Arthur White in Nichol and Rennell, *Tail-End Charlies*, 89.

97. See e.g. Arthur C. Smith, *Halifax Crew: The Story of a Wartime Bomber Crew* (Stevenage, UK: Carlton, 1983), 45; Sydney Percival Smith and David Scott Smith, *Lifting the Silence* (Toronto: Dundurn, 2010), 99.

98. See Colquhoun, *How Many for Breakfast*, 93; Archie Hall in *We, Also, Were There*, 33; D. Stafford-Clark, "Morale and Flying Experience: Results of a Wartime Study," *Journal of Mental Science* 95 (1949), 16.

99. Peter Constandelis, *8000 Feet over Hell* (Bloomington, IN: Trafford, 2008), 72.

100. David Zellmer, *The Spectator: A World War II Bomber Pilot's Journal of the Artist as Warrior* (Westport, CT: Praeger, 1999), 44.

101. Robert M. Littlefield interview, AFC/2001/001/10507, VHP.

102. Tripp, *Eighth Passenger*, 45–46.

103. See e.g. Clapham, *Night Be My Witness*, 233; Ted Park, *Angels Twenty* (St. Lucia, QLD: University of Queensland Press, 1994), 25; John Walsh, *Happy Landings*, 22, 12812, IWM.

104. Ironically, the batman actually thought this was a *good* thing in light of the superstition that bad things happen in threes. Stanley H. Mansbridge interview, UVic, accessed August 10, 2014, www.uvic.ca.

105. Desmond Scott, *One More Hour* (London: Hutchinson, 1989), 37.

106. MacKenzie, *Ten Men*, 32.

107. William C. Stewart in Bowman, *Echoes of England*, 154; see also e.g. John L. Sutton in *339th Fighter Group*, ed. G. P. Harry (Paducah, KY: Turner, 1991), 87; Bert Stiles, *Serenade to the Big Bird* (Carthage, TX: Howland, 1999), 26.

108. Arthur R. Hoyle, *Into the Darkness: One Young Australian's Journey from Sydney to the Deadly Skies over Germany, 1939–1945*, ed. David Vernon (Jamison Centre, ACT: Stringybark, 2012), 76; see also e.g. White, *King's Thunderbolts*, 173.

109. Peterson, *"The Saint,"* chapter 8, f. 4.

110. Oliver Guillot, narrative, 2, B24.Net, accessed October 24, 2014, b24.net /stories/Guillot.htm.

111. Alexander Nazemetz interview, ROHA, accessed September 26, 2015, oralhistory.rutgers.edu.

112. Q14a: "Do You Have Any Superstitions?," Gallup Survey 376-K, 16–21 August 1946, George H. Gallup, *The Gallup Poll: Public Opinion 1935–1971*, vol. 1, *1935–1938* (New York: Random House, 1972), 609.

113. Eddie S. Picardo, *Tales of a Tail Gunner: A Memoir of Seattle and World War II* (Seattle: Hara, 1996), 197–198.

114. McCrary and Scherman, *First of the Many*, 104, 110–111.

1. *Life* magazine, January 6, 1941, 72. On British visitors thinking of Americans as more superstitious, see *Saturday Evening Post*, October 4, 1948, 156.

2. Geoffrey Gorer, *Exploring English Character* (London: Cresset, 1955), 265.

3. E. A. W. Smith, *Spitfire Diary: The Boys of One-Two-Seven* (London: Kimber, 1988), 31.

4. Robert H. Sherwood, *Certified Brave* (Victoria, BC: Trafford, 2004), 30; see also e.g. Robert H. Hubbell in *The 390th Bomb Group in Action: An Anthology*, vol. 2, ed. Richard H. Perry, Wilbert H. Richarz, and William J. Robinson (Tucson, AZ: 390th Memorial Museum Foundation, 1985), 87; Curt M. Vogel narrative, 458th Bombardment Group (H), accessed October 24, 2014, 458bg.com. On 7 as lucky, see Steven Olderr, *Symbolism: A Comprehensive Dictionary* (Jefferson, NC: McFarland, 2012), 5–6.

5. Valarie Evans, *We That Are Left . . . Remember: New Brunswickers in the Air Force* (Saint John, NB: 250 RCAF [Saint John] Wing Air Force Association of Canada, 2002), 136.

6. Gregory G. Fletcher, *Intrepid Aviators: The True Story of USS* Intrepid's *Torpedo Squadron 18 and Its Epic Clash with the Superbattleship* Musashi (New York: NAL Caliber, 2012), 37.

7. Curt M. Vogel narrative, 458th Bombardment Group (H), accessed October 24, 2014, 458bg.com; Older, *Symbolism*, 8.

8. R. E. Peppy Blount, *We Band of Brothers* (Austin, TX: Eakin, 1984), 164.

9. See Harry M. Conley, *No Foxholes in the Sky*, ed. Mark H. Miller and Stuart G. Whittelsey Jr. (Trumbull, CT: FNP, 2002), 153; Bill Hancock in Pat Cunningham, *Fighter! Fighter! Corkscrew Port!* (Barnsley, UK: Pen & Sword Aviation, 2012), 65; Francis Bentinck Heffer, *From Cow Bells to Bell Bottoms: Wartime Experiences Extracted from Memoirs of an Ordinary Bloke* (Tauranga, NZ: Canrig, 1998), 170; Hugh Constant Godefroy, *Lucky Thirteen* (Stittsville, ON: Canada's Wings, 1983), 60; Simon Liberman interview TS, 4, ROHA, accessed September 26, 2015, oralhistory.rutgers.edu; Curt M. Vogel narrative, 458th Bombardment Group (H), accessed October 24, 2014, 458bg.com.

10. Don Berkus, *Another Soldier's Story: A Taste of a Great Generation* (Encino, CA: Berkus, 2010), 80.

11. Earl Benham memoir, 15, 2010.0213.0001, NMMEAF; see also e.g. William H. Bowen, *The Boy from Altheiner: From the Depression to the Boardroom* (Fayetteville: University of Arkansas Press, 2006), 25.

12. Robert W. Saunders in Perry et al., *The 390th Bomb Group Anthology*, vol. 2, 40.

13. Joe Foss as told to Walter Simmons, *Joe Foss, Flying Marine: The Story of His Flying Circus* (Washington, DC: Zenger, 1979), 36.

14. Bill Wallrich, "Superstition and the Air Force," *Western Folklore* 19 (1960), 14.

15. Donald Stones, *A Pilot's Passion: The Story of 'Dimsie'*, ed. Adrian Burt (London: Burt's, 2014), 56. Bomber pilot Stanley Mansbridge was assured the jinx of the quarters he was to occupy at an Operational Training Unit was lifted because three previous occupants already had been killed. Stanley H. Mansbridge interview, UVic, accessed August 10, 2014, uvic.ca.

16. James J. Mahoney and Brian H. Mahoney, *Reluctant Witness: Memoirs from the Last Year of the European Airwar, 1944–45* (Victoria, BC: Trafford, 2001), 232; see also e.g. Pat Y. Spillman interview TS, 65, OH 1319, UNT.

17. Richard Riley Johnson, *Twenty Five Milk Runs (And a Few Others): To Hell's Angels and Back* (Victoria, BC: Trafford, 2004), 176; see also e.g. Joseph W. Rutter, *Wreaking Havoc: A Year in an A-20* (College Station: Texas A&M University Press, 2004), 29.

18. Kenneth Brown Collings, "Pilots Are Superstitious," *Flying and Popular Aviation*, October 1941, 26.

19. Bill Albertson, *I Flew with Hell's Angels: Thirty-Six Combat Missions in a B-17 "Flying Fortress," 1944–1945* (Westminster, MD: Heritage, 2005), 102; see Nathaniel Lachenmeyer, *13: The Story of the World's Most Popular Superstition* (New York: Thunder's Mouth, 2004).

20. Joe Taylor in Stuart D. Ludlam, *They Turned the War Around at Coral Sea and Midway: Going to War with Yorktown's Air Group Five* (Bennington, VT: Merriam, 2006), 13.

21. John Howard McEniry, *A Marine Dive-Bomber Pilot at Guadalcanal* (Tuscaloosa: University of Alabama Press, 1987), 47.

22. Herschel H. Green, *Herky: Memoirs of a Checkertail Ace* (Atglen, PA: Schiffer, 1996), 26.

23. On a US plane maker avoiding thirteen in serial numbers, see Collings, "Pilots Are Superstitious," 25. On thirteen in a call sign, see e.g. Robert J. Goebel, *Mustang Ace: Memoirs of a P-51 Fighter Pilot* (Pacifica, CA: Pacifica, 1991), 114. On thirteenth crew in formation, see e.g. Lloyd Hall, My Service in the ETO, 2, 447th Bomb Group Association, accessed October 23, 2014, 447bg.com.

24. W. A. Wilson interview, UVic, accessed July 24, 2014, uvic.ca.

25. George Watt, *The Comet Connection: Escape from Hitler's Europe* (Lexington: University Press of Kentucky, 1990), 7.

26. Richard N. Bushong, *My Wars: B-17's to F-4's, WWII to Vietnam, with*

Speeds from 0 to Mach 2.1 (Raleigh, NC: lulu.com, 2008), 51; see also e.g. Robert L. Harcourt interview TS, 3, Oral History Collection, NMMEAF.

27. Godefroy, *Lucky Thirteen*, 131. On worrying about the thirteenth as an operational date, see also e.g. William P. Maher, *Fated to Survive: 401st Bombardment Group (H), Eighth Air Force: Memoirs of a B-17 Flying Fortress Pilot/Prisoner of War*, ed. Ed Y. Hall (Spartanburg, SC: Honoribus, 1992), 37.

28. George Gaines interview, EAA, accessed October 11, 2014, eaavideo.org. On Friday the 13th being considered unlucky, see also, e.g., A. B. Feuer, *General Chennault's Secret Weapon: The B-24 in China: Based on the Diary and Notes of Captain Elmer E. Haynes* (Westport, CT: Praeger, 1992), 53; William E. Heichel, *Milk Run: A Gunner's Tale* (Bloomington, IN: AuthorHouse, 2012), 58.

29. See Heffer, *Cow Bells to Bell Bottoms*, 170.

30. See e.g. Doy Duncan, *Abandoned at Leyte: The World War II Memories of Dr. Doy Duncan, Wildcat Pilot* (Fayetteville, AR: Phoenix, 2002), 16; Lloyd Hall, My Service in the ETO, 2, 447th Bomb Group Association, accessed October 23, 2014, 447bg.com; Richard B. Lewis, *Angel on My Wing: An Odyssey of Flying Combat with the 493rd Bomb Group, 8th Air Force in 1944* (Jacksonville Beach, FL: High Pitched Hum, 2009), 80.

31. Roger W. Armstrong, *U.S.A. the Hard Way: An Autobiography of a B-17 Crew Member*, ed. Ken Stone (Orange County, CA: Quail House, 1991), 60.

32. Robert M. Simmons in Ian McLachlan and Russell J. Zorn, *Eighth Air Force Bomber Stories: Eye-Witness Accounts from American Airmen and British Civilians of the Perils of War* (Sparkford, UK: Patrick Stephens, 1991), 16.

33. K. B. McGlashan, *Down to Earth: A Fighter Pilot's Experiences of Surviving Dunkirk, the Battle of Britain, Dieppe and D-Day* (London: Grub Street, 2007), 161.

34. Stan Bridgman in Laddie Lucas, *Out of the Blue: The Role of Luck in Air Warfare, 1917–1966* (London: Hutchinson, 1985), 283.

35. Walt Byrne in *The 390th Bomb Group in Action: An Anthology*, vol. 1, ed. Wilbert H. Richarz, Richard H. Perry, and William J. Robinson (Tucson, AZ: 390th Memorial Museum Foundation, 1983), 93–94.

36. John Kilbracken, *Bring Back My Stringbag: Swordfish Pilot at War, 1940–45*, rev. ed. (London: Leo Cooper, 1996), 163.

37. Gordon Colquhoun, *How Many for Breakfast?* (Seaton, UK: Motoprint, 1997), 98.

38. On planes going down on trip 13, see e.g. A. J. Padgett with Frank Padgett, *Mission over Indochine: A Story of Courage, Honor and Sacrifice* (Bloomington, IN: CreateSpace, 2012), 115–122; Ed Whitcomb, *On Celestial Wings* (Maxwell AFB, AL: Air University Press, 1995), 57. On worries about upcoming trip 13, see e.g.

Harry Barker in Martin Bowman, *RAF Bomber Command: Reflections of War*, vol. 2, *Live to Die Another Day* (Barnsley, UK: Pen & Sword Aviation, 2012), 123; Jack T. Brawley diary, 13, 2008.0507.0001, NMMEAF; Dawn Trimble Bunyak, *Our Last Mission: A World War II Prisoner in Germany* (Norman: University of Oklahoma Press, 2003), 52; Willie Chapman, *Booster McKeester and Other Expendables: 98th Heavy Bombardment Group, Ninth U.S. Army Air Force, Middle East Theater, 1942–43* (Collierville, TN: Global, 1994), 188; Al Dussleiere in *Hell's Angels Newsletter*, vol. 1, *Silver Anniversary Collection, 1976–2001*, ed. Eddie Deerfield (Palm Harbor, FL: 303rd Bomb Group [H] Association, 2002), 456; William C. Harris mission diary, May 8, 1944, 2010.0237.0001, NMMEAF; Duane Heath diary, June 14, 1944, accessed October 31, 2014, 492ndbombgroup.com; Carl W. Herdic diary, April 27, 1944, 2009.0006.0001, NMMEAF; Ralph R. Miller in Ivo de Jong, *Mission 85: The U.S. Eighth Air Force's Battle over Holland, August 19, 1943* (Mechanicsburg, PA: Stackpole, 2013), 44; E. E. Lovejoy, *Better Born Lucky Than Rich: The Diary of an Ordinary Airman* (Braunton, UK: Merlin, 1986), 65; Horace M. Meacomes Sr., The Military Career of Horace Melton Meacombes, ff. 40, 45, 2008.0657.0003, NMMEAF; Russell Meyne, One Mo' Time, 66, 2010.0128.0001, NMMEAF; Charles M. Olson, Life in the Service, diary entry, May 1, 1944, 2010.0210.0001, NMMEAF; Mel Rolfe, *To Hell and Back* (London: Grub Street, 1998), 18; Ed Gardner in Jay A. Stout, *Hell's Angels: The True Story of the 303rd Bomb Group in World War II* (New York: Berkley Caliber, 2015), 353; Boyd C. Smith, Memoirs of a Lucky Bastard, 12, 2014.002.0015, NMMEAF; Hal Turell, February 24, 1944—During 'Big Week,' 1, accessed October 31, 2014, 445bg.org/gotha.html; Frederick D. Worthen, *Against All Odds: Shot Down over Occupied Territory in World War II* (Santa Barbara, CA: Narrative, 2001), 69.

39. Truman Smith, *The Wrong Stuff: The Adventures and Misadventures of an 8th Air Force Aviator* (Norman: University of Oklahoma Press, 2002), 136.

40. Sam Honeycutt in Neal B. Dillon, *A Dying Breed: The True Story of a World War II Air Combat Crew's Courage, Camaraderie, Faith, and Spirit* (Grants Pass, OR: Hellgate, 2000), 166; see also e.g. Roy R. Fisher Jr., with Susan Fisher Anderson, *The Lucky Bastard Club: Letters to My Bride from the Left Seat* (Bloomington, IN: AuthorHouse, 2002), 111.

41. Charles Alling, *A Mighty Fortress: Lead Bomber over Europe* (Havertown, PA: Casemate, 2002), 72.

42. Marion E. Carl, *Pushing the Envelope: The Career of Fighter Ace and Test Pilot Marion Carl* (Annapolis, MD: Naval Institute Press, 1994), 34.

43. Jack Pitts, *P-47 Pilot: Scared, Bored, and Deadly* (San Antonio, TX: Pitts,

1997), 39; see also e.g. Ralph F. Coburn diary, August 19, 1944, in Deerfield, *Hell's Angels Newsletter*, vol. 1, 394.

44. See e.g. John Gee, Premonitions, RAFBCA, accessed April 26, 2014, raf bombercommand.com; Clarence Simonsen, *RAF and RCAF Aircraft Nose Art in World War II* (Ottringham, UK: Hikoki, 2001), 82.

45. William Dives, *A Bundu Boy in Bomber Command: Memoirs of a Royal Air Force Lancaster Pilot* (Victoria, BC: Trafford, 2003), 260; see also e.g. Rex Kimblin, *How Lucky I Was: 35 Missions in a Lancaster Bomber* (Toowong, QLD: Chambers, 2012), 181; Campbell Muirhead, *Diary of a Bomb Aimer: Training in America and Flying with 12 Squadron in WWII*, ed. Philip Swan (Barnsley, UK: Pen & Sword Aviation, 2009), 101; P. Hamilton Pollock, *Wings on the Cross: A Padre with the R.A.F.* (Dublin: Clanmore and Reynolds, 1954), 77; Miles Tripp, *The Eighth Passenger: A Flight of Recollection and Discovery* (London: Macmillan, 1969), 40; Graham White, *"The Long Road to the Sky": Night Fighter over Germany* (Barnsley, UK: Pen & Sword Aviation, 2006), 95.

46. Though there were certainly instances of "12A" in the USAAF: see e.g. Maurice Hackler in Deerfield, *Hell's Angels Newsletter*, I, 406–407; Paul Katz diary, March 18, 1945, in *Memories from the Out House Mouse: The Personal Diaries of One B-17 Crew*, ed. G. R. Harvey (Victoria, BC: Trafford, 2002), 85; Carl H. Moore, *Flying the B-26 Marauder over Europe: Memoir of a World War II Navigator*, 2nd ed. (Jefferson, NC: McFarland, 2013), 124.

47. Richard Bushong in Gary A. Best, *Belle of the Brawl: Letters Home from a B-17 Bombardier* (Portland, OR: Inkwater, 2010), 206; see also e.g. Andy Anderson, *One Pilot's Story: The Fabled 91st and Other 8th Airforce Memoirs* (Bloomington, IN: AuthorHouse, 2006), 9; Andrew Anderson, You Can Return, 1, 91st Bomb Group, accessed October 23, 2014, 91stbombgroup.com; Robert W. Schottel Korb mission diary, 41, 2010.0188.0001, NMMEAF; John L. Stewart, *The Forbidden Diary: A B-24 Navigator Remembers* (New York: McGraw-Hill, 1999), 113; Kenneth D. Jones memoir, 88, 2010.0228.0001, NMMEAF; Vern L. Moncur mission journal, February 21, 1944, 303rd Bomb Group (H) Association, accessed October 31, 2014, 303rdbga.com; Alexander Nazemetz interview TS, 32, ROHA, accessed September 26, 2015, oralhistory.rutgers.edu; Walter Peters, "The Birth of a Mission," *Yank*, January 21, 1944, 7.

48. Anthony Alberco and Kenneth Carey interview TS, 22, Oral History Collection, NMMEAF. On "12 ½," see e.g. Russell V. Meyne interview TS, 15, Oral History Collection, NMMEAF.

49. See Max Hastings, *Bomber Command* (London: Michael Joseph, 1979), 211.

50. Alan C. Deere, *Nine Lives* 2nd ed. (Canterbury, UK: Wingham, 1991), 163.

51. David Cox interview, 11510/3, IWM.

52. See Thomas G. Quinlan, *Corkscrew to Safety: A Tail-Gunner's Tour with 103 Squadron RAF 1944/5* (Bognor, UK: Woodfield, 2011), 34, 99.

53. Andrew R. B. Simpson, *'Ops': Victory at All Costs: On Operations over Hitler's Reich with the Crews of Bomber Command, Their War—Their Words* (Pulborough, UK: Tattered Flag, 2012), 105.

54. Harry Yates, *Luck and a Lancaster: Chance and Survival in World War II* (Shrewsbury, UK: Airlife, 1999), 9–10, 12, 82, 102–103, 105, 112, 113.

55. Edwin Watson in Kevin Wilson, *Journey's End: Bomber Command's Battle from Arnhem to Dresden and Beyond* (London: Weidenfeld & Nicolson, 2010), 244.

56. Don Feesey in Rolfe, *Hell and Back*, 89.

57. See Yates, *Luck and a Lancaster*, 199.

58. Byrne in *390th Bomb Group Anthology* I, 93.

59. Peter Townsend, *Duel of Eagles* (New York: Simon & Schuster, 1970), 366; Linda Piper, Mystery behind Pilot's Death, May 29, 2008, This is Local London, accessed October 3, 2015, thisislocallondon.co.uk.

60. Deere, *Nine Lives*, 163, 177.

61. Clayton Kelly Gross, *Live Bait: WWII Memories of an Undefeated Fighter Ace* (Portland, OR: Inkwater, 2006), 144.

62. Bill Turner, The Death of "F" for Fox, 705th Squadron, 446th Group, 2, 446th Bomb Group, accessed October 25, 2015, 446bg.com.

63. Paul Marable in *The 305th Bomb Group in Action: An Anthology*, ed. John V. Craven (Burleson, TX: 305th Bombardment Group [H] Memorial Association, 1990), 231. On fears about naming a plane after a living person, see e.g. Roscoe H. Johnson Jr., in Charles W. Richards, *The Second Was First: The Lives and Times of the Second Bombardment Group (Heavy) during World War II* (Bend, OR: Maverick, 1999), 41.

64. Joe Gaffney in C. C. Neal, *Gentlemen from Hell: Men of the 487th Bomb Group* (Paducah, KY: Turner, 2005), 83–84.

65. Ted Hallock quoted in Brendan Gill, "Young Man Behind Plexiglas," *New Yorker*, August 12, 1944, 30.

66. See Stuart J. Wright, *An Emotional Gauntlet: From Life in Peacetime America to the War in European Skies* (Madison: University of Wisconsin Press, 2004), 254.

67. John Comer, *Combat Crew: A True Story of Flying and Fighting in World War II* (New York: Morrow, 1988), 85–86, 90.

68. Norman "Bud" Fortier, *An Ace of the Eighth: An American Fighter Pilot's Air War in Europe* (New York: Presidio, 2003), 49.

69. In air-to-air combat, even the silhouettes of particular types of allied or

enemy planes might be difficult to distinguish from one another, leading to near misses or actual fratricide incidents. See e.g. Richard Townshend Bickers, *Friendly Fire: Accidents in Battle from Ancient Greece to the Gulf War* (London: Leo Cooper, 1994), 58, 93, 96; Andy Saunders, *Bader's Last Fight: An In-Depth Investigation of a Great WWII Mystery* (London: Grub Street, 2007).

70. Paul Marable in *The 305th Bomb Group in Action*, 221.

71. James L. Weaver in Charles W. Richards, *The Second Was First: The Lives and Times of the Second Bombardment Group (Heavy) during World War II* (Bend, OR: Maverick, 1999), 222.

72. Jackson Granholm, *The Day We Bombed Switzerland: Flying with the US Eighth Army Air Force in World War II* (Shrewsbury, UK: Airlife, 2000), 6; see also Mahoney, *Reluctant Witness*, 240.

73. Alan McGregor Peart, *From North Africa to the Arakan: The Engrossing Memoir of a WWII Spitfire Ace* (London: Grub Street, 2008), 87. Not all aural hallucinations were interpreted as bad news. See e.g. William J. Fox, *Passage to Valhalla: The Human Side of Aerial Combat over Nazi Germany* (Media, PA: Filcon, 1991), 126; Joe Thompson and Tom Delvaux, *Tiger Joe: A Photographic Diary of a World War II Reconnaisance Pilot* (Nashville, TN: Eveready, 2006), 73.

74. Bill Garrioch in Martin W. Bowman, *RAF Bomber Command at War: Reflections of War*, vol. 1, *Cover of Darkness* (Barnsley, UK: Pen & Sword Aviation, 2011), 107–108.

75. Maurice G. Lihou, *Out of the Italian Night: Wellington Bomber Operations 1944–45* (Shrewsbury, UK: Airlife, 2000), 94.

76. H. Nick Knilans, A Yank in the RCAF, 52, B2445, RAFM.

77. Colquhoun, *How Many for Breakfast*, 103–104.

78. Quinlan, *Corkscrew to Safety*, 57.

79. Thomas C. Wilcox, *One Man's Destiny* (Mogadore, OH: Telecraft, 1991), 87–88; Peart, *From North Africa to the Arakan*, 86.

80. Garrioch in Bowman, *RAF Bomber Command at War*, vol. 1, 108.

81. Colquhoun, *How Many for Breakfast*, 100–104.

82. Fred Slavar in Stephen Darlow, *D-Day Bombers: The Veterans' Story: RAF Bomber Command and the US Eighth Air Force Support to the Normandy Invasion 1944* (London: Grub Street, 2004), 186.

83. Jack Currie, *Echoes in the Air: A Chronicle of Aeronautical Ghost Stories* (Manchester, UK: Crécy, 1998), 77–80. For another case where "seeing things" occurred in the context of enormous operational stress—in this case a bail out over the English Channel—see Peter Horsley, *Sounds From Another Room* (London: Leo Cooper, 1997), 110–118, 125–131.

84. Knilans, Yank in the RCAF, RAFM, 52.

85. John Steinbeck, *Once There Was a War* (New York: Viking, 1958), 32. For another case of a vision likely caused by oxygen deprivation, see Philip Joubert de la Ferté, *Fun and Games* (London: Hutchinson, 1964), 110–112.

86. Peart, *From North Africa to the Arakan*, 88.

87. Colquhoun, *How Many for Breakfast*, 104; Garrioch in Bowman, *RAF Bomber Command at War*, vol. 1, 108.

88. See e.g. Horsley, *Sounds From Another Room*, 125–131.

89. Lihou, *Out of the Italian Night*, 94–95.

90. Knilans, Yank in the RCAF, RAFM, 52.

91. Quinlan, *Corkscrew to Safety*, 59.

CHAPTER 7: PREMONITIONS OF DISASTER

1. Mel Rolfe, *Flying into Hell: The Bomber Command Offensive as Seen Through the Eyes of Twenty Crews* (London: Grub Street, 2001), 14. On charms, rituals, and prayers as a regression to childhood magical thinking, see e.g. Roy R. Grinker and John P. Spiegel, *Men under Stress* (Philadelphia: Blakiston, 1945), 131.

2. Paul Richey, *Fighter Pilot: A Personal Record of the Campaign in France: September 8th, 1939, to June 13th, 1940* (London: Batsford, 1941), 78.

3. Mike Henry, *Air Gunner* (London: Foulis, 1964), 53–54.

4. This was a rare case of a premonition being connected with a positive outcome, in this case the pilot's first kill. Roger Hall, *Spitfire Pilot: An Extraordinary Tale of Combat in the Battle of Britain* (Stroud, UK: Amberley, 2012), 140–143.

5. Desmond Scott, *Typhoon Pilot* (London: Leo Cooper, 1980), 44.

6. Bob Horsley in Tony Iveson and Brian Milton, *Lancaster: The Biography* (London: Deutsch, 2009), 62–63.

7. George Moreton, *Doctor in Chains* (London: Corgi, 1980), 52–56.

8. Alan White, *The King's Thunderbolts: No. 44 (Rhodesia) Squadron Royal Air Force* (Lincoln, UK: Tucann, 2007), 95.

9. Henry "Hank" Adlam, *On and Off the Flight Deck: Reflections of a Naval Fighter Pilot in World War II* (Barnsley, UK: Pen & Sword Aviation, 2007), 81.

10. C. J. Sheddan with Norman Franks, *Tempest Pilot* (London: Grub Street, 1993), 40.

11. Bert W. Humphreys, Times of Our Lives (An Autobiography), vol. 3, pt. 1, 24–26, 91st Bomb Group (H), accessed October 30, 2014, 91stbombgroup .com.

12. P. Eldris in J. Kemp McGlauchlin, *The Mighty Eighth in WWII: A Memoir* (Lexington: University Press of Kentucky, 2000), 70–71.

13. Jack O. Luehrs in *The 305th Bomb Group in Action: An Anthology*, ed. John V. Craven (Burleson, TX: 305th Bomb Group [H] Memorial Association, 1990), 60.

14. John R. McCrary and David E. Sherman, *First of the Many: A Journal of Action with the Men of the Eighth Air Force* (New York: Simon & Schuster, 1944), 108, 110, 111.

15. Harry E. Slater, *Lingering Contrails of the Big Square A: A History of the 94th Bomb Group (H), 1942–1945* (Hadley, PA: Slater, 1980), 98.

16. J. Goff in *B-17s over Berlin: Personal Stories from the 95th Bomb Group (H)*, ed. Ian L. Hawkins (Washington, DC: Brassey's, 1990), 65.

17. Jack Novey, *The Cold Blue Sky: A B-17 Gunner in World War II* (Charlottesville, VA: Howell, 1997), 116.

18. Ray T. Matheny, *Rite of Passage: A Teenager's Chronicle of Combat and Captivity in Nazi Germany* (Clearfield, UT: American Legacy Media, 2009), 161–167.

19. Norman Noble in Tom Wingham, *Halifax Down! On the Run from the Gestapo, 1944* (London: Grub Street, 2009), 52.

20. William R. Cubbins, *The War of the Cottontails: A Bomber Pilot with the Fifteenth Air Force against Nazi Germany* (Chapel Hill, NC: Algonquin, 1989), 37; see also e.g. Robert H. Sherwood, *Certified Brave* (Victoria, BC: Trafford, 2004), 95–96, 100; John J. Shiver, *I Always Wanted to Fly: Memoirs of a World War II Flight Engineer/Gunner* (Atmore, AL: Shiver, 2012), 154.

21. R. Longo narrative, B24.Net, accessed October 24, 2014, www.b24net /stories/longo.htm.

22. Louis H. Breitenbach, Name? Rank? Serial Number? "For You the War Is Over," 12, 2010.0031.0001, NMMEAF.

23. Charles Bistline in *The Fight'n 451st Bomb Group (H)*, ed. Michael D. Hill (Paducah, KY: Turner, 1990), 124.

24. A. Bibbins in *388th Anthology*, vol. 2, *Tales of the 388th Bombardment Group (H) 1942–45*, ed. Janet Pack and Richard Singer (San Jose, CA: Writer's Club, 2001), 128.

25. Thomas C. Wilcox, *One Man's Destiny* (Mogadore, OH: Telecraft, 1991), 87.

26. J. Corbitt in *Missions Remembered: The Men of the Middle Tennessee WWII Fighter Pilots Association*, ed. John K. Breast (Brentwood, TN: JM Productions, 1995), 23–24.

27. William H. Sederwall in Ken Stone, *Triumphant We Fly: A 381st Bomb Group Anthology* (Paducah, KY: Turner, 1994), 124.

28. Jackson Granholm, *The Day We Bombed Switzerland: Flying with the US Eighth Army Air Force in World War II* (Shrewsbury, UK: Airlife, 2000), 111–112, 117–118.

29. Jim O'Leary, "Carl Ulrich's Nightmares Came True at Merseburg," in *Hell's Angels Newsletter*, vol. 2, *Silver Anniversary Collection, 1976–2001*, ed. Eddie Deerfield (Palm Harbor, FL: 303rd Bomb Group (H) Association, 2002), 5–6.

30. A. B. Feuer, *General Chennault's Secret Weapon: The B-24 in China: Based on the Diary and Notes of Captain Elmer E. Haynes* (Westport, CT: Praeger, 1992), 57.

31. Ibid., 60–66.

32. John Misterly Jr., *Over and Under* (New York: Carlton, 1987), 180.

33. Ibid., 182.

34. Doy Duncan, *Abandoned at Leyte: The World War II Memories of Dr. Doy Duncan, Wildcat Pilot* (Fayetteville, AR: Phoenix, 2002), 108.

35. Keith Gardner in Gerald W. Thomas, *Torpedo Squadron Four: A Cockpit View of World War II* (Las Cruces: New Mexico State University Press, 1991), 184.

36. Laurie Underwood in Mel Rolf, *Flying into Hell: The Bomber Command Offensive as Seen Through the Eyes of Twenty Crews* (London: Grub Street, 2001), 14–15.

37. James Kyle, *A Typhoon Tale* (Bognor, UK: New Horizon, 1984), 124.

38. Geoffrey P. Jones, *Raider: The Halifax and Its Flyers* (London: Kimber, 1979), 166–169.

39. Ralph Edwards, *In the Thick of It: The Autobiography of a Bomber Pilot* (Upton, UK: Images, 1994), 139.

40. Charles Alling, *A Mighty Fortress: Lead Bomber over Europe* (Havertown, PA: Casemate, 2002), 72–74.

41. Stephen E. Ambrose, *The Wild Blue: The Men and Boys Who Flew the B-24s over Germany* (New York: Simon & Schuster, 2001), 220–221.

42. Chuck Yeager and Leo Janos, *Yeager: An Autobiography* (New York: Bantam, 1985), 62.

43. T. Braidic in *B-17s over Berlin*, 272–273.

44. Mel Rolfe, *To Hell and Back* (London: Grub Street, 1998), 43–48.

45. Will Iredale, *The Kamikaze Hunters: Fighting for the Pacific, 1945* (London: Macmillan, 2015), 190.

46. Ron Johnson, *A Navigator's Tale* (Chippenham, UK: Irregular Records, 2000), 34–35.

47. John W. Gee, *Wingspan: The Recollections of a Bomber Pilot* (Wellesbourne, UK: Self-Publishing Association, 1988), 181–182.

48. See also e.g. George Allen in Max Arthur, *Lost Voices of the Royal Air Force* (London: Hodder, 2005), 116; Tony Bird, *Bird over Berlin* (Bognor, UK: Woodfield, 2000), 48, 79; George B. McLaughlin in Martin W. Bowman, *We Were Eagles: The Eighth Air Force at War*, vol. 2, *December 1943 to May 1944* (Stroud,

UK: Amberley, 2014), 228–229; Walter Clapham, *Night Be My Witness* (London: Cape, 1952), 240; William Dobson interview, UVic, accessed August 3, 2014, uvic.ca; Sean Feast, *Master Bombers: The Experiences of a Pathfinder Squadron at War, 1944–1945* (London: Grub Street, 2008), 119; Robert J. Goebel, *Mustang Ace: Memoirs of a P-51 Fighter Pilot* (Pacifica, CA: Pacifica, 1991), 95; W. E. "Bill" Goodman, *Of Stirlings and Stalags: An Air-Gunner's Tale* (London: PublishNation, 2013), 116; James Holland, *Dam Busters: The Race to Smash the Dams, 1943* (London: Bantam, 2012), 290; James Douglas Hudson, *There and Back Again: A Navigator's Story*, 3rd ed. (Lincoln, UK: Tucann, 2003), 168–169; Ian McLachlan, *Eighth Air Force Stories: A New Selection* (Stroud, UK: Sutton, 2004), 61–62; Kenje Ogata interview, AFC/2001/001/76800, VHP; Harold C. Rosser, *No Hurrahs for Me* (Sevierville, TN: Covenant House, 1994), 124–126; Joseph W. Rutter, *Wreaking Havoc: A Year in an A-20* (College Station: Texas A&M University Press, 2004), 52; Desmond Scott, *One More Hour* (London: Hutchinson, 1989), 39, 40–42; John Searby, *The Bomber Battle for Berlin* (Shrewsbury, UK: Airlife, 1991), 85; John Steinbeck, *Once There Was a War* (New York: Viking, 1958), 31; Jack Watts, *Nickels and Nightingales* (Burnstown, ON: GSPH, 1995), 277–278; Reid Thompson in Kevin Wilson, *Bomber Boys: The RAF Offensive of 1943* (London: Weidenfeld & Nicolson, 2005), 38; Douglas Hudson in Kevin Wilson, *Men of Air: The Doomed Youth of Bomber Command, 1944* (London: Weidenfeld & Nicolson, 2007), 272; Harold Wright transcript, 17, S00582, AWM; Royan Yule, *On a Wing and a Prayer* (Derby, UK: Derby Books, 2012), 96.

49. C. F. Rawnsley with Robert Wright, *Night Fighter* (London: Collins, 1957), 264.

50. Leslie E. Traughber in Breast, *Missions Remembered*, 132–133.

51. Pip Beck, *Keeping Watch: A WAAF in Bomber Command* (Manchester, UK: Crécy, 2004), 77.

52. Michael Bentine, *The Reluctant Jester* (London: Bantam, 1992), 135; ibid., *The Door Marked Summer* (London: Granada, 1981), 141; see also John Walsh, *Happy Landings*, 40, 12812, IWM.

53. Leslie Temple in *Into the Wind*, dir. Steven Hatton (Electric Egg, 2011).

54. See e.g. Willis Quigley in Currie, *Echoes in the Air*, 99; Miles Tripp, *The Eighth Passenger* (London: Macmillan, 1969), 79–81, 90–92, 134.

55. On the failure to certify the existence of a sixth sense, see e.g. Jonathan C. Smith, *Pseudoscience and Extraordinary Claims of the Paranormal: A Critical Thinker's Toolkit* (Malden, MA: Wiley-Blackwell, 2010), 245–267. See also, with reference to precognition, Stuart J. Ritchie, Richard Wiseman, and Christopher C. French, "Failing the Future: Three Unsuccessful Attempts to Replicate Bem's

'Retroactive Facilitation of Recall' Effect," *PLoS ONE* 7 (2012): 1–5; Klaus Fiedler and Joachim I. Krueger, "Afterthoughts on Precognition: No Cogent Evidence for Anomalous Influences of Consequent Events on Preceding Cognition," *Theory & Psychology* 23 (2013): 323–333. On premonitions not coming to pass, see e.g. Adlam, *On and Off the Flight Deck*, 81; Jim Auton, *RAF Liberator over the Eastern Front: A Bomb Aimer's Second World War and Cold War Story* (Barnsley, UK: Pen & Sword Aviation, 2008), 94; Richard C. Baynes, *Replacement Crew: The Training and Combat Experience of a Typical 8th Air Force Replacement Crew in 1944* (Irvine, CA: Baynes, 1993), 65; Fred Slevar in Stephen Darlow, *D-Day Bombers: The Veterans' Story: RAF Bomber Command and the US Eighth Air Force Support in the Normandy Invasion 1944* (London: Grub Street, 2004), 186; Albert M. Bell in *The 390th Bomb Group in Action: An Anthology*, vol. 1, ed. Wilbert H. Richarz, Richard H. Perry, and William J. Robinson (Tucson, AZ: 390th Memorial Museum Foundation, 1983), 259–260; Clapham, *Night Be My Witness*, 267; Dan Conway, *The Trenches in the Sky: What It Was Like Flying in RAF Bomber and Transport Commands in World War II* (Carlisle, WA: Hesperian, 1995), 144; Hugh Constance Godefroy, *Lucky Thirteen* (Stittsville, ON: Canada's Wings, 1983), 131–133; Arthur Eyeton-Jones, *Day Bomber* (Stroud, UK: Sutton, 1998), 97; Arthur Hoyle, *Into the Darkness: One Young Australian's Journey from Sydney to the Deadly Skies over Germany*, ed. David Vernon (Jamison Centre, ACT: Stringybark, 2012), 888–889; H. Nick Knilans, A Yank in the RCAF, 52, B2445, RAFM; Harry Lomas, *One Wing High: Halifax Bomber—The Navigator's Story* (Shrewsbury, UK: Airlife, 1995), 167; McGlauchlin, *Mighty Eighth*, 83–84; George Webster, *The Savage Sky: Life and Death in a Bomber over Germany in 1944* (Mechanicsburg, PA; Stackpole, 2007), 215, 218.

56. Leslie Mann, *And Some Fell on Stony Ground: A Day in the Life of an RAF Bomber Pilot* (London: Icon, 2014), 49; see also e.g. Bruce Halpenny, *Ghost Stations IV* (Chester-le-Street, UK: Casdec, 1993), 101–103; Clarence Henigman interview, UVic, accessed August 3, 2014, uvic.ca; Bill Stepp in Ian McLachlan and Russell J. Zorn, *Eighth Air Force Bomber Stories: Eye-Witness Accounts from American Airmen and British Civilians of the Perils of War* (Sparkford, UK: Patrick Stephens, 1991), 158.

57. Slater, *Lingering Contrails*, 98.

58. Bistline in *Fight'n 451st*, 124; Misterly, *Over and Under*, 180.

59. Graham Welsh in Gordon Thorburn, *A Century of Air Warfare with Nine (IX) Squadron RAF: Still Going Strong* (Barnsley, UK: Pen & Sword Aviation, 2014), 142.

60. Richard B. (Dick) Lewis, *Angel on My Wing: An Odyssey of Flying Combat with the 493rd Bomb Group, 8th Air Force in 1944* (Jacksonville Beach, FL: High Pitched Hum, 2009), 75.

61. Yeager, *Yeager*, 62.

62. Alling, *Mighty Fortress*, 72.

63. See Roger A. Freeman, *The American Airman in Europe* (Osceola, WI: Motorbooks, 1991), 97; Tim Hamilton, *The Life and Times of Pilot Officer Prune: Being the Official Story of Tee Emm* (London: HMSO, 1991), 77; see also e.g. Christine A. Butterworth and Susan C. Butterworth, *Life, Luck and Lancasters: Vivid Reminiscences of Louis Butler* (Rochdale, UK: Henham, 2013), 60.

64. Johnson, *It's Never Dark*, 139; see also e.g. Adge Boal in *Into the Wind*, dir. Steven Hatton (Electric Egg, 2011); Harry Hughes in Steve Darlow, *Five of the Many: Survivors of the Bomber Command Offensive from the Battle of Britain to Victory Tell Their Story* (Oxford: ISIS, 2009), 263–264; D. G. Hornsey, Here Today, Bomb Tomorrow, 386, 4559, IWM; Campbell Muirhead, *Diary of a Bomb Aimer: Training in America and Flying with 12 Squadron in WWII*, ed. Philip Swan (Barnsley, UK: Pen & Sword Aviation, 2009), 158.

65. See e.g. Bill Stepp in McLachlan and Zorn, *Eighth Air Force Bomber Stories*, 158; Thomas G. Quinlan, *Corkscrew to Safety* (Bognor, UK: Woodfield, 2011), 106–107.

66. Webster, *Savage Sky*, 213–15; P. Edris in McGlauchlin, *Mighty Eighth*, 70–71.

67. Kenneth G. Bergin, *Aviation Medicine: Its Theory and Application* (Bristol, UK: Wright, 1949), 362; see also Mark K. Wells, *Courage and Air Warfare: The Allied Aircrew Experience in the Second World War* (London: Cass, 1995), 60–83.

68. A few, to be sure, like Ben Heffer's friend, had a premonition that they would be killed before they entered combat—see also e.g. George G. Wells in Patricia Chapman Meder, *The True Story of Catch 22: The Real Men and Missions of Joseph Heller's 340th Bomb Group in World War II* (Philadelphia: Casemate, 2012), 108–109; Thomas, *Torpedo Squadron Four*, 184—which was likely due to lack of self-confidence: see Robin Olds with Christina Olds and Ed Rasimus, *Fighter Pilot: The Memoirs of Legendary Ace Robin Olds* (New York: St. Martin's, 2010), 86.

69. Richey, *Fighter Pilot*, 96; see also e.g. Adlam, *On and Off the Flight Deck*, 147.

70. Hall, *Spitfire Pilot*, 1–140.

71. Scott, *Typhoon Pilot*, 44.

72. Wilcox, *One Man's Destiny*, 87.

73. Ray Parker, *Down in Flames: A True Story* (Minneapolis: Mill City, 2009), 75.

74. D. Curo in Ivo de Jong, *Mission 85: The U.S. Eighth Air Force's Battle over Holland, August 19, 1943* (Mechanicsburg, PA: Stackpole, 2013), 120.

75. See e.g. Matthew Hugh Erdelyi, "The Interpretation of Dreams, and of Jokes," *Review of General Psychology* 18 (2014): 115–126; Andrea Rock, *The Mind at Night: The New Science of How and Why We Dream* (New York: Basic, 2004), 71–72, 93, 105–106, 114–117, 188; Daniel M. Wegner, Richard M. Wezlaff, and Megan Kozak, "Dream Rebound: The Return of Suppressed Thoughts in Dreams," *Psychological Science* 15 (2004): 232–236.

76. Henry R. Rollin, *Festina Lente: A Psychiatric Odyssey* (London: BMJ, 1990), 38; see e.g. John J. Briol, *Dead Engine Kids: World War II Diary of John J. Briol, B-17 Ball Turret Gunner, with Comments from Notes of Other Crew Members*, ed. John F. Welch (Rapid City, SD: Silver Wings Association, 1993), 44; Robert S. Carré, *Flying Colt: Liberator Pilot in Italy: Diary and History: World War II: 456th Bombardment Group (Heavy), 15th Air Force* (Alexandria, VA: Manor House, 1997), 93; Doug Mourton, *Lucky Doug: Memoirs of the RAF 1937–1946 and After* (Edinburgh: Pentland, 1999), 111. On combat nightmares, see also e.g. Bill Lundhal in Fiske Hanley, *History of the 504th Bomb Group (VH) in World War II* (Enfield, CT: 504th Bomb Group Association, 1992), 234; Walter F. Hughes, *A Bomber Pilot in WW II: From Farm Boy to Pilot: 35 Missions in the B-24 Liberator Bomber* (Fremont, CA: Hughes, 1994), 65; Brian D. O'Neill, *Half a Wing, Three Engines and a Prayer: B-17s over Germany*, special ed. (New York: McGraw-Hill, 1999), 289–290; Murray Peden, *A Thousand Shall Fall: A Pilot for 214* (Stittsville, ON: Canada's Wings, 1979), 413; Ron Smith, *Rear Gunner Pathfinders* (Manchester, UK: Crécy, 1987), 40; Harold J. Wright, *Pathfinder Squadron* (London: Kimber, 1987), 153.

77. See e.g. Max Böckermann, Annika Gieselmann, and Reinhard Pietrowsky, "What Does Nightmare Distress Mean? Factorial Structure and Psychometric Properties of the Nightmare Distress Questionnaire," *Dreaming* 24 (2014): 279–289; M. P. Martinez, Elena Miró, and Raimundo Arriaza, "Evaluation of the Distress and Effects Caused by Nightmares: A Study of the Psychometric Properties of the Nightmare Distress Questionnaire and the Nightmare Effects Survey," *Sleep and Hypnosis* 7 (2005): 29–41.

78. Duncan, *Abandoned at Leyte*, 108. On the non-precognitive nature of dreams in general, see Richard Wiseman, *Paranormality: Why We See What Isn't There* (London: Spin Solutions, 2010), 147–154.

79. See e.g. John T. Godfrey, *The Look of Eagles* (New York: Random House, 1958), 147.

80. McCrary, *First of the Many*, 104.

81. H. Turell narrative, 445th Bombardment Group (Heavy), accessed October 31, 2015, 445bg.org/gotha.html; Louis H. Breitenbach, Name? Rank? Serial Number? "For You the War Is Over," 12, 2010.0031.0001, NMMEAF.

82. William H. Sederwall in Stone, *Triumphant We Fly*, 124.

83. See Max Hastings, *Bomber Command* (London: Michael Joseph, 1979), 222.

84. See Smith, *Pseudoscience*, 153–154.

85. R. C. Anderson, "Neuropsychiatric Problems of the Flyer," *American Journal of Medicine* 4 (1948), 640; see also D. Bond, The Diagnosis and Disposition of Combat Crews Suffering from Emotional Disorders, 24 September 1944, 6, Reel 135071, AFHRA. See e.g. Ray Carré, *Maximum Effort* (Burbank, CA: National Literary Guild, 1984), 133; Robert H. Honeycutt interview, AFC/2001/001/20352, VHP.

86. See e.g. Adlam, *On and Off the Flight Deck*, 147; E. E. Barringer, '*Alone on a Wide, Wide Sea': The Story of 835 Naval Air Squadron in the Second World War* (London: Leo Cooper, 1995), 36; H. E. Bates, *The World in Ripeness: An Autobiography*, vol. 3 (London: Michael Joseph, 1972), 15–16; Dan Bowling, "*Follow P-D-I": My Experiences as an AAF B-25 Pilot during World War II* (Lomita, CA: Cambria, 2009), 70; Gordon Colquhoun, *How Many for Breakfast?* (Seaton, UK: Motoprint, 1977), 77; Charles Demoulin, *Firebirds! Flying the Typhoon in Action* (Shrewsbury, UK: Airlife, 1987), 69; J. Douglas Harvey, *Boys, Bombs and Brussels Sprouts: A Knees-Up, Wheels-Up Chronicle of World War II* (Toronto: McClelland & Stewart, 1981), 161; Johnnie Johnson, *Wing Leader* (Newton Abbot, UK: David and Charles, 1974), 187; S. H. Johnson, *It's Never Dark above the Clouds* (Trigg, WA: Johnson, 1994), 55; Nathan Lazenby, Lads Together, 9, X003–2966, RAFM; Thomas Cameron Tredwell interview, 10743/2, IWM; Harold Wright interview TS, 16, S00582, AWM.

87. Joan Beech, *One Waaf's War* (Tunbridge Wells, UK: Costello, 1989), 60.

88. Rawnsley, *Night Fighter*, 264.

89. Bentine, *Reluctant Jester*, 135; see Bentine, *Door Marked Summer*, 141.

90. See Maurice Chick interview, RAFBCA, accessed April 26, 2014, raf bombercommand.com; Robert Morgan with Ron Powers, *The Man Who Flew the Memphis Belle: Memoir of a WWII Bomber Pilot* (New York: Dutton, 2001), 134; T. Wingham in Mel Rolfe, *To Hell and Back* (London: Grub Street, 1998), 171; Walter R. Thompson, *Lancaster to Berlin* (Southside, UK: Goodall, 1997), 156; see also e.g. Roland Winfield, *The Sky Belongs to Them* (London: Kimber, 1976), 151–152.

91. Bill Jackson, *Three Stripes and Four Brownings* (North Battleford, SK: Turner-Warwick, 1990), 107–108.

92. On USAAF policies, see Link and Coleman, *Medical Support*, 662; Wells, *Courage and Air Warfare*, 79–80. On USAAF cases, see e.g. Bert Stiles, *Serenade to the Big Bird* (Carthage, TX: Howland, 1999), 52. On cases in the RAF being dealt with without the men concerned being branded LMF—Lack of Moral Fiber—see e.g. Brian Burnett, *A Pilot at Wimbledon: The Memoirs of Air Chief Marshal Sir Brian Burnett* (Codicote, UK: Blenheim, 2009), 73; Don Charlwood, *Journeys into Night* (Hawthorn, VIC: Hudson, 1991), 204; Conway, *Trenches in the Sky*, 147; Grace Hall, *We, Also, Were There: A Collection of Recollections of Wartime Women of Bomber Command* (Braunton, UK: Merlin, 1985), 40; Keith Hall in Pat Cunningham, *The Fear in the Sky: Vivid Memories of Operational Aircrew in World War Two* (Barnsley, UK: Pen & Sword Aviation, 2012), 40; Reginald J. Lane interview, UVic, accessed August 13, 2014, uvic.ca; Andy Black in Laddie Lucas, *Out of the Blue: The Role of Luck in Air Warfare, 1917–1966* (London: Hutchinson, 1985), 216; A. R. D. MacDonell, *From Dogfight to Diplomacy: A Spitfire Pilot's Log, 1932–1958* (Barnsley, UK: Pen & Sword Aviation, 2005), 47; Richard Passmore, *Blenheim Boy* (London: Harmsworth, 1981), 130; Welsh in Thorburn, *Century of Air Warfare*, 142; G. R. T. Willis, *No Hero, Just a Survivor: A Personal Story with Beaufighters and Mosquitos of 47 Squadron RAF over the Mediterranean and Burma, 1943–1945* (Emley, UK: Willis, 1999), 107. On a case in the RN, see Adlam, *On and Off the Flight Deck*, 136.

93. For flier premonitions in World War I, see e.g. D'Arcy Greig, *My Golden Flying Years: From 1918 over France through Iraq in the 1920s* (London: Basingstoke, UK Palgrave Macmillan, 2001), 118, 122; Joshua Levine, *On a Wing and a Prayer* (London: Collins, 2008), 314; Vivian Ross ['Roger Vee'], *Flying Minnows: Memoirs of a World War One Fighter Pilot, from Training in Canada to the Front Line, 1917–1918* (London: Arms & Armour, 1977), 110–111. For premonitions during the Vietnam War, see e.g. Jerry W. Cook, *Once a Fighter Pilot . . .* (New York: McGraw-Hill, 1996), 135; Mike McCarthy, *Phantom Reflections: The Education of an American Fighter Pilot in Vietnam* (Westport, CT: Praeger, 2007), 101; Marshall L. Michel III, *The Eleven Days of Christmas: America's Last Vietnam Air Battle* (San Francisco: Encounter, 2002), 191, 195–196.

CONCLUSION

1. On this conclusion, see e.g. John C. McManus, *Deadly Sky: The American Combat Airman in World War II* (Novato, CA: Presidio, 2000), 312; Andrew R. B. Simpson, *'Ops': Victory at All Costs: On Operations over Hitler's Reich with the*

Crews of Bomber Command, Their War—Their Words (Pulborough, UK: Tattered Flag, 2012), 105.

2. Tom Sawyer, *Only Owls and Bloody Fools Fly at Night* (London: Kimber, 1982), 55; see also e.g. Kenneth K. Blyth, *Cradle Crew: Royal Canadian Air Force World War II* (Manhattan, KS: Sunflower University Press, 1997), 80; William Dives, *A Bundu Boy in Bomber Command: Memoirs of a Royal Air Force Lancaster Pilot* (Victoria, BC: Trafford, 2003), 260; T. W. Fox, My Life with RAF Bomber Command during the 2nd World War, 12, 7811, IWM; Eric Harrison interview, 30002/6, IWM; Brian Johnson and H. I. Cozens, *Bombers: The Weapon of Total War* (London: Thames Methuen, 1984), 226.

3. Alvin E. Kotler as told to Jack Flynn, *We Came to Fight a War: The Story of a B-17 Radio Gunner and His Pilot* (Bennington, VT: Merriam, 2012), 58; see also e.g. Edwin E. Koch, "G.I. Lore: Lore of the Fifteenth Air Force," *New York Folklore Quarterly* 9 (1953): 59; David A. McCarthy, *Fear No More: A B-17 Navigator's Journey* (Pittsburgh: Cottage Wordsmiths, 1991), 145; David B. Dahlberg in C. C. Neal, *Gentlemen From Hell: Men of the 487th Bomb Group* (Paducah, KY: Turner, 2005), 146.

4. Quentin Aanenson, A Fighter Pilot's Story, p. 5, 2012.0055.0001, NMMEAF.

5. John Talbot Smith interview TS, 17, Oral History Collection, NMMEAF.

6. Ernie Pyle, *Brave Men* (New York: Henry Holt, 1944), 176.

7. Andy Anzanos, *My Combat Diary: With Eighth Air Force B-17s, 390th Bomb Group*, rev. ed. (Raleigh, NC: lulu.com, 2009), 45.

8. John Galvin in Eric Hammel, *Aces against Japan: The American Aces Speak* (Pacifica, CA: Pacifica, 2000), 205.

9. Kenneth A. Walsh in Mark Styling, *Corsair Aces of World War II* (Oxford: Osprey, 1995), 8–9.

10. See e.g. William Anderson, *Pathfinders* (London: Jarrolds, 1946); Denys A. Braithwaite, *Target for Tonight: Flying Long-range Reconnaissance and Pathfinder Missions in World War II* (Barnsley, UK: Pen & Sword Aviation, 2005); Hugh Dundas, *Flying Start: A Fighter Pilot's War Years* (Barnsley, UK: Pen & Sword Aviation, 2011); Vincent F. Fagan, *Liberator Pilot: The Cottontails' Battle for Oil* (Carlsbad, CA: California Aero, 1992); Carl Fyler, *Staying Alive: A B-17 Pilot's Experiences Flying Unescorted Bomber Missions by 8th Air Force Elements during World War II* (Leavenworth, KS: J. H. Johnston, 1995); Robert Grilley, *Return from Berlin: The Eye of a Navigator* (Madison: University of Wisconsin Press, 2003); Byron Lane, *Byron's War: I Never Will Be Young Again* (Central Point, OR: Hellgate, 1997); Frank D. Murphy, *Luck of the Draw: Reflections on the Air War in Europe* (Trumbull, CT: FNP, 2001); R. J. W. Passmore, *Out of the Darkness*

(Bristol, UK: Arrowsmith, 2011); Robert M. Slane, *Journey to Freedom and Beyond* (Victoria, BC: Trafford, 2004); Moritz Thomsen, *My Two Wars* (South Royalton, VT: Steerforth, 1996); Robert "Smoky" Vrilakas, *Look, Mom—I Can Fly! Memoirs of a World War II P-38 Fighter Pilot* (Tucson, AZ: Amethyst Moon, 2011).

11. See e.g. George F. Bailey interview TS, 7, Oral History Collection, NMMEAF; Martin Coffee interview TS, 5, 398th Bomb Group, accessed October 31, 2014, 398th.org; John Costigan interview, 13573/4, IWM; Russell Currier interview TS, 10, 398th Bomb Group, accessed October 31, 2014, 398th.org; Don Farrington interview, 32394/6, IWM; Harry D. Gobrecht interview TS, 13, Oral History Collection, NMMEAF; Jeffrey Goodwin interview, 27793/4, IWM; James R. Haas interview TS, 13, 398th Bomb Group, accessed October 31, 2014, 398th.org; Myron Howard Hails interview, AFC/2001/001/19881, VHP; John F. Homan interview, ROHA, accessed September 26, 2015, oralhistory.rutgers.edu; Henry Hooper interview, 27807/9, IWM; Donald R. Jenkins interview, ROHA, accessed September 26, 2015, oralhistory.rutgers.edu; Edward Jones interview TS, 3, 398th Bomb Group, accessed October 31, 2014, 398th.org; Donald D. Johnson interview TS, 4, Oral History Collection, NMMEAF; Richard M. Kennedy interview TS, 7, Oral History Collection, NMMEAF; Clarence King interview TS, 14, 398th Bomb Group, accessed October 31, 2014, 398th.org; Ernie Lummis interview, 27800/6, IWM; John W. Nipper interview TS, 43, Veterans Oral History Project, CSWS, accessed October 9, 2015, sws.utk.edu; Alan M. Neilson interview TS, 8, Oral History Collection, NMMEAF; John N. Anderson with Clint and Steve Sperry, *Thunderbolt to War: An American Fighter Pilot in England* (Stroud, UK: Fonthill, 2015), 77; Albert S. Porter interview TS, 20, Oral History Collection, NMMEAF; Robert Rowland interview TS, 4, 398th Bomb Group, accessed November 1, 2014, 398th.org; John W. Towle interview TS, 52, CSWS, accessed October 9, 2015, csws.utk.edu; John Wall interview, 27806/2, IWM; W. Bud Wentz interview TS, 11, Oral History Collection, NMMEAF.

12. Arthur Batten interview, 27802/14, IWM; see also e.g. John Costigan interview, 13573/4, IWM; see also e.g. Rex Kimblin, *How Lucky I Was: 35 Missions in a Lancaster Bomber* (Toowong, QLD: Chambers, 2012), 181.

13. Arnold Willis interview, EAA, accessed October 10, 2014, eaavideo.org; see also e.g. Edward P. Perry, *Recalling World War II: One Personal Experience* (New York: Vantage, 1992), 85; Jesse Richard Pitts, *Return to Base: Memoirs of a B-17 Copilot, Kimbolton, England, 1943–1944* (Charlottesville, VA: Howell, 2004), 159.

14. Robert G. Brown, *On the Edge: Personal Flying Experiences during the Second World War* (Burnstown, ON: GSPH, 1999), 76.

15. John Comer, *Combat Crew: A True Story of Flying and Fighting in World War II* (New York: William Morrow, 1988), 139; see also e.g. Julius Altvater, *Off We Go . . . Down in Flame* (Victoria, BC: Trafford, 2002), 102.

16. Albert M. Bell in *The 390th Bomb Group in Action: An Anthology*, vol. 1, ed. Wilbert H. Richarz, Richard H. Perry, and William J. Robinson (Tucson, AZ: 390th Memorial Museum Foundation, 1983), 169. On prayer seen as interfering with ship operations, see also e.g. Paul C. Grassey interview TS, 21, Oral History Collection, NMMEAF.

17. John Matthews in Mel Rolfe, *Flying into Hell: The Bomber Command Offensive as Seen Through the Eyes of Twenty Crews* (London: Grub Street, 2001), 39; see also e.g. Arthur Madelaine in ibid., 118.

18. Trevor Timperley interview, 27493/7, IWM; see also Brown, *On the Edge*, 76.

19. Max Hastings, *Bomber Command* (London: Michael Joseph, 1979), 222.

20. Ted Park, *Angels Twenty* (St. Lucia, QLD: University of Queensland Press, 1994), 25.

21. William M. Behrns with Kenneth Moore, *The San Joaquin Siren: An American Ace in WWII's CBI* (Tucson, AZ: Amethyst Moon, 2011), 125.

22. Geoffrey Willatt, *Bombs and Barbed Wire: My War in the RAF and Stalag Luft III* (Tunbridge Wells, UK: Parapress, 1995), 38.

23. John Walsh, Happy Landings, 22, 12812, IWM.

24. Dennis "Sandy" Slack in Pat Cunningham, *Bomb on the Red Markers* (Newbury, UK: Countryside, 2010), 15.

25. Wallace R. Foreman, *B-17 Nose Art Directory* (North Branch, MN: Phalanx, 1996), 26; Wallace R. Foreman, *B-24 Nose Art Directory* (North Branch, MN: Phalanx, 1996), 29.

26. Lloyd Krueger, *Come Fly With Me: Experiences of an Airman in World War II* (Dubuque, IA: Shepherd, 1990), 146–147, 155.

27. Sid Grantham, *The 13 Squadron Story* (Dee Why, NSW: Grantham, 1991), 158, back cover.

28. Tony Reick in Atholl Sutherland Brown, *Silently into the Midst of Things: 177 Squadron Royal Air Force in Burma, 1943–1945: History and Personal Narratives* (Lewes, UK: Book Guild, 1997), 156.

29. Foreman, *B-17 Nose Art;* Foreman, *B-24 Nose Art.*

30. Geoffrey Wellum, *First Light* (London: Viking, 2002).

31. Geoffrey Wellum in William Little, *The Psychic Tourist: A Voyage into the Curious World of Predicting the Future* (London: Icon, 2010), 274.

32. Leonard Carson, *Pursue and Destroy* (Granada Hills, CA: Sentry, 1978), 88.

33. See e.g. Roger W. Armstrong, *U.S.A. the Hard Way: An Autobiography of a B-17 Crew Member*, ed. Ken Stone (Orange County, CA: Quail House, 1991), 59–60; Gary A. Best, *Belle of the Brawl: Letters Home from a B-17 Bombardier* (Portland, OR: Inkwater, 2010), 206; Robert E. Haynes interview TS, 5, Oral History Collection, NMMEAF; Keith C. Schuyler, *Elusive Horizons* (Cranbury, NJ: A. S. Barnes, 1969), 153.

34. Herschel H. Green, *Herky: Memoirs of a Checkertail Ace* (Atglen, PA: Schiffer, 1996), 26.

35. Richard C. Greene interview TS, 5, Oral History Collection, NMMEAF; see also Anthony Alberco and Kenneth Carey interview TS, 23–24, Oral History Collection, NMMEAF.

36. Daniel H. Kalish interview TS, 11, Oral History Collection, NMMEAF.

37. Altvater, *Off We Go*, 103.

38. Robert C. Kensett, *A Walk in the Valley* (Burnstown, ON: GSPH, 2003), 53.

39. Daniel L. Becker, My Twenty-Eight Missions in the European Theater of Operations, November 7, 1943 to May 18, 1944, 23, 2009.0380.0001, NMMEAF.

40. John Talbot Smith interview TS, 59, ROHA, accessed September 26, 2015, oralhistory.rutgers.edu.

41. Harry Irons interview, 27796/3, IWM.

42. Tom Sawyer, *Only Owls and Bloody Fools Fly at Night* (London: Kimber, 1982), 55.

43. Don Collumbell interview TS, 23, S00509, AWM; see also e.g. Ron Fitch, *Recollections: A Lancaster Bomber Crew 55 Years On* (Annandale, NSW: Desert Pea, 2001), 38; Kensett, *Walk in the Valley*, 53.

44. Miles Tripp, *The Eighth Passenger: A Flight of Recollection and Discovery* (London: Macmillan, 1969), 135.

45. Vernon Wilkes in Simpson, *'Ops,'* 105; Vernon Wilkes in Roger A. Freeman, *The British Airman* (London: Arms & Armour, 1989), 89.

46. Lucien Thomas in Dunmore and Carter, *Reap the Whirlwind*, 191.

47. Robert V. Brulle, *Angels Zero: P-47 Close Air Support in Europe* (Washington, DC: Smithsonian, 2000), 132; Ken Adam in Max Arthur, *Lost Voices of the Royal Air Force* (London: Hodder, 2005), 217–218; see also e.g. Howard L. Abney in *Hells Angel's Newsletter: The Final Six Years*, ed. Eddie Deerfield (Palm Harbor, FL: 303rd Bomb Group [H] Association, 2007), February 2004, 16; Ted Hitchcock interview, 30005/4, IWM; Sam Lipfriend interview, 31462/4, IWM.

48. Edwin E. Koch, "G.I. Lore: Lore of the Fifteenth Air Force," *New York Folklore Quarterly* 9 (1953): 61.

49. Edward H. Tracy, The War Years: The Memoirs of Edward H. Tracy, 44, 2003.1617.0001, NMMEAF.

50. Norbert "Pete" Riegel, Papa Pete: "The Way It Was," 32, 2016.0251.0001, NMMEAF.

51. Len Bradfield in Martin W. Bowman, *Scramble: Memories of the RAF in the Second World War* (Stroud, UK: Tempus, 2006), 95.

52. See e.g. Bob Hutton and Andy Rooney, *Air Gunner* (New York: Farrar & Rinehart, 1944), 47–48, 82–83; Roy R. Grinker and John M. Spiegel, *Men under Stress* (Philadelphia: Blakiston, 1945), 131; D. Stafford-Clark, "Morale and Flying Experience: Results of a Wartime Study," *Journal of Mental Science* 95 (1949): 16; John Steinbeck, *Once There Was a War* (New York: Viking, 1958), 30–31.

53. Arthur White, *Bread and Butter Bomber Boys* (Upton on Severn, UK: Square One, 1995), 125.

54. Frank A. Armstrong, So Near Heaven and Surrounded by Hell, 13, Frank A. Armstrong Jr. Papers, ECU. Another example is the commander of the 487th Bomb Group, Beirne Lay, who among other things was triskaidekaphobic. See Beirne Lay Jr., *I Wanted Wings* (New York: Harper, 1937), 195.

55. William F. Halsey and J. Bryan III, *Admiral Halsey's Story* (New York: McGraw-Hill, 1947), 97.

56. See Najeeb E. Halaby, *Crosswinds: An Airman's Memoir* (New York: Doubleday, 1978), 80.

57. Bill Newton Dunn *Big Wing: The Biography of Air Chief Marshal Sir Trafford Leigh-Mallory* (Shrewsbury, UK: Airlife, 1992), 63.

58. *Nashua Telegraph*, October 14, 1943, 1.

59. See *Florence-Times News*, March 11, 1931, 1.

60. See Harry C. Butcher, *My Three Years with Eisenhower: The Personal Diary of Captain Harry C. Butcher, USNR, Naval Aide to General Eisenhower, 1942 to 1945* (New York: Simon & Schuster, 1946), 269.

61. Chaz Bowyer, *Guns in the Sky* (London: Dent, 1979), 35–36.

62. Arnold, Henry H. *American Air Power Comes of Age: General Henry H. "Hap" Arnold's World War II Diaries*, ed. John W. Huston (Maxwell AFB, AL: Air University Press, 2002), 329, 351 n. 82.

63. Doolittle had been a founding member of the Anti-Superstition Society in 1930 (see *Nashua Telegraph*, June 14, 1980, 6), while Harris referred to those who put their faith in magical thinking as "idiots" (R. V. Jones, *Most Secret War* [London: Penguin, 2009], 390).

64. See e.g. Keith Beattie in Max Lambert, *Night after Night: New Zealanders in*

Bomber Command (Auckland: HarperCollins, 2005), 102; Sidney Munns, *As Luck Would Have It: Reminiscences of a Retired RAF Observer/Navigator* (Northampton, UK: Friday File, 1992), 26; Jack Davenport in Ross A. Pearson, *Australians at War in the Air*, vol. 1 (Kenthurst, NSW: Kangaroo, 1995), 51; Jack Watts, *Nickels and Nightingales* (Burnstown, ON: GSPH, 1995), 123; Charlie Churchill in Alan White, *The King's Thunderbolts: No. 44 (Rhodesia) Squadron Royal Air Force* (Lincoln, UK: Tucann, 2007), 51. On the role of German sound locators, see Werner Muller, *Sound Locators, Fire Control Systems and Searchlights of the German Heavy Flak Units, 1939–1945* (Atglen, PA: Schiffer, 2004).

65. Thomas G. Quinlan, *Corkscrew to Safety: A Tail-Gunner's Tour with 103 Squadron RAF, 1944/5* (Bognor, UK: Woodfield, 2011), 68, 78, 131.

66. Ibid., 85, 112, 138.

67. See Werner Muller, *Ground Radar Systems of the Luftwaffe* (Atglen, PA: Schiffer, 2004), 29–30; The R1155 Info Page, accessed October 15, 2015, vq5x79. f2s.com/greenradio/Wireless21a.html.

68. See Bill Bailey, *Alone I Fly* (Barnsley, UK: Pen & Sword Aviation, 2009), 33; Peter McGrath in Pat Cunningham, *Fighter! Fighter! Corkscrew Port!* (Barnsley, UK: Pen & Sword Aviation, 2012), 192–193; G. P. Dawson, Wartime Memoirs, 29, 16764, IWM; G. I. Donnelly, *A Quest for Wings: From Tail-Gunner to Pilot* (Stroud, UK: Tempus, 2000), 47; A. O. Rankin, Research in Relation to Bomber Operations, July 23, 1941, AIR 14/3922, TNA; White, *King's Thunderbolts*, 69.

69. See Report on the Effect of I.F.F. on Searchlights, encl. 14A, AIR 14/3270, TNA.

70. John Slessor, *The Central Blue: The Autobiography of Sir John Slessor* (New York: Praeger, 1957), 374.

71. Jones, *Most Secret War*, 211, 390.

72. Arthur T. Harris, *Despatch on War Operations, 23rd February, 1942, to 8th May, 1945* (London: Frank Cass, 1995), 140.

73. On the development of the flak suit and reactions, see Mae Mills Link and Hubert A. Coleman, *Medical Support of the Army Air Forces in World War II* (Washington, DC: Office of the Surgeon General, USAF, 1955), 628; see also Curtis LeMay with MacKinlay Kantor, *Mission with LeMay* (Garden City, NY: Doubleday, 1965), 330–331. On bomber crews choosing to sit or stand on their body armor, see e.g. Carl Fyler, *Staying Alive: A B-17 Pilot's Experiences Flying Unescorted Bomber Missions by 8th Air Force Elements during World War II* (Leavenworth, KS: J. H. Johnson, 1995), 41; Jackson Granholm, *The Day We Bombed Switzerland: Flying with the US Eighth Army Air Force in World War II* (Shrewsbury, UK: Airlife, 2000), 66; Richard H. Hamilton interview, AFC/2001/001/61291, VHP;

Richard Riley Johnson, *Twenty Five Milk Runs (And a Few Others): To Hell's Angels and Back* (Victoria, BC: Trafford, 2004), 185; Krueger, *Come Fly With Me*, 142; Bill Simkins in Brian D. O'Neill, *Half a Wing, Three Engines and a Prayer: B-17s over Germany* (New York: McGraw-Hill, 1999), 325; A. B. De Jarnett in *388th Anthology*, vol. 2, *Tales of the 388th Bombardment Group (H) 1942–45*, ed. Janet Pack and Richard Singer (San Jose, CA: Writers Club, 2001), 56; Ben Smith Jr., *Chick's Crew: A Tale of the Eighth Air Force* (Tallahassee, FL: Rose, 1983), 54.

74. Andrew Wiseman with Sean Feast, *An Alien Sky: The Story of One Man's Remarkable Adventure in Bomber Command during the Second World War* (London: Grub Street, 2015), 49.

75. Charles Lamb, *To War in a Stringbag* (Garden City, NY: Doubleday, 1980), 115.

76. McManus, *Deadly Sky*, 306: see e.g. U.S. Militaria Forum, usmilitaria forum.com/forums/index.php?/topic/36421-lucky-bastard-club-certificates, accessed September 10, 2016.

77. Kenneth Thompson, *Memoirs of a WWII Fighter Pilot: And Some Modern Political Commentary* (Victoria, BC: Trafford, 2011), 39.

78. Tom Blackburn, *The Jolly Rogers: The Story of Tom Blackburn and Navy Fighting Squadron VF-17* (New York: Orion, 1989), 41.

79. Mark K. Wells, *Courage and Air Warfare: The Allied Aircrew Experience in the Second World War* (London: Frank Cass, 1995), 75–80; see Link and Coleman, *Medical Support*, 660–670; S. C. Rexford-Welch, *The Royal Air Force Medical Services*, vol. 2, *Commands* (London: HMSO, 1955), 123–137. On the often problematic evolution of psychiatric diagnosis and treatment in the military context, see Hans Binneveld, *From Shellshock to Combat Stress: A Comparative History of Military Psychiatry* (Amsterdam: Amsterdam University Press, 1997); Edgar Jones and Simon Wessely, *Shell Shock to PTSD: Military Psychiatry from 1900 to the Gulf War* (Hove, UK: Psychology Press, 2005); Ben Shephard, *A War of Nerves: Soldiers and Psychiatrists in the Twentieth Century* (Cambridge, MA: Harvard University Press, 2001).

80. Grinker and Spiegel, *Men under Stress*, 131; Stafford-Clark, "Morale and Flying Experience," 16. On other, less benign, symptoms of combat stress, see e.g. R. C. Anderson, "Neuropsychiatric Problems of the Flyer," *American Journal of Medicine* 4 (1948): 639–640; Kenneth G. Bergin, *Aviation Medicine: Its Theory and Application* (Bristol, UK: John Wright, 1949), 358–359; Norman A. Levy, *Personality Disturbances in Combat Fliers* (New York: Josiah Macy Jr., 1945), 12–13.

81. See Lysann Damisch, Barbara Stoberock, and Thomas Mussweiler, "Keep Your Fingers Crossed! How Superstition Improves Performance," *Psychological*

Science 21, 7 (2010): 1014–1020; Erez Siniver and Gideon Yaniv, "Kissing the Mezuzah and Cognitive Performance: Is There an Observable Benefit?" *Journal of Economic Behavior & Organization* 117 (2015): 40–46; see also Robert L. Park, *Superstition: Belief in the Age of Science* (Princeton: Princeton University Press, 2008), 121; Richard Wiseman and Caroline Watt, "Measuring Superstitious Belief: Why Lucky Charms Matter," *Personality and Individual Difference* 37 (2004): 1533–1541. The reverse also holds true, of course, meaning the decades-old Department of Defense policy of skipping the number 13 as a designator for sponsored military aircraft designs is not necessarily as irrational as it might seem. See Andreas Parsch, "Missing" USAF/DOD Aircraft Designations, accessed July 4, 2015, designation-systems.net/usmilav/missing-mds.html.

82. Malte Friese et al., "Personal Prayer Counteracts Self-control Depletion," *Consciousness and Cognition* 29 (2014): 90–95; Malte Friese and Michaela Wänke, "Personal Prayer Buffers Self-control Depletion," *Journal of Experimental Social Psychology* 51 (2014): 56–59.

83. Asking for divine intervention seems to have been more popular—or at least more openly engaged in—among American than British fliers, while the latter were more prone to the phobia about having their pictures taken.

84. Superstition was, however, apparently quite rare among British and Commonwealth crews assigned to anti-submarine work rather than strategic bombing, which can be explained by the lesser dangers encountered. A study of former RCAF aircrew from 1982 suggests the incidence of combat-related stress was significantly lower in Coastal Command than in Bomber Command or Fighter Command. Lisa Elizabeth Dwyer, "Wartime Operational Stress and Ischemic Heart Disease: The Manitoba Follow-Up Study, 1948–2005," MSc diss., University of Manitoba, 2005, 87, 89: see also Richard Kingsland, *Into the Midst of Things* (Canberra: Air Power Development Centre, 2010), 55. It did, however, still occur: see e.g. Eric Harrison interview, 30002/6, IWM: Donald Stewart MacNeil interview, Island Voices, accessed November 15, 2015, islandvoices.ca; John Millet, *View from the Turret* (Wollongong, NSW: Five Islands, 1994), 35.

85. William C. "Bill" Healy in Paul M. Sailer, *The Oranges Are Sweet: Major Don M. Beerbower and the 353rd Fighter Squadron, November 1942 to August 1944* (Wadena, MN: Loden, 2011), 282.

86. Levy, *Personality Disturbances*, 6.

87. Kelly Clayton Gross, *Live Bait: WWII Memories of an Undefeated Fighter Ace* (Portland, OR: Inkwater, 2006), 240. See also, however, Granholm, *Day We Bombed Switzerland*, 129.

88. See e.g. Kenneth Brown Collings, "Pilots Are Superstitious," *Flying and*

Popular Aviation, October 1941, 24–26, 86; Mike Klesius, "One More for the Checklist," *Air & Space Magazine*, September 2010, accessed December 10, 2014, airspacemag.com. In the United States in particular, superstitious behavior portrayed in Hollywood aviation films of the 1930s and 1940s might also be replicated by real fliers. See Barrett Tillman, "Omens, Augurs, Jinxes and Other Aviation Superstitions," *Air Progress*, April 1971, 27–29. There was also, over time, a tendency for the flier superstitions of one era to become part of a pattern that in some cases has lasted down to the present. See Rob Burgon, *Piano Burning and Other Fighter Pilot Traditions* (Salt Lake City: Slipstream, 2016). To take a couple of postwar British examples, fighter pilot Geoff Higgs was certain that trouble always came in threes (see G. R. Higgs, *Front Line and Experimental Flying with the Fleet Air Arm: "Purely by Chance"* [Barnsley, UK: Pen & Sword Aviation, 2010], 52–53, 55) while test pilot Roland Beamont was considered very brave by others to have taken the maiden flight of the RAF's Canberra jet bomber on Friday, May 13, 1949 (see Roland Beamont, *The Years Flew Past: 40 Years at the Leading Edge of Aviation* [Shrewsbury, UK: Airlife, 2001], 64; Mike Brooke, *Follow Me Through: The Ups and Downs of an RAF Flying Instructor* [Stroud, UK: History Press, 2013], 152–153).

89. On flying military jets as inherently dangerous and requiring luck even in peace, see e.g. Jerry Pooke, *Flying Freestyle: An RAF Fast Jet Pilot's Story* (Barnsley, UK: Pen & Sword Aviation, 2009), 34; Jay Lacklen, *Flying the Line: An Air Force Pilot's Journey* (Minneapolis: Two Harbors, 2013), 34–35. On the perils of civil aviation from the 1930s through the 1950s, see e.g. Ernest Kellogg Gann, *Fate Is the Hunter* (New York: Simon & Schuster, 1961).

90. Interview with Red Arrow Flight Lieutenant Mike Child, Sussex Life, 24 October 2012, accessed December 7, 2014, sussexlife.co.uk.

91. Peter Hunt, *Angles of Attack: An A-6 Intruder Pilot's War* (New York: Ballantine, 2002), 216.

92. On the growth of superstition in RAF Bomber Command, see Stafford-Clark, "Morale and Flying Experience," 16. On the growth of bomber crew anxiety reactions as losses mounted in the Eighth Air Force, see Douglas D. Bond, *The Love and Fear of Flying* (New York: International Universities Press, 1952), 126–129, 189; Statistical Survey of the Emotional Casualties of the Eighth Air Force Aircrews, 25 May 1945, Reel 135071, AFHRA.

93. Smith, *Chick's Crew*, 135.

94. Those academics who have dealt with the subject so far, such as Vanessa Ann Chambers and Martin Francis, have worked on broader canvases: in the former case, popular belief in the first half of the twentieth century; in the lat-

ter case, the place of the RAF flier within British culture during the war. Vanessa Ann Chambers, "Fighting Chance: War, Popular Belief and British Society, 1900–1951," PhD diss., University of London, 2007; Martin Francis, *The Flyer: British Culture and the Royal Air Force, 1939–1945* (Oxford: Oxford University Press, 2008).

95. On superstition and sports, see e.g. Judy Becker, "Superstition in Sport," *International Journal of Sport Psychology* 6 (1975): 148–152; Jerry M. Burger and Amy L. Lynn, "Superstitious Behavior among American and Japanese Professional Baseball Players," *Basic and Applied Social Psychology* 27 (2005): 71–76; Judy L. Van Raalte et al., "Chance Orientation and Superstitious Behavior on the Putting Green," *Journal of Sport Behavior* 14 (1991): 41–50; Michaéla C. Schippers and Paul A. M. Van Langer, "The Psychological Benefits of Superstitious Rituals in Top Sport: A Study Among Top Sportspersons," *Journal of Applied Social Psychology* 36 (2006): 2532–2553.

96. Grinker and Spiegel, *Men under Stress*, 131.

97. On ongoing conviction, see e.g. Chambers, "Fighting Chance," 87; Forrest S. Clark interview TS, 15, Oral History Collection, NMMEAF; Jack D. Rude interview TS, 10, Oral History Collection, NMMEAF; Charles W. Spencer and Darrell Gust in Brian D. O'Neill, *Half a Wing, Three Engines and a Prayer: B-17s over Germany* (New York: McGraw-Hill, 1999), 202, 334.

APPENDIX I: TOUR LENGTH

1. John Terraine, *The Right of the Line: The Role of the RAF in World War Two* (Barnsley, UK: Pen & Sword Military, 2010), 522–527; Arthur Eyeton-Jones, *Day Bomber* (Stroud, UK: Sutton, 1998), 25.

2. See Frank Broome, *Dead Before Dawn: A Heavy Bomber Tail-gunner in World War II* (Barnsley, UK: Pen & Sword Aviation, 2008), 283; Geoff D. Copeman, *Right-Hand Man: A Flight Engineer's Story* (Baldock, UK: Euro Slug, 1996), 44, 51, 77; Arthur Hoyle, *Into the Darkness: One Young Australian's Journey from Sydney to the Deadly Skies over Germany, 1939–1945*, ed. David Vernon (Jamison Centre, ACT: Stringybark, 2012), 147; Royan Yule, *On a Wing and a Prayer* (Derby, UK: Derby Books, 2012), 26.

3. See Jim Auton, *RAF Liberator over the Eastern Front: A Bomb Aimer's Second World War and Cold War Story* (Barnsley, UK: Pen & Sword Aviation, 2008), 88; Richard Stowers, *Wellingtons over the Med: A Kiwi Pilot's Story from the Mediterranean* (Hamilton, NZ: Stowers, 2012), 122.

4. See Atholl Sutherland Brown, *Silently into the Midst of Things: 177 Squadron Royal Air Force in Burma, 1943–1945: History and Personal Narratives* (Lewes, UK:

Book Guild, 1997), 74; Dennis Spencer, *Looking Backwards over Burma: Wartime Recollections of a RAF Beaufighter Navigator* (Bognor, UK: Woodfield, 2009), 150.

5. See Roy Lee Grover, *Incidents in the Life of a B-25 Pilot* (Bloomington, IN: AuthorHouse, 2006), 84; Garrett Middlebrook, *Air Combat at 20 Feet: Selected Missions from a Strafer Pilot's Diary* (Bloomington, IN: AuthorHouse, 2004), 533, 607.

6. Mae Mills Link and Hubert C. Coleman, *Medical Support of the Army Air Forces in World War II* (Washington, DC: Office of the Surgeon General, USAF, 1955), 661.

7. James H. "Jimmy" Doolittle with Carroll V. Glines, *I Could Never Be So Lucky Again* (New York: Bantam, 1992), 359–60; Gordon Graham, *Down for Double: Anecdotes of a Fighter Pilot* (White Stone, VA: Brandylane, 1996), 47.

8. Willie Chapman, *Booster McKeester and Other Expendables: 98th Heavy Bombardment Group, Ninth U.S. Army Air Force, Middle East Theater, 1942–43* (Collierville, TN: Global, 1994), 111; Vincent F. Fagan, *Liberator Pilot: The Cottontails' Battle for Oil* (Carlsbad, CA: California Aero, 1992), 69; John C. McManus, *Deadly Sky: The American Combat Airman in World War II* (Novato, CA: Presidio, 2000), 300; Jack R. Myers, *Shot at and Missed: Recollections of a World War II Bombardier* (Norman: University of Oklahoma Press, 2004), 189–90; Thomas C. Wilcox, *One Man's Destiny* (Mogadore, OH: Telecraft, 1991), 91. The tours of the small cadre of reconnissance pilots in the Ninth Air Force in 1944–1945 rose progressively from seventy-five to ninety missions. Joe Thompson and Tom Delvaux, *Tiger Joe: A Photographic Diary of a World War II Aerial Reconnaisance Pilot* (Nashville, TN: Eveready, 2006), 69.

9. See Howard "Tommy" Thompson in Elizabeth Cassen, *The Last Voices: World War II Veterans of the Air War Speak More Than Half a Century Later* (Seattle: CreateSpace, 2014), 82.

10. See A. J. Padgett with Frank Padgett, *Mission over Indochine: A Story of Courage, Honor and Sacrifice* (Bloomington, IN: AuthorHouse, 2012), 115; Walt Shiel, *Rough War: The Combat Story of Lt. Paul J. Eastman, a "Burma Banshee" P-40 and P-47 Pilot* (Jacobsville, MI: Jacobsville Books, 2011), 196.

11. See Chester Marshall, *Sky Giants over Japan: A Diary of a B-29 Combat Crew in WWII* (Winona, MN: Apollo, 1984), 180, 188; Van R. Parker, *Dear Folks* (Memphis, TN: Global, 1989), 243.

12. See John Boeman, *Morotai: A Memoir of War* (Garden City, NY: Doubleday, 1981), 104.

13. J. D. Brown, *Carrier Operations in World War II*, ed. David Hobbs (Barnsley, UK: Pen & Sword Aviation, 2009), 250.

14. Hank Adlam, *The Disastrous Fall and Triumphant Rise of the Fleet Air Arm from 1913–1945* (Barnsley, UK: Pen & Sword Aviation, 2014), 132; see e.g. E. E. Barringer, *"Alone on a Wide, Wide Sea": The Story of 835 Naval Air Squadron in the Second World War* (London: Leo Cooper, 1995), 109; Henry "Hank" Adlam, *On and Off the Flight Deck: Reflections of a Naval Fighter Pilot in World War II* (Barnsley, UK: Pen & Sword Aviation, 2007), 136, 179.

15. Byron C. Cook in *388th Anthology,* vol. 2, *Tales of the 388th Bombardment Group (H) 1942–45,* ed. Janet Pack and Richard Singer (San Jose, CA: Writers Club, 2001), 89; see also e.g. Keith C. Schuyler, *Elusive Horizons* (Cranbury, NJ: A. S. Barnes, 1969), 154.

16. Eric Cropper, *Back Bearings: A Navigator's Tale, 1942–1974* (Barnsley, UK: Pen & Sword Aviation, 2010), 43; see also e.g. Copeman, *Right-Hand Man,* 44; Campbell Muirhead, *Diary of a Bomb Aimer: Training in America and Flying with 12 Squadron in WWII,* ed. Philip Swan (Barnsley, UK: Pen & Sword Aviation, 2009), 100.

17. Marshall, *Sky Giants,* 188; see also e.g. Kevin Herbert, *Maximum Effort: The B-29's against Japan* (Manhattan, KS: Sunflower University Press, 1983), 60.

BIBLIOGRAPHY

INTERVIEWS

Abbott, J. (VHP); Alberco, A. (NMMEAF); Aldridge, J. (IWM); Alymore G. (bbc
.co.uk/ww2peopleswar/stories, accessed January 18, 2013); Anderson, K. (398th
.org, accessed October 31, 2014); Arrowsmith, D. (IWM); Bailey, G. (NMMEAF);
Bain, R. (IWM); Bartlett, L. (LC); Batten, A. (IWM); Biddle, J. (VHP); Bilton, G.
(IWM); Blower, W. (VHP); Boydston, R. (VHP); Candelaria, R. (lib/texas.edu
/voices, accessed May 1, 2015); Capen, R. (VHP); Carey, K. (NMMEAF); Carney,
D. (VHP); Cecil, B. (IWM); Charlwood, D. (AWM); Chick, M. (RAFBCA); Clark,
F. (ROHA; MNMEAF); Coffee, M. (398th.org, accessed October 31, 2014);
Collumbell, D. (AWM); Costigan, J. (IWM); Cox, D. (IWM); Culp, R. (VHP);
Currier, R. (398th.org, accessed October 31, 2014); Domski, E. (EAA); Donson,
W. (UVic); Dowden, W. (VHP); Drake, E. (UNT); Dyson, R. (LC); Easton, A.
(IWM); Edge, G. (IWM); Evans, D. (IWM); Everhart, J. (CAPS); Farrington,
D. (IWM); Fleming, D. (UNT); Gaines, G. (EAA); Gearing, E. (IWM); Gee, J.
(RAFBCA); Geraldi, J. (VHP); Gillespie, K. (VHP); Gobrecht, H. (NMMEAF);
Godfrey, L. (IWM); Gold, L. (VHP); Goodwin, J. (IWM); Gordon, E. (bbc.co
.uk/history/ww2peopleswar/stories, accessed January 19, 2013); Grant, N.
(NMMEAF); Grassey, P. (NMMEAF); Gray, K. (AWM); Greene, R. (NMMEAF);
Guest, F. (NMMEAF); Hails, M. (VHP); Harcourt, R. (NMMEAF); Harrison,
E. (IWM); Hass, J. (398th.org, accessed October 31, 2014); Hatfield, B. (VHP);
Haynes, R. (NMMEAF); Hays, E. (tankbooks.com/interviews/hays1.htm,
accessed May 1, 2015); Henderson, L. (TMP); Henigman, C. (UVic); Hitchcock,
T. (IWM); Homan, J. (ROHA); Honeycutt, R. (VHP); Hooper, H. (IWM);
Hudson, D. (UVic); Ingram, A. (NMMEAF); Irons, H. (IWM); Iveson, T.
(IWM); James, P. (IWM); Jayne, W. (NMMEAF); Jenkins, D. (ROHA); Jennings,
D. (AWM); Jessup, E. (NMMEAF); Johnson, D. (NMMEAF); Jones, H. (UNT);
Joseph, J. (398th.org, accessed October 31, 2014); Kalish, D. (NMMEAF);
Kearns, R. (IWM); Kelbrick, W. (IWM); King, C. (398th.org, accessed October
31, 2014); Keller, J. (NMMEAF); Kelly, R. (TMP); Kennedy, R. (NMMEAF);
Kilmer, R. (UNT); King, G. (IWM); Kling, V. (398th.org, accessed November 1,
2014); Kuehner, B. (EAA); Ladbury, R. (UVic); Lane, R. (UVic); Lasprogato,
M. (CAPS); Liberman, S. (ROHA); Le Marchant, H. (RAFBCA); Lipfriend,
S. (IWM); Littlefield, R. (VHP); Lohse, W. (NMMEAF); Lummis, E. (IWM);
Lundy, D. (NMMEAF); MacNeil, D. (islandvoices.ca, accessed November 18,

2015); Mahony, W. (VHP); Mann, H. (VHP); Mansbridge, S. (UVic); Masters, R. (UVic); McGillvray, J. (IWM); McGovern, F. (IWM); McGregor, J. (IWM); McLaughlin, J. (EAA); Mellor, G. (IWM); Mero, H. (398th.org, accessed October 31, 2014); Meyne, R. (NMMEAF); Moritz, F. (TMP); Nash, H. (RAFBCA); Nazemetz, A. (ROHA); Nealis, L. (NMMEAF); Neilson, A. (NMMEAF); Nelson, B. (398th.org, accessed November 1, 2014); Nipper, J. (CSWS); Ogata, K. (VHP); Ohr, F. (VHP); Peters, W. (VHP); Petrocine, P. (398th.org, accessed November 1, 2014); Porter, A. (NMMEAF); Pykto, S. (EAA); Rackley, L. (AWM); Rackley, W. (ww2online.org, accessed November 1, 2014); Reid, B. (RAFBCA); Ritter, R. (VHP); Roberts, G. (NMMEAF); Robinson, R. (VHP); Rosenthal, R. (100thbg .com, accessed October 25, 2014); Rowland, R. (398th.org, accessed November 1, 2014); Rude, J. (NMMEAF); Sample, D. (TMP); Seagraves, J. (UNT); Schaff, W. (VHP); Seesenguth, D. (VHP); Smith, J. (ROHA; NMMEAF); Smith, L. (EAA); Soper, B. (bbc.co.uk/history/ww2peopleswar/stories, accessed January 19, 2013); Stivender, J. (VHP); Stouffer, R. (EAA); Talbott, R. (398th.org, accessed November 1, 2014); Taylor, J. (IWM); Taylor, J. (NMMEAF); Tenger, V. (IWM); Timperley, T. (IWM); Towle, J. (CSWS); Tredwell, T. (IWM); Tye, E. (VHP); Vickers, R. (NMMEAF); Wall, J. (IWM); Walls, G. (UVic); Ward, N (IWM); Watson, A. (IWM); Wentz, W. (NMMEAF); Whitlow, W. (CAPS); Wilde, E. (UNT); Willis, A. (EAA); Williamson, L. (NMMEAF); Wilson, W. (UVic); Wiswall, F. (ROHA); Wright, H. (AWM); Zauner, W. (EAA).

UNPUBLISHED PAPERS

Aanenson, Q. (NMMEAF); Adler, B. (40thbombgroup.org, accessed January 19, 2015); Anderson, A. (91stbombgroup.com, accessed October 23, 2014); Armstrong, F. (ECU); Beasley, L. (NMMEAF); Becker, D. (NMMEAF); Benham, E. (NMMEAF); Brawley, J. (NMMEAF); Breitenbach, L. (NMMEAF); Brennan, O. (NMMEAF); Brown, F. (LC); Carson, J. (justinmuseum.com, accessed September 26, 2015); Colby, C. (458bg.com, accessed October 24, 2014); Conrad, W. (NMMEAF); Cook, A. (447bg.com, accessed October 23, 2014); Couch, W. (NMMEAF); Dawson, G. (IWM); Domke, M. (446bg.com, accessed October 24, 2014); Donahue, M. (NMMEAF); Dorsett, W. (NMMEAF); Etherington, G. (40thbombgroup.org, accessed January 19, 2015); Field, D. (IWM); Fox, T. (IWM); Frow, B. (RAFM); Golden, S. (388thbg.org, accessed November 8, 2014); Guillot, O. (b24.net, accessed October 24, 2014); Hahn, P. (NMMEAF); Hall, L. (447bg.com, accessed October 23, 2014); Hann, R. (CAPS); Harris, W. (NMMEAF); Hastings, D. (NMMEAF); Harvey, R. (RAFM); Heath, D. (492ndbombgroup.com, accessed October 31, 2014);

Herdic, C. (NMMEAF); Hockaday, N. (IWM); Hornsey, D. (IWM); Hudson, C. (91stbombgroup.com, accessed October 23, 2014); Humphries, B. (91stbomb group.com, accessed October 23, 2014); Hutchens, D. (381st.org, accessed October 31, 2014); Ingram, A. (NMMEAF); Johnson, A. (91stbombgroup.com, accessed October 23, 2014); Jones, K. (NMMEAF); Jule, B. (NMMEAF); Kahne, D. (NMMEAF); Keilman, M. (b24.net, accessed October 24, 2014); Knilans, H. (RAFM); Lamb, K. (NMMEAF); Lazenby, N. (RAFM); Longo, R. (b24.net, accessed October 24, 2014); Maddock, T. (IWM); Malone, W. (303rdbga.com, accessed October 31, 2014); Marshall, W. (NMMEAF); May, J. (NMMEAF); McFarland, L. (447bg.com, accessed October 23, 2014); Meacomes, H. (NMMEAF); Meyne, R. (NMMEAF); Miller, R. (376hbgva.com, accessed October 25, 2014); Moncur, V. (303rdbga.com, accessed October 31, 2014); Muirhead, G. (40thbombgroup.org, accessed January 19, 2015); Olson, C. (NMMEAF); Oncur, V. (303rdbga.com, accessed October 31, 2014); Platt, A. (91stbombgroup.com, accessed October 23, 2014); Randolph, B. (justin museum.com, accessed September 26, 2015); Redfeldt, G. (NMMEAF); Riegel, N. (NMMEAF); Ross, J. (b24.net, accessed October 24, 2014); Rossman, J. (NMMEAF); Schlesinger, B. (NMMEAF); Schmidt, B. (b24.net, accessed October 24, 2014); Schottel Korb, R. (NMMEAF); Simester, R. (NMMEAF); Smith, B. (NMMEAF); Smith, D. (NMMEAF); Stout, M. (453rd.com, accessed October 31, 2014); Tays, R. (NMMEAF); Tracy, E. (NMMEAF); Turell, H. (445bg .org, accessed October 31, 2014); Turner, W. (446bg.com, accessed October 25, 2014); Vogel, C. (458bg.com, accessed October 24, 2014); Walsh, J. (IWM); West, B. (320thbg.org, accessed October 31, 2014); Weir, G. (NMMEAF); Wood, J. (RAFM); Woods, V. (91stbombgroup.com, accessed October 23, 2014).

AIR FORCE HISTORICAL RESEARCH AGENCY
Reel 135071

MASS-OBSERVATION
FR 975—Report on Superstition, November 26, 1941

THE NATIONAL ARCHIVES
AIR 14, 18

DISSERTATIONS
Chambers, Vanessa Ann. "Fighting Chance: War, Popular Belief and British Society, 1900–1951." PhD diss., University of London, 2007.

Dwyer, Lisa Elizabeth. "Wartime Operational Stress and Ischemic Heart Disease: The Manitoba Follow-Up Study, 1948–2005." MSc. diss., University of Manitoba, 2005.

BOOKS AND ARTICLES

Abner, Alan K. *Dead Reckoning: Experiences of a World War II Fighter Pilot.* Shippensburg, PA: Burd Street, 1997.

Adair, Lawrens. *Glass Houses: Paper Men.* Brisbane, QLD: CopyRight Publishing, 1992.

Adlam, Hank. *The Disastrous Fall and Triumphant Rise of the Fleet Air Arm from 1913–1945: Sea Eagles Led by Penguins.* Barnsley, UK: Pen & Sword Aviation, 2014.

Adlam, Henry (Hank). *On and Off the Flight Deck: Reflections of a Naval Fighter Pilot in World War II.* Barnsley, UK: Pen & Sword Aviation, 2007.

Aircrew Association, Vancouver Island Branch. *Aircrew Memories.* Victoria, BC: Victoria Publishing, 1999.

Albertson, Bill. *I Flew with Hell's Angels: Thirty-Six Combat Missions in a B-17 "Flying Fortress," 1944–1945.* Westminster, MD: Heritage, 2005.

Aldridge, Arthur, with Mark Ryan. *The Last Torpedo Flyers.* London: Simon & Schuster, 2013.

Alexander, Richard L. *They Called Me Dixie.* Hemet, CA: Robinson Typographics, 1988.

Alling, Charles. *A Mighty Fortress: Lead Bomber over Europe.* Havertown, PA: Casemate, 2002.

Allison, Robert. *One Man's War.* Seattle: CreateSpace, 2012.

Altvater, Julius (Al). *Off We Go . . . Down in Flame.* Victoria, BC: Trafford, 2002.

Ambrose, Stephen E. *The Wild Blue: The Men and Boys Who Flew the B-24s over Germany.* New York: Simon & Schuster, 2001.

Anderson, Andy. *One Pilot's Story: The Fabled 91st and Other 8th Airforce Memoirs.* Bloomington, IN: AuthorHouse, 2006.

Anderson, Clarence E. (Bud), with Joseph P. Hamelin. *To Fly and Fight: Memoirs of a Triple Ace.* New York: St. Martin's, 1990.

Anderson, John N., with Clint and Steve Sperry. *Thunderbolt to War: An American Fighter Pilot in England.* Stroud, UK: Fonthill, 2015.

Anderson, R. C. "Neuropsychiatric Problems of the Flyer." *American Journal of Medicine* 4 (1948): 636–644.

Anderson, William. *Pathfinders.* London: Jarrolds, 1946.

Anzanos, Andy. *My Combat Diary: With Eighth Air Force B-17s, 390th Bomb Group*. Rev. ed. Raleigh, NC: lulu.com, 2009.

Archer, Henry, and Edward Pine. *To Perish Never*. London: Cassell, 1954.

Ardery, Philip. *Bomber Pilot: A Memoir of World War II*. Lexington: University Press of Kentucky, 1978.

Armitage, Michael. *The Royal Air Force*. London: Brockhampton, 1995.

Armstrong, James Edwin. *Escape! An American Airman's Escape from Hitler's Fortress Europe*. Spartanburg, SC: Honoribus, 2002.

Armstrong, Roger W. *U.S.A. the Hard Way: An Autobiography of a B-17 Crew Member*. Edited by Ken Stone. Orange County, CA: Quail House, 1991.

Arnold, Henry H. *American Air Power Comes of Age: General Henry H. "Hap" Arnold's World War II Diaries*. Vol 2. Edited by John W. Huston. Maxwell AFB, AL: Air University Press, 2002.

Arthur, Max. *Lost Voices of the Royal Air Force*. London: Hodder, 2005.

Asch, Alfred, with David Asch. *The Whole Nine Yards . . . and Then Some*. Franklin, TN: Done Wise, 2013.

Ashman, R. V. *Spitfire against the Odds*. Wellingborough, UK: Patrick Stephens, 1989.

Ashton, J. Norman. *Only Birds and Fools: Flight Engineer, Avro Lancaster, World War II*. Shrewsbury, UK: Airlife, 2000.

Atkinson, William C. *The Jolly Roger: An Airman's Tale of Survival in World War II*. Indianapolis, IN: Dog Ear, 2015.

Austin, R. L. *High Adventure—Navigator at War*. Chichester, UK: Barry Rose, 1989.

Auton, Jim. *RAF Liberator over the Eastern Front: A Bomb Aimer's Second World War and Cold War Story*. Barnsley, UK: Pen & Sword Aviation, 2008.

Aveni, Anthony. *Behind the Crystal Ball: Magic, Science, and the Occult from Antiquity through the New Age*. New York: Random House, 1996.

Aviation History Unit. *The Navy's Air War: A Mission Completed*. Edited by A. R. Buchanan. New York: Harper, 1946.

Ayres, Travis L. *The Bomber Boys: Heroes Who Flew the B-17s in World War II*. New York: NAL Caliber, 2009.

Bailey, Bill. *Alone I Fly*. Barnsley, UK: Pen & Sword Aviation, 2009.

Bailey, John C. *Buffalos, Boomerangs and Kittyhawks: Memoirs of an RAAF WWII Pilot*. Mandurah, WA: DB, 2009.

Baker, Joseph O., and Scott Draper. "Diverse Supernatural Portfolios: Certitude, Exclusivity, and the Curvilinear Relationship between Religiosity and

Paranormal Beliefs." *Journal of the Scientific Study of Religion* 49 (2010): 413–424.

Baldwin, Sherman. *Ironclaw: A Navy Carrier Pilot's Gulf War Experience*. New York: William Murrow, 1996.

Balgrove, Mark, Christopher C. French, and Gareth Jones. "Probabilistic Reasoning, Affirmative Bias and Belief in Precognitive Dreams." *Applied Cognitive Psychology* 20 (2006): 65–83.

Ballard, Jack Stokes. *War Bird Ace: The Great War Exploits of Capt. Field E. Kindley*. College Station: Texas A&M University Press, 2007.

Banta, Theodore Michael. *Vignettes of a B-17 Combat Crew*. New York: Banta, 1997.

Barclay, George. *Fighter Pilot*. London: William Kimber, 1976.

Barringer, E. E. *"Alone on a Wide, Wide Sea": The Story of 835 Naval Air Squadron in the Second World War*. London: Leo Cooper, 1995.

Bates, H. E. *The World in Ripeness: An Autobiography*. Vol. 3. London: Michael Joseph, 1972.

———. [Flying Officer "X"]. *Something in the Air: Comprising* The Greatest People in the World *and* How Sleep the Brave. London: Jonathan Cape, 1944.

Bauchman, Perry. *Spitfire Pilot*. Hantsport, NS: Lancelot, 1996.

Baynes, Richard C. *Replacement Crew: The Training and Combat Experience of a Typical 8th Air Force Replacement Crew in 1944*. Irvine, CA: Baynes, 1993.

Beamont, Roland (Bee). *The Years Flew Past: 40 Years at the Leading Edge of Aviation*. Shrewsbury, UK: Airlife, 2001.

Beaton, Cecil. *Winged Squadrons*. London: Hutchinson, 1942.

Beck, Pip. *Keeping Watch: A WAAF in Bomber Command*. Manchester, UK: Crécy, 2004.

Becker, Judy. "Superstition in Sport." *International Journal of Sport Psychology* 6 (1975): 148–152.

Beech, Joan. *One Waaf's War*. Tunbridge Wells, UK: Costello, 1989.

Beede, John. *They Hosed Them Out*. London: Tandem, 1971.

Behrns, William M., with Kenneth Moore. *The San Joaquin Siren: An American Ace in WWII's CBI*. Tucson, AZ: Amethyst Moon, 2011.

Benbow, Tim, ed. *British Naval Aviation: The First 100 Years*. London: Ashgate, 2011.

Bendiner, Elmer. *The Fall of Fortresses: A Personal Account of the Most Daring—and Deadly—American Air Battles of World War II*. New York: Putnam's, 1980.

Bentine, Michael. *The Reluctant Jester*. London: Bantam, 1992.

————. *The Door Marked Summer*. London: Granada, 1981.

Berkus, Don. *Another Soldier's Story: A Taste of a Great Generation*. Encino, CA: Published by the author, 2010.

Best, Gary A. *Belle of the Brawl: Letters Home from a B-17 Bombardier*. Portland, OR: Inkwater, 2010.

Bewsher, Paul. *"Green Balls": The Adventures of a Night-Bomber*. Edinburgh: Blackwood, 1919.

Bickers, Richard Townshend. *Friendly Fire: Accidents in Battle from Ancient Greece to the Gulf War*. London: Leo Cooper, 1994.

Binneveld, Hans. *From Shell Shock to Combat Stress: A Comparative History of Military Psychiatry*. Translated by John O'Kane. Amsterdam: Amsterdam University Press, 1997.

Bird, Tony. *A Bird over Berlin: A World War Two RAF Pilot's Remarkable Story of Survival*. Bognor: Woodfield, 2000.

Bishop, Patrick. *Bomber Boys: Fighting Back 1940–1945*. London: HarperPress, 2007.

Blackburn, Tom. *The Jolly Rogers: The Story of Tom Blackburn and Navy Fighting Squadron VF-17*. New York: Orion, 1989.

Bledsoe, Marvin. *Thunderbolt: Memoirs of a World War II Fighter Pilot*. New York: Van Norstrand Reinhold, 1982.

Bloemertz, Gunther. *Heaven Next Stop: Impressions of a German Fighter Pilot*. London: Kimber, 1953.

Blount, R. E. (Peppy). *We Band of Brothers*. Austin, TX: Eakin, 1984.

Bloyd, Dean M. *Flak at 12 O'Clock: A Teenage Farm Boy's Experiences That Led to His Becoming a B-17 Co-Pilot; In the 8th Air Force during the Final Months of World War II*. San Jose, CA: Writers Club, 2001.

Blyth, Kenneth K. *Cradle Crew: Royal Canadian Air Force World War II*. Manhattan, KS: Sunflower University Press, 1997.

Böckermann, Max, Annika Gieselmann, and Reinhard Pietrowsky. "What Does Nightmare Distress Mean? Factorial Structure and Psychometric Properties of the Nightmare Distress Questionnaire." *Dreaming* 24 (2014): 279–289.

Boeman, John. *Morotai: A Memoir of War*. Garden City, NY: Doubleday, 1981.

Boiten, Theo. *Nachtjagd: The Night Fighter versus Bomber War over the Third Reich*. Marlborough: Crowood, 1997.

Botsko, Michael. *A Hero Not Forgotten: The Combat Diary of Sgt. Michael Botsko*. Edited by R. J. Kluba. Lexington, KY: CreateSpace, 2013.

Bowen, William H. *The Boy from Altheimer: From the Depression to the Boardroom*. Fayetteville: University of Arkansas Press, 2006.

Bowling, Dan. *"Follow P-D-I": My Experiences as an AAF B-25 Pilot during World War II.* Lomita, CA: Cambria, 2009.

Bowman, Martin W. *We Were Eagles: The Eighth Air Force at War.* 4 vols. Stroud, UK: Amberley, 2014.

———. *RAF Bomber Command: Reflections of War.* 5 vols. Barnsley, UK: Pen & Sword Aviation, 2011–2014.

———. *Echoes of England: The 8th Air Force in World War II.* Stroud, UK: Tempus, 2006.

———. *Scramble: Memories of the RAF in the Second World War.* Stroud, UK: Tempus, 2006.

Bowyer, Chaz. *Tales from the Bombers.* London: William Kimber, 1985.

———. *Guns in the Sky.* London: Dent, 1979.

Boyne, Walter J. Jr. *Beyond the Wild Blue.* 2nd ed. New York: Thomas Dunne, 2007.

Braithwaite, Denys A. *Target for Tonight: Flying Long-range Reconnaissance and Pathfinder Missions in World War II.* Barnsley, UK: Pen & Sword Aviation, 2005.

Brandon, Sydney. "LMF in Bomber Command, 1939–45: Diagnosis or Denouncement?" In *150 Years of British Psychiatry.* Vol. 2, *The Aftermath,* edited by Hugh Freeman and German E. Berrios, 119–129. London: Athlone, 1996.

Breast, John K., ed. *Missions Remembered: The Men of the Middle Tennessee WWII Fighter Pilots Association.* Brentwood, TN: J. M. Productions, 1995.

Briol, John J. *Dead Engine Kids: World War II Diary of John J. Briol, B-17 Ball Turret Gunner with Comments from Notes of Other Crew Members.* Edited by John F. Welch. Rapid City, SD: Silver Wings Association, 1993.

Brooke, J. H. *No Bacon and Eggs Tonight.* Southport, UK: Creativelines, 2002.

Brooke, Mike. *Follow Me Through: The Ups and Downs of an RAF Flying Instructor.* Stroud, UK: History Press, 2013.

Broome, Frank. *Dead Before Dawn: A Heavy Bomber Tail-gunner in World War II.* Barnsley, UK: Pen & Sword Aviation, 2008.

Broughton, Irv. *Hanger Talk: Interviews with Fliers, 1920s–1990s.* Cheney: Eastern Washington University Press, 1998.

Broughton, Irv, ed. *Forever Remembered: The Fliers of WWII.* Spokane: Eastern Washington University Press, 2001.

Brown, Atholl Sutherland. *Silently into the Midst of Things: 177 Squadron Royal Air Force in Burma, 1943–1945: History and Personal Narratives.* Lewes, UK: Book Guild, 1997.

Brown, Gregory, and Basil Spiller. *Halifax Navigator: An Oral and Extended History of Flying Officer Basil Spiller's Years at War*. Howrah, TAS: CreateSpace, 2013.

Brown, James Good. *The Mighty Men of the 381st: Heroes All*. 2nd ed. Salt Lake City: Publishers Press, 1986.

Brown, Kenneth T. *Marauder Man: World War II in the Crucial but Little-Known B-26 Marauder: A Memoir/History*. Pacifica, CA: Pacifica, 2001.

Brown, Robert G. *On the Edge: Personal Flying Experiences during the Second World War*. Burnstown, ON: GSPH, 1999.

Brownwell, R. J. *From Khaki to Blue*. Canberra: Military Historical Society, 1978.

Bruce, Steve. *God Is Dead: Secularization in the West*. Oxford: Blackwell, 2002.

Brulle, Robert V. *Angels Zero: P-47 Close Air Support in Europe*. Washington, DC: Smithsonian, 2000.

Bryan, J., III, and Philip Reed. *Mission Beyond Darkness*. New York: Duell, Sloan and Pearce, 1945.

Buchanan, A. R., ed. *The Navy's Air War: A Mission Completed*. New York: Harper, 1946.

Buckley, John. *Air Power in the Age of Total War*. London: University College London, 2009.

Buell, Harold L. *Dauntless Helldivers: A Dive-Bomber Pilot's Epic Story of the Carrier Battles*. New York: Orion, 1991.

Bunyak, Dawn Trimble. *Our Last Mission: A World War II Prisoner in Germany*. Norman: University of Oklahoma Press, 2003.

Burger, Jerry M., and Amy L. Lynn. "Superstitious Behavior among American and Japanese Baseball Players." *Basic and Applied Social Psychology* 27 (2005): 71–76.

Burgon, Rob. *Piano Burning and Other Fighter Pilot Traditions*. Salt Lake City: Slipstream, 2016.

Burnett, Brian. *A Pilot at Wimbledon: The Memoirs of Air Chief Marshal Sir Brian Burnett*. Codicote, UK: Blenheim, 2009.

Bury, George. *Wellingtons of 115 Squadron over Europe: Life in the Royal Air Force in War and Peace*. Swindon, UK: Air Force Publishing Services, 1994.

Busha, James P. *The Fight in the Clouds: The Extraordinary Combat Experience of P-51 Mustang Pilots during World War II*. Minneapolis: Zenith, 2014.

Bushby, John. *Gunner's Moon*. London: Ian Allan, 1972.

Bushong, Richard B. *My Wars: B-17's to F-4's, WWII to Vietnam, with Speeds 0 to Mach 2.1*. Raleigh, NC: Lulu, 2008.

Butcher, Harry C. *My Three Years with Eisenhower: The Personal Diary of Captain Harry C. Butcher, USNR, Naval Aide to General Eisenhower, 1942 to 1945.* New York: Simon & Schuster, 1946.

Butterworth, Christine A., and Susan C. Butterworth. *Life, Luck and Lancasters: Vivid Wartime Reminiscences of Louis Butler.* Rochdale, UK: Henham, 2013.

Byers, Richard G. *Attack.* Sandy, UT: Aardvark, 1984.

Byers, Roland O. *Flak Dodger: A Story of the 457th Bomb Group, 1943–1945.* Moscow, ID: Pawpaw, 1985.

Cachart, Ted, assisted by Alan and Barbara Parr et al. *Ted the Lad: A Schoolboy Who Went to War.* Derby, UK: JoTe, 2007.

Cameron, Rebecca. *Training to Fly: Military Flight Training, 1907–1945.* Washington, DC: Air Force History and Museums, 1999.

Campbell, James. *Maximum Effort.* London: Alison & Busby, 1957.

Capps, Robert S. *Flying Colt: Liberator Pilot in Italy.* Alexandria, VA: Manor House, 1997.

Carigan, William. *Ad Lib: Flying the B-24 Liberator in World War II.* Manhattan, KS: Sunflower University Press, 1988.

Carl, Marion E. *Pushing the Envelope: The Career of Fighter Ace and Test Pilot Marion Carl.* Annapolis, MD: Naval Institute Press, 1994.

Carré, Ray. *Maximum Effort.* Burbank, CA: National Literary Guild, 1984.

Carson, Gene T. *Wing Ding.* Bloomington, IN: Xlibris, 2000.

Carson, Leonard (Kit). *Pursue and Destroy.* Granada Hills, CA: Sentry, 1978.

Casey, Donald E. *To Fight for My Country, Sir! Memoirs of a 19 Year Old B-17 Navigator Shot Down in Nazi Germany and Imprisoned in the WWII "Great Escape" Prison Camp.* Chicago: CreateSpace, 2009.

Cassen, Elizabeth. *The Last Voices: World War II Veterans of the Air War Speak More than Half a Century Later.* Seattle: CreateSpace, 2014.

Cathcart, Timothy J. "On Angels' Wings: The Religious Origins of the US Air Force." In *The Martial Imagination: Cultural Aspects of American Warfare,* edited by Jimmy L. Bryan Jr., 168–180. College Station: Texas A&M University Press, 2013.

Chapman, Willie. *Booster McKeester and Other Expendables.* Colliersville, TN: Global, 1994.

Charlwood, Don. *No Moon Tonight.* Manchester, UK: Crécy, 2000.

———. *Journeys into Night.* Hawthorn, VIC: Hudson, 1991.

Cheshire, Leonard. *Bomber Pilot.* London: Hutchinson, 1943.

Chisolm, Gary. *One Eyed Gunner.* Chester, NS: Bryler, 2010.

Chorley, W. R. *To See the Dawn Breaking: 76 Squadron Operations.* Ottery St. Mary, UK: Chorley, 1981.

Clapham, Walter. *Night Be My Witness.* London: Cape, 1952.

Clark, John A. *An Eighth Air Force Combat Diary: A First-Person, Contemporaneous Account of Combat Missions Flown with the 100th Bomb Group, England, 1944–1945.* Ann Arbor, MI: Proctor, 2001.

Clarke, Kenneth. *The Trip Back: World War II as Seen from the Belly of a B-17.* Austin, TX: 1st World Library, 2004.

Clodfelter, Michael. *Warfare and Armed Conflicts: A Statistical Reference.* Vol. 2, *1900–1999.* Jefferson, NC: McFarland, 1992.

Coates, Edward. *Lone Evader: The Escape from France of RAAF Sergeant Pilot Ted Coates, 1942–1943.* Loftus, NSW: Australian Military History Publications, 1995.

Colgan, William B. *Allied Strafing in World War II: A Cockpit View of Air to Ground Battle.* Jefferson, NC: McFarland, 2010.

———. *World War II Fighter-Bomber Pilot.* 3rd ed. Westminster, MD: Heritage, 2008.

Collings, Kenneth Brown. "Pilots Are Superstitious." *Flying and Popular Aviation* (October 1941): 24–26, 86.

Colquhoun, Gordon. *How Many for Breakfast?* Seaton, UK: Motoprint, 1997.

Comer, John. *Combat Crew: A True Story of Flying and Fighting in World War II.* New York: William Morrow, 1988.

Condreras, Frank J. *The Lady from Hell: Memories of a WWII B-17 Top Turret Gunner.* Charleston, SC: BookSurge, 2005.

Conklin, Edmund S. "Superstitious Belief and Practice among College Students." *American Journal of Psychology* 30 (1919): 83–102.

Conley, Harry M. *No Foxholes in the Sky.* Edited by Mark H. Miller and Stuart Whittelsey Jr. Trumbull, CT: FNP, 2002.

Connelly, Mark. *Reaching for the Stars: A New History of Bomber Command.* London: I. B. Tauris, 2001.

Constandelis, Peter. *8000 Feet over Hell.* Bloomington, IN: Trafford, 2008.

Constein, Carl Frey. *Born to Fly the Hump: A WWII Memoir.* Bloomington, IN: 1st Books, 2001.

Conway, Dan. *The Trenches in the Sky: What It Was Like Flying in RAF Bomber and Transport Commands in World War II.* Carlisle, WA: Hesperian, 1995.

Cook, Jerry W. *Once a Fighter Pilot. . . .* New York: McGraw-Hill, 1996.

Cook, Tim. "Grave Beliefs: Stories of the Supernatural and the Uncanny among

Canada's Great War Trench Soldiers." *Journal of Military History* 77 (2013): 521–542.

Copeman, Geoff D. *Right-Hand Man: A Flight Engineer's Story.* Baldock, UK: Euro Slug, 1996.

Corbin, Jimmy. *Last of the Ten Fighter Boys.* Stroud, UK: Sutton, 2007.

Cotton, M. C. (Bush). *Hurricanes over Burma: The Story of an Australian Fighter Pilot in the Royal Air Force.* Oberon, NSW: Titania, 1988.

Cowie, Ian, Dim Jones, and Chris Long, comps. and eds. *Out of the Blue: The Sometimes Scary and Often Funny World of Flying in the Royal Air Force—As Told by Some of Those Who Were There.* Farnborough, UK: Halldale, 2011.

Cox, Bryan. *Too Young to Die: The Story of a New Zealand Fighter Pilot in the Pacific War.* Ames: Iowa State University Press, 1989.

Crane, Conrad C. *American Airpower Strategy in World War II: Bombs, Cities, Civilians, and Oil.* Lawrence: University Press of Kansas, 2016.

Craven, John V., ed. *The 305th Bomb Group in Action: An Anthology.* Burleson, TX: 305th Bombardment Group (H) Memorial Association, 1990.

Craven, Wesley Frank, and James Lea Cate, eds. *The Army Air Forces in World War II.* Vol. 6, *Men and Planes.* Washington, DC: Office of Air Force History, 1983.

Creech, William T. (Bill). *The 3rd Greatest Fighter Pilot.* Bloomington, IN: AuthorHouse, 2005.

Crisp, N. J. *Yesterday's Gone.* London: Macdonald, 1983.

Cronkite, Walter. *A Reporter's Life.* New York: Knopf, 1996.

Crosby, Donald F. *Battlefield Chaplains: Catholic Priests in World War II.* Lawrence: University Press of Kansas, 1994.

Crosby, Harry H. *A Wing and a Prayer: The "Bloody 100th" Bomb Group of the U.S. Eighth Air Force over Europe in World War II.* San Jose, CA: iUniverse, 2000.

Cubbins, William R. *The War of the Cottontails: A Bomber Pilot with the Fifteenth Air Force against Germany.* Chapel Hill, NC: Algonquin, 1989.

Culler, Dan. *Black Hole of Wauwilermoos.* Tucson, AZ: Ghost River Images, 1995.

Cunningham, Pat. *The Fear in the Sky: Vivid Memories of Operational Aircrew in World War Two.* Barnsley, UK: Pen & Sword Aviation, 2012.

———. *Fighter! Fighter! Corkscrew Port!* Barnsley, UK: Pen & Sword Aviation, 2012.

———. *Bomb on the Red Markers.* Newbury, UK: Countryside, 2010.

Cunningham, Randy, with Jeff Ethell. *Fox Two: The Story of America's First Ace in Vietnam.* Mesa, AZ: Champlin Fighter Museum, 1984.

Currie, Jack. *Echoes in the Air: A Chronicle of Aeronautical Ghost Stories.* Manchester, UK: Crécy, 1998.

———. *Lancaster Target: The Story of a Crew Who Flew from Wickenby.* London: Goodhall, 1981.

Currier, Donald R. *50 Mission Crush.* Shippensburg, PA: Burd Street, 1992.

Curtis, Bob. *What Did You Do in the War Grandpa? The Wartime Experiences of Bob Curtis, RAAF 1941–1945.* Frenchs Forest, NSW: Curtis, 1995.

Curtis, Richard K. *Dumb but Lucky! Confessions of a P-51 Fighter Pilot in World War II.* New York: Ballantine, 2005.

Dagnall, Neil, et al. "Misperception of Chance, Conjunction, Belief in the Paranormal and Reality Testing: A Reappraisal." *Applied Cognitive Psychology* 28 (2014): 711–719.

Dahl, Roald. *The Gremlins.* New York: Random House, 1943.

Damisch, Lysann, Barbara Stoberock, and Thomas Mussweiler. "Keep Your Fingers Crossed! How Superstition Improves Performance." *Psychological Science* 21 (2010): 1014–1020.

Darling, Ian. *Amazing Airmen: Canadian Flyers in the Second World War II.* Toronto: Dundurn, 2009.

Darlow, Steve. *Five of the Many: Survivors of the Bomber Command Offensive from the Battle of Britain to Victory Tell Their Story.* Oxford: ISIS, 2009.

———. *Five of the Few: Survivors of the Battle of Britain and the Blitz Tell Their Story.* London: Grub Street, 2006.

———. *Victory Fighters: The Veterans' Story; Winning the Battle for Supremacy in the Skies over Western Europe, 1941–1945.* London: Grub Street, 2005.

———. *D-Day Bombers: The Veterans' Story; RAF Bomber Command and the US Eighth Air Force Support to the Normandy Invasion 1944.* London: Grub Street, 2004.

Daso, Dik Alan. *Hap Arnold and the Evolution of American Air Power.* Washington, DC: Smithsonian, 2000.

Davenport, Phil. *Hurrah for the Next Man.* Swansea, TAS: Beachcomber, 2009.

Davies, E. W. (Bill), ed. *Recollections and Reminiscences: Some Reminiscences and Recollections of W.W.2: A Collection of Stories Written by Members of the Aircrew Association of South Australia.* Hyde Park, SA: Aircrew Association of South Australia, 1997.

Davis, Burke. *War Bird: The Life and Times of Elliott White Springs.* Chapel Hill: University of North Carolina Press, 1987.

Davis, James M. *In Hostile Skies: An American B-24 Pilot in World War II.* Edited by David I. Snead. Denton: University of North Texas Press, 2006.

Davis, Richard G. *Carl A. Spaatz and the Air War in Europe.* Washington, DC: Smithsonian, 1992.

Deane, Laurence. *A Pathfinder's War and Peace.* Braunton, UK: Merlin, 1993.

Deere, Alan C. *Nine Lives.* 2nd ed. Canterbury, UK: Wingham, 1991.

Deerfield, Eddie, ed. *Hell's Angels Newsletter: The Final Six Years, 2002–2007.* Palm Harbor, FL: 303rd Bomb Group Association, 2007.

———. *Hell's Angels Newsletter: Silver Anniversary Collection, 1976–2001.* Vols. 1–2. Palm Harbor, FL: 303rd Bomb Group (H), 2002.

De Jong, Ivo. *Mission 85: The U.S. Eighth Air Force's Battle over Holland, August 19, 1943.* Mechanicsburg, PA: Stackpole, 2013.

———. *Mission 376: Battle over the Reich, May 28, 1944.* Mechanicsburg, PA: Stackpole, 2003.

De Lys, Claudia. *A Treasury of American Superstitions.* New York: Philosophical Library, 1958.

Demoulin, Charles. *Firebirds! Flying the Typhoon in Action.* Shrewsbury, UK: Airlife, 1987.

Detwiler, Ross C. *The Great Muckrock and Rosie.* Bloomington, IN: Abbott, 2013.

Dickinson, Jack. *The Time of My Life, 1940–1945: Life with 218 and 623 Squadrons.* Preston, UK: Compaid, 1999.

Dillon, Neal B. *A Dying Breed: The True Story of a World War II Air Combat Crew's Courage, Camaraderie, Faith, and Spirit.* Grants Pass, OR: Hellgate, 2000.

Dives, William. *A Bundu Boy in Bomber Command: Memoirs of a Royal Air Force Lancaster Pilot.* Victoria, BC: Trafford, 2003.

Docherty, Thomas G. *No. 7 Bomber Squadron RAF in World War II.* Barnsley: Pen & Sword Aviation, 2007.

Done, T. E. *All Our Mates.* Candelo, NSW: Widgeram, 1995.

Donnelly, G. I. *A Quest for Wings: From Tail-Gunner to Pilot.* Stroud, UK: Tempus, 2000.

Doolittle, James H. "Jimmy," with Carroll V. Glines. *I Could Never Be So Lucky Again.* New York: Bantam, 1992.

Douglas, Sholto. *Years of Combat.* London: Collins, 1963.

Drabkin, Artem. *Barbarossa and the Retreat to Moscow: Recollections of Fighter Pilots on the Eastern Front.* Barnsley, UK: Pen & Sword Military, 2007.

Drinnon, Kenneth C. *Wings of Tru Love: A WWII B17 Ball-Turret Gunner Memoir.* Bloomington, IN: Xlibris, 2011.

Drury, Clifford M. *The History of the Chaplain Corps, United States Navy.* Vol. 2, *1939–1949.* Washington, DC: Department of the Navy, 1949.

Dudycha, George J. "The Superstitious Beliefs of College Students." *Journal of Abnormal Psychology* 27 (1933): 457–464.

Duke, Neville, in collaboration with Alan W. Mitchell. *Test Pilot*. London: Grub Street, 1992.

Duncan, Alex. *Sweating the Metal*. London: Hodder & Stoughton, 2011.

Duncan, Doy. *Abandoned at Leyte: The World War II Memories of Dr. Doy Duncan, Wildcat Pilot*. Fayettville, AK: Phoenix, 2002.

Dundas, Hugh. *Flying Start: A Fighter Pilot's War Years*. Barnsley, UK: Pen & Sword Aviation, 2011.

Dunmore, Spencer, and William Carter. *Reap the Whirlwind: The Untold Story of 6 Group, Canada's Bomber Force of World War*. Toronto: McClelland & Stewart, 1991.

Dunn, Bill Newton. *Big Wing: The Biography of Air Chief Marshal Sir Trafford Leigh-Mallory*. Shrewsbury, UK: Airlife, 1992.

Dunn, William R. *Fighter Pilot: The First American Ace of World War II*. Lexington: University Press of Kentucky, 1982.

Dye, Thomas G. *Private to WWII Pilot*. Victoria, BC: Trafford, 2004.

Dyreborg, Erik. *The Lucky Ones: Airmen of the Mighty Eighth*. San Jose, CA: Writers Club, 2002.

Dyson, Freeman. *Disturbing the Universe*. New York: Basic, 1979.

Edwards, Ralph. *In the Thick of It: The Autobiography of a Bomber Pilot*. Upton, UK: Images, 1994.

Eeles, Tom. *A Passion for Flying: 8,000 Hours of RAF Flying*. Barnsley, UK: Pen & Sword Aviation, 2008.

Ehlers, Robert S., Jr. *The Mediterranean Air War: Airpower and Allied Victory in World War II*. Lawrence: University Press of Kansas, 2015.

———. *Targeting the Third Reich: Air Intelligence and the Allied Bombing Campaigns*. Lawrence: University Press of Kansas, 2009.

Eliot, Mark. *Jimmy Stewart: A Biography*. New York: Harmony, 2006.

Emerick, Joanne Pfannenstiel. *Courage before Every Danger, Honor Before All Men: The History of the 31st Bombardment Squadron (H) in World War II . . . In Their Own Words*. Colby, KS: Leroy's, 2010.

English, Alan D. *The Cream of the Crop: Canadian Aircrew, 1939–1945*. Montreal/Kingston: McGill-Queen's University Press, 1996.

Enzer, Hyman A. *The Most Exciting Year of Our Lives: Memoir of a World War II B-24 Co-Pilot*. Seattle: CreateSpace, 2011.

Erdleyi, Matthew Hugh. "The Interpretation of Dreams, and of Jokes." *Review of General Psychology* 18 (2014): 115–126.

Ethell, Jeffrey, and Alfred Price. *Target Berlin: Mission 250: 6 March 1944*. London: Brassey's, 1981.

Evans, Valerie. *We That Are Left . . . Remember: New Brunswickers in the Air Force*. Saint John, NB: 250 RCAF (Saint John) Wing Air Force Association of Canada, 2002.

Eyeton-Jones, Arthur. *Day Bomber*. Stroud, UK: Sutton, 1998.

Fagan, Vincent F. *Liberator Pilot: The Cottontails' Battle for Oil*. Carlsbad, CA: California Aero, 1991.

Fahrenwald, Ted. *Wot a Way to Run a War! The World War II Exploits and Escapades of a Pilot in the 352nd Fighter Group*. Havertown, PA: Casemate, 2014.

Farr, Frank. *Flak Happy*. Bloomington, IN: AuthorHouse, 2011.

Farrell, Bud. *"No Sweat": B-29 Aircraft # 44–70134, 93rd Bomb Squadron, 19th Bomb Group, Korean War 1952–53*. Bloomington, IN: 1st Books, 2004.

Feast, Sean. *Master Bombers: The Experiences of a Pathfinder Squadron at War 1944–1945*. London: Grub Street, 2008.

Feesey, Donald W. (Don). *The Fly by Nights: RAF Bomber Command Sorties 1944–45*. Barnsley: Pen & Sword Aviation, 2007.

Feuer, A. B. *General Chennault's Secret Weapon: The B-24 in China: Based on the Diary and Notes of Captain Elmer E. Haynes*. Westport, CT: Praeger, 1992.

Fiedler, Klaus, and Joachim I. Krueger. "Afterthoughts on Precognition: No Cogent Evidence for Anomalous Influences of Consequent Events on Preceding Cognition." *Theory & Psychology* 23 (2013): 323–333.

Fili, William J. *Passage to Valhalla: The Human Side of Aerial Combat over Nazi Occupied Europe*. Media, PA: Filcon, 1991.

Fisher, Clayton E. *Hooked: Tales and Adventures of a Tailhook Warrior*. Denver, CO: Outskirts, 2009.

Fisher, Roy R., Jr., with Susan Fisher Anderson. *The Lucky Bastard Club: Letters to My Bride from the Left Seat*. Bloomington, IN: AuthorHouse, 2003.

Fitch, Ron. *Recollections: A Lancaster Crew 55 Years On*. Annandale, NSW: Desert Pea, 2001.

Fleming, Samuel P., as told to Ed Y. Hall. *Flying with the "Hell's Angels": Memoirs of a B-17 Flying Fortress Navigator*. Spartanburg, SC: Honoribus, 1992.

Fletcher, Charles J. *Quest for Survival*. Aurora, CO: Glenbridge, 2002.

Fletcher, Eugene. *Fletcher's Gang: A B-17 Crew in Europe*. Seattle: University of Washington Press, 1988.

Fletcher, Gregory G. *Intrepid Aviators: The True Story of USS* Interpid*'s Torpedo Squadron 18 and Its Epic Clash with the Superbattleship* Musashi. New York: NAL Caliber, 2012.

Fogg, Richard, and Janet Fogg. *Fogg in the Cockpit: Howard Fogg, Master Railroad Artist, World War II Fighter Pilot: Wartime Diaries, October 1943 to September 1944*. Philadelphia: Casemate, 2011.

Foisie, Jack. "U.S. Pilots Fly Modern Jets but Cling to Superstitions." *Western Folklore* 30 (1971): 140.

Ford, Harry X. *Mud, Wings, and Wire: A Memoir*. Los Altos, CA: Enthusiast, 2006.

Foreman, Wallace R. *B-17 Nose Art Name Directory*. North Branch, MN: Phalanx, 1996.

———. *B-24 Nose Art Name Directory*. North Branch, MN: Phalanx, 1996.

Fortier, Norman (Bud). *An Ace of the Eighth: An American Fighter Pilot's Air War in Europe*. New York: Presidio, 2003.

Foss, Joe, as told to Walter Simmons. *Joe Foss, Flying Marine: The Story of His Flying Circus*. Washington, DC: Zenger, 1979.

Foster, John M. *Hell in the Heavens: The True Combat Adventures of a Marine Fighter Pilot in World War Two*. Washington, DC: Zenger, 1981.

Francis, Martin. *The Flyer: British Culture and the Royal Air Force, 1939–1945*. Oxford: Oxford University Press, 2008.

Frankhouser, Bill. *World War II Odyssey: Pennsylvania Dutch Farm Boy Becomes 8th Air Force Navigator*. Bedford, VA: Hamilton's, 1997.

Freeman, Roger A. *The American Airman in Europe*. Osceola, WI: Motorbooks, 1991.

———. *The British Airman*. London: Arms & Armour, 1989.

French, Gerald M. *Liberal Lady I-IV: Reflections of a Military Pilot*. Seattle: BookSurge, 2007.

Friese, Malte, et al. "Personal Prayer Counteracts Self-control Depletion." *Consciousness and Cognition* 29 (2014): 90–95.

Friese, Malte, and Michaela Wänke. "Personal Prayer Buffers Self-control Depletion." *Journal of Experimental Social Psychology* 51 (2014): 56–59.

Furey, Charles. *Going Back: A Navy Airman in the Pacific War*. Annapolis, MD: Naval Institute Press, 1997.

Fussell, Paul. *Wartime: Understanding and Behavior in the Second World War*. New York: Oxford University Press, 1989.

———. *The Great War and Modern Memory*. New York: Oxford University Press, 1975.

Fydenchuk, Peter W. *Immigrants of War: Americans Serving with the Royal Air Force and Royal Canadian Air Force during World War II*. Crediton, ON: WPF Publications, 2006.

Fyler, Carl. *Staying Alive: A B-17 Pilot's Experiences Flying Unescorted Bomber Missions by 8th Air Force Elements during World War II.* Leavenworth, KS: J. H. Johnston, 1995.

Gabreski, Francis, as told to Carl Molesworth. *Gabby: A Fighter Pilot's Life.* New York: Orion, 1991.

Gadbois, Robert (Gabby). *Hellcat Tales: A U.S. Navy Fighter Pilot in World War II.* Bennington, VT: Merriam, 2005.

Gaillard, Ernest. *Flight Surgeon: Complete and Unabridged Diary of Medical Detachment, 1943–1944, 242nd Medical Dispensary, Eighth Army Air Forces, 381st Bomb Group, Station 167, Ridgewell, Essex, England, 1943–1944.* Edited by William N. Gaillard. Bloomington, IN: 1st Books, 2005.

Gallup, George H. *The Gallup Poll: Public Opinion 1935–1971.* Vol. 1, *1935–1948.* New York: Random House, 1972.

Gallup, George, Jr. *The Gallup Poll: Public Opinion, 1991.* Wilmington, DE: Scholarly Resources, 1993.

Gann, Ernest Kellogg. *Fate Is the Hunter.* New York: Simon & Schuster, 1961.

Gaskell, William M. *Fighter Pilot: World War II in the South Pacific.* Manhattan, KS: Sunflower University Press, 1997.

Gaustad, Edwin S. "America's Institutions of Faith: A Statistical Postscript." In *Religion in America,* edited by William G. McLoughlin and Robert N. Bellah, 111–113. Boston: Houghton Mifflin, 1968.

Gay, George. *Sole Survivor: A Personal Story about the Battle of Midway.* Rev. ed. Naples, FL: Midway, 1986.

Gee, John W. *Wingspan: The Recollections of a Bomber Pilot.* Wellesbourne, UK: Self-Publishing Association, 1988.

George, Harry D., and Harry D. George Jr. *Georgio Italiano: An American B-25 Pilot's Unlikely Tuscan Adventure.* Victoria, BC: Trafford, 2000.

Giering, Edward J. *B-17 Bomber Crew Diary.* Edited by Abigail T. Siddall. Manhattan, KS: Sunflower University Press, 1985.

Gill, Brendan. "Young Man Behind Plexiglas." *New Yorker,* August 12, 1944, 26–36.

Gillum, Eugene M. "What's in a Name." *AAHS Journal* 47 (2002): 28–34.

Gilmore, David D. *Misogyny: The Male Malady.* Philadelphia: University of Pennsylvania Press, 2001.

Gladman, Brad William. *Intelligence and Anglo-American Air Support in World War II: The Western Desert and Tunisia, 1940–1943.* Basingstoke, UK: Palgrave Macmillan, 2009.

Gleed, Ian. *Arise to Conquer.* New York: Random House, 1942.

Glemby, Kenneth Lane, as told to Norman Auslander. *"Flyboy": Memoirs of a P-47 Pilot*. Seattle: CreateSpace, 2015.

Godefroy, Hugh Constant. *Lucky Thirteen*. Stittsville, ON: Canada's Wings, 1983.

Godfrey, John T. *The Look of Eagles*. New York: Random House, 1958.

Goebel, Robert J. *Mustang Ace: Memoirs of a P-51 Pilot*. Pacifica, CA: Pacifica, 1991.

Golley, John. *The Day of the Typhoon: Flying with the RAF Tankbusters in Normandy*. Wellingborough, UK: Patrick Stephens, 1986.

Goodman, W. E. (Bill). *Of Stirlings and Stalags: An Air-Gunner's Tale*. London: PublishNation, 2013.

Goodson, James A. *Tumult in the Clouds*. New York: St. Martin's, 1983.

Gorer, Geoffrey. *Exploring English Character*. London: Cresset, 1955.

Gorsuch, Richard L. "On the Limits of Scientific Investigation: Miracles and Intercessory Prayer." In *Miracles: God, Science, and Psychology in the Paranormal*. Vol. 1, *Religious and Spiritual Events*, edited by J. Harold Ellens, 280–299. Westport, CT: Praeger, 2008.

Grady, Walter Anthony Jr. *The Moral Domain of War: A View from the Cockpit*. Maxwell AFB, AL: Air University Press, 1993.

Graham, Gordon M. *Down for Double: Anecdotes of a Fighter Pilot*. White Stone, VA: Brandylane, 1996.

Granholm, Jackson. *The Day We Bombed Switzerland: Flying with the US Eighth Army Air Force in World War II*. Shrewsbury, UK: Airlife, 2000.

Grantham, Sid. *The 13 Squadron Story*. Dee Why, NSW: Grantham, 1991.

Gray, Gilbert. *Green Markers Ahead Skipper*. Swindon, UK: Newton, 1993.

Gray, Philip. *Ghosts of Targets Past*. Edited by E. J. Coulter. London: Grub Street, 1995.

Green, Herschel H. *Herky: The Memoirs of a Checkertail Ace*. Atglen, PA: Schiffer, 1996.

Greig, D'Arcy. *My Golden Flying Years: From 1918 over France through Iraq in the 1920s*. London: Grub Street, 2010.

Grierson, Bill. *We Band of Brothers*. Hailsham, UK: J&KH, 1997.

Griffith, Thomas E., Jr. *MacArthur's Airman: General George C. Kenney and the War in the Southwest Pacific*. Lawrence: University Press of Kansas, 1998.

Grilley, Robert. *Return from Berlin: The Eye of a Navigator*. Madison: University of Wisconsin Press, 2003.

Grinker, Roy R., and John P. Spiegel. *Men Under Stress*. Philadelphia: Blakiston, 1945.

Gross, Clayton Kelly. *Live Bait: WWII Memories of an Undefeated Fighter Ace*. Portland, OR: Inkwater, 2006.

Grover, Roy Lee. *Incidents in the Life of a B-25 Pilot*. Bloomington, IN: AuthorHouse, 2006.

Gushwa, Robert L. *The Best and the Worst of Times: The United States Army Chaplaincy, 1920–1945*. Washington, DC: Office of the Chief of Chaplains, Department of the Army, 1977.

Haarmeyer, Arthur L. *Into the Land of Darkness: A Bombardier-Navigator's Story*. Sacramento, CA: Haarmeyer, 2013.

Halaby, Najeeb E. *Crosswinds: An Airman's Memoir*. New York: Doubleday, 1978.

Hall, David Ian. *Strategy for Victory: The Development of British Tactical Air Power, 1919–1943*. Westport, CT: Praeger, 2008.

Hall, Grace (Archie). *We, Also, Were There: A Collection of Recollections of Wartime Women of Bomber Command*. Braunton, UK: Merlin, 1985.

Hall, Grover C. *1000 Destroyed: The Life and Times of the 4th Fighter Group*. Fallbrook, CA: Aero, 1978.

Hall, Roger. *Spitfire Pilot: An Extraordinary True Story of Combat in the Battle of Britain*. Stroud, UK: Amberley, 2012.

Halpenny, Bruce Barrymore. *Ghost Stations VII: True Stories of the Supernatural*. Durham, UK: Casdec, 1995.

———. *Ghost Stations IV*. Chester-le-Street, UK: Casdec, 1993.

———. *Ghost Stations III*. Chester-le-Street, UK: Casdec, 1990.

———. *Ghost Stations*. Braunton, UK: Merlin, 1986.

Halsey, William F., and J. Bryan III. *Admiral Halsey's Story*. New York: McGraw-Hill, 1947.

Hamerman, Eric J., and Carey K. Morewedge. "Reliance on Luck: Which Achievement Goals Elicit Superstitious Behavior." *Personality and Social Psychology Bulletin* 41 (2015): 323–335.

Hamilton, Tim. *The Life and Times of Pilot Officer Prune: Being the Official Story of Tee Emm*. London: HMSO, 1991.

Hammel, Eric. *Aces against Japan: The American Aces Speak*. Pacifica, CA: Pacifica, 2000.

Hammersley, Roland. *Into Battle with 57 Squadron*. Bovington, UK: Hammersley, 1992.

Hammond, James T. *Tom's War: Flying with the U.S. Eighth Army Air Force in Europe, 1944*. Bloomington, IN: iUniverse, 2007.

Hamner, Christopher H. *Enduring Battle: American Soldiers in Three Wars, 1776–1945*. Lawrence: University Press of Kansas, 2011.

Hanley, Fiske. *History of the 504th Bomb Group (VH)*. Enfield, CT: 504th Bomb Group, 1992.

Hansen, Randall. *Fire and Fury: The Allied Bombing of Germany, 1942–45.* Toronto: Doubleday, 2008.

Hanson, Norman. *Carrier Pilot: An Unforgettable True Story of Wartime Flying.* Cambridge, UK: Patrick Stephens, 1979.

Hardie, Jack. *From Timaru to Stalag VIIB: A New Zealand Pilot's Wartime Story.* Wellington, NZ: Steele Roberts, 2009.

Harding, John. *The Dancin' Navigator.* Guelph, ON: Asterisk, 1988.

Harris, Arthur. *Bomber Offensive.* London: Collins, 1947.

Harris, Arthur T. *Despatch on War Operations, 23rd February, 1942, to 8th May, 1945.* London: Frank Cass, 1995.

Harris, Craig, ed. *Fait Accompli III: A Historical Anthology of the 457th Bomb Group (H): The Fireball Outfit.* Compiled by James L. Bass. Nashville, TN: JM Press, 2000.

Harris, Samuel Russ, Jr. *B-29s over Japan: A Group Commander's Diary.* Edited by Robert A. Mann. Jefferson, NC: McFarland, 2011.

Harry, G. P., ed. *339th Fighter Group.* Paducah, KY: Turner, 1991.

Hart, Jason W., et al. "Is Any Explanation Better Than No Explanation? Intolerance of Uncertainty and Paranormal Beliefs." *Social Behavior and Personality* 41 (2013): 343–344.

Hartney, Harold E. *Wings over France.* Edited by Stanley M. Ulanoff. Folkestone, UK: Bailey & Swifen, 1974.

Harvey, G. R., comp. *Memories from the Out House Mouse: The Personal Diaries of One B-17 Crew.* Victoria, BC: Trafford, 2002.

Harvey, J. Douglas. *Boys, Bombs and Brussels Sprouts: A Knees-up, Wheels-up Chronicle of WWII.* Toronto: McClelland & Stewart, 1981.

Harvey, W. J. (Night-Hawk). *Rover of the Night Sky.* London: Greenhill, 1984.

Hasey, Casey. *My Bombsight View of WWII.* Bloomington, IN: AuthorHouse, 2011.

Hassner, Ron E. *Religion on the Battlefield.* Ithaca, NY: Cornell University Press, 2016.

Hastings, Donald W., David G. Wright, and Bernard C. Glueck. *Psychiatric Experiences of the Eighth Air Force: First Year of Combat (July 4, 1942–July 4, 1943).* New York: Josiah Macy Jr., 1944.

Hastings, Max. *Bomber Command.* London: Michael Joseph, 1979.

Hatch, Herbert (Stubb). *An Ace and His Angel: Memoirs of a World War II Fighter Pilot.* Paducah, KY: Turner, 2000.

Hawkins, Ian L., ed. *B-17s over Berlin: Personal Stories from the 95th Bomb Group (H).* Washington, DC: Brassey's, 1990.

Hazzard, S. B., and D. F. E. C. Dean. *They're Not Shooting at You Now, Grandad.* Braunton, UK: Merlin, 1991.

Heaton, Colin D., and Anne-Marie Lewis. *The Star of Africa: The Story of Hans Marseille, the Rogue Luftwaffe Ace Who Dominated the WWII Skies.* Minneapolis: Zenith, 2012.

———. *The German Aces Speak: World War II Through the Eyes of Four of the Luftwaffe's Most Important Commanders.* Minneapolis: Zenith, 2011.

Hedtke, James R. *The Freckleton, England, Air Disaster: The B-24 Crash That Killed 38 Preschoolers and 23 Adults, August 23, 1944.* Jefferson, NC: McFarland, 2014.

Heffer, Francis Bentinck. *From Cow Bells to Bell Bottoms: Wartime Experiences Extracted from Memoirs of an Ordinary Bloke.* Tauranga, NZ: Canrig, 1998.

Heichel, William E. *Milk Run: A Gunner's Tale.* Bloomington, IN: AuthorHouse, 2012.

Helm, Warren G. *Big War, Little People.* El Paso, TX: Helm, 2009.

Hemmingway, Kenneth. *Wings over Burma.* London: Quality, 1944.

Henry, Mike. *Air Gunner.* London: Foulis, 1964.

Herbert, Kevin. *Maximum Effort: The B-29's against Japan.* Manhattan, KS: Sunflower University Press, 1983.

Herman, Leonard, with Rob Morris. *Combat Bombardier: Memoirs of Two Combat Tours in the Skies over Europe in World War Two.* Bloomington, IN: Xlibris, 2007.

Higgs, G. R. *Front-Line and Experimental Flying with the Fleet Air Arm: "Purely by Chance."* Barnsley, UK: Pen & Sword Aviation, 2010.

Hill, Michael D., ed. *The Fight'n 451st Bomb Group (H).* Paducah, KY: Turner, 1990.

Hinchliffe, Peter. *The Other Battle: Luftwaffe Night Aces versus Bomber Command.* Edison, NJ: Castle, 2001.

Hindle, Brooke. *Lucky Lady and the Navy Mystique.* New York: Vantage, 1991.

Hinton, Charles W. *Korea: A Short Time in a Small War; A Combat Story in the B-26 in the Korean War.* Satellite Beach, FL: Hinton, 2014.

Hipperson, Carol Edgemon. *The Belly Gunner.* Brookfield, CT: Twenty-First Century, 2001.

Hoare, John. *Tumult in the Clouds: A Story of the Fleet Air Arm.* London: Michael Joseph, 1976.

Holden, Wendy. *Shell Shock: The Psychological Impact of War.* London: Channel 4, 1998.

Holland, Jack. *Misogyny: The World's Oldest Prejudice.* London: Robinson, 2006.

Holland, James. *Dam Busters: The Race to Smash the Dams, 1943*. London: Bantam, 2012.

———. *Twenty-One: Coming of Age in the Second World War*. London: HarperCollins, 2006.

Hook, Franklin. *Pinky: The Story of North Dakota's First Aerial Combat Ace Flying on Guadalcanal*. Hot Springs, SD: Fall River, 2014.

Horsley, Peter. *Sounds from Another Room*. London: Leo Cooper, 1997.

Houlton, Johnnie. *Spitfire Strikes: A New Zealand Fighter Pilot's Story*. London: John Murray, 1985.

Howard, Bill. *What the RAF Airman Took to War*. Oxford: Shire, 2015.

Howard, James H. *Roar of the Tiger*. New York: Orion, 1991.

Hoyle, Arthur R. *Into the Darkness: One Young Australian's Journey from Sydney to the Deadly Skies over Germany, 1939–1945*. Edited by David Vernon. Jamison Centre, ACT: Stringybark, 2012.

Hudson, Charles S., and Ross R. Oleny. *Combat, He Wrote. . . .* Coalinga, CA: Airborne, 1994.

Hudson, James Douglas. *There and Back Again: A Navigator's Story*. 3rd ed. Lincoln, UK: Tucann, 2003.

Huggett, Richard. *Supernatural on Stage: Ghosts and Superstitions of the Theatre*. New York: Taplinger, 1975.

Hughes, Walter F. *A Bomber Pilot in WWII: From Farm Boy to Pilot; 35 Missions in the B-24 Liberator Bomber*. Fremont, CA: Hughes, 1994.

Humphries, Harry. *Living With Heroes: The Story of the Dam Busters*. Norwich, UK: Erskine, 2003.

Hunt, Peter. *Angles of Attack: An A-6 Intruder Pilot's War*. New York: Ballantine, 2002.

Hunter, William James. *From Coastal Command to Captivity*. Barnsley, UK: Leo Cooper, 2003.

Hurley, Gordon James. *Corkscrew Starboard*. York, UK: Field House, 2009.

Hutchinson, James Lee. *The Boys in the B-17*. Bloomington, IN: AuthorHouse, 2011.

Hutton, Bud, and Andy Rooney. *Air Gunner*. New York: Farrar & Rinehart, 1944.

Ingalls, David S. *Hero of the Angry Sky: The World War I Diary and Letters of David S. Ingalls, America's First Naval Ace*. Edited by Geoffrey L. Rossano. Athens: Ohio University Press, 2013.

Iredale, Will. *The Kamikaze Hunters: Fighting for the Pacific, 1945*. London: Macmillan, 2015.

Iveson, Tony, and Brian Milton. *Lancaster: The Biography*. London: Deutsch, 2009.

Jackson, Bill. *Three Stripes and Four Brownings*. North Battleford, SK: Turner-Warwick, 1990.

Jacobs, Peter, with Les Bartlett. *Bomb Aimer over Berlin: The Wartime Memoirs of Les Bartlett*. Barnsley, UK: Pen & Sword Aviation, 2007.

Jenks, Andrew L. *The Cosmonaut Who Couldn't Stop Smiling: The Life and Legend of Yuri Gagarin*. De Kalb: Northern Illinois University Press, 2012.

Johnson, Brian, and H. I. Cozens. *Bombers: The Weapon of Total War*. London: Thames Methuen, 1984.

Johnson, E. J. *Hann's Crew*. Paducah, KY: Turner, 2000.

Johnson, George (Johnny). *The Last British Dambuster*. London: Ebury, 2014.

Johnson, Gerald W., with John C. McClure and Charlotte S. McClure. *Called to Command: A World War II Fighter Ace's Adventurous Journey*. Paducah, KY: Turner, 1996.

Johnson, J. E. (Johnnie). *Wing Leader*. Newton Abbot, UK: David & Charles, 1974.

Johnson, John R., Jr. *Un-Armed, Un-Armored and Un-Escorted: A World War II C-47 Airborne Troop Carrier Pilot Remembers*. Bennington, VT: Merriam, 2014.

Johnson, Richard Riley. *Twenty Five Milk Runs (and a Few Others): To Hell's Angels and Back*. Victoria, BC: Trafford, 2004.

Johnson, Robert S., with Martin Caidin. *Thunderbolt!* New York: Rinehart, 1958.

Johnson, Ron. *A Navigator's Tale*. Chippenham, UK: Irregular Records, 2000.

Johnson, S. H. *It's Never Dark Above the Clouds*. Trigg, WA: Johnson, 1994.

Johnston, Doug. *From Air Gunner to Prisoner of War*. Toronto: Laing MacDowell, 1994.

Jones, Andrew. *The Corsair Years*. Paducah, KY: Turner, 1995.

Jones, Edgar. "'LMF': The Use of Psychiatric Stigma in the Royal Air Force during the Second World War." *Journal of Military History* 70 (2006): 439–458.

Jones, Edgar, and Simon Wessely. *Shell Shock to PTSD: Military Psychiatry from 1990 to the Gulf War*. Hove, UK: Psychology Press, 2005.

Jones, Geoffrey P. *Raider: The Halifax and Its Flyers*. London: Kimber, 1978.

Jones, Harlow. *Bomber Pilot: A Canadian Youth's War*. St. Catherines, ON: Vanwell, 2001.

Jones, Laurie. *A Pilot's Story: Of Flying in War and Peace*. Wahroonga, NSW: L. R., 1996.

Jones, R. V. *Most Secret War*. London: Penguin, 2009.

Jorgensen, Daniel B. *The Service of Chaplains to Army Air Units, 1917–1946*. Washington, DC: Office, Chief of Air Force Chaplains, 1961.

Joubert de la Ferté, Philip. *Fun and Games*. London: Hutchinson, 1964.

Kantor, Linda Audrey. *Emil's Story: Memoir of a WWII Bomber Pilot*. Lexington, KY: CreateSpace, 2012.

Kaplan, Philip, and Jack Currie. *Round the Clock: The Experience of the Allied Bomber Crews Who Flew by Day and Night from England in the Second World War*. London: Cassell, 1993.

Keeffe, James H., III. *Two Gold Coins and a Prayer: The Epic Journey of a World War II Bomber Pilot and POW*. Fall City, WA: Appell, 2010.

Keinan, Giora. "The Effect of Stress and Desire for Control on Superstitious Behavior." *Personality and Social Psychology Bulletin* 28 (2002): 102–108.

———. "Effects of Stress and Tolerance of Ambiguity on Magical Thinking." *Journal of Personality and Social Psychology* 67 (1994): 48–55.

Kellett, Anthony. *Combat Motivation: The Behavior of Soldiers in Battle*. Boston: Kluwer, 1982.

Kelly, Carol Adele, ed. *Voices of my Comrades: America's Reserve Officers Remember World War II*. New York: Fordham University Press, 2007.

Kennett, Lee. *G.I.: The American Soldier in World War II*. New York: Scribner's, 1987.

Kensett, Robert C. *A Walk in the Valley*. Burnstown, ON: GSPH, 2003.

Kent, Rade Petrović. *Is It Just Poor Memory . . . Or Just One More Treason?* Lausanne: L'Age d'Homme, 1998.

Kilbracken, John. *Bring Back My Stringbag: Swordfish Pilot at War, 1940–1945*. Rev. ed. London: Leo Cooper, 1996.

Kimblin, Rex. *How Lucky I Was: 35 Missions in a Lancaster Bomber*. Toowong, QLD: Chambers, 2012.

Kindsvatter, Peter S. *American Soldiers: Ground Combat in the World Wars, Korea, and Vietnam*. Lawrence: University Press of Kansas, 2003.

King, Dan. *The Last Zero Fighter: Firsthand Accounts from WWII Japanese Naval Pilots*. Irvine, CA: Pacific, 2012.

Kingsford, A. R. *Night of the Raiders: Being the Experiences of a Night Flying Pilot, Who Raided Hunland on Many Dark Nights during the War*. London: Greenhill, 1988.

Kingsford-Smith, Rollo. *I Wouldn't Have Missed It for Quids*. Exeter, NSW: Kingsford-Smith, 1999.

Kingsland, Richard. *Into the Midst of Things*. Canberra: Air Power Development Centre, 2010.

Kinney, John F. *Wake Island Pilot: A World War II Memoir.* Washington, DC: Potomac, 2005.

Knaresborough, John. *R.A.F. Chaplains Look Ahead: Report of some R.A.F. Chaplains' Conferences, 1944.* London: Society for Promoting Christian Knowledge, 1945.

Koch, Edwin E. "G.I. Lore: Lore of the Fifteenth Air Force." *New York Folklore Quarterly* 9 (1953): 59–70.

Koger, Fred. *Countdown!* Chapel Hill, NC: Algonquin, 1990.

Köthe, Martina, and Reinhard Pietrowsky. "Behavioral Effects of Nightmares and Their Correlations to Personality Patterns." *Dreaming* 11 (2001): 43–52.

Kotler, Alvin E., as told to Jack Flynn. *We Came to Fight a War: The Story of a B-17 Radio Gunner and His Pilot.* Bennington, VT: Merriam, 2012.

Krosnick, Gerald. "Anxiety Reaction in Fighter Pilots." In *Observations on Combat Flying Personnel.* Edited by David G. Wright, 53–62. New York: Josiah Macy Jr., 1944.

Krueger, Lloyd O. *Enjoy, Lest Tomorrow Flees.* Victoria, BC: Trafford, 2002.

———. *Come Fly with Me: Experiences of an Airman in World War II.* Dubuque, IA: Shepherd, 1990.

Kyle, James. *A Typhoon Tale.* Bognor, UK: New Horizon, 1984.

Lachenmeyer, Nathaniel. *13: The Story of the World's Most Popular Superstition.* New York: Thunder's Mouth, 2004.

Lacklen, Jay. *Flying the Line: An Air Force Pilot's Journey.* Minneapolis: Two Harbors, 2013.

Lamb, Charles. *To War in a Stringbag.* Garden City, NY: Doubleday, 1980.

Lambert, Bill. *Combat Report.* London: William Kimber, 1973.

Lambert, Max. *Night After Night: New Zealanders in Bomber Command.* Auckland: HarperCollins, 2005.

Lancashire, Thomas, and Stuart Burbridge. *A Trenchard Brat at War.* Oxford: ISIS, 2010.

Lande, D. A. *From Somewhere in England.* Osceola, WI: Motorbooks, 1990.

Lane, Byron. *Byron's War: I Never Will Be Young Again.* Central Point, OR: Hellgate, 1997.

Lang, Noella, comp. *The Rest of My Life with 50 Squadron: From the Diaries and Letters of F/O P. W. Rowling.* Northbridge, WA: Access, 1997.

Lay, Beirne, Jr. *Presumed Dead: The Survival of a Bomb Group Commander.* New York: Dodd, Mead, 1980.

———. *I Wanted Wings.* New York: Harper, 1937.

Lee, Arthur Gould. *Open Cockpit.* London: Grub Street, 2012.

Lee, Wright. *Not as Briefed: Memoirs of a B-24 Navigator/Prisoner of War, 1943–1945.* Spartanburg, SC: Honoribus, 1995.

LeMay, Curtis E., with MacKinlay Kantor. *Mission with LeMay.* Garden City, NY: Doubleday, 1965.

Lester, John R. (Bob). *Frontline Airline: Troop Carrier Pilot in World War II.* Manhattan, KS: Sunflower University Press, 1994.

Leuthner, Stuart, and Oliver Jensen. *High Honor: Recollections by Men and Women of World War II Aviation.* Washington, DC: Smithsonian, 1989.

Levine, Joshua. *On a Wing and a Prayer.* London: Collins, 2008.

Levitt, Eugene E. "Superstitions: Twenty-Five Years Ago and Today." *American Journal of Psychology* 65 (1952): 443–449.

Levy, Norman A. *Personality Disturbances in Combat Fliers.* New York: Josiah Macy Jr., 1945.

Lewis, Damien. *The Dog Who Could Fly: The Incredible True Story of a WWII Airman and the Four-Legged Hero Who Flew at His Side.* New York: Atria, 2013.

Lewis, Richard B. (Dick). *Angel on My Wing: An Odyssey of Flying Combat with the 493rd Bomb Group, 8th Air Force in 1944.* Jacksonville Beach, FL: High Pitched Hum, 2009.

Lihou, Maurice G. *Out of the Italian Night: Wellington Bomber Operations, 1944–45.* Shrewsbury, UK: Airlife, 2000.

Link, Mae Mills, and Hubert A. Coleman. *Medical Support of the Army Air Forces in World War II.* Washington, DC: Office of the Surgeon General, USAF, 1955.

Little, William. *The Psychic Tourist: A Voyage into the Curious World of Predicting the Future.* London: Icon, 2010.

Logan, Edward F., Jr. *"Jump, Damn It, Jump!" Memoir of a Downed B-17 Pilot in World War II.* Jefferson, NC: McFarland, 2006.

Lomas, Harry. *One Wing High: Halifax Bomber: The Navigator's Story.* Shrewsbury, UK: Airlife, 1995.

Lovejoy, E. E. *Better Born Lucky Than Rich: The Diary of an Ordinary Airman.* Braunton, UK: Merlin, 1986.

Loving, George G. *Woodbine Red Leader: A P-51 Mustang Ace in the Mediterranean Theater.* New York: Presidio, 2003.

Lucas, Laddie. *Out of the Blue: The Role of Luck in Air Warfare, 1917–1966.* London: Hutchinson, 1985.

Luckett, Perry D., and Charles L. Byler. *Tempered Steel: The Three Wars of Triple Air Force Cross Winner Jim Kasler.* Dulles, VA: Potomac, 2005.

Ludlam, Stuart D. *They Turned the War Around at Coral Sea and Midway: Going to War with* Yorktown*'s Air Group Five.* Bennington, VT: Merriam, 2006.

MacKenzie, Emmett G. (Mac). *Ten Men, a "Flying Boxcar," and a War: A Journal of B-24 Crew 313, 1944 to 1945*. New York: iUniverse, 2005.

Maddox, Joey. *Bleeding Sky: The Story of Captain Fletcher E. Adams and the 357th Fighter Group*. Bloomington, IN: Xlibris, 2009.

Maher, William P. *Fated to Survive: 401st Bombardment Group (H), Eighth Air Force: Memoirs of a B-17 Flying Fortress Pilot/Prisoner of War*. Edited by Ed Y. Hall. Spartanburg, SC: Honoribus, 1992.

Mahoney, James J., and Brian H. Mahoney. *Reluctant Witness: Memoirs from the Last Year of the European Airwar, 1944–45*. Victoria, BC: Trafford, 2001.

Maitland, Andrew. *Through the Bombsight*. London: Kimber, 1986.

Mann, Leslie. *And Some Fell on Stony Ground: A Day in the Life of an RAF Bomber Pilot*. London: Icon, 2014.

Mann, Robert A. *The B-29 Superfortress: A Comprehensive Registry of the Planes and Their Missions*. Jefferson, NC: McFarland, 2005.

Margerison, Russell. *Boys at War*. Bolton: Ross Anderson, 1986.

Markey, Morris. *Well Done! An Aircraft Carrier in Battle Action*. New York: Appleton-Century, 1945.

Marshall, Chester. *Sky Giants over Japan: A Diary of a B-29 Combat Crew in WWII*. Winona, MN: Apollo, 1984.

Martin, Alfie. *Bale Out! Escaping Occupied France with the Resistance*. Newtonards, NI: Colourpoint, 2005.

Martin, B. W. *War Memories of an Engineer Officer in Bomber Command*. Hailsham, UK: J&KH, 1998.

Martinez, M. P., Elena Miró, and Raimundo Arriaza. "Evaluation of the Distress and Effects Caused by Nightmares: A Study of the Psychometric Properties of the Nightmare Distress Questionnaire and the Nightmare Effects Survey." *Sleep and Hypnosis* 7 (2005): 29–41.

Mason, Keith W. *My War in Italy: On the Ground and in Flight with the 15th Air Force*. Columbia: University of Missouri Press, 2016.

Mason, Pablo. *Pablo's War*. London: Bloomsbury, 1992.

Mass-Observation. *Puzzled People: A Study in Attitudes to Religion, Ethics, Progress and Politics in a London Borough*. London: Gollancz, 1948.

Masters, Ken S., Glen I. Spielmans, and Jason T. Goodson. "Are There Demonstrable Effects of Distant Intercessory Prayer? A Meta-analytic Review." *Annals of Behavioral Medicine* 32 (2006): 21–26.

Matenkoski, Gregory J. *Lucky Penny's Tail: The True Story of Edmund Survilla, Tail Gunner 453rd Bomb Group, January 1944 to June 1944*. Lexington, KY: MD, 2010.

Matheny, Ray T. *Rite of Passage: A Teenager's Chronicle of Combat and Captivity in Nazi Germany*. Clearfield, UT: American Legacy, 2009.

Matt, John. *Crewdog: A Saga of a Young American*. Hamilton, VA: Waterford, 1992.

Mayhill, Ron. *Bombs on Target: A Compelling Eye-Witness Account of Bomber Command Operations*. Sparkford: Stephens, 1991.

McCadden, Helen M. "Folklore in the Schools: Folk Beliefs: Current Report." *New York Folklore Quarterly* 3 (1947): 330–340.

McCarthy, David A. *Fear No More: A B-17 Navigator's Journey*. Pittsburgh: Cottage Wordsmiths, 1991.

McCarthy, John. "Aircrew and 'Lack of Moral Fibre' in the Second World War." *War & Society* 2 (1984): 87–101.

McCarthy, Mike. *Phantom Reflections: The Education of an American Fighter Pilot in Vietnam*. Westport, CT: Praeger, 2007.

McCrary, John R., and David E. Scherman. *First of the Many: A Journal of Action with the Men of the Eighth Air Force*. New York: Simon & Schuster, 1944.

McCrea, Bill. *A Chequer-Board of Nights*. Longton, UK: Compaid, 2003.

McDonald, Paul. *Winged Warriors: The Cold War from the Cockpit*. Barnsley: Pen & Sword Aviation, 2012.

McDonnell, A. R. D. *From Dogfight to Diplomacy: A Spitfire Pilot's Log, 1932–1958*. Barnsley, UK: Pen & Sword Aviation, 2005.

McEniry, John Howard. *A Marine Dive-Bomber Pilot at Guadalcanal*. Tuscaloosa: University of Alabama Press, 1987.

McGindle, Ted. *Pimpernel Squadron: An Anecdotal History of 462 Squadron R.A.A.F., August 1944–May 1945*. Beechworth, VIC: McGindle, 2000.

McGlashan, K. B. *Down to Earth: A Fighter Pilot's Experiences of Surviving Dunkirk, the Battle of Britain, Dieppe and D-Day*. London: Grub Street, 2007.

McGlauchlin, J. Kemp. *The Mighty Eighth in WWII: A Memoir*. Lexington: University Press of Kentucky, 2000.

McGuire, Melvin W., and Robert Hadley. *Bloody Skies: A 15th AAF B-17 Combat Crew: How They Lived and Died*. Las Cruces, NM: Yucca Tree, 1993.

McIntosh, Dave. *Terror in the Starboard Seat*. Don Mills, ON: General, 1980.

McKay, Russell. *One of the Many*. Burnstown, ON: GSPH, 1980.

McLachlan, Ian. *Eighth Air Force Bomber Stories: A New Selection*. Stroud, UK: Sutton, 2004.

McLachlan, Ian, and Russell J. Zorn. *Eighth Air Force Bomber Reflections: Eye-Witness Accounts from American Airmen and British Civilians of the Perils of War*. Sparkford, UK: Patrick Stephens, 1991.

McManus, John C. *Deadly Sky: The American Combat Airman in World War II.* Novato, CA: Presidio, 2000.

McPartland, Virginia C. *Brothers at Daybreak: World War II Crew Beats the Odds over Pacific Waters.* Los Gatos, CA: Robertson, 2013.

McWilliams, Caitlin. "Camaraderie, Morale and Material Culture: Reflections on the Nose Art of No. 6 Group, Royal Canadian Air Force." *Canadian Military History* 19 (2010): 20–30.

Mears, Dwight S. "The Catch-22 Effect: The Lasting Stigma of Wartime Cowardice in the U.S. Army Air Forces." *Journal of Military History* 77 (2013): 1025–1054.

Meder, Patricia Chapman. *The True Story of Catch-22: The Real Men and Missions of Joseph Heller's 340th Bomb Group in World War II.* Philadelphia: Casemate, 2012.

Melvin, Carl (Mel). *The Journey: From Farm Boy to World War II Pilot to Los Angeles Cabbie.* Los Angeles: Melvin, 2010.

Meyher, Charles R. *Memoirs of a B-29 Pilot.* Bennington, VT: Merriam, 2008.

Michel, Marshall L., III. *The Eleven Days of Christmas: America's Last Vietnam Air Battle.* San Francisco: Encounter, 2002.

Middlebrook, Garrett. *Air Combat at 20 Feet: Selected Missions from a Strafer Pilot's Diary.* Bloomington, IN: AuthorHouse, 2004.

Middlebrook, Martin. *The Nuremberg Raid.* London: Penguin, 1986.

———. *The Schweinfurt-Regensburg Mission.* New York: Scribner's, 1983.

Millett, John. *View from the Turret.* Wollongong, NSW: Five Islands, 1994.

Mireless, Anthony J. *Fatal Army Air Forces Aviation Accidents in the United States, 1941–1945.* Vol. 1. Jefferson, NC: McFarland, 2006.

Misterly, John, Jr. *Over and Under.* New York: Carlton, 1987.

Mocan, Naci, and Luiza Pogorelova. "Compulsory Schooling Laws and Formation of Beliefs: Education, Religion and Superstition." Working Paper 20557, October 2014, National Bureau of Economic Research, accessed October 19, 2014, nber.org/papers.w20557.

Moore, Carl H. *Flying the B-26 Marauder over Europe: Memoir of a World War II Navigator.* 2nd ed. Jefferson, NC: McFarland, 2013.

Morehead, James B. *In My Sights: The Memoir of a P-40 Ace.* Novato, CA: Presidio, 1998.

Moreton, George. *Doctor in Chains.* London: Corgi, 1980.

Morgan, David H. S. *Hostile Skies: The Falklands Conflict Through the Eyes of a Sea Harrier Pilot.* London: Weidenfeld & Nicolson, 2006.

Morgan, Robert, with Ron Powers. *The Man Who Flew the* Memphis Belle: *Memoir of a WWII Bomber Pilot*. New York: Dutton, 2001.

Morris, Jerrold. *Canadian Artists and Airmen, 1940–45: A Wartime Memoir*. Toronto: Morris Gallery, 1974.

Morrison, Les. *Of Luck and War: From Squeegee Kid to Bomber Pilot in World War II*. Burnstown, ON: GSPH, 1999.

Mossop, Jack. *A Pathfinder's Story: The Life and Death of Jack Mossop*. Edited by Bill Robertson. Barnsley, UK: Pen & Sword Aviation, 2007.

Mourton, Doug. *Lucky Doug: Memoirs of the RAF, 1937–1946 and After*. Edinburgh: Pentland, 1999.

Mrazek, Robert J. *To Kingdom Come: An Epic Saga of Survival in the Air War over Germany*. New York: NAL Caliber, 2011.

Muirhead, Campbell. *Diary of a Bomb Aimer: Training in America and Flying with 12 Squadron in WWII*. Edited by Philip Swan. Barnsley, UK: Pen & Sword Aviation, 2009.

Muirhead, John. *Those Who Fall*. New York: Random House, 1986.

Muller, Werner. *Sound Locators, Fire Control Systems and Searchlights of the German Heavy Flak Units, 1939–1945*. Atglen, PA: Schiffer, 2004.

———. *Ground Radar Systems of the German Luftwaffe to 1945*. Atglen, PA: Schiffer, 1998.

Munns, Sidney. *As Luck Would Have It: Reminiscences of a Retired RAF Observer/ Navigator*. Northampton, UK: Friday File, 1992.

Murphy, Frank D. *Luck of the Draw: Reflections on the Air War in Europe*. Trumbull, CT: FNP, 2001.

Murray, Robert N. *Lest We Forget: The Experiences of World War II Westindian Ex-Service Personnel*. Nottingham, UK: Westindian Combined Ex-Servicemen's Association, 1996.

Musch, Jochen, and Katja Ehrenberg. "Probability Misjudgment, Cognitive Ability, and Belief in the Paranormal." *British Journal of Psychology* (2002): 169–177.

Musgrove, Frank. *Dresden and the Heavy Bombers*. Barnsley, UK: Pen & Sword Aviation, 2005.

Myers, Jack R. *Shot at and Missed: Recollections of a World War II Bombardier*. Norman: University of Oklahoma Press, 2004.

Napier, Michael. *Tornado over the Tigris: Recollections of a Fast Jet Pilot*. Barnsley, UK: Pen & Sword Aviation, 2015.

Naydler, Meron. *Young Man, You'll Never Die*. Barnsley, UK: Pen & Sword Aviation, 2005.

Neal, C. C. *Gentlemen From Hell: Men of the 487th Bomb Group*. Paducah, TN: Turner, 2005.

Nelson, Earle M. *If Winter Comes*. Lovely Banks, VIC: Nelson, 1989.

Nelson, Hank. *Chased by the Sun: Courageous Australians in Bomber Command in World War II*. Sydney: ABC, 2002.

Nelson, Ted. *A Survivor's Tale: The True Life of a Wireless Operator/Air Gunner from Enlistment in 1940 to Demobilisation in 1946*. Cowbit, UK: Old Forge, 2009.

Newby, Leroy W. *Target Ploesti: View from a Bombsight*. Novato, CA: Presidio, 1983.

Nichols, J. A. *B-24 Bomber Crew: A True Story of the Pacific War with Japan*. New York: Vantage, 1997.

Nicol, John. *The Red Line*. London: Collins, 2013.

Nicol, John, and Tony Rennell. *Tail-End Charlies: The Last Battles of the Bomber War, 1944–45*. London: Viking, 2004.

Nielsen, Robert S. *With the Stars Above*. Olympia, WA: JENN, 1984.

Nixon, H. K. "Popular Answers to Some Psychological Questions." *American Journal of Psychology* 36 (1925): 418–423.

Noles, James L., and James L. Noles Jr. *Mighty by Sacrifice: The Destruction of an American Bomber Squadron, August 29, 1944*. Tuscaloosa: University of Alabama Press, 2009.

Novak, Paul. *Into Hostile Skies: An Anthology*. Seattle: CreateSpace, 2013.

Novey, Jack. *The Cold Blue Sky: A B-17 Gunner in World War Two*. Edited by Fryar Calhoun. Charlottesville, VA: Howell, 1997.

Office of Statistical Control. *Army Air Forces Statistical Digest: World War II*. Washington, DC: Office of Statistical Control, 1945.

Office of the Chief of Naval Operations. *United States Naval Aviation, 1910–1970*. Washington, DC: Department of the Navy, 1970.

Ohnuki-Tierney, Emiko. *Kamikaze Diaries*. Chicago: University of Chicago Press, 2010.

Okerstrom, Dennis R. *The Final Mission of Bottoms Up: A World War II Pilot's Story*. Columbia: University of Missouri Press, 2011.

Olderr, Steven. *Symbolism: A Comprehensive Dictionary*. Jefferson, NC: McFarland, 2012.

Olds, Robin, with Christina Olds and Ed Rasimus. *Fighter Pilot: The Memoirs of Legendary Ace Robin Olds*. New York: St. Martin's, 2010.

Oleson, James A. *In Their Own Words: True Stories and Adventures of the American Fighter Ace*. New York: iUniverse, 2007.

Olive, Gordon. *Spitfire Ace: My Life as a Battle of Britain Pilot*. Edited by Dennis Newton. Stroud, UK: Amberley, 2015.

O'Neill, Brian D. *Half a Wing, Three Engines and a Prayer: B-17s Over Germany*. Special ed. New York: McGraw-Hill, 1999.

Ono, Kiochi. "Superstitious Behavior in Humans." *Journal of the Experimental Analysis of Behavior* 47 (1987): 261–271.

Orange, Vincent. *Dowding of Fighter Command*. London: Grub Street, 2008.

Orchard, Ade, with James Barrington. *Joint Force Harrier*. London: Michael Joseph, 2008.

Overy, Richard. *The Bombing War: Europe 1939–1945*. London: Allen Lane, 2013.

———. *Bomber Command, 1939–1945*. London: HarperCollins, 1997.

Pack, Janet, and Richard Singer, comps. and eds. *388th Anthology, Vols. 1–2: Tales of the 388th Bombardment Group (H) 1942–45*. San Jose, CA: Writers Club, 2001.

Padgett, A. J., with Frank Padgett. *Mission over Indochine: A Story of Courage, Honor and Sacrifice*. Seattle: CreateSpace, 2012.

Padgett, Vernon R., and Dale O. Jorgenson. "Superstition and Economic Threat: Germany, 1918–1940." *Personality and Social Psychology Bulletin* 8 (1982): 736–741.

Paisley, Melvyn, with Vicki Paisley. *Ace! Autobiography of a Fighter Pilot, World War II*. Boston: Branden, 1992.

Papple, Fred J. *Seventy Five Percent Luck: An Anecdotal History of 640 Squadron R.A.F., January 1944–May 1945*. Warrandale, SA: Papple, 1997.

Pargament, Kenneth I. "The Bitter and the Sweet: An Evaluation of the Costs and Benefits of Religiousness." *Psychological Inquiry* 13 (2002): 168–181.

Park, Robert L. *Superstition: Belief in the Age of Science*. Princeton: Princeton University Press, 2008.

Park, Ted. *Angels Twenty*. St. Lucia, QLD: University of Queensland Press, 1994.

Parker, Ray. *Down in Flames: A True Story*. Minneapolis: Mill City, 2009.

Parker, Van R. *Dear Folks*. Memphis, TN: Global, 1989.

Parsons, Edwin C. *I Flew With the Lafayette Escadrille*. New York: Arno, 1972.

Passmore, Richard. *Out of the Darkness*. Bristol, UK: Arrowsmith, 2011.

———. *Blenheim Boy*. London: Thomas Harmsworth, 1981.

Pearce, David H. *Dark Skies and Dead Reckoning*. Moe, VIC: Pearce, 2000.

Pearce, William George. *The Wing Is Clipped: A Real Life Adventure with the RAAF*. Margate, QLD: Slipstream, 2000.

Pearson, Ross A. *Australians at War in the Air*. Vol. 1. Kenthurst, NSW: Kangaroo, 1995.

Peart, Alan McGregor. *From North Africa to the Arakan: The Engrossing Memoir of a WWII Spitfire Ace*. London: Grub Street, 2008.

Peden, Murray. *A Thousand Shall Fall: A Pilot for 214*. Stittsville, ON: Canada's Wings, 1979.

Perkins, L. W., comp. *Flight into Yesterday: A Memory or Two from Members of the Wartime Aircrew Club of Kelowna*. Victoria, BC: Trafford, 2002.

Perry, Edward P. *Recalling World War II: One Personal Experience*. New York: Vantage, 1992.

Perry, Richard H., Wilbert H. Richarz, and William J. Robinson, eds. *The 390th Bomb Group in Action: An Anthology*. Vol. 2. Tucson, AZ: 390th Memorial Museum Foundation, 1985.

Peters, Walter. "The Birth of a Mission." *Yank*, January 21, 1944: 6–8.

Peterson, Ralph L. *Fly a Big Tin Bird: 379th Bombardment Group*. Victoria, BC: Trafford, 2000.

Peterson, Stanley A. *"The Saint": Stories by the Navigator of a B-17*. Lexington, KY: CreateSpace, 2014.

Picardo, Eddie S. *Tales of a Tail Gunner: A Memoir of Seattle and World War II*. Seattle: Hara, 1996.

Pindak, Frank F., William S. Tune, and Loy A. Dickinson. *Mission No. 263: Second Bombardment Group, Fifteenth Air Force, August 29, 1944*. Denver, CO: Dickinson, 1997.

Pisanos, Steve N. *The Flying Greek: An Immigrant Fighter Ace's WWII Odyssey with the RAF, USAAF, and French Resistance*. Washington, DC: Potomac, 2008.

Pishioneri, Albert F. *Me, Mom, and World War II*. Bloomington, IN: AuthorHouse, 2008.

Pitts, Jack. *P-47 Pilot: Scared, Bored, and Deadly*. San Antonio, TX: Pitts, 1997.

Pitts, Jesse Richard. *Return to Base: Memoirs of a B-17 Copilot, Kimbolton, England, 1943–1944*. Charlottesville, VA: Howell, 2004.

Plate, Wilmer A. *The Storm Clouds of War: Reflections of a WWII Bomber Pilot*. Portsmouth, NH: Vilnius, 2014.

Platt, Charles. *Popular Superstitions*. London: Herbert Jenkins, 1925.

Pollock, P. Hamilton. *Wings on the Cross: A Padre with the R.A.F.* Dublin: Clanmore and Reynolds, 1954.

Pooke, Jerry. *Flying Freestyle: An RAF Jet Pilot's Story*. Barnsley, UK: Pen & Sword Aviation, 2009.

Popham, Hugh. *Sea Flight: A Fleet Air Arm Pilot's Story*. London: Kimber, 1954.

Porter, Bob. *The Long Return*. Burnaby, BC: Porter, 1997.

Porter, R. Bruce, with Eric Hammel. *Ace! A Marine Night-Fighter Pilot in World War II*. Pacifica, CA: Pacifica, 1985.

Preston-Hough, Peter. *Commanding Far Eastern Skies: A Critical Analysis of the Royal Air Force Air Superiority Campaign in India, Burma and Malaya, 1941–1945*. Solihull: Helion, 2015.

Prince, Catheryn J. *Shot from the Sky: American POWs in Switzerland*. Annapolis, MD: Naval Institute Press, 2003.

Pyle, Ernie. *Here Is Your War: Story of G.I. Joe*. Lincoln: University of Nebraska Press, 2004.

———. *Brave Men*. New York: Henry Holt, 1944.

Quinlan, Thomas G. *Corkscrew to Safety: A Tail-Gunner's Tour with 103 Squadron RAF 1944/5*. Bognor, UK: Woodfield, 2011.

Rains, Calvin E., Sr. *The Story of One Navy Fighter Pilot*. Bloomington, IN: AuthorHouse, 2006.

Rainsford, F. F. *Memoirs of an Accidental Airman*. London: Harmsworth, 1986.

Ralph, Wayne. *Aces, Warriors and Wingmen: Firsthand Accounts of Canada's Fighter Pilots in the Second World War*. Mississauga, ON: Wiley, 2005.

Rasimus, Ed. *When Thunder Rolled: A F-105 Pilot over North Vietnam*. Washington, DC: Smithsonian, 2003.

Rasmussen, Randall L. *Hell's Belle: From a B-17 to Stalag 17B*. Santa Fe, NM: Sunstone, 2003.

Rawnsley, C. F., with Robert Wright. *Night Fighter*. London: Collins, 1957.

Rayla, Lynn L. "Some Surprising Beliefs Concerning Human Nature among Pre-Medical Psychology Students." *British Journal of Educational Psychology* 15 (1945): 70–75.

Rea, Robert R. *Wings of Gold: An Account of Naval Aviation Training in World War II*. Edited by Wesley Phillips Newton and Robert R. Rea. Tuscaloosa: University of Alabama Press, 1987.

Redding, Tony. *Flying for Freedom: Life and Death in Bomber Command*. Bristol, UK: Cerberus, 2005.

Rees, Ken, with Karen Arrandale. *Lie in the Dark and Listen: The Remarkable Exploits of a WWII Bomber Pilot and Great Escaper*. London: Grub Street, 2004.

Rehr, Louis S., with Carleton R. Rehr. *Marauder: Memoir of a B-26 Pilot in Europe in World War II*. Jefferson, NC: McFarland, 2004.

Rein, Christopher M. *The North African Air Campaign: U.S. Army Air Forces from El Alamein to Salerno*. Lawrence: University Press of Kansas, 2012.

Renaut, Micael. *Terror by Night: A Bomber Pilot's Story*. London: Kimber, 1982.

Rexford-Welch, S. C. *The Royal Air Force Medical Services*. Vol. 2, *Commands*. London: HMSO, 1955.

Reynolds, Thomas P. *Belle of the Brawl: A Biographical Memoir of Walter Malone Baskin*. Paducah, KY: Turner, 1996.

Rice, Tom W. "Believe It or Not: Religious and Other Paranormal Beliefs in the United States." *Journal for the Scientific Study of Religion* 42 (2003): 95–106.

Richards, Charles W. *The Second Was First: The Lives and Times of the Second Bombardment Group (Heavy) during World War II*. Bend, OR: Maverick, 1999.

Richardson, Wilbur. *Aluminum Castles: WWII from a Gunner's View*. Chino Hills, CA: Cantemos, 2012.

Richarz, Wilbert H., Richard H. Perry, and William J. Robinson, eds. *The 390th Bomb Group Anthology*. Vol. 1. Tucson, AZ: 390th Memorial Museum Foundation, 1983.

Richer, Leo. *I Flew the Lancaster Bomber*. Windermere, BC: Richer, 1998.

Richey, Paul. *Fighter Pilot: A Personal Record of the Campaign in France: September 8th, 1939, to June 13th, 1940*. London: Batsford, 1941.

Richman, Harvey, and Courtney Bell. "Paranormal Beliefs Then and Now." *North American Journal of Psychology* 14 (2012): 197–206.

Rimell, Raymond Lawrence. *The Airship VC: The Life of Captain William Leefe Robinson*. Bourne End, UK: Aston, 1989.

Ritchie, Stuart J., Richard Wiseman, and Christopher C. French. "Failing the Future: Three Unsuccessful Attempts to Replicate Bem's 'Retroactive Facilitation of Recall' Effect." *PLoS ONE* 7 (2012): 1–5.

Rivaz, R. C. *Tail Gunner*. Stroud, UK: Sutton, 1996.

Roberts, E. M. *A Flying Fighter: An American Above the Lines in France*. London: Greenhill, 1988.

Roberts, Leanne, Irshad Ahmed, and Andrew Davidson. "Intercessory Prayer for the Alleviation of Ill Health." Cochrane Library. onlinelibrary.wiley.com (accessed November 5, 2015).

Robertson, Gordon Bennett, Jr. *Bringing the Thunder: The Missions of a World War II B-29 Pilot in the Pacific*. Mechanicsburg, PA: Stackpole, 2006.

Rochlin, Fred. *Old Man in a Baseball Cap: A Memoir of World War II*. New York: HarperCollins, 1999.

Rock, Andrea. *The Mind at Night: The New Science of How and Why We Dream*. New York: Basic, 2004.

Rodgers, C. Wade *There's No Future in It*. Orford, TAS: Rodgers, 1988.

Rodgers, Jack. *Navigator's Log of a Tour in Bomber Command*. Braunton, UK: Merlin, 1985.

Roe, Chris A. "Critical Thinking and Belief in the Paranormal: A Re-evaluation." *British Journal of Psychology* 90 (1999): 85–98.

Rogers, Paul, Tiffany Davis, and John Fisk. "Paranormal Belief and Susceptibility to the Conjunction Fallacy." *Applied Cognitive Psychology* 23 (2009): 524–542.

Rolf, Mel. *Looking into Hell: Experiences of the Bomber Command War*. London: Rigel, 2004.

———. *Gunning for the Enemy: Wallace McIntosh*. London: Grub Street, 2003.

———. *Flying into Hell: The Bomber Command Offensive as Seen Through the Experiences of Twenty Crews*. London: Grub Street, 2001.

———. *Hell on Earth: Dramatic First Hand Experiences of Bomber Command at War*. London: Grub Street, 1999.

———. *To Hell and Back*. London: Grub Street, 1998.

Rollin, Henry R. *Festina Lente: A Psychiatric Odyssey*. London: BMJ, 1990.

Rooney, Andy. *My War*. New York: Times Books, 1995.

Ross, Vivian (Roger Vee). *Flying Minnows: Memoirs of a World War One Fighter Pilot, from Training in Canada to the Front Line, 1917–1918*. London: Arms & Armour, 1977.

Rosser, Harold C. *No Hurrahs for Me*. Sevierville, TN: Covenant House, 1994.

Roud, Steve. *A Pocket Guide to Superstitions of the British Isles*. London: Penguin, 2004.

Rowland, John. *Return Flights in War and Peace*. Barnsley, UK: Pen & Sword Aviation, 2011.

Rudski, Jeffrey. "The Illusion of Control, Superstitious Belief, and Optimism." *Current Psychology: Developmental, Learning, Personality, Social* 22 (2004): 306–315.

Russell, Peter. *Flying in Defiance of the Reich: A Lancaster Pilot's Rites of Passage*. Barnsley, UK: Pen & Sword Aviation, 2007.

Rutter, Joseph W. *Wreaking Havoc: A Year in an A-20*. College Station: Texas A&M University Press, 2004.

Sailer, Paul M. *The Oranges Are Sweet: Major Don M. Beerbower and the 353rd Fighter Squadron, November 1942 to August 1944*. Wadena, MN: Loden, 2011.

Sakia, Saburo, with Martin Caiden and Fred Saito. *Samurai!* New York: Ballantine, 1958.

Salter, James. *Burning the Days: Recollection*. New York: Random House, 1997.

Samuel, Wolfgang W. E. *I Always Wanted to Fly: America's Cold War Airmen.* Jackson: University Press of Mississippi, 2001.

Sanders, James. *Of Wind and Water: A Kiwi Pilot in Coastal Command.* Shrewsbury, UK: Airlife, 1989.

Sandstedt, L. Roger. *My B-29 Story.* St. Louis, MO: Sandstedt, 2003.

Saunders, Andy. *Bader's Last Fight: An In-Depth Investigation of a Great WWII Mystery.* London: Grub Street, 2007.

Savage, Mark A. *"Those Were the Days": Aviation Adventures in World War II.* Dublin, OH: Markas, 1993.

Sawyer, Tom. *Only Owls and Bloody Fools Fly at Night.* London: Kimber, 1982.

Scearce, Phil. *Finish Forty and Home: The Untold World War II Story of B-24s in the Pacific.* Denton: University of North Texas Press, 2011.

Schippers, Michaéla C., and Paul A. M. Van Lange. "The Psychological Benefits of Superstitious Rituals in Top Sport: A Study among Top Sportspersons." *Journal of Applied Social Psychology* 36 (2006): 2532–2553.

Schneck, Donald R., and Ralph H. Schneck. *Cheerio and Best Wishes: Letters from a World War II Hoosier Pilot.* West Lafayette, IN: Purdue University Press, 2013.

Schreiber, Irving. *The War Years: My Participation in the Second World War.* Rockville, MD: Schreiber, 2012.

Schuyler, Keith C. *Elusive Horizons.* Cranbury, NJ: A. S. Barnes, 1969.

Scott, Desmond. *One More Hour.* London: Hutchinson, 1989.

———. *Typhoon Pilot.* London: Leo Cooper, 1980.

Scott, Robert L., Jr. *God Is My Co-Pilot.* New York: Scribner's, 1943.

Scranton, Dennis. *Crew One: A World War II Memoir of VPB-108.* Bennington, VT: Merriam, 2001.

Searby, John. *The Bomber Battle for Berlin.* Shrewsbury, UK: Airlife, 1991.

Shaffer, Laurance D., et al. "Surveys of Experiences of Returned Personnel." In *Army Air Forces Aviation Psychology Program Research Reports: Psychological Problems of Redistribution: Report No. 14,* edited by Frederic Wickert, 122–162. Washington, DC: US Government Printing Office, 1946.

Sheddan, C. J., with Norman Franks. *Tempest Pilot.* London: Grub Street, 1993.

Shephard, Ben. *A War of Nerves: Soldiers and Psychiatrists in the Twentieth Century.* Cambridge, MA: Harvard University Press, 2001.

Sheridan, Jerome W. *American Airman in the Belgian Resistance: Gerald E. Sorensen and the Transatlantic Alliance.* Jefferson, NC: McFarland, 2014.

Shermer, Michael. *The Believing Brain.* New York: Times Books, 2011.

Sherrod, Robert. *History of Marine Corps Aviation in World War II.* San Rafael, CA: Presidio, 1980.

Sherwood, Robert H. *Certified Brave.* Victoria, BC: Trafford, 2004.

Shiel, Walt. *Rough War: The Combat Story of Lt. Paul Eastman, a "Burma Banshee" P-40 and P-47 Pilot.* Jacobsville, MI: Jacobsville, 2011.

Shiver, John J., Jr. *I Always Wanted to Fly: Memoirs of a World War II Flight Engineer/Gunner.* Atmore, AL: Shiver, 2012.

Shook, Hal. *Fighter Pilot Jazz: Role of the P-47 and Spirited Guys in Winning the Air-Ground War in Normandy, 1944.* Huntington, WV: Humanomics, 2005.

Silbert, Eric. *Dinkum Mishpochah.* Perth, WA: Artlook, 1981.

Simonsen, Clarence. *RAF and RCAF Aircraft Nose Art in World War II.* Ottringham, UK: Hikoki, 2001.

Simpson, Andrew R. B. *'Ops': Victory at All Costs: On Operations over Hitler's Reich with the Crews of Bomber Command, Their War—Their Words.* Pulborough, UK: Tattered Flag, 2012.

Singer, Jack. *Grandpa's War in Bomber Command.* Ottawa: War Amps, 2012.

Siniver, Erez, and Gideon Yaniv. "Kissing the Mezuzah and Cognitive Performance: Is There an Observable Benefit?" *Journal of Economic Behavior & Organization* 117 (2015): 40–46.

Skinner, B. F. "Superstition in the Pigeon." *Journal of Experimental Psychology* 38 (1948): 168–172.

Skipper, Robert C. *On a Wing and a Prayer: Until Our Last Mission.* Chatham, ON: Chamberlain Mercury, 1991.

Slade, Robert M. *Journey to Freedom and Beyond.* Victoria, BC: Trafford, 2004.

Slater, Harry E. *Lingering Contrails of the Big Square A: A History of the 94th Bomb Group (H), 1942–1945.* Hadley, PA: Slater, 1980.

Slessor, John. *The Central Blue: The Autobiography of Sir John Slessor, Marshal of the RAF.* New York: Praeger, 1957.

Sloan, John S. *The Route as Briefed: The History of the 92nd Bombardment Group USAAF, 1942–1945.* Cleveland, OH: Argus, 1946.

Sloan, Richard P., and Rajasekhar Ramakrishnan. "Science, Medicine, and Intercessory Prayer." *Perspectives in Biology and Medicine* 49 (2006): 504–514.

Smallwood, J. W. *Tomlin's Crew: A Bombardier's Story.* Manhattan, KS: Sunflower University Press, 1992.

Smallwood, William L. *Warthog: Flying the A-10 in the Gulf War.* Washington, DC: Brassey's, 1993.

Smith, Arthur C. *Halifax Crew: The Story of a Wartime Bomber Crew.* Stevenage, UK: Carlton, 1983.

Smith, Ben, Jr. *Chick's Crew: A Tale of the Eighth Air Force.* Tallahassee, FL: Rose, 1983.

Smith, Dale O. *Screaming Eagle: Memoirs of a B-17 Group Commander.* Chapel Hill: Algonquin, 1990.

Smith, E. A. W. *Spitfire Diary: The Boys of One-Two-Seven.* London: Kimber, 1988.

Smith, John F. *Hellcats over the Philippine Deep.* Manhattan, KS: Sunflower University Press, 1995.

Smith, Ron. *Rear Gunner Pathfinders.* Manchester, UK: Crécy, 1987.

Smith, Sydney Percival, and David Scott Smith. *Lifting the Silence.* Toronto: Dundurn, 2010.

Smith, Truman. *The Wrong Stuff: The Adventures and Misadventures of an 8th Air Force Aviator.* Norman: University of Oklahoma Press, 2002.

Snape, Michael. *God and Uncle Sam: Religion and America's Armed Forces in World War II.* Woodbridge, UK: Boydell, 2015.

———. *God and the British Soldier: Religion and the British Army in the First and Second World Wars.* London: Routledge, 2005.

Snyder, Earl. *General Leemy's Circus: A Navigator's Story of the 20th Air Force in World War II.* New York: Exposition, 1955.

Snyder, Steve. *Shot Down: The True Story of the Pilot Howard Snyder and the Crew of the B-17* Susan Ruth. Seal Beach, CA: Sea Breeze, 2015.

Somers, William F. *Fortress Fighters: An Autobiography of a B-17 Aerial Gunner.* Tempe, AZ: Somers, 2000.

Speer, Frank. *One Down, One Dead: The Personal Adventures of Two Fourth Fighter Group Combat Pilots as They Face the Luftwaffe over Germany.* Bloomington, IN: Xlibris, 2003.

———. *Wingman.* New York: Hearthstone, 1993.

Spencer, Dennis. *Looking Backwards over Burma: Wartime Recollections of a RAF Beaufighter Navigator.* Bognor, UK: Woodfield, 2009.

Spiller, H. J. *Ticket to Freedom.* London: Kimber, 1988.

Springer, Joseph A. *Inferno: The Life and Death Struggle of the USS* Franklin *in World War II.* Minneapolis: Zenith, 2011.

Springs, Elliott White. *War Birds: Diary of an Unknown Airman.* New York: Grosset & Dunlap, 1926.

Stein, Allan T. *Into the Wild Blue Yonder: My Life in the Air Force.* College Station: Texas A&M University Press, 2005.

Steinbeck, John. *Once There Was a War.* New York: Viking, 1958.

Stephens, Allan. *The Royal Australian Air Force.* Melbourne: Oxford University Press, 2001.

Stevens, Charles N. *An Innocent at Polebrook: A Memoir of an 8th Air Force Bombardier*. Bloomington, IN: 1st Books, 2004.

Stewart, John L. *The Forbidden Diary: A B-24 Navigator Remembers*. New York: McGraw-Hill, 1998.

Stiles, Bert. *Serenade to the Big Bird*. Carthage, TX: Howland Associates, 1999.

Stoker, Brian. *If the Flak Doesn't Get You the Fighters Will*. Hailsham, UK: J&KH, 1995.

Stone, Ken. *Triumphant We Fly: A 381st Bomb Group Anthology, 1943–1945*. Edited by Ken Stone. Paducah, KY: Turner, 1994.

Stones, Donald. *A Pilot's Passion: The Story of "Dimsie."* Edited by Adrian Burt. London: Burt's, 2014.

Stouffer, Samuel A., et al. *The American Soldier: Combat and Its Aftermath*. Princeton: Princeton University Press, 1949.

Stout, Jay A. *Hell's Angels: The True Story of the 303rd Bomb Group in World War II*. New York: Berkley Caliber, 2015.

———. *Unsung Eagles: True Stories of America's Citizen Airmen in the Skies of World War II*. Philadelphia: Casemate, 2013.

———. *Fighter Group: The 352nd; "Blue-Nosed Bastards" in World War II*. Mechanicsburg, PA: Stackpole, 2012.

Stowers, Richard. *Wellingtons over the Med: A Kiwi Pilot's Story from the Mediterranean*. Hamilton, NZ: Stowers, 2012.

Styling, Mark. *Corsair Aces of World War II*. Oxford: Osprey, 1995.

Taylor, Geoff. *Piece of Cake*. London: Corgi, 1980.

Taylor, Gordon. *The Sea Chaplains: A History of the Chaplains of the Royal Navy*. Oxford: Oxford Illustrated, 1978.

Taylor, James, and Martin Davidson. *Bomber Crew*. London: Hodder and Stoughton, 2004.

TenHaken, Mel. *Bail-Out! POW, 1944–1945*. Manhattan, KS: Sunflower University Press, 1990.

Terraine, John. *The Right of the Line: The Role of the RAF in World War Two*. Barnsley, UK: Pen & Sword, 2010.

Thixton, Marshall J., George E. Moffat, and John J. O'Neil. *Bombs Away: By Pathfinders of the Eighth Air Force*. Trumbull, CT: FNP, 1998.

Thomas, Gerald W. *Torpedo Squadron Four: A Cockpit View of World War II*. Las Cruces: New Mexico State University, 1991.

Thomas, Rowan T. *Born in Battle: Round the World Adventures of the 513th Bombardment Squadron*. Philadelphia: Winston, 1944.

Thompson, Henry J. *The Buccaneers of Henry Sears: The History of Navy Bombing Squadron 104, World War II, April 1943 to April 1944.* Harper, TX: Charlie Horse, 1997.

Thompson, Jack E. *Bomber Crew.* 2nd ed. Victoria, BC: Trafford, 2005.

Thompson, Joe, and Tom Delvaux. *Tiger Joe: A Photographic Diary of an Aerial Reconnaissance Pilot.* Nashville, TN: Everready, 2006.

Thompson, Kenneth. *Memoirs of a WWII Fighter Pilot: And Some Modern Political Commentary.* Victoria, BC: Trafford, 2011.

Thompson, Walter R. *Lancaster to Berlin.* Southside, UK: Goodall, 1997.

Thomsen, Moritz. *My Two Wars.* South Royalton, VT: Steerforth, 1996.

Thorburn, Gordon. *A Century of Air Warfare with Nine (IX) Squadron, RAF: Still Going Strong.* Barnsley, UK: Pen & Sword Aviation, 2014.

———. *Bombers First and Last.* London: Robson, 2006.

Thorsness, Leo. *Surviving Hell.* New York: Encounter, 2008.

Tillman, Barrett. *Forgotten Fifteenth: The Daring Airmen Who Crippled Hitler's War Machine.* Washington, DC: Regnery, 2014.

———. *Clash of the Carriers: The True Story of the Marianas Turkey Shoot of World War II.* New York: NAL Caliber, 2005.

Timberlake, Richard H., Jr. *They Never Saw Me Then.* Philadelphia: Xlibris, 2001.

Toliver, Raymond F., and Trevor J. Constable. *The Blond Knight of Germany: A Biography of Erich Hartmann.* Blue Ridge Summit, PA: Aero, 1970.

Townsend, Peter. *Duel of Eagles.* New York: Simon & Schuster, 1970.

Timofeeva-Ogorova, Anna. *Over Fields of Fire: Flying the Sturmovik in Action on the Eastern Front, 1942–45.* Edited by Sergey Anisomov. Translated by Vladimir Kroupnik. Solihull, UK: Helio, 2010.

Trask, Harry E. *Harry's War: A Memoir of World War II by a Navigator of a B-29 in the Pacific Theater.* Brockton, MA: One Tiny Pizza, 2004.

Trent, Ken. *Bomb Doors Open: From East End Boy to Lancaster Bomber Pilot with 617 "Dambusters" Squadron.* St. Mary, UK: Seeker, 2016.

Tripp, Miles. *The Eighth Passenger: A Flight of Recollection and Discovery.* London: Macmillan, 1969.

———. *Faith Is a Windsock.* London: Peter Davis, 1952.

Truluck, John H., Jr. *And So It Was: Memories of a World War II Fighter Pilot.* Walterboro, SC: Press and Standard, 1989.

Tuck, Harley H., Sr., with Ann I. Clizer. *Angel on My Shoulder: I've Joined the Lucky Bastard Club.* Bloomington, IN: AuthorHouse, 2015.

Tucker, Kenneth S., and Wanda Tucker Goodwin. *Last Roll Call*. Southport, FL: Priority, 2009.

Turham, Keith M. *Death Denied*. San Diego: Fairdale, 2007.

Turner, Richard E. *Big Friend, Little Friend: Memoirs of a World War II Fighter Pilot*. Garden City, NY: Doubleday, 1969.

Van Ralte, Judy L., et al. "Chance Orientation and Superstitious Behavior on the Putting Green." *Journal of Sport Behavior* 14 (1991): 41–50.

Vernon, James W. *The Hostile Sky: A Hellcat Flier in World War II*. Annapolis, MD: Naval Institute Press, 2003.

Vigors, Tim. *Life's Too Short to Cry: The Compelling Memoir of a Battle of Britain Ace*. London: Grub Street, 2006.

Vrilakas, Robert. *Look, Mom—I Can Fly! Memoirs of a World War II P-38 Fighter Pilot*. Tucson, AZ: Amethyst Moon, 2011.

Vyse, Stuart. *Believing in Magic*. Updated ed. New York: Oxford University Press, 2014.

Wainwright, John. *Tail-End Charlie*. London: Macmillan, 1978.

Waite, Ronnie. *Death or Decoration*. Cowden, UK: Newton, 1991.

Wakelam, Randall T. *The Science of Bombing: Operational Research in RAF Bomber Command*. Toronto: University of Toronto Press, 2009.

Walcott, John W. *One Fighter Pilot's War*. Bloomington, IN: iUniverse, 2015.

Wallrich, Bill. "Superstition and the Air Force." *Western Folklore* 19 (1960): 11–16.

Walter, John C. *My War: The True Experiences of a U.S. Army Air Force Pilot in World War II*. Bloomington, IN: AuthorHouse, 2004.

Wannop, Robert E. *Chocks Away*. Worcester, UK: Square One, 1989.

Warburg, F. W. "Beliefs Concerning Human Nature among Students in a University Department of Education." *British Journal of Educational Psychology* 26 (1956): 156–162.

Warner, Wayne A. *One Trip Too Many: A Pilot's Memoirs of 38 Months in Combat over Laos and Vietnam*. Seattle: CreateSpace, 2011.

Watson, Alexander. *Enduring the Great War: Combat, Morale and Collapse in the German and British Armies, 1914–1918*. Cambridge, UK: Cambridge University Press, 2008.

Watson, John. *Johnny Kinsman*. London: Cassell, 1955.

Watt, George. *The Comet Connection: Escape from Hitler's Europe*. Lexington: University Press of Kentucky, 1990.

Watts, Jack. *Nickels and Nightingales*. Burnstown, ON: GSPH, 1995.

Webster, George. *The Savage Sky: Life and Death on a Bomber over Germany in 1944*. Mechanicsburg, PA: Stackpole, 2007.

Weekley, Harold D., and James B. Zazas. *The Last of the Combat B-17 Drivers*. Carthage, NC: Flying Fortress International, 2007.

Wegmann, Rolph, and Bo Widfeldt. *Making For Sweden, Part 1: The Royal Air Force*. Walton on Thames, UK: Air Research, 1997.

Wegner, Daniel M., Richard M. Wezlaff, and Megan Kozak. "Dream Rebound: The Return of Suppressed Thoughts in Dreams." *Psychological Science* 15 (2004): 232–236.

Wellham, John. *With Naval Wings: The Autobiography of a Fleet Air Arm Pilot in World War II*. Staplehurst, UK: Spellmount, 2003.

Wellum, Geoffrey. *First Light*. London: Viking, 2002.

Whitcomb, Ed. *On Celestial Wings*. Maxwell AFB, AL: Air University Press, 1995.

White, Alan. *The King's Thunderbolts: No 44 (Rhodesia) Squadron Royal Air Force: An Operational Record and Roll of Honour, 1917–1982*. Lincoln: Tucann, 2007.

White, Arthur. *Bread and Butter Bomber Boys*. Upton on Severn, UK: Square One, 1995.

White, Graham. *"The Long Road to the Sky": Night Fighter over Germany*. Barnsley, UK: Pen & Sword Aviation, 2006.

Wiessner, Richard (Dick). *The Real World of War*. Edited by Ruth Welsh. Edina, MN: Beaver's Pond, 2015.

Wilcox, Thomas C. *One Man's Destiny*. Mogadore, OH: Telecraft, 1991.

Willatt, Geoffrey. *Bombs and Barbed Wire: My War in the RAF and Stalag Luft III*. Tunbridge Wells, UK: Parapress, 1995.

Williams, Bill. *Five Miles High and Forty Below: Fifty Missions of a B-17 Bomber Crew, June–August 1944*. Bonanza, OR: CP Media, 2009.

Williams, Ernest H. L. (H. W.). *Sh! Gremlins!* London: Crowther, 1942.

Williams, Geoffrey. *Flying Backwards: Memoirs of a Rear Gunner*. Loftus, NSW: Publishing Services, 2001.

Willis, G. R. T. *No Hero, Just a Survivor: A Personal Story with Beaufighters and Mosquitos of 47 Squadron RAF over the Mediterranean and Burma, 1943–1945*. Emley, UK: Willis, 1999.

Wilson, Bradford P. *Everyday P.O.W.: A Rural California Boy's Story of Going to War*. Pollock Pines, CA: Storyteller, 2010.

Wilson, Kevin. *Journey's End: Bomber Command's Battle from Arnhem to Dresden and Beyond*. London: Weidenfeld & Nicolson, 2010.

————. *Men of Air: Doomed Youth of Bomber Command, 1944.* London: Weidenfeld & Nicolson, 2007.

————. *Bomber Boys: The RAF Offensive of 1943.* London: Weidenfeld & Nicolson, 2005.

Winfield, Roland. *The Sky Belongs to Them.* London: Kimber, 1976.

Wingham, Tom. *Halifax Down! On the Run from the Gestapo, 1944.* London: Grub Street, 2009.

Wink, Gene. *Born to Fly.* Bloomington, IN: AuthorHouse, 2006.

Winston, Robert A. *Fighting Squadron: A Sequel to Dive Bomber.* New York: Holiday, 1946.

Winters, Hugh. *Skipper: Confessions of a Fighter Squadron Commander.* Meza, AZ: Champlin Fighter Museum, 1985.

Wiseman, Andrew, with Sean Feast. *An Alien Sky: The Story of One Man's Remarkable Adventure in Bomber Command during the Second World War.* London: Grub Street, 2015.

Wiseman, Richard. *Paranormality: Why We See What Isn't There.* London: Spin Solutions, 2010.

Wiseman, Richard, and Caroline Watt. "Measuring Superstitious Belief: Why Lucky Charms Matter." *Personality and Individual Differences* 37 (2004): 1533–1541.

Wolffe, John. *God and Greater Britain: Religion and National Life in Britain and Ireland 1843–1945.* London: Routledge, 1994.

Wolk, Herman S. *Cataclysm: General Hap Arnold and the Defeat of Japan.* Denton: University of North Texas Press, 2010.

Wood, Richard A., and Robert S. Bee, eds. *War Stories of the O & W: A History of the 486th Bomb Group (Heavy).* Columbus, OH: RSB, 1996.

Woods, Laurie. *Flying into the Mouth of Hell.* Loftus, NSW: Australian Military History Publications, 2003.

Woodward, Ellis M. *Flying School: Combat Hell.* Baltimore, MD: American Literary Press, 1998.

Worthen, Frederick D. *Against All Odds: Shot Down over Occupied Territory in World War II.* Santa Barbara, CA: Narrative, 1996.

Wright, David G., ed. *Observations on Combat Flying Personnel.* New York: Josiah Macy Jr., 1944.

Wright, Harold J. *Pathfinder Squadron.* London: Kimber, 1987.

Wright, Stuart J. *An Emotional Gauntlet: From Life in Peacetime America to the War in European Skies.* Madison: University of Wisconsin Press, 2004.

Wright, William Thomas. *My Three Years in the Army Air Forces in World War II: December 9, 1942, to December 8, 1945*. Raleigh, NC: Lulu, 2014.

Wynn, Humphrey. *Darkness Shall Cover Me: Night Bombing over the Western Front, 1918*. Shrewsbury, UK: Airlife, 1989.

Yaeger, Chuck, and Leo Janos. *Yaeger: The Autobiography*. New York: Bantam, 1985.

Yasuo, Kuwahara, and Gordon T. Allred. *Kamikaze*. 7th ed. Clearfield, UT: American Legacy Media, 2007.

Yates, Harry. *Luck and a Lancaster: Chance and Survival in World War II*. Shrewsbury, UK: Airlife, 1999.

Yeates, V. M. *Winged Victory*. London: Cape, 1961.

Yule, Royan. *On a Wing and a Prayer*. Derby, UK: Derby Books, 2012.

Zellmer, David. *The Spectator: A World War II Bomber Pilot's Journal of the Artist as Warrior*. Westport, CT: Praeger, 1999.

Zlaten, Al. *By the Grace of God: Or It Ain't All Luck*. Longmont, CO: Zlaten, 2000.

Zucker, Ray F. *??Remember??* Knoxville, TN: Tennessee Valley, 1993.

Zverev, S. E. "Military Superstition as an Attempt at Rationalizing Stressful Reality." *Military Thought* 23 (2014): 65–74.

DOCUMENTARIES

Bomber Command (dir. M. Liddell: ITV, 2012).

Into the Wind (dir. S. Hatton: Electric Egg, 2011).

The Valour and the Horror: Death by Moonlight (dir. B. McKenna: Gala Films, 1992).

INDEX